P9-CKN-480

Constructing Accessible Web Sites

Jim Thatcher

Paul Bohman

Michael Burks

Shawn Lawton Henry

Bob Regan

Sarah Swierenga

Mark D. Urban

Cynthia D. Waddell

© 2002 glasshaus

Published by glasshaus Ltd,
Arden House,
1102 Warwick Road,
Acocks Green,
Birmingham,
B27 6BH, UK

Printed in the United States
ISBN 1-904151-00-0

Constructing Accessible Web Sites

All rights reserved. No part of this book may be reproduced, stored in a retrieval system, or transmitted in any form or by any means, without the prior written permission of the publisher, except in the case of brief quotations embodied in critical articles or reviews.

The authors and publisher have made every effort in the preparation of this book to ensure the accuracy of the information. However, the information contained in this book is sold without warranty, either express or implied. Neither the authors, glasshaus, nor its dealers or distributors will be held liable for any damages caused or alleged to be caused either directly or indirectly by this book.

web professional to web professional

© 2002 glasshaus

Trademark Acknowledgements

glasshaus has endeavoured to provide trademark information about all the companies and products mentioned in this book by the appropriate use of capitals. However, glasshaus cannot guarantee the accuracy of this information.

Credits

Authors
Jim Thatcher
Paul Bohman
Michael Burks
Shawn Lawton Henry
Bob Regan
Sarah Swierenga
Mark D. Urban
Cynthia D. Waddell

Commissioning Editor
Eleanor Baylis

Lead Editor
Alessandro Ansa

Technical Editors
Sarah Larder
Chris Mills
Gareth Oakley
Daniel Walker

Project Manager
Sophie Edwards

Proof Reader
Agnes Wiggers

Brand Visionary
Bruce Lawson

Technical Reviewers
Michael Burks
Wendy Chisholm
Michael Delcasino
Jon Duckett
Dani Harris
Julie Howell
Jeremy Hurst
Devin Lunsford
Bob Regan
Terry Robinson
David Schultz
Peter Seebach

Managing Editor
Liz Toy

Production Coordinator
Pip Wonson

Production Assistant
Rachel Taylor

Cover
Dawn Chellingworth

Indexer
Bill Johncocks

Cover Image

Humid Tropics Biome – from the Eden Project series (for full series, go to *http://www.les.stclair.btinternet.co.uk /*). Photo taken by, and used by kind permission of Les St. Clair (contact: *les.stclair@btinternet.com*).

The Eden project is a series of huge covered conservatories, called Biomes, built in a giant crater in Cornwall, England, within which grow plants from the Mediterranean, South Africa, and California, and other parts of the world.

About the Authors

Jim Thatcher

Dr. Jim Thatcher received his PhD from the University of Michigan in 1963, one of the first PhDs in Computer Science. Together with his thesis advisor, Dr. Jesse Wright, Jim then joined the Mathematical Sciences Department of IBM Research, where he stayed until 1996.

His research area was mathematical computer science, including automata theory, semantics, and data abstraction. Jim began moving away from the abstract and toward the practical when he and Dr. Wright, who is blind, started working on an "audio access system" for the IBM Personal Computer.

This work culminated in the development of one of the first screen readers for DOS in 1984-85, called IBM Screen Reader. (Such access systems are now known as "screen readers"!) He later led the development of IBM Screen Reader/2, the first screen reader for a graphical user interface on the PC. Jim was intimately involved in the development of IBM Home Page Reader, a talking web browser for the blind and visually impaired.

In 1996 Dr. Thatcher joined the IBM Accessibility Center in Austin, TX, where he led the effort to include accessibility in the IBM development process. A key part of that effort was the establishment of the IBM Accessibility Guidelines specifically for use within IBM's development community.

Jim served as Vice-Chair of the Electronic and Information Technology Access Advisory Committee (EITAAC) which was empanelled by the Access Board to propose standards for Section 508; he chaired the subcommittee on software standards. Later he wrote the course on Web Accessibility for Section 508 for ITTATC, the Information Technology Technical Assistance and Training Center, which was funded in support of Section 508.

Dr. Thatcher received numerous awards for technical work over his 37 year career with IBM. He received a Distinguished Service award from The National Federation of the Blind in 1994 and the Vice President's Hammer Award for his work with the Department of Education on the development of Software Accessibility Standards in 1999. Jim retired in March, 2000, becoming an independent consultant in the area of accessibility.

Paul Bohman

Paul Bohman, M.S. is the Technology Coordinator for WebAIM (Web Accessibility in Mind), a project at the Center for Persons with Disabilities at Utah State University. He specializes in training Web developers and IT professionals in accessible web design skills. Over the years, he has provided web accessibility training at numerous universities, colleges, conferences, corporate settings, media events, and workshops. He has also written a broad range of documents, tutorials, articles, checklists, guides, and other materials, many of which are featured on the WebAIM site (*www.webaim.org*).

Michael Burks

Michael Burks currently serves as AT&T Network Product Manager and Expert on Accessibility of AT&T Web-Based Products and electronic and information technology.

He is also the Webmaster and Public Information Officer of the International Center for Disability Resources on the Internet (*http://www.icdri.org*), a non-profit organization dedicated to presenting disability resources and information to those who are dealing with disability issues.

He works with the Internet Society (*http://www.isoc.org*) on disability issues and has made presentations and taught tutorials on web accessibility and disability issues around the world.

He is married and has a 15 year old son.

Shawn Lawton Henry

Shawn Lawton Henry (*www.uiaccess.com/profile.html*) helps organizations develop and implement strategies to optimize design for usability and accessibility. For over a decade, she has worked with international standards bodies, research centers, government agencies, non-profit organizations, education providers, and Fortune 500 companies to advance user interface design. Shawn developed accessibility resource http://www.UIAccess.com.

Bob Regan

Bob Regan is the product manager for accessibility at Macromedia. In that role, he works with designers, developers, and engineers from around the world to communicate existing strategies for accessibility as well as develop new strategies. He works with engineers and designers within Macromedia to develop new techniques and improve the accessibility of Macromedia tools.

Bob has a Masters degree from Columbia University in Education. He is currently a doctoral student in Education at the University of Wisconsin – Madison. His dissertation research looks at accessibility policy implementation strategies.

Bob spent six years as a teacher and technology leader in Chicago and New York City. Working with teachers and students across a range of ages and subject matter, he has extensive knowledge of elementary and secondary education. Bob spent two years teaching web design and accessibility at the University of Wisconsin – Madison.

Sarah Swierenga

Dr. Sarah Swierenga is both an experienced researcher and a practitioner, who has almost 20 years of experience in the scientific study of users in both commercial and military environments. She has extensive skills in user interface design, data collection tools, and methodologies including usability tests, questionnaires, and focus groups.

Additionally, Sarah led a corporate accessibility compliance initiative, providing technical consulting on over 50 products, creating an organizational strategy for implementing Section 508 of the Rehabilitation Act standards, developing technical guidelines for applying the regulation, and raising company-wide awareness of accessibility compliance issues.

Sarah holds a Ph.D. in Human Factors Psychology with a concentration in human-computer interaction from the University of South Dakota, and a B.A. in Psychology from Calvin College. She is also a Certified Professional Ergonomist (C.P.E.). She can be contacted on *sarahswierenga@yahoo.com*.

Acknowledgements: I want to thank my web designer, Eileen Quenin, for creating several of the stylesheet examples from the montanaboat.com web site. I appreciate her assistance with this chapter, as well as her inspiration and encouragement for this effort. Thanks to Tim Orr, consulting software engineer, for reviewing the chapter and providing technical feedback. Most importantly, I would like to thank my family, Toni, Kiah, and Sydney, for their love and support as I wrote this chapter in "my spare time."

Mark D. Urban

Mark D. Urban of Raleigh is Chairman of the North Carolina (USA) Governor's Advocacy Council for Persons with Disabilities.

He is currently chairman of the board of directors for the International Center for Disability Resources on the Internet (*http://www.icdri.org*), and vice-chairman of the InterNational Committee for Information Technology Standards, V2 (IT Access Interfaces).

He is the author of several papers and presentations worldwide on IT access in government and industry, and is active in the US federal Accessibility Forum, as well as the W3C's Web Accessibility Initiative. He worked as senior information technology architect for accessibility with North Carolina's Information Technology Services and served on the Information Resource Management Commission work group on accessibility. Urban was chairman of the Board of Selectmen (mayor) for the town of Shutesbury, Mass from 1992-1994. He served as a member of the United States Navy Reserves as a Fleet Marine Force corpsman until his diagnosis with Type 1 Diabetes in 2000.

Mr. Urban currently does private consulting on accessibility matters with federal, state, and local agencies and the businesses that supply them.

Cynthia Waddell

In the world of accessibility, Cynthia D. Waddell, JD, is a nationally and internationally recognized expert in the field of electronic and information technology as well as employment and construction. During the past decade, Cynthia Waddell has worked as an ADA consultant for university and government entities and has lectured at various universities, presented at international conferences, received numerous awards, served on several boards, and published a number of papers on law and policy for information technology.

As the author of the first accessible web design standard for US local government, Cynthia Waddell's accessibility efforts in the international arena have included participation on the Portuguese International Accessibility Board; an effort that led to Portugal's adoption of the Portuguese Accessibility Guidelines for web sites.

In addition, she participated several years in the "Boosting the UK Digital Economy- A Virtual Think Tank" event and at the invitation of the Japan Executive Committee of The Internet Society, presented at the "Global Everyone Access" INET2000 in Yokohama, Japan, and currently participates in the European Union "Design for All" initiative. In order to dedicate all of her time to promoting accessibility on a national level, Cynthia Waddell cofounded ACE and is a Principal Consultant and Accessibility Subject Matter Expert.

As a key member of the ACE team, Cynthia Waddell combines her expertise in disability legislation and technology to provide education and professional consulting services for access to electronic and information technology for persons with disabilities. She was the subject of a feature story "Enabling Technology" in the February 2001 issue of **Government Technology Magazine**. In addition, as one of the world's leading experts, she was the sole US speaker at the 2001 "Design for All European Day of Disabled People" at the invitation of the European Commission and the European Disability Forum. Recently in the US, the National Council on Disability cited her influential paper "Applying the ADA to the Internet" in their impact report **The Accessible Future**.

Along with the ACE team, Cynthia Waddell participates on the federal US General Services Administration Section 508 Accessibility Forum. She is an ADA Mediator for the US Department of Justice Key Bridge project and a member of the National Task Forces on Technology and Disability. She also serves on the National Committee for Information Technology Standards (NCITS) V2 IT Access Interfaces Technical Committee. Current appointments include service as Chair of the Santa Clara County Advisory Commission for People with Disabilities and Vice-Chair of the State of California Building Code Access Committee. She is an active participant on the World Wide Web Consortium Web Accessibility Initiative Interest Group, The Internet Society, and the National Association of State Chief Information Officer workgroup on accessibility.

Table of Contents

Table of Contents

Table of Contents

Table of Contents

Introduction

When the World Wide Web was invented it was not envisioned that it would evolve into what it is today. While some may decry this evolution, it surely has helped to increase the availability of knowledge and has surely improved communication on a global scale. Because of this evolution and progress in improving communications, it is all the more important that this technology should reach the largest audience possible, regardless of disability, language barriers, devices being used, or bandwidth issues, to name just a few factors that affect the use of the Web and its technology.

The idea of accessibility of web-based technology is based on far more than the implementation of standards and technological solutions. It embodies the idea that everyone has the right to information and that everyone has the right to be included in society, regardless of disability, geographical location, language barriers, or any other factor. Accessibility of web pages is one part; one step in the inclusion of all in the benefits of the Information Society in particular and in society as a whole.

The people who have written and contributed to this volume are some of the leading experts in accessible web design – as such they are helping to make great strides in including many more people in the "Information Age."

What is in the Book

This book not only contains a detailed discussion of technical issues surrounding web accessibility, but also covers legal and policy issues, as well as the practicalities of implementing web accessibility, and integrating this technology into an organization. We will cover these areas in a thorough and comprehensive way, using plenty of practical and real-world examples, so that you can make your site fully accessible to people with disabilities.

Let's have a more detailed look into the fundamental areas of web accessibility:

What is an Accessible Web Site?

In Chapter 1, the basic ideas and concepts behind the current state of accessibility are presented for those who still need to be persuaded of the advantages, or want to know the history behind accessible web technology. This chapter clearly defines accessibility in the context of usability and how this applies to web design. A site that is accessible will, by definition, also be usable, increasing its overall effectiveness. It is important to realize that making your web site accessible not only benefits people who are disabled, but also users who have situational limitations such as those accessing your web site on a mobile device with no mouse, or in constraining circumstances such as while driving.

Legal Issues

The legal issues are no longer confined to the US, although to some degree the US is still used as a model. We cover legal issues in the US in some detail and also address accessibility laws and policies on a global scale.

The legal chapters (2 and 13) are presented in language that is clear and easy to understand by both legal experts and laymen. These chapters are invaluable both for those who need to understand the legal and policy issues in general and those who will have to deal with them in more depth.

The implementation in the US in June of 2000 of the Section 508 Guidelines, requiring all electronic and information technology (including web sites) to be accessible to people with disabilities, has most definitely served as an impetus increasing awareness of the need for accessible web-based technology. We have included both legal and technical sections in this book that deal with this subject specifically.

Cynthia Waddell, who wrote the legal and policy chapters, also wrote what were some of the first web accessibility guidelines, in fact, they were *the* first guidelines ever produced.

> *"As early as 1995, technical accessibility issues centered around access to content on the World Wide Web and web-based technology. Accessibility barriers were being created by the shift from a text-based environment to a robust, multi-media environment. In order to address these barriers, Cynthia Waddell authored the first accessible web design standard for local government in the US, for the City of San José, California. This standard quickly led to recognition as a best practice by the US government and adoption by governments in the US and abroad."*

(Taken from the Membership Briefing document for The Internet Society: *http://www.isoc.org/briefings/002/*)

How Do You Make a Web Site Accessible?

In Chapters 3 to 7 of this book, we attempt to demonstrate exactly how to create an accessible web site. The way in which your content is designed can make it completely inaccessible to a user who is visually impaired with a screen reader, yet a few simple changes to the HTML code can make all the difference. Not only does the content itself need to be accessible, but also the navigation, both within individual pages and around the site as a whole. Consider how confusing a poorly structured web site with badly designed navigation can be for a sighted person; this problem is further compounded for a person who is visually impaired.

In addition to offering solutions to these problems, we will also illustrate how to make forms completely accessible to users who are disabled and how to test your web site for accessibility.

This section of the book thoroughly documents how the popular screen readers and voice browsers, such as JAWS for Windows (JFW), Window-Eyes, and IBM's Home Page Reader, handle web pages.

Integrating Accessible Solutions into an Organization

One of the biggest problems today is implementing accessible web technology in organizations. This book gives you not only the tools to implement the technology, but also deals directly with building a model to address implementing accessibility within your organization in an efficient and cost-effective manner. This is explained in Chapter 11.

This chapter provides a model of how to implement accessible web technology across your organization in a consistent manner. In this chapter, we also introduce the tools available to help spur on implementation of accessible sites, and discuss some of their advantages and disadvantages.

Quick Tips

A set of quick tips that are tied directly to the content of the book has been provided. It will allow all involved to get a good, quick look at the issues that must be addressed without going into massive detail.

Who Is This Book for?

This book is essential for a variety of people involved in web-based business/services. It can, of course, be used by those who simply need to raise their awareness of what issues are involved in producing accessible web-based products and services.

- This book is a thorough technical reference for any web developer implementing specific accessibility techniques. Clear and practical examples cover the major issues, as well as more subtle accessibility problems. It is suitable in and of itself as a technical reference for both beginners and experienced web professionals.

- Top management must have a good overview of the issues and the obligations that their organizations face in order to set the policy and direction the origination must take.

- Managers at all levels must be aware of the issues so they can choose the proper way to manage these concerns to the benefit of their customers and the organization. They must know what they are expected to do, and what resources must be applied to accomplish the end result. They must understand the issues involved, so they can assess the progress being made in the implementation of accessible web-based technology in the production of their goods and services.

- Marketing personnel are critical in ensuring that goods and services meet the needs of customers. If they do not understand the issues, and if they do not understand that a market exists for these products and services, then a critical part is being left out of the picture.

- The legal section will be vital to legal personnel and policy makers, who must base decisions on existing laws and policies.

Using the book as an overall planning guide will assist in the efficient integration of accessible web design into an organization and will keep the cost to a minimum while maximizing human and technical resources – which are always scarce.

Why Do You Need This Book?

With the advent of Section 508 in the US and several other accessibility laws and policies around the world (as detailed in *Chapters 2* and 13) accessibility has become a more prominent issue both for those who are building government sites and those who are not. E-commerce is growing and people with disabilities are expecting to be able to use all the web facilities that everyone else is using. In some respects, the ability to use e-commerce is even more critical for those who are faced with transportation difficulties. The Web and e-commerce offer many people with and without disabilities a wider range of goods and services than has ever been available to them before.

Because of the economics of this situation and the fact that more and more people with disabilities are going online, the market is growing. No one should be excluded and those with disabilities are no exception.

No matter what phase your organization is at in its implementation of web-based technology, this book will provide the answers you need to make it accessible to the widest audience possible – disabled or not. This expanding audience will include not only people with disabilities, but those using alternative access devices such as cell phones and PDAs, as well as others in circumstances best served by accessible design, such as those using ATMs, information kiosks and other products and services that will utilize web-based technologies.

This book will help in the initial planning phase of individual projects and overall policy. By planning for accessibility from both the individual project standpoint and from the overall organizational standpoint, you will not only address the technical issues and maximize the utilization of technical resources, but you will be able to implement this technology in legacy areas in an ordered and cost effective manner.

It will also be useful in building organizational models to help support the accessibility effort in a way that will maximize the utilization of your organizations' resources at a minimum of cost.

> *It is cheaper to build sites in an accessible manner from the beginning; it is cheaper to build the technology to implement features on the sites so that it can be used in an accessible manner; it is the right thing to do, and in many cases it is going to become a question of law.*

One last thought: obviously no book will be completely relevant forever, but because this book is not just a book on technology but deals with legal, policy, technical, and organizational issues, it will have relevance for a long time to come. To a large degree it is about making information, products, services and anything based on an emerging technology available to as many people as possible. It is about inclusion of the largest number possible of people in the expanding world of information technology.

> *To put it in Cynthia Waddell's words – "Technology Changes, But Civil Rights Do Not".*

Support/Feedback

At glasshaus, we aim to make our books as helpful and informative as possible. However, no matter how many edits we subject our chapters to, a few errors are bound to slip through. We would like to apologize in advance for any errors that reach the published version in advance. However, all is not lost. If you spot an error in this book, please submit it to us by e-mailing it to support@glasshaus.com. We will then check out the error, and put it up on the Constructing Accessible Web Sites errata page if it is something that will help out other readers too. The errata page can be found on *http://www.glasshaus.com*.

This address can also be used to access our support network. We are dedicated to helping your career at every stage, not just up until the book hits the shelves. If you have trouble running any of the code in this book, or have a related question that you feel that the book didn't answer, please mail your problem to the above address, in addition quoting the title of the book, the last 4 digits of its ISBN, and the chapter/page number your query relates to.

Web Support

Feel free to go visit our website, at *http://www.glasshaus.com/*. Here, you will find a wealth of useful resources:

- **Code Download**: The example code for this, and every other glasshaus book, can be downloaded from our site.

- **An online glossary** of the terms in this book is being provided. The glossary will be a living document that can be updated on a regular basis, remaining up-to-date with the advances in accessible technology.

1

- Accessibility-usability synergy
- Reasons for providing accessible web sites
- Debunking myths

Author: Shawn Lawton Henry

Understanding Web Accessibility

At the most basic level, web accessibility is about people being able to get and use web content. It is about designing web pages that people can present and interact with according to their needs and preferences. A primary focus of accessibility is access by people with disabilities. The larger scope of accessibility includes benefits to people without disabilities. While accessibility is presented here in its relationship to usability, it is important to remember that the fundamental point is the ability to access web content at all. What is nice to have for some people is required by other people for them to be able to access web sites at all.

This chapter introduces web accessibility, with a focus on the synergy between usability and accessibility. It covers the benefits of accessibility, beyond access for people with disabilities. Some common myths are addressed and the conclusion touches on opportunities related to web accessibility. References for more information are included throughout the chapter text and in a reference list at the end.

Accessibility – Usability Synergy

Accessibility is a subset of a more general pursuit: usability. Put simply, usability means designing a user interface that is effective, efficient, and satisfying. Important elements of web site usability are:

- **Learnability**: Can visitors use the web site effectively the first time they visit it without becoming frustrated?

- **Memorability**: Will visitors remember how to use the web site the next time?

- **Effectiveness**: Can visitors easily navigate through the web site, determine what to do next, and understand the content? Is the design consistent and predictable?

- **Efficiency**: Can visitors find what they need and accomplish their goal in a reasonable amount of time?

- **Satisfaction**: Do visitors have a good feeling about using the web site? Will they use it again? Is the content presented effectively?

Certainly all of these usability elements are good for accessibility, as well. In the context of usability, *accessibility* means designing a user interface to be effective, efficient, and satisfying **for more people in more situations**. However, satisfaction is much less an issue with accessibility. Accessibility is more concerned with making web sites **perceivable**, **operable**, and **understandable.** That web interaction is effective and efficient becomes more important when it is part of education and employment.

Usable Accessibility

While many would agree with the concept of accessibility being related to usability, that is often not how accessibility is approached in practice. Many designers and developers were recently introduced to accessibility because of regulations such as Section 508 of the Rehabilitation Act in the US. In such cases, the focus of accessibility is often limited to meeting standards and guidelines. Often this means technical aspects get emphasized at the expense of the human interaction aspect. (This problem can also be seen in some assistive technologies and early web sites that were developed specifically for people with disabilities. While being accessible to some, they demonstrated a clear lack of usability.)

A simplified example of something that can "pass" an automated check for accessibility and still not be usable is alternative text for an image (adding an `alt` attribute to the `<img>` element that describes the graphic; there's more about this below). Alternative text can be provided that does not help users without access to the image at all. The `alt` text must be meaningful in the context of the page for the page to be usable without images.

This problem can be avoided by adopting the broader definition of accessibility as a guiding principle. Instead of focusing only on the technical aspects, it is important to recognize that usability is also an important aspect of accessibility. Consciously addressing '*usable accessibility*' helps to clarify the difference between what meets minimum accessibility standards and what is usable by people with disabilities.

Setting a goal of usable accessibility will impact how you develop and evaluate solutions. It has been said that you can meet Section 508 accessibility standards by focusing only on the markup. However, to evaluate for usable accessibility, you need to actually interact with the rendered web pages in various configurations, preferably including usability testing that involves participants with disabilities.

In this way you go beyond technical accessibility to achieve usable accessibility.

Concrete Example of Web Accessibility

A large proportion of accessibility standards and accessibility testing software tools address the more technical aspects of accessibility. These tend to be easier to understand, quantify, and test. Indeed one such aspect, text equivalents for images, is one of the most common and powerful examples of incorporating accessibility on the Web. (Text equivalents are also a common example of an accessibility technique that is of great benefit beyond accessibility to people with disabilities – including indexing, search, and mobile computing.)

Web pages often include images, but many web page visitors cannot see images. Some are blind and use a screen reader, which reads aloud the text on a screen. Others have turned off image downloading because they have a slow Internet connection, or they are working with a handheld device that cannot display images.

Viewing pages without images is addressed when web designers include equivalent text descriptions for images. Called 'alt text', short for alternative text, these text descriptions are:

- Displayed when the mouse pointer hovers over the image (by most visual browsers)

- Displayed when images are not downloaded (by most visual browsers)

- Read by screen readers and voice browsers

The figures below are examples of how alt text is rendered by three different browser configurations. The first is Internet Explorer with images loaded and the mouse hovering over an image, which displays the alt text in a popup:

Day	Mon	Tues	Wed	Thur	Fri
Outlook	☀	⛅	🌧	🌦	🌨
High (°C)	25°	20°	15°	10° rain 5°	
Low (°C)	15°	10°	5°	0°	-5°

The next figure shows the same page in Opera with images turned off in the browser settings. For images with alt text provided, the alt text is displayed. Where alt text is missing (the middle image), "*IMAGE*" is displayed.

Day	Mon	Tues	Wed	Thur	Fri
Outlook	sunny	partly cloudy	IMAGE	rain	snow
High (°C)	25°	20°	15°	10°	5°
Low (°C)	15°	10°	5°	0°	-5°

The third figure shows the display of IBM Home Page Reader, a voice browser, set to read images without alt text. The text in the bottom pane indicates what a person using the voice browser would hear. (At the time of the screen capture, it was reading the middle image, thus it is highlighted and the information at the top and bottom of the page is not visible in the bottom text pane.) Notice that it reads the file name of the image that is missing alt text:

Day	Mon	Tues	Wed	Thur	Fri
Outlook	☼	⛅	⛈	🌧	🌨
High (°C)	25°	20°	15°	10°	5°
Low (°C)	15°	10°	5°	0°	-5°

Outlook
[sunny.]
[partly cloudy.]
[Image with no alt text: example%20of%20alt%20text/thunder.gif.]
[rain.]
[snow.]
High (°C)

The figures demonstrate that if there is no `alt` text, the usefulness and usability of the page is dramatically reduced for visitors not able to access images. With equivalent `alt` text, the page is equally usable with or without images.

Alternative text is primarily discussed in terms of its usefulness to people who are blind and use screen readers. This clearly is an accessibility issue for people with disabilities. At the same time, alternative text can also be useful to people without disabilities, such as those using a handheld device. `alt` text can also increase usability. Most visual browsers display the `alt` text for an image as the image is downloading. For long downloads, this helps both with user perceptions and with interactions. That is, users are likely to be less aware of a slow image download because they are getting some information about the content from its `alt` text. The fact that there are benefits of accessibility improvements to people without disabilities is one of the complications of distinguishing between usability and accessibility.

Differentiating Between Usability and Accessibility

When designing web sites, it is rarely useful to differentiate between usability and accessibility. There are times when such a distinction is considered, such as when looking at discrimination against people with disabilities and when defining and addressing specific accessibility standards and guidelines. The following problems illustrate the difference between usability and accessibility:

- Usability problems impact all users equally, regardless of ability. That is, a person with a disability is not disadvantaged to a greater extent by usability issues than a person without a disability.

- Accessibility problems hinder access to a web site by people with disabilities. When a person with a disability is at a disadvantage relative to a person without a disability, that is an accessibility issue.

The distinction between usability and accessibility is especially difficult to define when considering cognitive and language disabilities. It is further blurred by the fact that features and functionality for people with disabilities benefit people without disabilities because of situational limitations (as described in the *Functional and Situational Limitations* section). The overlap between the processes of designing for usability and designing for accessibility, addressed in the next section, demonstrates the synergy between usability and accessibility.

Accessibility As a Process

User-Centered Design (**UCD**) is an established and proven (although unfortunately not universally followed) process for designing mainstream hardware, software, and web interfaces. (A list of resources for more information on UCD is included at the end of this chapter.) UCD considers usability goals and the users' characteristics, environment, tasks, and workflow in the design of an interface.

While usability and UCD have been topics in books, conference presentations, and education programs over the last decade, design that considers the needs of people with disabilities is still relatively uncommon in education and practice. As a result, the range of users who can use products and the situations in which products can be used are both less inclusive than if the needs of people with disabilities were considered in design. At issue is the range of user characteristics and enviroments that designers define in the design process, consciously or unconsciously.

Without a formal process for considering others, it is common to design for ourselves. Therefore, many web sites are designed based on the individual designer's preferences, abilites, and environment. A large percentage of web site designers are young, without disabilities, experienced with computers, and operating with the latest technologies. Thus, all too often, that is the user profile they tend to design for.

Even when specific user analysis is conducted, the range of users considered is often too narrow. Primarily because of a simple lack or awareness, designers tend not to include people with disabilities and people operating in more unusual environments in their user analysis.

In order to design inclusively, designers need to consider the widest range of possible users and environments. The **Web Content Accessibility Guidelines** (**WCAG**) notes that many users may be operating in contexts very different from the designers' context:

- They may not be able to see, hear, move, or may not be able to process some types of information easily or at all.

- They may have difficulty reading or comprehending text.

- They may not have or be able to use a keyboard or mouse.

- They may have a text-only screen, a small screen, or a slow Internet connection.

- They may not speak or adequately understand the language in which the document is written.

- They may be in a situation where their eyes, ears, or hands are busy or interfered with (for example, driving to work, or working in a loud environment).

- They may have an early version of a browser, a different browser entirely, a voice browser, or a different operating system.

These are taken from the World Wide Web Consortium (W3C) Web Accessibility Initiative (WAI) Web Accessibility Content Guidelines (WCAG) 1.0 www.w3.org/TR/WCAG10/

When all possible users and environments are considered in web site design, the process can be called inclusive design. (This does not mean that all user circumstances should be given equal weight in design. Certainly it is best that designs are optimized for the most common configurations *and* are flexible enough to accommodate other configurations.) Inclusive design, as the integration of accessibility into a UCD process, is similar to "design for all" (commonly used in Europe) and "universal design" (more broadly used in the US).

Universal Design

The term *universal design* was originally used in association with buildings, and has more recently been used in describing an approach to accessibility for information and communication technologies (ICT). Gregg C. Vanderheiden of the Trace Research & Development Center has defined it as such:

> *"Universal design is the process of creating products (devices, environments, systems, and processes) which are usable by people with the widest possible range of abilities, operating within the widest possible range of situations (environments, conditions, and circumstances), as is commercially practical."*
>
> *Universal Design of Consumer Products: Current Industry Practice and Perceptions*
> *http://trace.wisc.edu/docs/ud_consumer_products_hfes2000/index.htm.*

Universal design refers to a process, rather than the resulting product. When implementing such a process, it becomes clear that some design elements which are merely good, nice-to-haves for usability, are very important when considering access by people with disabilities.

Good for Some People, Required for Others

The beginning of this chapter listed elements of usability and noted that they are good for accessibility as well. The converse is also true, as demonstrated by looking at formal accessibility guidelines. For example, consider the following guidelines from the WCAG:

- 9.4: Create a logical tab order...

- 12.3: Divide large blocks of information into more manageable groups...

- 13.4: Use navigation mechanisms in a consistent manner

- 13.6: Group related links...

- 13.8: Place distinguishing information at the beginning of headings...

- 14.1: Use the clearest and simplest language appropriate...

- 14.3: Create a style of presentation that is consistent across pages

It would be good if all web sites followed these guidelines. They are aspects of usability, yet, these specific guidelines come from the Web Content Accessibility Guidelines (WCAG); they are web **accessibility** guidelines.

Certainly, in developing guidelines specifically for accessibility, it is often difficult to distinguish between usability and accessibility. It becomes clear that many design aspects that are **good** for general usability are **required** for accessibility.

Consistent Navigation and Presentation Example

Consistent navigation and presentation across a web site is one example of a design aspect that is good for usability and much more important for accessibility. Imagine using a site where the navigation is inconsistent. You have to skim the page to find the navigation in a different location each time. If you have good vision and are using the site on a high-resolution monitor, inconsistent navigation presentation is a minor inconvenience. It only requires visually skimming the page, or maybe one or two mouse clicks to scroll down it.

However, if you have no vision, the inconsistency is a much greater problem; you cannot visually skim the page. People who are blind and use a screen reader hear only one word at a time, rather than seeing the entire web page at once. People with other visual impairments, such as people using significant screen magnification or people with extreme tunnel vision (which is rather like looking through a drinking straw) may see only a small portion of a web page at a time.

People without disabilities can face similar constraints. Web phones and personal digital assistants (PDAs) – which are increasingly being used to access web sites – have very small display screens. Web page navigation that may be visible in one screen on a common monitor may not fit in one screen on a different device.

In all these cases, consistent navigation impacts the usability of the web site even more when the user is operating under constraints from disabilities or devices. This parallelism between constraints from disabilities and constraints from devices is addressed in the next section.

Functional and Situational Limitations

The *Differentiating Between Usability and Accessibility* section distinguished accessibility as related to disability. Subsequent sections showed areas where this distinction is blurred. A broader definition of accessibility, provided below, is more suitable in most circumstances.

Accessibility can be defined as the quality of a web site that makes it possible for people to use it – to find it navigable and understandable – even when they are working under limiting conditions or constraints.

> *Accessibility is about designing so that **more people** can use your web site **effectively** in **more situations**.*

Although most people consider accessibility in terms of disability, that is not the whole picture. A more broad definition of accessibility covers people operating under situational limitations as well as functional limitations:

- **Functional limitations** pertain to disabilities, such as blindness or limited use of the hands. Functional limitations can be visual, auditory, physical, or cognitive (which includes language and learning disabilities).

- **Situational limitations** relate to the prevailing circumstances, environment, or device. These limitations can affect anybody, not just people with disabilities. Examples include mobile devices and device limitations, such as having no mouse, or constraining circumstances, such as interacting with a web site through a computer integrated into a car's dashboard, where use of the hands and eyes is limited.

Most of the legal requirements for accessibility are concerned with meeting the needs of people with functional limitations, or disabilities. Understanding the benefits of accessibility to people who are operating with situational limitations, clarifies some of the benefits to people without disabilities and the related business benefits of accessibility.

Two Categories, One Solution

Some business benefits of accessibility are realized because of the relationship between functional limitations and situational limitations. Two seemingly different objectives – designing systems that work in a wide range of environments, and designing systems for a wide range of user characteristics – have similar solutions, as discussed in *User Interfaces for All: Concepts, Methods, and Tools* (*Vanderheiden and Henry, Lawrence Erlbaum Associates, ISBN: 0805829679*).

The issues of accessible design are essentially the same, whether you are concerned about designing a mobile Internet appliance with input and output limitations, designing a public kiosk to be accessible to people with disabilities, or designing a web application targeted at seniors. Accessible web sites include those that can be used hands-free, eyes-free, or ears-free (requirements of many mobile products) and by people who are in noisy or dark environments.

> *If we design a system that is truly universal and mobile, we will have created a system that is accessible to almost anyone with a physical or sensory disability.*
>
> User Interfaces for All *(Vanderheiden and Henry, Lawrence Erlbaum Associates, ISBN: 0805829679).*

Curb cuts, the slope from a sidewalk to a street, are a common example from the physical world of how solutions for disability access are similar to solutions for situational limitation access. Curb cuts are primarily intended to accommodate people in wheelchairs. Curb cuts also benefit people with situational limitations that make it difficult to get over a curb. In fact, most curb cuts are used more often by people without physical disabilities – pushing strollers or shopping carts, riding a bicycle or roller blades, pulling luggage or appliance dollies – than by people in wheelchairs.

The curb cuts example illustrates how people without disabilities benefit from a design for people with disabilities. The next section addresses other benefits of web accessibility.

Many Reasons To Provide Accessible Web Sites

The previous section provides examples of how increasing accessibility for people with disabilities can increase usability for people without disabilities. This section discusses several other motivations for accessibility, including:

- **Compliance with regulatory and legal requirements**

- **Exposure to more people: people with disabilities and seniors**

- **Exposure to more situations: new places, new devices**

- **Better design and implementation**

- **Cost savings**

- **It makes you look good**

- **Enlightened self interest**

A Brief Aside On the History of Web Accessibility Awareness

Web accessibility is not a new thing. In the 1990s, web accessibility information was available from organizations such as the **Trace Research and Development Center** and companies such as IBM. The City of San José Web Page Disability Access Design Standard was developed in 1996, and the **AUS Standards for Accessible Web Design** (*http://www.lawlink.nsw.gov.au/lawlink.nsf/pages/aus_standards*) were available online in 1997. (For a list of other guidelines, see the references at the end of *http://trace.wisc.edu/archive/html_guidelines/version8.htm*.) Also in 1997, the World Wide Web Consortium established the **Web Accessibility Initiative** (**WAI** – see *http://www.w3.org/wai*) and in 1999 the **Web Content Accessibility Guidelines** (**WCAG**) 1.0 were finalized as a Recommendation.

Despite the extensive web accessibility work completed in a few areas, the majority of web site designers and developers were, in the recent past, not aware of accessibility issues at all. Awareness gradually increased with media articles on accessibility, in newspapers (such as the Washington Post and USA Today) and sites for designers and developers (such as Jakob Nielsen's Alertbox and *http://builder.com.com/*) and also as accessibility began showing up in conference topics – such as at web design conferences by CMP Media and Thunder Lizard, Human Factors and the Web conference, and at the Usability Professionals Association conference. (A list of resources for more information on cited examples is included at the end of this chapter.)

While more people began to hear about accessibility, the majority of web sites still did little to implement it. There are several reasons why so many web sites were not accessible besides lack of awareness. Most designers, developers, and managers did not understand the benefits of providing accessible sites and so were not convinced that it was important for their business. Even those who did want to incorporate accessibility had difficulty finding the resources to do so. Recent legal and regulatory activity changed that.

Compliance with Regulatory and Legal Requirements

Increasingly, legal concerns are providing the primary impetus for organizations to pay attention to accessibility issues. Governments issued guidelines for accessibility, including the Canadian Common Look and Feel Standards and Guidelines, and the Irish Recommended Guidelines for Public Sector Organisations. Many people consider accessibility a civil right. In Australia, an individual won a complaint of web inaccessibility against the Sydney Organizing Committee for the Olympic Games under the Disability Discrimination Act (DDA). Similarly, in the US, applicability of the Americans with Disabilities Act (ADA) to web sites has been addressed in documents and case law. America Online (AOL) settled a lawsuit with the National Federation of the Blind (NFB), and major US banks signed agreements to provide accessible online banking. (A list of resources for more information on cited examples is included at the end of this chapter.)

Section 508 of the Rehabilitation Act and the accompanying Electronic and Information Technology Accessibility Standards, which directly address web accessibility, have arguably been the largest catalyst for motivating accessibility work in government and commercial organizations. For more details on legal issues, see *http://www.uiaccess.com/resources.html#resources-legal*, and Chapter 13 in this book.

Even when the primary motivation for addressing accessibility is legal, organizations can get more out of their accessibility efforts if they realize the additional benefits discussed below, such as increasing the number of people who can use the web site.

More People: People with Disabilities and Seniors

Between 15% and 30% of the general population have functional limitations that can affect their ability to use technology products. That represents an estimated 50 million people in the US alone, and over 750 million worldwide. (Source of these statistics – *http://www.infouse.com/disabilitydata/p4.textgfx.html* and World Health Organization, respectively.) It is estimated that people with disabilities control a discretionary income of over $175 billion annually in the US alone (*http://www.isoc.org/briefings/002/*). For businesses, accessibility is also about increasing sales by addressing the range of constraints that could limit customers' use of your web site.

> Accessible web sites accommodate a wider range of customers and constituents, increasing the number of people who can effectively use your web site.

At one time, only a very few people had access to the Internet. As the Internet grew in popularity, an early segment of Internet users were members of "Generation X". A stereotype emerged in the mid-1990s of mainly affluent young men spending inordinate amounts of time on the Internet. This is no longer the case; these days more people, including people with disabilities and older people, are using the Internet. Organizations are implementing web applications for employees, vendors, and customers. Computers are now available in many schools, public libraries, and senior activity centers. The recent focus on the "digital divide" points out the large number of people who currently have computer access as well as efforts to increase that availability throughout society.

In fact, some people with disabilities and older people have additional motivations for using the Internet. People who cannot drive, who have difficulty walking, or have difficulty carrying packages are more likely to find accessible online shopping an attractive alternative to shopping in "bricks and mortar" stores. Almost 10% of Internet users reported having a disability, in a user survey carried out by the *Georgia Institute of Technology Graphic, Visualization, & Usability Center,* (*http://www.gvu.gatech.edu/user_surveys/survey-1998-10/graphs/general/q12.htm*).

Computerworld reported back in 1999 that:

- The age group with the highest concentration of online buyers is the 50 to 64 segment, with over 25% making online purchases – and the fastest-growing segment is the 65 and over group.

- Altogether, almost 7 in 10 online buyers are over 40, according to a survey by Ernst & Young and the National Retail Federation.

  (*http://www.computerworld.com/cwi/story/0,1199,NAV47_STO42944,00.html*)

In addition to shopping, employment opportunities exist with accessible technology. Some disabilities will prevent people from performing a number of jobs. However, those same people can excel at jobs that primarily require computer interaction. So providing accessible web applications externally increases the number of potential customers and providing accessible web applications internally increases the number of potential employees.

Seniors

The statistics and trends point to an ever-increasing number of people with functional limitations in the future. As we age, most people experience a decrease in vision, hearing, physical abilities, and cognitive abilities. The pie charts below show the increase in disability with aging:

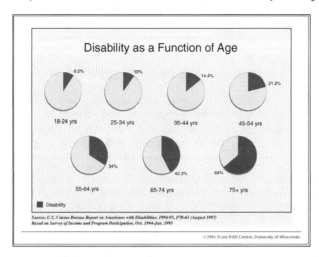

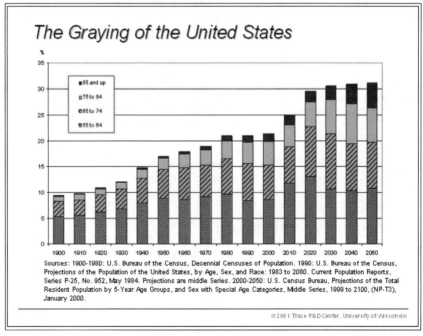

[Printed with permission from the Trace R&D Center.
http://trace.wisc.edu/docs/function-aging/]

As shown in the graph overleaf, the portion of the population considered "senior" is dramatically increasing, particularly in places where use of technology is pervasive. This has created greater interest in technologies that reduce the impact of various impairments. Older users with diminishing hearing, sight, physical, and cognitive abilities are an important market for many organizations online. For example, in Europe, people past retirement age number about 100 million, according to the Tiresias site: *http://www.tiresias.org/reports/hdti1.htm*.

More Situations: New Places, New Devices

Situational limitations are increasingly issues for people without disabilities (as well as people with disabilities).

> Accessible web sites accommodate people in a wider range of situations, increasing the situations in which your web site can be used effectively.

Various situational constraints from environments or circumstance are impacting the design of emerging technologies. Sometimes the limitation is inherent in the product, for example, PDAs, mobile phones, and other handheld devices are increasingly able to access the Internet. These devices have limited input and output options, such as small displays without color. Following accessibility guidelines can optimize interaction with such devices.

For example, in 1999, *http://www.optavia.com* was designed to meet accessibility guidelines and provide usable accessibility, but without thought given to the possibility of access by PDAs and such devices. In 2001, Optavia's president checked out the site on her new web-enabled mobile phone. She was delighted to find that the site as designed worked well on the phone display. It turned out that the effort that went into making the site accessible also made it work on the web phone.

It bears noting that new devices tend to be purchased by affluent buyers, a desirable market segment for most businesses. Examples include an executive buying a gift via a hand-held device, or a stock analyst checking the market from a web-enabled mobile phone. Yet these technologies are not only for the rich. Like mobile phones before them, PDAs and other wireless devices are beginning to spread into common use.

Understanding and using accessibility techniques now will better position your organization to capture the benefits of these and other emerging technologies as their use increases. However, you don't have to wait for the future to realize the additional benefits of accessibility.

Better Design and Implementation

Most of the improvements you make for accessibility result in better design and implementation overall. As discussed previously, accessibility improvements can increase usability for all users, with and without disabilities. Accessible design can also help with technical and maintenance issues. This section describes how accessibility improvements lead to better design and implementation by:

- Using HMTL for structure and stylesheets for presentation
- Providing textual information as text rather than images

The example of situational limitations opposite relates to a fundamental principle of accessible web site design, that is to *transform gracefully*. When a web site transforms gracefully, it is usable in different modes and configurations. So, it works just as well when used on a large monitor set at 640 x 480 screen resolution, a screen reader, or a PDA. "Pages that transform gracefully remain accessible despite any of the constraints...including physical, sensory, and cognitive disabilities, work constraints, and technological barriers." (*Web Content Accessibility Guidelines 1.0, http://www.w3.org/TR/WCAG/#transform-gracefully*)

Of primary importance in achieving graceful transformation is *separation of structure and presentation* (which is further discussed in Chapter 9). HTML was originally intended to merely mark up the content of technical documents in such a way that they could be efficiently transmitted and accessed by multiple platforms. However, once the Internet began to be used more as a marketing tool, web site designers wanted more control over the visual representation of information. As a result, HTML was misused to defining visual representation rather than the intended structural information.

Current technologies such as Cascading Style Sheets (CSS) were designed to provide web site designers with a dedicated method to influence presentation while using HTML only for structure (for more on using CSS to improve Accessibility, see *Chapter 9*). Consider, for example, a web page in which the main heading is "About Acme." You should not use HTML to mark up the presentation or appearance, which is a common mistake. Instead, you should use HTML to mark up the structure. Specifically, the heading should be marked up with an `<h1>` tag, rather than with `<font>`, as shown below:

Correct (HTML for structure):

```
<h1>About Acme</h1>
<strong> (usually rendered as bold)
<em> (for emphasis, usually rendered as italic)
```

Incorrect (HTML for presentation):

```
<font size="14pt"><b>About Acme</b></font>
<b> (for bold)
<i> (for italic)
```

Many of the old features of HTML that were used to mark up appearance have been deprecated in favor of using CSS to define presentation. As shown above, HTML elements such as `<b>` and `<i>` define presentation, and therefore should not be used. Instead, elements such as `<strong>` and `<em>` should be used to mark up the structure and content.

For a list of tags and the role of each (structure or presentation), see "Index of HTML elements and attributes" in Techniques for Web Content Accessibility Guidelines at http://www.w3.org/TR/WAI-WEBCONTENT-TECHS/#html-index.

Deprecated elements and attributes are listed at: http://www.w3.org/TR/REC-html40/appendix/changes.html#h-A.3.1.2 and http://www.w3.org/TR/REC-html40/index/attributes.html.

It is important to use HTML to mark up document structure so that assistive technologies can provide appropriate information to users. A well-designed page will have visually distinct groups of information with headings. People who can see can get an overview of a web page's content by visually skimming the page. People who cannot see are not able to do this. One technique that non-visual users can use to get such an overview is to listen to the headings. Most screen readers and voice browsers have a feature that lets users jump to headings on a page. The screenshot below shows the *Headings Reading Mode* in IBM Home Page Reader:

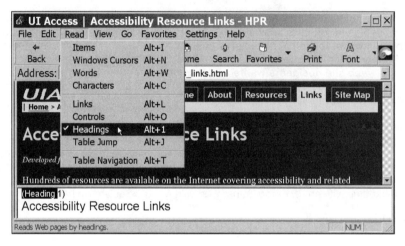

One way to check headings is with HTML validator (*http://validator.w3.org*). Below is an outline generated by HMTL validator from heading tags:

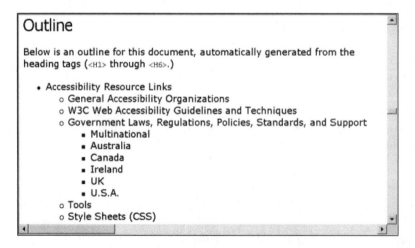

When headings are not marked up properly as headings, this information is not available to assistive technologies. While a page could appear to have headings when viewed in a graphical browser, Home Page Reader will say, "No headings on this page". A page without headings marked up properly would show no outline in HTML validator, as shown:

Stylesheets let web developers mark up headings in correct HTML and change the way browsers present them visually.

Implementation with Stylesheets

Using stylesheets also provides additional advantages, such as helping to manage consistency across multiple pages, upholding site-wide standards, and simplifying maintenance. For example, consider the case where heading colors are blue for first-level headings and red for second-level headings. Then, some time later, the heading colors need to be changed to reflect marketing's branding change. If the colors were marked up in HMTL, the update would require finding and changing every instance of the headings in every page on the site. If instead the colors are defined in a stylesheet that the pages reference, the change is as simple as changing the singlestyle sheet.

Another advantage to stylesheets is in performance. Using stylesheets rather than HTML to define presentation can result in smaller files, thus slightly increasing page transmission rates by reducing use of bandwidth. This increase in download speed is an important issue for many web sites. Another best practice for accessibility that increases download speed is using text rather than images to present textual information.

Text As Text, Not Images

One way that designers attempt to control the way a web page looks is by using images rather than text to present textual information. However, if we look at an example, we can immediately see the accessibility problems we run into when using this method. The first two examples show the navigation text in images. The second two show the navigation text as text. The following screenshot shows a web page that uses images to present some of the navigation, with the browser set to use smaller fonts:

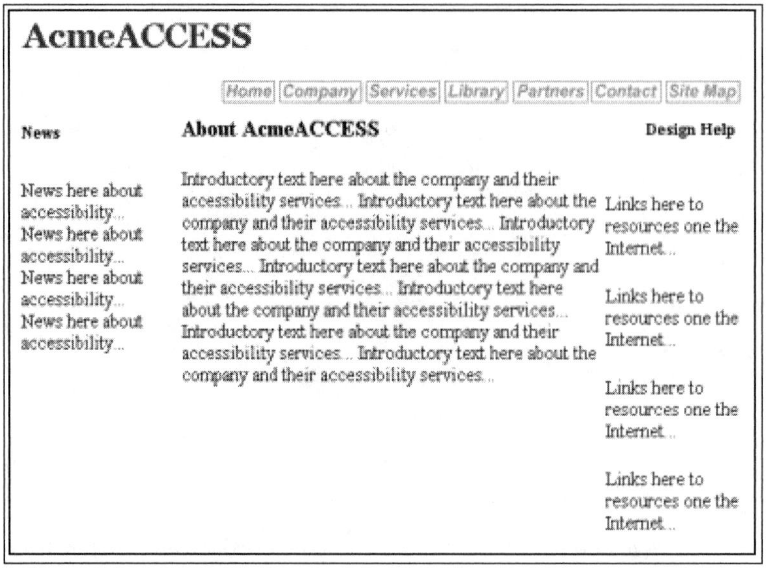

AcmeACCESS

Home | Company | Services | Library | Partners | Contact | Site Map

News

About AcmeACCESS

Design Help

News here about accessibility...
News here about accessibility...
News here about accessibility...
News here about accessibility...

Introductory text here about the company and their accessibility services... Introductory text here about the company and their accessibility services... Introductory text here about the company and their accessibility services... Introductory text here about the company and their accessibility services... Introductory text here about the company and their accessibility services... Introductory text here about the company and their accessibility services... Introductory text here about the company and their accessibility services...

Links here to resources one the Internet...

Links here to resources one the Internet...

Links here to resources one the Internet...

Links here to resources one the Internet...

The screenshot below shows the same web page with fonts set to largest in the browser. Notice that the text that is in images – the primary navigation – does not resize:

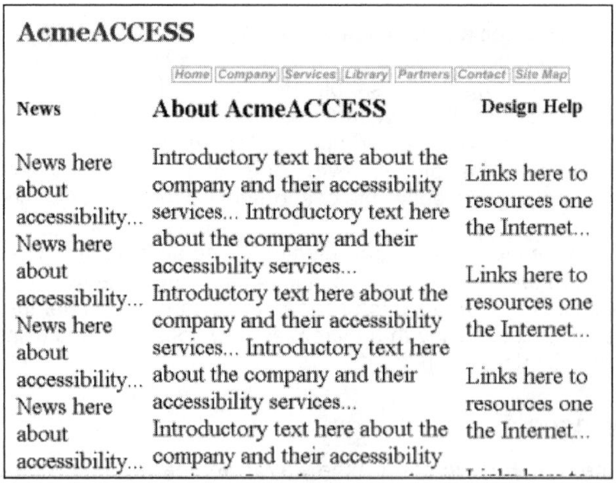

AcmeACCESS

Home | Company | Services | Library | Partners | Contact | Site Map

News

About AcmeACCESS

Design Help

News here about accessibility...
News here about accessibility...
News here about accessibility...
News here about accessibility...

Introductory text here about the company and their accessibility services... Introductory text here about the company and their accessibility services... Introductory text here about the company and their accessibility services... Introductory text here about the company and their accessibility

Links here to resources one the Internet...

Links here to resources one the Internet...

Links here to resources one the Internet...

The following two screenshots show the UIAccess page that uses similar looking navigation. Notice that between the two screenshots with fonts set to smaller and largest, the text on the navigation bar resizes:

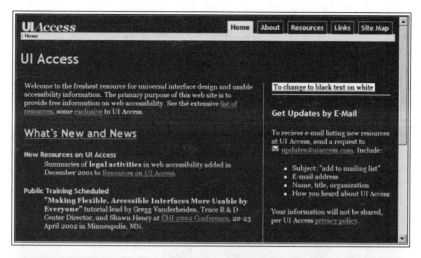

Obviously, the text in the image is not resized in the first example, therefore limiting the accessibility of the page to some people with visual impairments – if scalable text was used, we would not run into this problem. Text that is fixed size, rather than a relative size, also will not resize in most browsers, as shown with the left-side text in the following screenshots with small and largest font settings:

Providing text as true text and not images has additional benefits beyond accessibility, helping with data mining, and the visibility of a site to search engines. Presenting text as text also helps with redesign and providing multiple languages. As you may expect, when text is presented in images, stylesheets cannot be used to modify them. A similar situation exists in providing multiple languages – images have to be redesigned to provide the text they contain in different languages, and also, any automatic translators will not be able to translate text in images. These examples also show areas for cost savings from addressing accessibility, another advantage of accessibility beyond disability access.

Cost Savings

Initially, understanding and implementing accessibility will take time and money. At the same time, some of the accessibility improvements will reduce overall web site costs, for example, because accessibility improvements increase general usability, online sales are likely to increase and support calls and costs will go down. In fact, in the long-term, you will likely achieve cost savings and revenue increases from the investments you make in accessibility. For example, we have already talked about using stylesheets effectively in web development to reduce maintenance.

Another aspect of accessibility is providing information in plain text, in addition to other multimedia as appropriate. Generally, textual information is easier and cheaper to manage, update, and migrate compared to information contained in graphics. Consider localization, which is the provision of multiple languages.

Providing accessible online products and services can reduce other expenditures for access to people with disabilities. For example, companies that provide accessible online statements (such as telephone, utility, credit card, bank) will likely be able to significantly cut the cost of providing alternative formats such as Braille and large print statements, as customers are drawn online by the flexibility and convenience of online access.

Incorporating accessibility is much more cost-effective when it is addressed from the beginning, and throughout a project. Waiting until the end of a project to consider accessibility significantly increases the time and effort required. Also considering accessibility can help you discover other issues earlier in the project life cycle, saving money and time relative to correcting problems later in the project.

Finally, providing accessible web sites could also save you from some legal costs, as addressed in Chapter 13, and sales could increase following positive press coverage.

Boosting Your Reputation

A commitment to accessibility can be very positive for an organization's image. Take advantage of your accessibility work as an example of being a good "corporate citizen" and meeting the needs of your customers or constituents. Once your web site meets accessibility standards and guidelines and provides usable accessibility, by all means, include it in marketing materials. Businesses such as Adobe have issued press releases on the accessibility of their web-related products. Banks have received valuable local news coverage for their "talking ATMs" (automated teller machines). You can promote your site's accessibility by including the following logos:

- W3C web Content Accessibility Guidelines Conformance Logos: *http://www.w3.org/WAI/WCAG1-Conformance.html*

- W3C HTML logo: *http://www.w3.org/Icons/valid-html40*

- W3C CSS logo: *http://jigsaw.w3.org/css-validator/images/vcss.gif*

- W3C CSS buttons: *http://www.w3.org/Style/CSS/Buttons/Menu*

- CAST Bobby icon guidelines: *http://www.cast.org/bobby/index.cfm?i=317*

- NCAM web accessibility symbol: *http://ncam.wgbh.org/webaccess/symbolwinner.html*

You can also list accessible products at places such as:

- List of (self-reported) Bobby-approved sites: *http://www.cast.org/Bobby/ApprovedSites318.cfm*

- List of NCAM symbol sites: *http://ncam.wgbh.org/webaccess/symbolsites.html*

- WeMedia: *http://www.wemedia.com* – Media company covering issues important to people with disabilities

- Half the Planet: *http://www.halftheplanet.com* – Lists disability-related services and products, news, and more

- List of Health and Disability Portals: http://*www.icdri.org/Portals.htm*

Furthermore, web accessibility proponents and designers are eager to share the web addresses (URLs) of good examples of accessible web sites. Positive coverage is another way that addressing accessibility is in an organization's self-interest.

Enlightened Self-Interest

Incorporating accessibility is **an act of enlightened self-interest**, both for organizations and individuals. That is, if individuals and organizations are aware of the benefits of accessibility (they are "enlightened"), they will address accessibility issues in order to benefit themselves (as well as others). For example, while some people are born with a disability, others acquire disabilities from accident, illness, disease, or aging. Most people will experience temporary or permanent disability in their lifetime, and can benefit from technology that is accessible. The acronym TAB for *temporarily able-bodied* addresses the myth that accessibility only helps people who currently have disabilities.

Debunking Myths

Another aspect of being enlightened about web accessibility is learning enough to separate the myths from reality, as covered in this section.

In Chapter 13, we debunk some legal myths of web accessibility.

Myth: Accessible Pages Have To Be Plain

Many people have the misconception that to make a web site accessible, you have to take out images and color, make it boring, or "dumb it down" in terms of design sophistication. That is not true. We do not want to limit designs for accessibility, and taking away visual appeal does not serve the best interests of the overall audience. In fact, part of the accessibility-usability synthesis is making the web site usable, aesthetically pleasing **and** commercially viable to all users. It is pointless to design web sites that are accessible, but cannot succeed in the market.

In fact, using images and color often increases usability for some people with cognitive disabilities, while also benefiting people who are cognitively average. WCAG checkpoint 14.2 specifically mandates this:

"Supplement text with graphic or auditory presentations where they will facilitate comprehension of the page. [Priority 3]."

An example of using color to increase usability is in navigation areas of web pages. When navigation links are on a light-colored background and content is on a white background, as in the example web page opposite, it is easier cognitively to distinguish between the navigation area and content area. Furthermore, integrating corporate colors in such a design can increase branding and visual appeal.

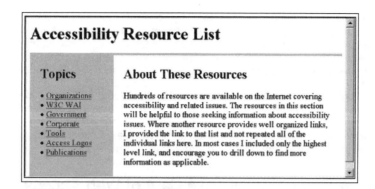

Myth: Just Add a Text-Only Version

A common approach to providing accessible web pages is to design a site, and then make a separate accessible site, that is, *text-only version*. The issue of text-only versions crosses into the idea of separate versus inclusive design. In today's environment, providing separately developed sites is rarely the best approach for accessibility, or for business. (However, providing truly equivalent information that can be accessed graphically or textually from the same content source is advantageous.)

In the past, common assistive technologies were not able to handle complex web page designs. For example, screen readers read across the screen, so multi-column newspaper-style layouts were not usable. It was nearly impossible at one time to provide visually appealing, complex, dynamic web sites that were also accessible. Therefore, designers were faced with the choice of either significant constraints on their design or providing a text-only version. Now, technologies let you develop visually appealing, complex, dynamic web sites that are also accessible. Stylesheets offer more presentation functionality, assistive technologies can handle layout tables, and browsers provide text resizing. Many recent technologies from the W3C such as **Scaleable Vector Graphics** (**SVG**) actually provide more flexibility for presentation as well as accessibility support.

There are several problems with providing a separate accessible site:

- Separate versions are rarely equal. When there are two versions of the site, invariably, the text-only version does not get updated as frequently as the main version. Even when organizations and individuals have the best intentions of keeping two sites synchronized, the realities of deadlines and limited resources interfere. As discussed overleaf, emerging technologies and methodologies are minimizing this problem.

- The primary version often lacks even the most basic accessibility. Commonly, developers of alternative accessible test-only sites spend little effort in making the primary site accessible. The alternative site is often optimized for screen readers, with all information provided linearly and without graphics and color. However, some people would be better off using an accessible primary site.

Some new tools generate both a primary site and a text-only site from a single source of content, supposedly eliminating the first problem mentioned, that of separate sites not being synchronized. In one such implementation that I reviewed, the text-only site was fairly close in content to the primary site. However, the alternative site was missing promotional material. Therefore, users of the text-only version missed out on special offers offered through the web site. Clearly this was discriminatory.

Certainly technologies and development efforts are beginning to provide the tools and methodologies needed to ensure that truly equivalent multiple versions of a site can be provided. For example, using XSLT to transform XML documents into other markup more suited for specific configurations or ASP to dynamically generate pages from database or XML files. Organizations such as SmartForce are creating multiple versions from a single content source. This is a promising development.

Myth: Assistive Technologies Take Care of Web Access

Successful web accessibility implementation requires cooperation among diverse areas. Disability groups, standards organizations, government regulators, attorneys, vendors of web development tools, developers of browsers and other user agents, assistive technology developers, and content providers all have roles to play in designing for accessibility. When one of these groups acts unilaterally, or fails to fulfill its responsibilities, it lowers the prospects for a Web that is universally accessible.

Timing of technology advancements also figures in the equation. Some technology advancements provide opportunities to increase accessibility. However, for content providers to take advantage of the new technologies, customers must use them. Some organizations have technology change management systems that impede their rapid adoption of the latest browsers and browser plug-ins. Similar reasons of cost and compatibility, especially with assistive technologies, also make some individuals reluctant to upgrade.

Browser and tool developers are supporting accessibility to a greater extent in new versions of the products, making it easier for content developers to implement accessibility in their web sites. Judy Brewer, Director of the Web Accessibility Initiative (WAI) International Program Office at the W3C, commented as follows:

> "Implementations of either of the web software guidelines (the latter two guidelines) (Authoring Tool Accessibility Guidelines and User Agent Accessibility Guidelines) make it easier for web designers to implement the Web Content Accessibility Guidelines. For instance, as browsers develop more capabilities to support accessibility, web site designers need to do less to make their pages accessible. Likewise, as authoring tools automate more of the production of accessible web content, site designers will be able to produce accessible web sites with little effort."
>
> (Quote taken from http://commdocs.house.gov/committees/judiciary/hju65010.000/ hju65010_0.htm)

Despite this trend, implementing accessibility in a web site still requires careful attention by the content developers. While it will get easier in the future, content developers will always have a role in accessibility implementation, regardless of technology advancements. The alt text example that opened this chapter illustrates the continuing responsibility of content developers. Standards can define the alt attribute in HTML, user agents (browsers and assistive technologies) can properly provide alt text to users, development tools can encourage or even require you to assign them, and testing tools can validate that they are included — yet only content developers can ensure that the text is equivalent, meaningful, and useful. Therein lies the responsibility and opportunity for all involved.

For more on implementation of accessible web sites, see Chapter 11.

Opportunity

Accessible web sites provide opportunity. For organizations and businesses, there is opportunity to make web sites work for more people and in more situations, to excel over competitors, and to get more business. Designing accessible web sites prepares organizations to take advantage of emerging technologies. For people with disabilities, web sites provide opportunities to participate in work, entertainment, and social activities in ways not otherwise available. With accessible web sites, more people can do ordinary things: children can learn, teenagers can flirt, adults can make a living, and seniors can read about their grandchildren.

Accessible web sites are one opportunity to further empower people – all people. Implementing accessibility is not always easy, and the right attitude is needed to overcome the challenges.

When people embrace the importance of accessibility, understand the benefits to themselves, to their organization, to other individuals, and to society, view accessibility as an exciting challenge, see the opportunity to improve their products and their individual skills, and when they are proud of their accomplishments, then efforts to construct accessible web sites can be a resounding success.

Citations and Resources for More Information

- *Accessibility Resource Links: http://www.uiaccess.com/access_links.html*

- *Thirty-Something (Million) – Should They Be Exceptions?: http://trace.wisc.edu/docs/30_some/30_some.htm*

- *The Growing Digital Divide In Access For People With Disabilities: Overcoming Barriers To Participation In The Digital Economy: http://www.icdri.org/the_digital_divide.htm*

- *Disability as a Function of Age: http://trace.wisc.edu/docs/function-aging/*

User-Centered Design: Books

- *Usability Engineering (Jakob Nielsen, Morgan Kauffman Publishers, ISBN: 0125184069)*

- *User-Centered Design: An Integrated Approach (Karel Vredenburg et al, Prentice Hall, ISBN: 0130912956)*

- *User-Centered Web Development (Jonathan Lazar, Jones and Bartlett Pub, ISBN: 0763714313)*

- *User-Centered Web Design (Jon Cato, Addison Westley Professional, ISBN: 0201398605)*

User-Centered Design: Online

- *User-Centered Design: http://www-3.ibm.com/ibm/easy/eou_ext.nsf/Publish/570*

- *User-Centered Design and Web Development: www.stcsig.org/usability/topics/articles/ucd%20_web_devel.html*

Conferences

- *Annual Usability Professionals' Association (UPA) conference: http://www.upassoc.org/*

- *ACM Conference on Universal Usability: http://www.acm.org/sigchi/cuu/*

- Annual SIGCHI Conference: Human Factors in Computing Systems:
  http://www.acm.org/sigchi/conferences/

Legal Activities Cited

- *Chapter 13* of this book: US Law in Depth

- *Chapter 2* of this book: Overview of Law and Guidelines

- *Applicability of the Americans With Disabilities Act (ADA) to Private Internet Sites*:
  http://commdocs.house.gov/committees/judiciary/hju65010.000/hju65010_0f.htm

- *Applying the ADA to the Internet:* A Web Accessibility Standard*:*
  http://www.rit.edu/~easi/law/weblaw1.htm

- *National Federation of the Blind/America Online Accessibility Agreement*:
  http://www.nfb.org/Tech/accessibility.htm

- *NFB Sues AOL: http://www.nfb.org/bm/bm99/bm991201.htm*

- *Reader's guide to Sydney Olympics accessibility complaint*:
  http://www.contenu.nu/socog.html

- *Bruce Lindsay Maguire v Sydney Organising Committee for the Olympic Games*:
  http://scaleplus.law.gov.au/html/ddadec/0/2000/0/DD000120.htm

- *Bruce Lindsay Maguire v. Sydney Organising Committee for the Olympic Games
  (Respondent): http://scaleplus.law.gov.au/html/ddadec/0/2000/0/DD000200.htm*

- *[Canadian] Common Look and Feel Standards and Guidelines*:
  http://www.cio-dpi.gc.ca/clf-upe/apr_e.asp

- *[Irish] Recommended Guidelines for Public Sector Organisations*:
  http://www.irlgov.ie/taoiseach/publication/webpg/guidelines.htm

- *[US] Section255 of the Telecommunications Act*: see *http://www.fcc.gov/telecom.html* and
  http://www.access-board.gov/telecomm/html/telfinal.htm

- *[US] Section 508 of the Rehabilitation Act*: see *http://www.access-board.gov/508.htm* and
  http://www.section508.gov/index.cfm?FuseAction=Content&ID=3

- *Resources on Laws, Regulations, Standards, Guidelines*:
  http://www.uiaccess.com/resources.html#resources-legal

Articles Cited

- *Disabled Accessibility: The Pragmatic Approach, Jakob Nielsen's Alertbox*:
  http://www.useit.com/alertbox/990613.html

- *"Software lets the blind browse the Web" in USA Today*:
  http://www.usatoday.com/life/cyber/tech/ct747.htm

- *"Web can aid deaf shoppers, E-mail helps buyer, seller communicate" USA Today, Apr 27,
  1999*

- *Giving the Disabled Increased E-Access, Washington Post*:
  *http://www.washingtonpost.com/ac2/wp-dyn?pagename=article&node=&contentId=A13415-
  2000Aug23*

- *Designing for Differences at builder.com*:
  http://builder.cnet.com/webbuilding/pages/Authoring/Shafer/080497/

Press Releases and Papers Cited

- *Microsoft Accessibility in the News: http://www.microsoft.com/enable/news/press.htm*

- *Adobe Enhances Accessibility of Adobe Acrobat Software for the Disability Community*:
  http://www.adobe.com/aboutadobe/pressroom/pressreleases/200004/20000418acr.html

- *SmartForce Announces Major Achievements in Accessibility and Conformance with Section
  508 Standards*:
  http://www.smartforce.com/corp/marketing/about_sf/press_releases_02/jan_24_02.htm

- *Achievements in accessibility: SmartForce case study, by Optavia Corporation*:
  http://www.optavia.com/smtf_access_achievements.htm

- *News on Talking ATMs, Resource Summary Page,
  http://www.icdri.org/news_on_talking_atms.htm*

2

- Complaints filed due to inaccessible web design
- Development of accessible web design guidelines and laws

Author: Cynthia D. Waddell

Overview of Law and Guidelines

Throughout history, disability law and public policy have reflected the norms of the many governments of the world and the varying socio-economic environments. But one common thread in many societies has been the tendency to isolate and segregate persons with disabilities because of ignorance, neglect, superstition, or fear. Within this social environment, disability policy has evolved from the early social welfare approach, under the medical model of institutional care, to rehabilitation and education.

Since World War II, a new concept of integration has emerged along with a growing awareness of the capabilities of persons with disabilities. For example, the 1960s saw the United Nations re-evaluating their policy and establishing the foundation for the human rights of people with disabilities and their full participation society.

Raising the alarm, the United Nations noted that more than half a billion persons were disabled worldwide and that approximately 80 per cent of this population lived in developing countries. Declaring a "silent crisis," the United Nations said that the public policy issue "affects not only disabled persons themselves and their families, but also the economic and social development of entire societies, where a significant reservoir of human potential often goes untapped." See *United Nations Commitment to Advancement of the Status of Persons with Disabilities*, *http://www.un.org/esa/socdev/enable/disun.htm*.

The 1980s brought the formulation of the current **World Programme of Action** (**WPA**) concerning Disabled Persons, adopted by the General Assembly in December 1982 (*General Assembly resolution 37/52*). The theme of the WPA is the equalization of opportunities for persons with disabilities and the need to approach disability from a human rights perspective:

> *One of the most important concerns is **accessibility: to new technologies, in particular information and communications technologies, as well as to the physical environment**. The notion of "mainstreaming" will also be given prominence, that is, including a **disability dimension in policy recommendations** covering a wide spectrum of social and economic concerns.*

See United Nations Commitment to Advancement of the Status of Persons with Disabilities, http://www.un.org/esa/socdev/enable/disun.htm (emphasis added).

As a result, Rule 5 of the *Standard Rules on the Equalization of Opportunities for People with Disabilities* (*General Assembly resolution 48/96 of 20 December 1993, annex*) addresses "Accessibility" and measures to provide access to the physical environment as well as access to information and communication. See *http://www.un.org/esa/socdev/enable/dissre04.htm.*

Other examples of public policy initiatives include the European Union activities discussed in this chapter, as well as various initiatives addressing the global digital divide – for example, see *http://www.bridges.org.*

Because of the growing body of laws and public policies requiring the accessible design of products and web sites, policymakers and designers of technology and communication networks need to be able to recognize barriers in technology and how to comply with these laws and policies. Just as security, cyber crime, privacy, and copyright are important issues for technologists, so too is accessible web design.

This chapter will introduce you to the emergence of global legal and policy issues for accessible web design standards. Since many jurisdictions now require adherence to standards of accessibility in web design, it is important for the web designer to understand which technical standards to apply. Below we see the following:

- A general introduction to the legal and public policy issues leads the reader to a discussion of two disability rights complaints, which serve to illustrate inaccessible web design.

- We then conclude with an introduction to the current standards established by the World Wide Web Consortium (W3C), as well as the new US legislation addressing Electronic and Information Technology Accessibility Standards.

What Is the Problem?

It now appears that a significant crossroads has been reached where our global policies, technologies, and purchasing choices will determine whether or not every person will benefit from, and directly participate in, the digital economy. The explosive growth of electronic commerce continues to erect new barriers to participation for people with disabilities as well as for anyone without the latest technology.

We are now seeing a significant shift, from using the Web to post essentially static information, to using it for dynamic applications. The impact is systemic and reaches all sectors of our economy. Whether or not the web application is for e-Government (communications, services, and Internet voting), e-Commerce (shopping, kiosks, personal digital assistants, and product design), e-Banking (online banking), or e-Education (long distance learning and research), a shift in methodology is in progress, impacting the delivery of communications and services. For a detailed discussion of this issue and the new barriers being created, see *The Growing Digital Divide in Access for People with Disabilities: Overcoming Barriers to Participation* commissioned by the US Department of Commerce, National Science Foundation, and authored by Cynthia D. Waddell at *http://www.icdri.org/the_digital_divide.htm.*

Information technology has evolved from command-line text interfaces, through Graphical User Interfaces, and today to other modalities such as speech input and output. By mainstreaming modalities historically available through assistive computer technologies, the widest possible audience can benefit regardless of disability, age, or limitations of the end user's technology. As the Internet evolves and technology advances, it is important for managers and public policy technologists to understand accessible web design so that they can recognize public policy issues as they arise.

One particular example of a public policy problem is the language used to establish contract formation on the Web in the US Electronic Signatures in Global and National Commerce Act passed in 2000. The language of this digital signature Act not only creates problems for enabling accessible contract formation on the web, but it also has an adverse impact on the use of alternative Internet access devices such as cell phones and Personal Digital Assistants (PDAs). See The Internet Society Press Release, *Landmark US Digital Signature Legislation Falls Short with Regard to Persons with Disabilities*, at *http://www.isoc.org/isoc/media/releases/000703pr.shtml*, and related June 2000 commentary on *Questions about Electronic Signature Bill: Will Everyone Be Able to Participate?* at *http://www.icdri.org/questions_about_electronic_signa.htm*.

Nevertheless, the growing recognition that disability rights laws demand equal access to information and online services and programs has contributed to the development of accessible web design standards. In fact, the development of these standards, user agent accessibility guidelines and web authoring tool accessibility guidelines, acknowledges the practical and public policy needs for functionality and interoperability for the Web. This book is timely in that it provides the premier tools necessary for constructing accessible web sites for a sustainable infrastructure.

Complaints Filed Due To Inaccessible Web Design

At least two types of complaints can be filed against entities for creating and maintaining inaccessible web sites. We will take a look at two examples and examine the facts of these cases. Having done so, the web developer, manager, or public policymaker may better understand the legal liability and disability rights issues that can arise from failure to design an accessible web site. These cases illustrate some of the public policy reasons for why it is important to design accessibly. Decisions made at the design phase for a web site can have a profound impact on its navigation and usability, as well as legal liability for certain jurisdictions.

First, we will go back in Internet pioneering time to 1995 and the Wild, Wild Web – where there were no laws and every frontier web site was on its own. At the time an Americans with Disabilities Act (ADA) administrative complaint was filed against the City of San José. It was the resolution of that complaint that led to the first accessible web design standard for local government in the US. Next, we will fast-forward to 1999-2000 and examine the facts of the first fully adjudicated case in the world on the issue of constructing accessible web sites. This case is the 1999 Australian complaint filed against the Sydney, Australia Organising Committee for the Olympic Games.

ADA Complaint Against the City of San José, California, USA

In 1995 I served as the ADA Compliance Officer for the City of San José, CA, and was responsible for citywide compliance with State and Federal disability access laws. In that capacity, I was also designated to receive, investigate, and resolve ADA administrative complaints filed against the City. These complaints would be filed by, or on behalf of, people with disabilities who alleged discrimination on the basis of disability in their access to City programs, services, and facilities. San José was the third largest city in the State of California and the 11th largest in the nation.

At that time, my office received an ADA complaint against the City of San José for operating an inaccessible web site. A City Commissioner, who was blind complained that she was unable to access City Council documents as part of her City Council advisory role because the documents were posted in an inaccessible format, that is, Portable Document Format (PDF). This was a case where the posting of inaccessible City Council documents violated the "effective communication" requirement of the ADA. Because the ADA is a civil right, it did not matter if the webmaster did not know that the format was inaccessible. The mere fact that the Commissioner was discriminated against was enough.

Even four years later in 1999, the US Department of Education reported on the accessibility challenges of posting documents in Adobe Acrobat's PDF format:

> "The Portable Document Format (PDF) has provided one of the most controversial accessibility problems of the decade. ... Unfortunately, documents displayed by the Adobe suite of products are totally unusable by those using screen reader technology to retrieve information from a computer display." For more, go to http://www.usdoj.gov/crt/508/report/web.htm#N_20_.

This accessibility problem remains a difficulty even today as discussed in more detail in *Chapter 13, US Web Accessibility Law in Depth*.

At the time the web access complaint was filed, my office was familiar with screen reader access since we had initiated the practice of e-mailing Commission agendas and supporting documentation to the Chair of the San José Disability Advisory Commission – he also was blind. Not only did this practice eliminate the staff time, cost, and delivery delay for creating an audiotaped document, but also the electronic version provided word searchability not available to the Commissioner with the audiotape format.

As I researched the web access complaint, I found that I, too, was a stakeholder in the accessible web effort, since I needed captioning to understand web casts and audio streaming. As a person with a lifetime significant hearing loss, who had taken years and years of speech and lip-reading lessons, I found it simply impossible to lip-read audio on the Web!

In my capacity as a city manager, it was imperative that a policy be developed to manage the ADA violation on a proactive, rather than reactive basis. My legal analysis found that web sites constituted a program or service of the City and were thus subject to the ADA. Already, a growing number of administrative complaints were being filed against US entities operating inaccessible web sites. Not until the following year was my legal analysis confirmed by a policy ruling from the US Department of Justice. (See *Chapter 13* for further information).

By June 1996 I had written the *City of San José Web Page Disability Access Design Standard*. This standard was developed in response to the monitoring of ADA Internet complaints and the need to incorporate City ADA implementation policies. Seven minimum requirements were identified for web accessibility and it was understood that these standards would evolve as new technologies and information systems emerged to solve the problem:

1. Provide an Access Instruction page for visitors (explaining the accessibility features of the web site and providing an e-mail hyperlink for visitors to communicate problems with web page accessibility)

2. Provide support for text browsers and descriptive hyperlinks (links such as "this" and "click here" do not alone convey the nature of the target link)

3. Attach `alt` text to graphic images so that screen readers can identify the content

4. For each photograph contributing meaningful content to the page, provide a "*D*" hyperlink to a page providing descriptive text of the image

5. Provide text transcriptions or descriptions for all audio and video clips

6. Provide alternative mechanisms for online forms since forms are not supported by all browsers (such as e-mail or voice/TTY phone numbers)

7. Avoid access barriers such as the posting of documents in PDF, non-linear format, Frame format or requiring visitors to download software for access to content. If posting in PDF, then accessible HTML or ASCII must also be posted by the webmaster converting the document

In 1996 the City of San José Accessible Web Design Standard was the first governmental policy to be implemented in the US and was adopted by jurisdictions both in the US and abroad. Designated as a 'best practice' by the federal government, the standard was featured in former President Clinton's January 1997 inauguration as a virtual technology bridge to the Presidential Technology Tent on the mall.

Maguire v. Sydney Organizing Committee for the Olympic Games

In 1999 Mr. Maguire, a blind citizen of Australia, tried to request a ticket book in Braille format for the Olympic Games. He was told that blind people could have access to it if it was available on the Internet. Mr. Maguire, a user of refreshable Braille technology, explained that he could only access information if it was presented in accordance with international accessibility guidelines. He also stated that since the Sydney Organising Committee for the Olympic Games (SOCOG) web site did not comply with those guidelines, a lot of information was not accessible to him. The SOCOG response was that he should seek assistance from a sighted person.

On 7 June 1999 Mr. Maguire filed a complaint with the Australian Disability Discrimination Act (DDA) enforcement agency – the Human Rights and Equal Opportunity Commission (HREOC). His complaint alleged that he was unlawfully discriminated against by SOCOG in three respects:

- Failure to provide Braille copies of the information required to place orders for Olympic Games tickets

- Failure to provide Braille copies of the Olympic Games souvenir programme

- Failure to provide a web site which was accessible to the complainant

The ticket book and souvenir programme allegations were dealt with separately and are not the subject of this discussion.

Ultimately, in August 2000 the Sydney Organising Committee for the Olympic Games was found to have discriminated against the complainant in breach of Section 24 of the DDA in that the web site did not include `alt` text on all images and image maps links, the Index to Sports could not be accessed from the Schedule page, and the Results Tables were inaccessible. The SOCOG was ordered to make the web site accessible by the start of the Sydney Olympics but because they were found only partly compliant in November 2000, damages were awarded in the amount of $20,000.

For more, see:

http://www.hreoc.gov.au/disability_rights/decisions/comdec/Maguire%20v%20SOCOG3.htm.

By unlawfully breaching Section 24 of the DDA, the SOCOG decision confirmed the view that the DDA applied to the online provision of goods, services, or facilities to the public in Australia, whether or not for payment. According to the August 2000 press release of the Internet Industry Association:

> *"Disability access is therefore a serious consideration for any Australian business wanting to establish a presence on the Net. Sites which targeted customers overseas might also be liable under equivalent legislation in the US, Canada, the UK, and elsewhere." See* http://www.iia.net.au/news/000805.html.

There are a few points that should be highlighted from the case; although it is recommended that the reader review the entire decision of *Maguire v. Sydney Organising Committee for the Olympic Games* at *http://scaleplus.law.gov.au/html/ddadec/0/2000/0/DD000120.htm.*

First, it is important to note that the HREOC held that Mr. Maguire was subject to direct discrimination and rejected the argument that he was not treated less favorably in respect of the web site than a person who was not blind:

> *"The respondent in constructing its web site (and its Ticket Book) was intending to offer a service to the public. In the case of the web site that service consisted in the provision of a large body of information. By the form and content of its web site the respondent sought to make the information available. Because of the manner in which that information was made available, it could be accessed by a sighted person. Because of the manner in which that information was made available it could not be accessed by a blind person because of his or her disability." See page 9 of the decision.*

Second, although the respondent argued that remediation of the web site constituted unjustifiable hardship, this defence was rejected. The decision noted that the respondent argued that the W3C Web Content Accessibility Guidelines 1.0 had been released by the W3C on 5 May 1999, just the previous month, and that they *"appeared subsequent to the planning and 'substantial implementation' of its site."*

However, the HREOC noted that the web site had been in the process of continual development until the day of the decision in August 2000. For an example of the accessibility difficulties at the web site, see Mr. Worthington's demonstration and link to expert testimony at *http://www.tomw.net.au/2000/sports.html.*

Additional facts presented by both sides on the issue of unjustifiable hardship versus remediation demonstrate a significant variance in web site analysis. The respondent made a number of arguments for unjustifiable hardship, including the following:

- There were 1295 sports web templates

- That the Table of Results was made up of data sources from a number of different databases for each of the 37 sporting disciplines and that the tables contained wrapped text within cells

- That making the web site accessible would require the development of a new or separate site

- That extensive changes to infrastructure were required as well as specialized skills, both of which were limited and expensive

- That it would require one person to work 8 hours a day for 368 days

- That $2.2 million of additional infrastructure would be required to separately host the additional designs necessary for an accessible Table of Results

In contrast, Maguire offered a number of arguments for web site remediation, including:

- The number of templates was significantly less than 1295 and that the reformatting of the templates would take considerably less than the 2 hours for each alleged by the respondent – in fact 10 minutes each

- That wrapping in each cell could be addressed by simply including an invisible end of cell character for the screen reader to signal the end of the text in each cell

- That the cost of making the site accessible was a modest amount

- No new infrastructure would be required because it was in place

- A team of one experienced developer with a group of 5-10 assistants could provide an accessible site at W3C Level A compliance within 4 weeks.

Lastly, of interest was the comment by HREOC that according to Ms. Treviranus, if accessible web design had been addressed early in the web development process, the cost would have been less than one percent of the total effort. See page 12 of decision.

Expert witnesses for accessible web design on Maguire's behalf were Mr. Worthington and Ms. Treviranus. Mr. Worthington was the first Webmaster for the Australian Department of Defence. He was also one of the architects of the Commonwealth Government's Internet and web strategy. Ms. Treviranus was from the University of Toronto where she is the manager of the Adaptive Technology Resource Center at the University. She also chairs the W3C Authoring Tool Guidelines Group.

Development of Accessible Web Design Guidelines and Laws

Across the globe there are now public policies and laws protecting the rights of people with disabilities to access the content of the Web. However, at this time there are two types of specifications for accessible web design. The first – **World Wide Web Consortium Web Content Accessibility Guidelines 1.0 (WCAG)** – is a stable international specification developed through a voluntary industry consensus. This specification was released in May 1999 and has since been adopted by many countries as discussed overleaf.

The US Access Board published the second specification – Electronic and Information Technology Accessibility Standards – on December 21, 2000, pursuant to the US rulemaking process as required by **Section 508 of the Rehabilitation Act Amendments of 1998 (Section 508)**. See *36 CFR 1194, Electronic and Information Technology Accessibility Standards, Final Rule* (*http://www.access-board.gov/sec508/508standards.htm*).

These standards became effective on June 21, 2001, and are broad in scope, covering technical standards in the following areas:

- Software applications and operating systems

- Web-based intranet and Internet information and applications

- Telecommunications products

- Video and multimedia products

- Self contained, closed products

- Desktop and portable computers

The Electronic and Information Technology Accessibility Standards also include a section on Functional Performance Criteria as well as a section on Information, Documentation, and Support. Technologists responsible for Help Desk assistance should particularly note the rules under the latter section.

Web developers and managers creating or maintaining web sites for US entities subject to Section 508 must implement these standards in order to participate in the US market. Careful attention must be paid to the following Section 508 standards: software applications and operating systems; web-based intranet and Internet information and applications; and Information, Documentation, and Support.

Because Section 508 is based on the W3C WCAG 1.0, let us first turn to the W3C Web Accessibility Initiative and adoption by countries. We will then conclude with an introductory discussion on Section 508. For an in-depth discussion, please see *Chapter 13* on *US Web Accessibility Law in Depth*.

W3C Web Accessibility Initiative and Adoption By Countries

In April 1997 the W3C announced the launch of the **Web Accessibility Initiative** (**WAI**) to "*promote and achieve Web functionality for people with disabilities.*" (See the press release at *http://www.w3.org/Press/WAI-Launch.html*). The project began with a WAI workshop on Sunday, 6 April, 1997, which I attended by invitation and provided assistive technology for presenters with hearing loss, as well as copies of the first accessible web design standard written for the City of San José, California in 1996.

The W3C WAI envisioned the establishment of an International Program Office (IPO), and in October 1997 one was launched. In the press release about the launch, Tim Berners-Lee, W3C Director, commented that "*the power of the Web is in its universality. Access by everyone regardless of disability is an essential aspect. The IPO will ensure the Web can be accessed through different combinations of senses and physical capabilities just as other W3C activities ensure its operation across different hardware and software platforms, media, cultures, and countries.*"

This press release also announced the appointment of Judy Brewer as Director of the IPO and noted that the IPO was sponsored by a partnership of government, industry, research, and disability organizations (see press release *http://www.w3.org/Press/IPO-announce*).

Currently, the WAI (*http://www.w3.org/WAI/*), in coordination with organizations around the world, pursues accessibility of the Web through five primary areas of work: technology, guidelines, tools, education and outreach, and research and development. WAI is supported in part by:

- The US Department of Education's National Institute on Disability and Rehabilitation Research: *http://www.ed.gov/offices/OSERS/NIDRR/*

- European Commission's Information Society Technologies Programme: *http://europa.eu.int/comm/information_society/ist/index_en.htm*

- Canada's Assistive Devices Industry Office: *http://strategis.ic.gc.ca/SSG/as00011e.html*

- Elisa Communications: *http://www.elisa.fi/*

- Microsoft Corporation: *http://www.microsoft.com*

- IBM: *http://www-3.ibm.com/able/*

- SAP: *http://www.sap.com/*

- Verizon Foundation: *http://foundation.verizon.com/*

- Wells Fargo: *http://www.wellsfargo.com/*

The W3C WAI technical activity has produced many significant work products including:

- Web Content Accessibility Guidelines 1.0 – W3C Recommendation 5 May 1999. See *http://www.w3.org/TR/WCAG10/* (WCAG-accessible web design standards)

- Authoring Tool Accessibility Guidelines 1.0 – W3C Recommendation 3 February 2000. See *http://www.w3.org/TR/ATAG10/* (web content authoring tool guidelines that facilitate accessible web design, including making the tool interfaces accessible)

- User Agent Accessibility Guidelines 1.0 – W3C Candidate Recommendation 12 September 2001 *http://www.w3.org/TR/UAAG10/* (web user agent guidelines for any software that retrieves and renders web content for users such as browsers, media players, plug-ins and other programs, including assistive technologies)

WCAG Priorities

The WCAG has three priorities and each checkpoint has a priority level assigned by the Working Group based on the checkpoint's impact on accessibility, as follows:

[Priority 1] A web content developer **must** satisfy this checkpoint. Otherwise, one or more groups will find it impossible to access information in the document. Satisfying this checkpoint is a basic requirement for some groups to be able to use web documents.

[Priority 2] A web content developer **should** satisfy this checkpoint. Otherwise, one or more groups will find it difficult to access information in the document. Satisfying this checkpoint will remove significant barriers to accessing web documents.

[Priority 3] A web content developer **may** address this checkpoint. Otherwise, one or more groups will find it somewhat difficult to access information in the document. Satisfying this checkpoint will improve access to web documents.

Some checkpoints specify a priority level that may change under certain (indicated) conditions. The complete list of WACG checkpoints and their priority level can be found at *http://www.w3.org/TR/1999/WAI-WEBCONTENT-19990505/full-checklist*.

Today, governments around the world have adopted or are in the process of implementing W3C Web Content Accessibility Guidelines 1.0, as discussed below.

Australia

W3C WCAG is primary resource for minimum web site standards. Online information and services must be accessible to people with disabilities under the Disability Discrimination Act 1992 (DDA). This law requires that people with disabilities have access to employment, education, goods, services, and facilities on the same basis as the community in general. The Human Rights and Equal Opportunity Commission (HREOC) has the responsibility for ensuring that Commonwealth web sites are accessible to all.

In their Disability Discrimination Act Advisory Notes, the HREOC states that the DDA applies to any information or service provided through the Internet whether or not payment is required. In addition, the DDA applies to:

> "...any individual or organization developing a World Wide Web page in Australia, or placing or maintaining a web page on an Australian server. This includes pages developed or maintained for purposes relating to employment; education; provision of services including professional services, banking, insurance or financial services, entertainment or recreation, telecommunications services, public transport services, or government services; sale or rental of real estate, sport; activities of voluntary associations; or administration of Commonwealth laws or programs." See http://www.hreoc.gov.au/disability_rights/standards/www_3/www_3.html.

Timetable

From 1 June 2000, all web sites were to be tested by agencies for accessibility; all new contracts for web sites were to include accessibility as a key performance measure. From 1 December 2000, all web sites must follow the W3C WCAG so that they pass recognized tests of accessibility. See *http://www.govonline.gov.au/projects/standards/accessibility.htm*.

Canada

In May 2000, the government of Canada adopted a policy for all federal government organizations that requires conformance to W3C WCAG Priority 1 and 2 Checkpoints. This "Common Look and Feel for the Internet" policy is found at *http://www.cio-dpi.gc.ca/clf-upe/*.

Timetable

Government departments and agencies have until December 31, 2002, to fully implement the policy. This is not legislation but it is anticipated that this policy will be extended to the government of Canada intranets and extranets.

European Union e-Europe Initiative

In June 2000 the Feira European Council adopted the e-Europe Action Plan 2002 which includes steps to address access to the web for people with disabilities. As early as 1994 the European Union has recognized the importance of web accessibility through various action projects.

The 25 September 2001 *Communication from the Commission to the Council, The European Parliament, The Economic and Social Committee and The Committee of Regions, e-Europe 2002: Accessibility of Public Web Sites and their Content*, emphasizes that "*Public sector web sites and their content in Member States and in the European institutions must be designed to be accessible to ensure that citizens with disabilities can access information and take full advantage of the potential for e-government.*" See page 7 at *http://europa.eu.int/eur-lex/en/com/cnc/2001/com2001_0529en01.pdf*.

On 27 February 2002 a press release announced that the **European Economic and Social Committee (ESC)** had welcomed the Commission's communication on the accessibility of public web sites and their content as referenced above. According to the press release:

> "*The ESC also took the opportunity to rebut some misunderstandings relating to the time and cost involved in making public web sites compatible with the needs of disabled and elderly people. 'In many Member States the objection has been raised that the process of implementation of the WAI (web accessibility initiative) guidelines will constitute an excessive financial engagement. This assumption is simply wrong, because implementing the accessibility guidelines from the first is only a little more expensive than not implementing them,' says the opinion, which suggests that national funding be earmarked for implementation of the communication's provisions.*"

Also according to the press release, the ESC indicated that work was needed to make the new version of their web site, Europa II, accessible; especially with the upcoming European Year of Disabled People in 2003. See: *http://dbs.cordis.lu/cgi-bin/srchidadb?CALLER=NHP_EN_NEWS&ACTION=D&SESSION=&RCN=EN_RCN_ID:18053*.

The European Commission is currently working to improve the accessibility of web-based services and is following W3C WCAG, Priority Level One. The European Commission also reports the following Member States status (see below) on W3C WCAG conformance as of 17 July 2001 (referred to as "The Guidelines" in the 25 September 2001 Communication, Annex 3 at the above URL).

Belgium

Web Accessibility is included in the e-government concept but detailed specifications have not yet been addressed.

Accessibility was already an issue in the Tele-administration projects funded by the Flemish government that ran until 2001: see *http://www.vlaanderen.be/ned/sites/teleadmin/*. The research group on Document Architectures of the Katholieke Universiteit Leuven (see *http://go.to/docarch*) was in charge of consulting the Tele-administration projects on accessibility issues. The Guidelines on web accessibility have been promoted.

In April 2001, the non-governmental organization called Blindenzorg Licht en Liefde set up a Blindsurfer logo for Flemish language web sites. It is attributed after a human checking of the whole Web site, based on the Guidelines. Details about the logo will be available soon from: *http://www.blindenzorglichtenliefde.be*.

Denmark

The Guidelines have been included in the national guidelines for accessible web design; standards for accessible public publications; and advisory activity between public web masters. The Guidelines have also been used when providing information on accessible web design for web designers. Checks are being made on the accessibility of public web sites in different public sectors, and the results are published on the web at: *http://www.bedstpaanettet.dk*. All web pages on public web sites are being checked over a three-year period. The last check in 2001 will take place in August. User panels including persons with disabilities take part in the assessment of the public web sites. A national prize has been instituted for exemplary accessible web site design. This prize is open to commercial sites as well as public sites.

Finland

The Guidelines have been adopted as part of the Public Administration Recommendations in the *JHS 129 Guidelines* concerning development of *e*-Services, Ministry of the Interior, December 2000. See *http://www.intermin.fi/juhta/suositukset/jhs129.htm*.

JHS129 emphasizes equality of access for different users using different technologies; it makes a requirement of testing pages with several browsers and operating systems; it makes specific web page design recommendations; it also requires that there must be alternatives to web-based public services (for example telephone services).

France

In application of the 12th October 1999 administrative guidelines (circulaire), the "Mission pour les Technologies de l'Information et de la Communication" (MTIC) of the Prime Minister has published standards for accessibility of public web sites. This action aims to promote the following documentation and tools among public sector Webmasters, which are already available on MTIC's web site at *http://www.atica.pm.gouv.fr/interop/accessibilite/index.shtml*:

- The 'circulaire' on Internet sites of public services and administrations

- The recommendation of the W3C on the Guidelines

- The white paper of BrailleNet entitled "*Towards a more accessible web*"

- The free web browser Braillesurf

- Tools to verify the accessibility of web sites

- The existing labels

- The recommendations of the Council of Europe

Germany

The federal government and the governments of the Länder are working on taking up the Guidelines. A particular role in this context is with non-governmental organizations and initiatives, especially from the disability sector, to support this process.

Greece

Official adoption of the Guidelines and the practical implementation plan for existing and future public web sites are currently the subject of deliberations under the auspices of the Secretary for Information Society of the Hellenic Ministry of National Economy.

Ireland

Recommended Government Guidelines on Web Publication for Public Sector Organisations have been published, which include guidelines in relation to accessibility. A target has been set for all government Department web sites to achieve level A compliance by the end of April 2001, with achievement of level AA compliance as a target for the end of 2001. A Webmasters Network Group representing all government departments is making progress on these objectives.

Italy

On March 13th, 2001, the Ministry of Public Function signed a Cabinet Resolution with the title: "Linee Guida per l'organizzazione, l'usabilità e l'accessibilità dei siti Web delle Pubbliche Amministrazioni". See the following web sites:

- *http://www.funzionepubblica.it/download/pdf/accessibilita.pdf*

- *http://www.governo.it/sez_dossier/linee_web/direttiva.html*

This document has been developed by an inter-departmental working group, established in September 2000, that has the purpose of preparing national guidelines for both usability and accessibility of web sites of the public administration, in line with the Guidelines (WCAG 1.0) and to promote the application of the e-Europe programme concerning the accessibility in the framework of the Italian e-government plan.

Another working group was set up by the Authority for Information Technology in the Public Administration (AIPA) in July 2000 with the purpose of planning initiatives to promote and to facilitate the application of accessibility to both public web sites and hardware/software used for departmental activities of the public administration. In 2001, a national conference on the subject was organised, and a CD-ROM published.

Other initiatives are currently being planned by the AIPA group: a survey, a variety of templates, customized repair tools for existing public sites, another national conference, a course, a training plan, and an assessment of the impact of accessibility on the activities of the public administration.

Some important public web sites, such as that of the Italian government (*http://www.governo.it/*) and that of the Department of Public Function (*http://www.funzionepubblica.it*), have been completely redesigned, and are now accessible. Other public web sites, such as that of the Chamber of Deputies (*http://wai.camera.it/*), are available in an accessible version.

Luxemburg

In February 2001, the government adopted a national action plan: e-Luxembourg. The Guidelines will be included in the e-government concept (one of the six main targets of the e-Luxembourg programme).

Netherlands

The Guidelines have been recommended by the Minister of Public Health, Welfare, and Sport in February 2001. There is ongoing development of adoption plans.

Portugal

The Web Accessibility Initiative has already been adopted within the framework of the National Initiative for Citizens with Special Needs in Information Society (Iniciativa Nacional para os Cidadãos com Necessidades Especiais na Sociedade da Informação), by Cabinet Resolution 96 in August 1999 and Cabinet Resolution 97/99 – Accessibility to the Public Administration web sites.

An Access Unit (Unidade Acesso) has been created within the Ministry of Science and Technology, which develops coordination activities and communicates information about projects within the ambit of the above-mentioned National Initiative (Iniciativa Nacional), as well as training and the creation of skills for citizens with special needs. The following actions have been carried out or are in progress:

- Visitability requirements

- An "Accessibility of Web Public Administration" conference, held in November 2000

- Training courses on designing web accessibility

- Helpdesk of web accessibility to public web sites' webmasters

- An Accessibility of Public Administration Web Sites Report

- A Web Accessibility Evaluation Methodology

- An accessibility prize: *Portugal@cessível*

- A users panel

- An Accessibility Gallery

Spain

The WAI is being considered by parliament, and a standards working group is working with the Guidelines. A group in the Ministerio de Trabajo y Asuntos Sociales provides support on accessible web site implementation based on the Guidelines.

Sweden

Accessibility to information is included in the government bill "From patient to citizen – a national action plan for disability policy". The bill emphasizes that the state should set an example and that public authorities should ensure that their operations, information, and premises are accessible to people with disabilities.

A government ordinance concerning state government authorities and their responsibility for implementing the disability policy has recently been issued. According to the ordinance, which comes into force on September 1st, 2001, authorities have to take account of accessibility to people with disabilities in the design of their buildings, information, and other. In the work with accessibility issues, the authorities have to draw up action plans. The point of departure should be the United Nations Standard Rules.

The Guidelines have been recommended by the Swedish Handicap Institute (SHI) since February 2001. Educational activities on web accessibility and the guidelines are being arranged by the SHI.

The Swedish Agency for Administrative Development states in its report "Criteria for 24/7 agencies in the networked public administration" that the agencies' services for people with disabilities should be designed with a broad perspective, taking into account the variations related to special requirements. The Government has recently decided to commission the Agency to stimulate the development of 24/7 agencies. In this work, the needs of people with disabilities should be taken into consideration. No group of citizens should be excluded.

UK

The current guidelines for UK government web sites were published in late 1999. Chapter 4.4 deals with accessibility and points to the W3C WAI web site and tools such as Bobby. These guidelines are currently being investigated by the Office of the e-Envoy, and a draft is available at *http://www.open.gov.uk/dev/neil/*.

In an effort to increase awareness of web accessibility issues, the e-Envoy's office has expanded greatly on the amount of accessibility information available, and has established a mandatory level – the application of the Guidelines' level A – to all new or redesigned government web sites. For this, ministerial approval has been obtained. The draft guidance is at: *http://www.open.gov.uk/dev/neil/guide/chapt-8-4.htm.*

Update (as of publication)

On 26 February 2002 the Disability Rights commission published the new, revised Code of Practice for implementing the Disability Discrimination Act of 1995 (DDA). This statutory code, agreed by Parliament, expressly provides that accessible web sites are a type of auxiliary aid or service that enables people with disabilities to have access to goods, facilities, and services.

In particular, Paragraphs 5.23 and 5.26 of the Code of Practice state that an accessible web site is a type of auxiliary aid or service for people with hearing and visual disabilities. See *http://www.drc.org.uk/drc/InformationAndLegislation/Page331a.asp.*

The following example is provided at Paragraph 2.17 of the Code:

> *An airline company provides a flight reservation and booking service to the public on its web site. This is a provision of a service and is subject to the Act.*

Additional information can be found about the DDA at *http://www.drc-gb.org.*

Japan

A web accessibility guideline for the removal of information barriers was first announced in May, 1999, by the Telecommunication Accessibility Panel. This guideline contained some of the rules from W3C WCAG. Members of the panel included the Ministry of Posts and Telecommunications and the Ministry of Health and Welfare. See "*The Guidelines to make Web Content Accessible*" at *http://www.soumu.go.jp/joho_tsusin/policyreports/japanese/group/tsusin/90531x51.html* (Japanese).

The following year brought a report from the same panel recommending that a web accessibility evaluation tool (J-WAS) be developed in order to promote accessible web design. Issued on 23 May 2000, the report noted that the nature of Japanese language characters as well as the popular use of cell phones for the Web warranted attention to this matter. The report also noted the importance of including the opinions of the elderly and people with disabilities in the system planning. See *The plan to assist the use of the information and communication technology, and secure the web accessibility for elderly and disabled individuals* at *http://www.soumu.go.jp/joho_tsusin/pressrelease/japanese/tsusin/000523j501.html* (Japanese). See also *http://www.icdri.org/japanpress.htm* (English).

By 6 November 2000, the government declared that web sites of all ministries and the national public sector should apply the web accessibility guideline. At this Joint Meeting of the IT Strategy Council and the IT Strategy Headquarters (The Fifth conference) it was also decided that the web accessibility evaluation tool (J-WAS) should be developed and used by government organizations to increase the accessibility of their web pages after April 2001. See *http://www.kantei.go.jp/jp/it/goudoukaigi/dai5/5siryou7-1.html* (Japanese).

In addition, November 2000 also brought Japanese legislation impacting IT law entitled *Basic Law on the Formation of an Advanced Information and Telecommunications Network Society*. Also known as *Basic IT Law*, Article 8 provided the basis for addressing accessible web design:

> *"Article 8. In forming an advanced information and telecommunications network society, it is necessary to make active efforts to correct gaps in opportunities and skills for use of information and telecommunications technology that are caused by geographical restrictions, age, physical circumstances, and other factors, considering that such gaps may noticeably obstruct the smooth and uninterrupted formation of an advanced information and telecommunications network society." Approved by the Japanese Diet on 29 November 2000, the law became effective 6 January 2001. See http://www.kantei.go.jp/foreign/it/it_basiclaw/it_basiclaw.html. (English)*

The e-Japan Policy program for barrier-free access has resulted in significant policies impacting the accessible web. On 29 March 2001, the government IT Strategy Headquarters announced a number of policies, such as:

- Web sites of ministries and agencies shall be accessible so that government information on the Web can be easily utilized by people with visual disabilities

- Official Gazettes distributed over the Web will be tailored to the needs of people with visual disabilities

- So that people with visual and hearing disabilities can enjoy broadcast services just like people without disabilities, R&D activities on production technologies for broadcast programming will be conducted with the costs of programming for closed captions, explanatory narration, and sign languages to be subsidized

- School environments for children who are blind or deaf and with other disabilities will be addressed so that computers can be utilized by the students

- R&D activities will be conducted to provide children in hospital with the ability to study through the Web

- IT equipment and systems that can be easily used by the elderly and people with disabilities shall be developed

- Technologies will be developed to enable the elderly and people with disabilities to use the Internet easily, an accessibility checking system of web sites will be created, and verification experiments will be conducted for the promotion of a barrier-free environment of information access.

See *http://www.kantei.go.jp/foreign/it/network/priority-all/8.html* (English) and scroll to down "VII. Crosscutting Issues" to "2) Overcoming Age and Physical Constraints" under "2. Closing the Digital Divide."

Lastly, ongoing work for the development of J-WAS, the web accessibility evaluation tool, continued until it went public on the Web with a trial experiment in September 2001. The Web Accessibility Working Group, also known as the J-WAS Project, expects to conclude the first trial experiment in March 2002, improve the tool, and then begin the second phase from April 2002 to March 2003. See *http://www.jsas.gr.jp/index.html* (Japanese).

The September 2001 trial experiment, found at *http://www.jwas.gr.jp/activity/event/contents/jimukyoku.pdf* (Japanese), resulted in the following findings:

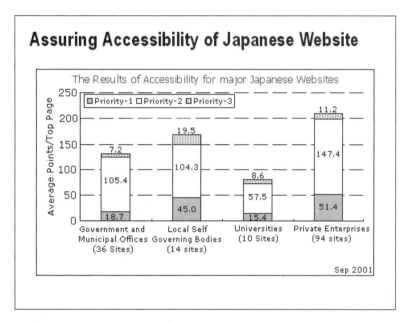

Published with permission from Uchida, H., Ando, M., Ohta, K., Shimizu, H., Hayashi, Y., Ichihara, Y.G. & Yamazaki, R.: Research And Improving Web Accessibility in Japan, Slide 7 – "The Results of Accessibility for Major Japanese Web Sites," Internet Imaging III Proceeding of SPIE, Vol. 4672, pp. 46-54, 2002.

According to Masaya Ando of Allied Brains, Inc., one of the accessibility difficulties unique to the Japanese language is mispronunciation by screen readers. For example, one Kanji (Chinese character) can be pronounced in several different ways. It is also difficult to complete a sentence with Kanji that can be understood by everyone. This is because the Japanese language consists of three different kinds of characters – Kanji (Chinese character), Katakana and Hiragana – and although there is a standard for Kanji used in everyday life, the individual's comprehension level will vary due to age, generation, and education. Moreover, in the Japanese writing system, words are not separated by spacing and so the screen reader will not pronounce a word correctly when a space exists within the word.

I would like to especially thank Kaoruko M. Nakano, Vice President & Secretary of Pacific, Prologue Corporation of San Jose, California USA and Masaya Ando of Allied Brains, Inc., Tokyo, Japan, for providing source documentation and various translations for this section on the accessible web effort in Japan.

New Zealand

Policy development is currently underway due to the establishment of the e-government programme on 1 July 2000 for four years. At present, a draft policy document proposing guidelines for New Zealand government web sites contains recommendations to follow W3C WCAG as a primary source, although there are exceptions to certain W3C WCAG specifications. Further information can be found on Web Guidelines Version 1.0, dated 30 June 2001 at: *http://www.e-government.govt.nz/guidelines/web-guidelines/.*

Singapore

On 5 February 2002 The **National Internet Advisory Committee** (**NIAC**), appointed by the Ministry of Information and the Arts, announced the launch of two major initiatives to address concerns about data protection and undesirable content on the Net. Please see *http://www.sba.gov.sg/sba/detailed.jsp?artid=362&typeid=1&cid=0&bSubmitBy=true.*

At the above URL, the NIAC released their 2001 report that discusses disability issues including greater education and promotion of web accessibility requirements at Paragraph 4.11 of the report. The NIAC noted the availability of guidelines to assist web site designers in designing accessible web sites and encourages their use.

Section 508: US Web-Based Accessibility Standards

Rather than adopt W3C WCAG, the US has taken a different track by legislating Electronic and Information Technology Accessibility Standards. As we will see in *Chapter 13* on *US Web Accessibility in Depth*, although a majority of the Web Section 508 rules are based on Priority Level 1 of the W3C WCAG 1.0, there are additional rules particular to US law. In fact, it will be important for the web developer and decision maker to understand when to follow the technical specifications for W3C WCAG and when to follow Section 508.

Introduction To Section 508

On August 7, 1998, the US Congress enacted Public Law 105-220 – the Rehabilitation Act Amendments of 1998. This law significantly expanded and strengthened the technology access requirements of Section 508 of the Rehabilitation Act of 1973 (Section 508).

Today US Federal agencies and covered entities must make their electronic and information technology accessible to people with disabilities. As we have seen in the earlier discussion on web site disability discrimination complaints, inaccessible technology interferes with an individual's ability to obtain and use information quickly and easily. Section 508 was enacted to eliminate barriers in information technology, to make available new opportunities for people with disabilities, and to encourage development of technologies that will help achieve these goals. As a result, accessible web design falls within the scope of Section 508.

The law applies to all covered entities whenever they develop, procure, maintain, or use electronic and information technology. The scope of electronic and information technology is expansively defined. It includes computers (such as hardware and software, and accessible data such as web pages), facsimile machines, copiers, information transaction machines or kiosks, telephones, and other equipment used for transmitting, receiving, using, or storing information.

Section 508 requires Federal agencies to give disabled employees and members of the public access to information that is comparable to the access available to others. Federal agencies do not have to comply with the technology access standards if it would impose an undue burden to do so. This is consistent with language expressed in the ADA and other US disability rights legislation, where the term "*undue burden*" is defined as "*significant difficulty or expense.*" However, agencies shall continue to have long-standing obligations under Sections 501 and 504 of the Rehabilitation Act to provide reasonable accommodation to qualified individuals with disabilities upon request.

For the first time in US history, Section 508 seeks to create a marketplace incentive for accessible technologies and utilizes the power of the Federal government purse to require accessible web design. A ripple effect is currently underway throughout US State and local government – Section 508 now informs State and local governments on how to meet their ADA obligations to provide accessible web sites for their citizens. Already we see States adopting Section 508 policies as part of their institutional electronic and information technology standards. See *http://www.resna.org/taproject/policy/initiatives/508/508Stateactions.htm*.

Summary

In this chapter you were introduced to the emergence of global law and policy guidelines pertaining to accessible web design. You learned that a significant crossroad has been reached where our global policies, technologies and purchasing choices determine whether or not every person can participate on the Web. You discovered the following:

- The United Nations World Programme of Action seeks the equalization of opportunities for persons with disabilities and that access to information and communication is a human right

- The global emergence of accessible web design laws and policies are a product of disability rights laws demanding equal access to information and online services and programs

- There are two types of approaches to specifications for accessible web design: W3C WCAG, an international voluntary standard, and Section 508, a US legislative mandate for Electronic and Information Technology Accessibility Standards

- It is important for the web developer and decision maker to understand which accessible web design guideline or standard they should apply for their client

- Depending on the laws of the jurisdiction, complaints can be filed by people with disabilities against institutions that develop, procure, maintain or use an inaccessible web site

As for the future of the Web, today's outreach and education on this important issue provides the foundation for tomorrow's accessible design of new technologies. By designing accessibly, everyone will benefit from this effort.

3

- Screen readers
- Voice browsers
- Screen magnification
- Using your browser to check for accessibility

Author: Jim Thatcher

Assistive Technology Browsers and Accessibility

Assistive technologies are an indispensable assessment tool for the web developer. It is not possible to determine a web site's compliance with most of the requirements of accessible web design using a conventional browser alone. Most requirements are *indirect*, in that they require information to be available to the user *through* his or her assistive technology. This information is not exposed by conventional browsers.

An example of this is the requirement for markup in data tables to indicate which cells are heading cells (Section 508 provisions §1194.22(g, h) and WCAG checkpoints 5.1 and 5.2). Sometimes this markup is reflected in the visual presentation, for example if the `<th>` element is used to define the heading cells then the text contained in them will be bold and centered by default. If, instead, the `headers` attribute is used to indicate heading cells there will be no visual manifestation. Another example is that text equivalents for non-text elements may or may not be available for normal visual examination.

There are also guidelines that are quite subjective, for example the WCAG Checkpoint 14.1 to use the clearest and simplest language appropriate for a site's content. The decision about whether a site complies with this or not can only be reached after careful assessment.

Screen readers are the primary assistive technology through which web site content is funneled. People who are blind use them to have the information that is displayed on the computer screen spoken to them with synthesized speech.

This chapter will provide a brief overview of the assistive technologies used in later chapters for exemplifying and examining accessible web techniques, and will also illustrate how to assess a web site's accessibility with a standard browser. We will be covering:

- Screen readers and the IBM Home Page Reader voice browser

- Screen Magnification software and hardware

- Ways in which standard browsers can be used to assess web page accessibility.

Screen Readers

Screen reader products in the DOS days literally read the 80x25 display buffer to speak the screen. The ASCII codes stored in it were exactly what was sent to a hardware device to produce synthesized speech. With the advent of the graphical user interface, screen readers had to become a lot smarter. Now they can capture text as it is written to the display through display driver software. These sophisticated technologies create what is called an off-screen model (OSM) that is, in effect, a database of all the text displayed on the graphical screen. When a screen reader user requests information, it is read from this database, the OSM, rather than from the screen itself.

Even speech synthesis has changed. The first developments in speech synthesis were hardware synthesizers that would cost around a thousand dollars. Now speech synthesizer software is included in screen readers and voice browsers and has even been built into operating systems, such as the MacOS.

With the advent of the web, the way in which screen readers work has changed yet again. Now screen readers look at the document object model (DOM) of the page to know what the browser would display. For the web, as well as for some other applications, screen readers are not reading the screen any more, not even reading what was written to the screen; instead, the screen reader is using the object model to provide a speech rendering of data that is a web page.

A screen reader must present the two-dimensional graphical web page to a user who is blind as a one-dimensional stream of characters which is usually fed to a speech synthesizer. There are alternative media that people who are blind can use to access content, such as refreshable Braille displays which typically have 20, 40, or 80 individual eight-dot Braille cells where the individual dots are raised and lowered with tiny solenoids. Four Braille cells are shown in the figure below from Robotron, Australia, *http://www.sensorytools.com*:

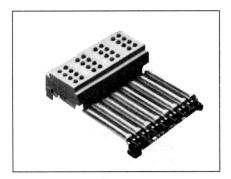

It is very important to recognize that this screen reading process is converting a two-dimensional page to a one-dimensional text string, whether spoken or displayed in Braille. This is aptly called **linearizing** the page. If you are familiar with HTML, then the simplest way of picturing linearization is by imagining an HTML document stripped of all its tags, leaving just the text together with the textual values of some attributes like `alt` and `title`. The resulting text file is the linearized version of the page. Different parts of that text document can be presented to a user who is blind with synthesized speech or Braille.

Another way to picture the linearization process is to read the page from left to right and from top to bottom. Tables are read left to right and top to bottom before continuing, and each cell is read completely before continuing to the next cell. Of course, there is more to this linear view than just characters. It must also include form elements and links in order to capture the function of the page.

It seems those users that are blind rarely listen to a page in full. Usually they navigate to the content and controls of the page. *TAB* and *SHIFT+TAB* move forward and backwards through the active elements of the page, that is, the links and form controls. Screen readers have key commands to read by characters, by words, by lines, and by sentences.

Screen readers do much more than read web pages; they can be used with any software running on the computer, therefore they must be keyboard-compatible with that software. This makes screen reader key combinations complicated and even arcane. For example, to move around the cells of a table with JAWS for Windows you need to use *CTRL+ALT+ARROW*, to go into table mode with Window-Eyes you need to use *INS+PLUS* then *INS+ARROW* to move around the table.

It is in this linearized world that some of the accessibility requirements begin to make better sense. Clearly, the images that are on the visual page need to be replaced with the text equivalents, the `alt` text, otherwise the information they contain will be lost.

Additional help is essential. If the user is reading in the middle of a data table, the screen reader technology needs a way of informing them of the current headers. Try to imagine, in this linearized text world, making an on-line order. Having selected the product you want to purchase, you reach the checkout page only to find several fields where you are required to enter your details, but no clue as to which data goes where. This is the kind of information that must be included in web page markup to make it accessible to a person who is blind.

> *You can find an excellent short video demonstration of how screen readers work on the University of Wisconsin, Learning Technology and Distance Education web site,* http://wiscinfo.doit.wisc.edu/ltde/, *"Introduction to the Screen Reader" with Neal Ewers of the Trace Research Center (*http://trace.wisc.edu*)* http://wiscinfo.doit.wisc.edu/ltde/access/ewers.htm.

Specific Screen Readers

In later chapters, two screen readers will be used to illustrate techniques for addressing web accessibility requirements. JAWS for Windows and Window-Eyes are used by probably over 90% of users of the Web who are blind.

JAWS for Windows (JFW) is the most popular screen reader. JAWS, an acronym for "Jobs Access With Speech", is developed by Freedom Scientific, *http://www.freedomscientific.com/*. The cost of JAWS is between $795 and $1395, depending on the version of the Windows operating system. You can download a limited functionality version to test, which will only operate for a limited amount of time without re-booting. The tests in the later chapters were run with JFW version 4.00.

The second screen reader is Window-Eyes, developed by GW Micro, *http://www.gwmicro.com/*. Window-Eyes costs $595 and runs on the Windows 9x and ME platforms. A beta version of Window-Eyes Professional is available that runs on Windows 2000 and XP. A timed demonstration is available from GW Micro. Window-Eyes version 4.11 was used for examples in later chapters.

There is one commercial screen reader for the Apple Macintosh. OutSpoken by the Alva Access Group, *http://www.aagi.com/*, was the first screen reader to provide access to the graphical user interface (in 1988). Unfortunately, OutSpoken has not kept up with Windows screen readers, especially in the way web information is handled. This has happened in part because of the lack of accessibility hooks and features in the Mac OS.

The picture for Unix is even bleaker. There are no commercial screen readers for X-Windows, the windowing system for Unix, although there are shareware attempts at accessing X-Windows for people who are blind. The structure of the X-Windows system is not conducive to screen reading, because of the lack of focus and object information. There is at least one sophisticated access system for text-based Unix, Emacsspeak, but that environment is usually accessed with terminal software under Windows, using Windows screen readers.

The EmacsSpeak homepage is http://www.cs.cornell.edu/home/raman/emacspeak/.

The bottom line here is that when we talk about access to the web for people who are blind, we are talking about the Windows platforms. Examples and samples in subsequent chapters are all taken from Windows, using Microsoft Internet Explorer, or Netscape Navigator. Between those browsers, only IE is effective with screen readers because of the way it exposes the Document Object Model (DOM) and provides information through Microsoft Active Accessibility (MSAA) (*http://www.microsoft.com/enable*).

Using the Screen Readers

In later chapters we will describe techniques for using screen readers in special circumstances, especially for forms, tables, and skipping bocks of links. Here are some screen reader basics.

JAWS for Windows

Each of the screen readers has a specialized **web mode** for reading web pages. In JAWS this is known as Virtual Pc Cursor mode (VPC). The screen reader automatically switches to VPC when Microsoft Internet Explorer is the foreground process. VPC can be turned on and off manually using *INSERT+Z,* which is a useful command to know when things aren't working quite right and you need to toggle between modes.

When JAWS for Windows loads a page, it announces the title, the number of links, and begins reading from the top. The *CTRL* button stops speech. The *DOWN arrow* and the *UP arrow* give you the next and previous line. *INSERT+DOWN ARROW* reads the rest of the page.

To find form controls, use *CTRL+INSERT+HOME* to go to the first input element and then *CTRL+INSERT+TAB* to move through the controls (to go backwards use *CTRL+INSERT+SHIFT+TAB*). You have to hit *ENTER* to go into forms mode to use input fields and then NUMPAD *PLUS* exits forms mode and returns to VPC on.

It is possible to obtain a copy of what JAWS *will* read, that is, JAWS' text view of the page. When the page loads, stop speech with *CTRL*, then use *CTRL+SHIFT+END* to select all, and use *CTRL+C* to copy all the text to the clipboard. Now you can paste (*CTRL+V*) into a word processor or text editor.

Window-Eyes

For Window-Eyes, the special "web mode" is "MSAA Application Mode" and it is toggled with *CTRL+SHIFT+A.*

Like JAWS, Window-Eyes switches to web mode automatically when Microsoft Internet Explorer is the foreground process. When the page is loaded, Window-Eyes announces, "loading page", then, "load done", and begins speaking with an announcement of the number of tables, followed by the text of the page.

The *ESC* button stops speech, and the *UP* and *DOWN arrow* keys speak the previous and next line. *CTRL+HOME* takes you to the beginning of the document, and *CTRL+END* takes you to the end. The *CTRL+SHIFT+R* command causes Window-Eyes to read from the current point to the end.

To get the Window-Eyes text view of the web page, use *CTRL+A* to select all, *CTRL+C* to copy to the clipboard and then use *CTRL+V* to paste the text into a text editor or word processor. This is an excellent way for a sighted developer or tester to study the web content for accessibility, especially because the screen reader is unfamiliar, and the synthesized speech may be difficult to understand.

Use *INS+TAB* when viewing any page and Window-Eyes brings up a dialog containing a list of all the links on the web page:

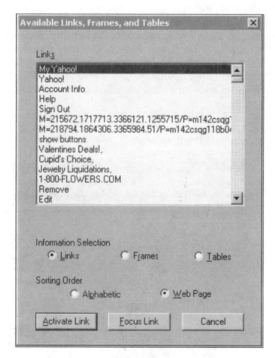

You can activate any link by moving to it and pressing *Enter* because *Activate Link* is the default push button. Alternatively, you can move to the link in the web page with the *Focus Link* push button. The same dialog that brings up the list of links also provides the option to see lists of tables or frames.

With both screen readers (and HPR in the next section) the active elements of a page, including links and form controls, can be navigated with the *TAB* key (*SHIFT+TAB* goes backwards). The order in which these links and form elements appear in the *TAB* sequence is the same as the linearized page unless the attribute `tabindex` is used in the HTML source of the document. Then those active elements with valid `tabindex` attributes appear first and according to the number assigned as the value of the `tabindex`. The active elements without the `tabindex` attribute are placed at the end of the sequence. `tabindex` is supported by JAWS with virtual PC cursor off, and by Window-Eyes when MSAA mode is off. HPR does not currently support `tabindex`.

Voice Browsers

Screen readers are inherently difficult to use because they have to be able to read, and therefore be compatible with any application. This results in incredibly complex keyboard commands that don't clash with any other application commands, but which are difficult to remember. If you don't have to use a screen reader and if you don't use it every day, then the chances are that you will have a hard time working with one.

There is a way of checking for accessibility with assistive technology and understanding how your web page sounds to someone who is blind. Voice browsers are technologies designed specifically to speak web pages. One of the first voice browsers was pwWebSpeak by Productivity Works, but was discontinued in Jan 2001. Currently the most commonly used voice browser is Home Page Reader from IBM (*http://www.ibm.com/able/hpr.html*) which costs $129 for an electronic download, and $149 for a CD. A 30-day trial is available from the IBM Accessibility Center (*http://www.ibm.com/able*). HPR is available in five languages; Brazilian Portuguese, French, German, Italian, and English and it is also available in Japanese as a separate product. It will recognize language changes specified in HTML (the `lang` attribute). When *Automatic Language Detection* is enabled, HPR uses a heuristic algorithm to switch between spoken languages even when the language of the page is not specified.

HPR was originally designed by a blind IBM researcher, Chieko Asakawa, and was first produced in Japanese in 1997. Asakawa was motivated to develop Home Page Reader by the fact that Japanese screen readers did not accommodate the Web at all.

Using the IBM Home Page Reader (HPR) is a much easier way for sighted developers to understand the view of the web experienced by a user who is blind. This is because HPR is a normal Windows application for speaking the Web with conventional menus and much simpler keyboard commands:

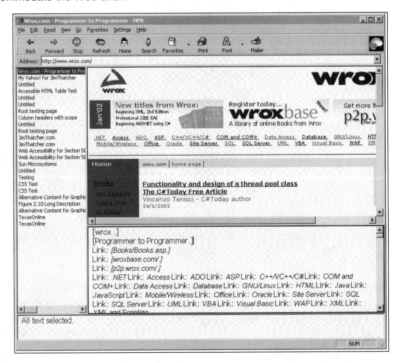

As shown above, HPR has four main sub-windows: a graphical browser window on the top right, a text window on the bottom right, a history view to the left, and an information view at the bottom of the screen. The important windows for this discussion are the graphical view and the text view. The other two can be closed through the *View* menu.

When HPR opens a web page it begins speaking and the text it is speaking is displayed in the text view. About eight or ten lines are displayed, and as speaking proceeds, the display is refreshed. If you would like to see all the text of the page, as a linearized or text view, put focus on the text view, use *CTRL+A* (for select all) and then you can copy (*CTRL+C*) the resulting text to your favorite word processor. This is a useful tool for studying the accessibility of your page, as it is with the screen readers.

When using HPR, the *SPACE* bar begins reading from the current point. As was mentioned above, people rarely listen to the whole page, but they navigate around the content instead. HPR's philosophy for navigation is to always use the arrow keys; left for previous, right for next, and down for current. In **reading mode** (in the *Read* menu) you can specify the size of "chunk" you move to with the navigation keys, the options available are character, word, line, paragraph (item), link, control, heading, and table. There is a special reading mode for reading tables, and in this case all four arrow keys navigate the cells of the table.

There is no question that IBM Home Page Reader is the easiest assistive technology for sighted people to learn to use. If you want to test your forms or tables for accessibility, then try them with HPR.

A Text Browser

If you have never seen Lynx then you are in for a surprise. Lynx is a text browser that is available on Unix, DOS, and Windows (through DOS emulation). Because it doesn't support graphics, dynamic HTML, or CSS, it is incredibly fast. When you enter a URL for opening a page with LYNX, the page is displayed almost immediately.

Like HPR and the screen readers, Lynx (*http://lynx.browser.org*) uses a linearized view of the page. In case you don't want to try Lynx, you can visit *http://www.delorie.com/web/lynxview.html* and there submit a URL in order to see what your page looks like as if it were viewed with Lynx, that is, when it is linearized.

Here is the Lynx screen for *http://www.wrox.com*:

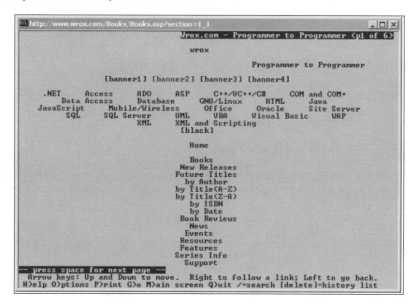

The user interface for Lynx is first and foremost command keys, including *G* (Go) for entering a URL to open, *O* (Options) for setting user preferences, and *H* (Help) for an extensive help document. A page is navigated with *UP* and *DOWN* arrows to move through the links on the page. After passing the bottom of the current screen, the next screen full of information is presented.

The current link is highlighted in red. The down arrow key moves through the links, *banner3*, *banner4*, (which is uninformative alternative text), *.NET* and so on. To follow a link, use the right arrow and to return to the previous page, use the left arrow. *Page Up* takes you to the previous screen if you have moved past the first screen display. Normal text is black while links are blue if they don't have focus. These are, of course, default settings which can be changed using the options ("*O*") command.

Any time there is need for text input, for example when a URL needs to be entered as a result of the *go* command, a command line opens up three lines above the bottom of the window. Text can be entered in that command line.

As mentioned above, Lynx does not support graphics, plug-ins, JavaScript, Java, or CSS. Thus it is an excellent test vehicle to evaluate whether or not your page is usable and readable with these technologies turned off.

Screen Magnification

Various hardware and software is available to increase the size of the display for people with some degree of visual impairment.

Screen magnification software uses standard display monitors. It increases the size of everything in the display, including text and images in a web page. Screen magnification software provides various degrees of magnification, typically between 1.5x and 32x. Because of the physical limitations of the monitor, the greater the magnification, the smaller the amount of content that is shown.

Some people have a visual impairment called 'tunnel vision' in which they have very limited field of vision, or peripheral vision. While they can have very high visual acuity, this condition has some of the same issues as with screen magnification, that is, seeing only a small area of content at one time.

The primary issues when using screen magnification software are:

- Small display area preventing users from getting the big picture view of a page

- Missing the context around the visible area

- Difficulty in finding page elements, such as navigation

Screen magnifiers provide multiple settings for magnification. Some also provide a split screen that shows both the magnified page and a non-magnified page, as shown opposite with 4x magnification:

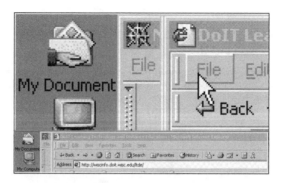

Consistent layout is a very important design consideration for users who depend on screen magnifiers. Placing the navigation links in the same position on every page, for example, will make it considerably easier for users who can only see a small portion of the screen at once to find their way around your site.

Some users view the magnified and non-magnified page simultaneously. This lets them see the general layout of the page in the non-magnified section and the details in the magnified section. Some users will view a page at less magnification first to get the big picture, then increase the magnification to read the text.

Large Display Hardware

Another assistive technology used by people with reduced vision is large display hardware, such as large monitors and Fresnel lenses. Users can also project the screen display onto a large desk area or a wall. Such solutions may not be feasible based on the environment. For example, you probably would not want your co-workers to be able to see your display from across the room. Large displays do not have the same problem with limited area as do screen magnifiers.

Using Your Browser To Check Accessibility

There are several ways in which the visual web browser can be used to assess how accessible a web site is. Certain sites provide an online analysis of active pages, and browser settings can be modified to simulate the way in which a user with disabilities experiences a page.

Web Sites That Analyze a Page

You can visit some web sites that will help you analyze a live web page. In the previous section, we mentioned the Delorie Software site for obtaining the Lynx view of a page, *http://www.delorie.com/web/lynxview.html*. The Lynx view from Delorie Software may not be completely faithful to what the current Lynx browser displays. The Wrox home page viewed with the Lynx browser shown earlier comes up completely empty in the Lynx viewer. This may be a version dependency; the Lynx Viewer is based on Lynx version 2.7.1 and the Wrox page shown above was viewed in Lynx version 2.8.3. Additionally, the Wrox page uses JavaScript and Lynx does not support JavaScript. This may explain the empty display in the Lynx viewer.

Whatever the reason for that failure, you can be sure that if your web site displays and performs well through the Lynx viewer, then it is readable and usable with scripting and CSS disabled.

In Chapter 7, we will discuss two web based accessibility evaluation tools, and each has a trial version on the web. These are Bobby from CAST (http://www.cast.org/bobby) and LIFT Online from UsableNet (http://www.UsableNet.com).

Another interesting web assessment tool is called the WAVE developed by the late Dr. Leonard Kasday (*http://www.temple.edu/inst_disabilities/piat/wave/*) at Temple University, Institute on Disabilities. To use WAVE, you simply enter the URL of a page to be analyzed:

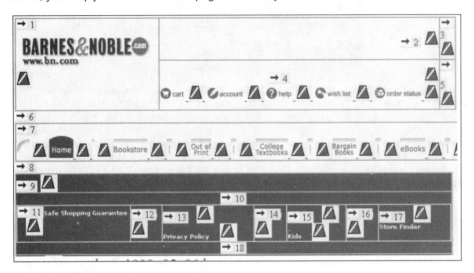

As shown above, WAVE analyzes the page and provides lots of accessibility information. The following table describes the function of each of the icons used by WAVE:

Icon	Function
➡	The reading order in the linearized page is displayed by the arrow icon, followed by a numeral. The numerals indicate the order in which the page will be read by a screen reader, voice browser, or text browser.
◿	The warning icon, indicates an image without alternative text
◿Txt	This icon is used to flag existing alternative text (note that this icon does not appear in the screenshot above).

Testing a Page with a Browser

One method of assessing how a screen reader will handle a page is by browsing it with images turned off.

In Microsoft Internet Explorer, use *Tools | Internet Options*, and then click the *Advanced* tab. In the resulting list, check *Always expand alt text for images* at the top of the list, and then down two pages in the list, under *Multimedia*, uncheck the item *Show Pictures*. With these settings, images will not be displayed and alternative text will appear instead.

The screenshot below illustrates the same page as analyzed by the WAVE tool above, except this time it is viewed with Internet Explorer with images turned off:

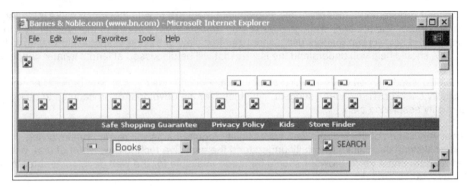

The small rectangles, each with an icon or part of an icon, are placeholders where images would be. Only one of these has alternative text, *SEARCH*.

When you want to turn off images in Netscape, use the *Edit* menu, and the *Preferences* submenu. There select the *Advanced* category and uncheck *Automatically load images*. Like the screenshot above, images will be replaced with rectangles and the alternative text if it is available.

There are two special considerations for this process of turning off images with Netscape. First, when you carry out the procedure above, you need to clear the cache (*Preferences | Advanced | Cache*) and then restart Netscape, otherwise recently viewed pages will still show images. Secondly, the size of the placeholder rectangles is determined by the image height and width. If there is not enough room to display the alternative text, it will *not* be displayed at all. This is why the option, *Always expand alt text for images*, was enabled in the Microsoft Internet Explorer process above. With this option selected, IE will expand the rectangle to accommodate the alternative text when that option was selected.

There are other browser features that can be turned off to check for accessibility. In Chapter 4 we will discuss the requirement that web pages be usable with cascading style sheets (CSS) turned off (Section 508 provision §1194.22(d) and Web Content Accessibility Checkpoint 6.1). There is no way to turn off stylesheets with Internet Explorer but there is a checkbox in Netscape's *Advanced* preferences, *Enable Style Sheets,* which does the job.

The WCAG checkpoint (6.3) on JavaScript requires that pages are usable when scripting is turned off. Again, Netscape has a simple checkbox, *Enable JavaScript*, on the *Advanced preferences* page. To disable JavaScript in Internet Explorer you need to visit the Security page of the Internet Options dialog. On that page select the "*Custom Level...*" In the resulting list of settings select the *Disable* radio button under *Active Scripting*.

Summary

The "indirect" requirements for accessible web development are mostly those that make information available to users who are blind through their screen readers. One purpose of this chapter was to help you understand how screen readers use a linearized text view of a page to speak information to their users. This should help you understand the issues that will be discussed at length in later chapters.

We also discussed several ways in which a web developer can use the standard browser as an accessibility checker. These ideas suggest "sniff tests" for the developer or procedures to be integrated into a quality assurance plan.

The best verification of the indirect web accessibility requirements will result from involving professionals with disabilities who fully understand the assistive technology. Short of that, one or more screen readers and a voice browser should be made available for the web development team and the quality assurance process.

4

- Text equivalents
- Color
- Creating accessible tables

Author: Jim Thatcher

Creating Accessible Content

The subject of accessibility on the Web can be divided into three main categories: accessible web content, accessible navigation, and accessible interaction. This chapter addresses the first of these: creating accessible content including the text, images, or audio files that might be available on a web page.

Content is only accessible if it can be "viewed" or accessed by people with disabilities. Accessible content must be compatible with assistive technologies, screen readers in particular. There have to be alternatives to pure visual content for people who can't see, and pure auditory content for people who can't hear; otherwise it becomes meaningless for people with physical disabilities.

There are three important sets of guidelines for accessible web development. In order to share in the wisdom of the corresponding community of experts and to give context to our discussion, each of our topics will be prefaced with a review of what the three guidelines have to say on the subject.

The most prominent of the three are the Web Content Accessibility Guidelines (WCAG), Version 1.0, from the Web Accessibility Initiative (WAI) of the World Web Consortium (W3C), which became an official Recommendation of the World Wide Web Consortium on May 5th 1999. WCAG consists of fourteen guidelines, or principles of accessible design. Each guideline includes a set of checkpoints that explain how the guideline applies to web development. The checkpoints (*http://www.w3.org/TR/WCAG10/full-checklist.html*) are prioritized according to the following criteria:

> *[Priority 1]* *A web content developer* **must** *satisfy this checkpoint. Otherwise, one or more groups will find it impossible to access information in the document. Satisfying this checkpoint is a basic requirement for some groups to be able to use web documents.*

> *[Priority 2]* *A web content developer* **should** *satisfy this checkpoint. Otherwise, one or more groups will find it difficult to access information in the document. Satisfying this checkpoint will remove significant barriers to accessing web documents.*

[Priority 3] A web content developer **may** *address this checkpoint. Otherwise, one or more groups will find it somewhat difficult to access information in the document. Satisfying this checkpoint will improve access to web documents.*

There are 65 checkpoints in all; 16 of them are priority 1, 30 are priority 2, and 19 are priority 3.

The United States Federal Access Board (*http://www.access-board.gov*) has issued access standards (*http://www.access-board.gov/sec508/508standards.htm*) for federal electronic and information technology as required under Section 508 of the Rehabilitation Act.

The Electronic and Information Technology Accessibility Standards, 36 CFR Part 1194, Web-based Intranet and Internet Information and Applications (1194.22), http://www.access-board.gov/sec508/508standards.htm.

The Access Board is also publishing an on-line guide (*http://www.access-board.gov/sec508/guide/index.htm*) for all the standards and this site is the easiest route to view the sixteen provisions of the Section 508 standards for the Web.

The force of the Section 508 standards is that electronic and information technology purchased by the U.S. federal government must comply with these provisions. Because of that force of law, these provisions are seen as playing an important role in defining accessibility, especially in the United States.

Many of the Section 508 provisions correspond to priority 1 Web Content Accessibility checkpoints with minor changes for regulatory wording. Some of the priority 1 checkpoints were deemed by the Access Board to be too restrictive on web development or too difficult to judge for compliance. In addition, the 508 standards add provisions that combine WCAG checkpoints of lower priorities, like the Section 508 provision for accessible forms.

The Association of Tech Act Projects (*http://www.ataporg.org/*) is a detailed side-by-side comparison (*http://www.jimthatcher.com/sidebyside.htm*) of the Section 508 provisions and the priority 1 WCAG checkpoints.

Finally, IBM has a collection of accessibility guidelines for Software, Hardware, Lotus Notes, Java and the Web (*http://www.ibm.com/able/guidelines.html*). These guidelines have been available since December 1999.

The IBM Web Accessibility Guidelines, Version 3.0, April 30, 2001, http://www.ibm.com/able/accessweb.html.

Although not in one-to-one correspondence, the sixteen IBM web accessibility guidelines (*http://www-3.ibm.com/able/accessweb.html*) cover all the same areas as the Section 508 provisions.

To explain issues and solutions for accessibility we will use three assistive technologies that we discussed in Chapter 3, one talking browser and two screen readers. All are intended to be used by people with very limited or no useful vision. There are demonstration versions of these products available on the respective web sites.

- IBM Home Page Reader, Version 3.0, *http://www.ibm.com/able/hpr.html*.

- JAWS for Windows by Freedom Scientific, Version 4.0, *http://www.freedomscientific.com/fs_products/software_jaws.asp*.

- Window-Eyes by GW Micro, Version 4.11, *http://www.gwmicro.com/*.

This chapter will address the individual guidelines and Section 508 web accessibility provisions and show how each one can be met. Here are the topics we will cover in this chapter:

- Text equivalents for images

- Text equivalents for audio

- Conveying information with color

- Contrast

- Creating accessible tables

- Avoiding flashing and flicker

We will cover accessible navigation in Chapter 5 and accessible data input in Chapter 6. In addition to these basic treatments of accessibility for the web see also the advanced topics including CSS in Chapter 9 .

Text equivalents

The one accessibility issue that is probably more important than all others is providing text information for web content that is non-textual. Non-text items include images, image maps, image buttons, audio files, and multimedia files that provide both audio and video.

The reason text is so important is that people with sensory disabilities have ways of accessing text even if they are unable to access the non-text content. If there is a textual equivalent for an image, then users who are blind will be able listen to that text with their screen reader or talking browser. Most images on web pages are simple and so their text equivalents are simple too. Even when the images carry more information – as with charts or graphs – there are techniques we will explore for conveying that information textually.

A person who is hearing impaired may find it difficult or impossible to get information from an audio file. The text equivalent of an audio file is a word-for-word transcript. The transcript can be read by itself or viewed while listening to the audio. In this way, the person who is hearing impaired can get the equivalent information.

It would be convenient if there were a concept for creating some sort of word-for-word transcript of an image, but of course there is no such thing. Therefore, the process of providing adequate and useful alternative text for images, which does not over-burden the user, requires judgment and style. This will be further discussed below.

The Guidelines and Standards

One measure of the perceived importance of the text equivalents can be gleaned from the fact that the requirement for text equivalents is the first item in most guideline lists.

WCAG

The first checkpoint in the Web Accessibility Initiative (WAI) Web Content Accessibility Guidelines (WCAG) deals with providing text equivalents for non-text elements.

> *1.1 Provide a text equivalent for every non-text element (for example, via "alt", "longdesc", or in element content). This includes: images, graphical representations of text (including symbols), image map regions, animations (for example, animated GIFs), applets and programmatic objects, ascii art, frames, scripts, images used as list bullets, spacers, graphical buttons, sounds (played with or without user interaction), stand-alone audio files, audio tracks of video, and video.*

This checkpoint from the Guidelines Working Group of the Web Accessibility Initiative lists more types of non-text elements than we will be considering in this chapter. Applets and programmatic objects, frames, scripts, and multimedia will be covered elsewhere.

There are also duplications in the WCAG list of non-text elements. Images, graphical representations of text, animations, images used as list bullets, and spacers are all instances of uses of the <img> element. Our classification of non-text elements will be discussed below.

Applets, programming objects, and scripts can often be very textual. The issues with these kinds of content are much more serious than suggested by including them amongst the candidates for alternative text.

Section 508

The first provision of the Section 508 Standards for web content accessibility is very similar to the WCAG, but without the "*This includes*" remarks.

> *§1194.22(a) A text equivalent for every non-text element shall be provided (e.g., via "alt", "longdesc", or in element content).*

The guides for the Section 508 accessibility standards are published by the Access Board (*http://www.access-board.gov/sec508/guide/index.htm*). The guide for this provision (*http://www.access-board.gov/sec508/guide/1194.22.htm#(a)*) includes mention of most of the examples included in WCAG checkpoint 1.1. The guide also mentions "check boxes" in the discussion of non-text elements.

IBM

The IBM Web Accessibility Guidelines – Version 3.0, April 30, 2001, begins with recommendations to use the alt attribute for images and animations.

> *1. Images and animations. Use the* alt="text" *attribute to provide text equivalents for images. Use* alt="" *for images that do not convey important information or convey redundant information.*

In those guidelines, there are three separate checkpoints that include the need for text equivalents for non-text elements. The second guideline addresses image maps in general and alternative text for image map hot spots (areas) in particular. A deeper discussion of the topic of image maps will be the basis of a separate discussion in Chapter 5 – *Accessible Navigation*. Here we will just address the especially important topic of providing text equivalents for image map areas or hot spots.

2. Image Maps. *Use client-side image maps with alternative text for image map hot spots. If you use server-side maps, provide equivalent text links.*

The third IBM guideline relating to text equivalents is aimed at the special case where images contain detailed information that needs to be presented to users who are visually impaired through the long description attribute.

3. Graphs and Charts. *Summarize the content of each graph and chart, or use the* `longdesc` *attribute to link to the description or data.*

Finally, Number 4 of the IBM guidelines includes the need for text equivalents for audio and video.

4. Multimedia. *Provide captions or transcripts of important audio content. Provide text or audio descriptions of important video content.*

Classification of Images

Images, including animated GIFs, are most of the pictures we see on web pages. They are also pictures we do not see, so called spacer images that are used for formatting purposes.

Text equivalents for images are provided through the `alt` attribute on the `<img>` element:

```
<IMG src= "logo.gif" width="120" height="60" alt= "company logo">
```

Every `<img>` element, should have alternative text specified in the `alt` attribute, thus referred to as "`alt` text" (in case you are wondering, we will see how to handle special images, such as spacers, shortly). Basically, the alternative text should convey the information about the image.

Let's look at different types of images:

1. Image links. These are images inside an anchor tag, like the following sample.

```
<a href="default.cfm" class="black">
    <img border="0" src="images/cordalogo.gif" width="95"
        height="82" alt="CORDA logo">
</a>
```

2. Image map hot spots. This is an image (IMG) with the usemap attribute whose value is the name of a `<map>` element.

Homepage | Services | Contact Us | Search

```
<IMG src="banner.gif" width="500" alt="navigation banner"
    usemap="#banner">
<MAP name="banner">
  <AREA href="home.htm" alt="homepage"
        shape="rect" coords="0,0 110,24" >
  <AREA href="services.htm" alt="services"
        shape="rect" coords="111,0 215,24">
  <AREA href="comntact.htm" alt="contact us"
        shape="rect" coords="216,0 326,24" >
  <AREA href="search.htm" alt="search"
        shape="rect" coords="327,0 435,24" >
</MAP>
```

3. Image buttons. An image button is an `<input>` element with `type="image"`. The source of the picture is also specified with the `src` attribute of the `<input>` element:

[**LOG ON ▸**]

```
<INPUT type="image" src= "images\logon.gif" alt="log on"
       name="logon">
```

4. Images which are primarily for visual appeal, for decoration, or that carry absolutely no information like "spacer" images used for formatting:

```
<IMG src="images/1-pix.gif" border="0" width="1" height="1" alt="">
```

5. Images that carry lots of information, like charts or graphs:

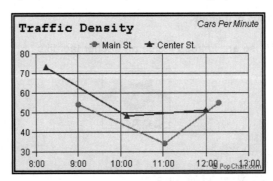

```
<IMG src="images/traffic.gif" width="360" height="220" border="0"
     alt="traffic density on main and centers streets" longdesc="traffic.htm">
```

Image Links

Images that play some active role in the navigation of the site must have meaningful and simple `alt` text because, without that text, users with disabilities will not be able to navigate or otherwise interact with your site. Since a user who is blind will be listening to the links, it is very important to make those alternative text strings simple and short while still clear.

Typical of this kind of image are the ones that look like buttons for navigation. Here are some examples.

This image typifies groups of images looking like the horizontal tabs on file folders.

Here is what the code for this image **should** look like:

```
<IMG src="… elec-tab.gif" width=39 … alt="Electronics">
```

I say, "should", because in fact this simple image does not have any alternative text at all on the site where it was found.

Since there isn't any `alt` text, the screen reader must try to hunt for some information about the image elsewhere. When there is no `alt` text the next place to look is the `href` attribute of the anchor element `<a>`.

Here is the `href` attribute (in elided form) for the link in this case:

```
href="exec/obidos/tg/browse/-/172282/ref=tab_gw_e_4/104-9411283-4768702"
```

Because values of `href` attributes are often very long and complicated (as in this case) with many initial segments that are redundant and do not carry information, IBM Home Page Reader tries to pick a part of the `href` that is shorter and will hopefully carry some information to the user. Here is the result in this case:

HPR:
ref=tab_gw_e_4/104-9411283-4768702

This is, of course, still meaningless, and so the visually impaired user with HPR will not be able to participate in this navigation. Things are no better for the Window-Eyes user, who gets to hear the whole `href`:

Window-Eyes:
exec/obidos/tg/browse/-/172282/ref=tab_gw_e_4/104-9411283-4768702

JAWS for Windows takes a different approach, which in this case is more helpful. It tries to read a part of the `src` attribute of the image. Here is the `src` attribute (slightly elided):

```
src="http://… /G/01/nav/personalized/tabs/electronics-off-sliced.gif"
```

The part that JAWS reads is remarkably good:

JAWS for Windows:
tabs/electronics-off-sliced.gif

However, this is probably the result of fortune rather than foresight, and is still really far from ideal! Accessibility should not rely on the use of comprehensible file names in your web page. (Not that they are a bad idea, but clear and simple `alt` text is the real answer.) Because this page does not have `alt` text where it needs it, the link becomes completely incomprehensible for both the HPR and the Window-Eyes user, and even JAWS users are left guessing to some extent.

After pulling this terribly inaccessible example into pieces, let's look at a simple example of a nicely accessible image link. This button-like navigation link, which appears on a major technology company web site, is the kind of thing that is very common on the web:

This image link is correctly coded with the `alt` text `"Corporate"`.

```
<IMG border= … alt="Corporate" src="… gen_corp_tab_off_us.gif">
```

Each assistive technology handles this link in pretty much the same way – in the way that the web author intended and the way that the user can understand. Here are the results:

HPR:	[Corporate]
W-E:	Link Corporate
JFW:	Link Graphic Corporate

The fact that an item is a link is (by default) indicated with HPR speaking in a female voice. Windows-Eyes and JAWS both speak some variation of the word "link". (Visually HPR displays `alt` text in square brackets.)

This is why `alt` text for images is so very important: it is important because the necessary information is quickly and clearly conveyed to the user and it is important for the web owner because without it, visitors who use screen readers or talking browsers will not be able to understand their site.

Image Map Hot Spots

The importance of text equivalents for image map hot spots is just as great as that for the image links we talked about in the last section. The difference is the form that these maps take.

Let's begin with an accessible client-side image instead of an inaccessible one – it's more fun that way. Here is the image from the University of Arizona *"Web Resources Page"*.

This image is specified in the HTML code as an `<IMG>` element with the `usemap` attribute as follows.

```
<IMG src=" …" alt="Web Resources at The University of Arizona" ...
    usemap="#banner">
```

Notice that the image does have `alt` text as it should, but the image itself is not the important accessibility issue. The important issue is the fact that the image is specified as a client-side image map by the `usemap` attribute.

Then the `<map>` with `name="banner"` specifies areas of the image that will be hot spots. In this example all the areas are simple rectangles (`shape="rect"`).

> A `<map>` element can be placed anywhere on the page; its position is irrelevant to the position of an image.

The six hot-spot rectangles specified by the `<area>` elements in the map surround the text headings in the image. Each rectangle is given x/y pixel coordinates where (0,0) is the top left and, in this case, (588, 81) is the bottom right.

If you visit the site (*http://uaweb.arizona.edu/resources/accessibility.shtml*) – or any site with image maps, for that matter – using a traditional browser like Internet Explorer or Netscape, the user is shown the `href` of the different areas in the browser status window as they move their mouse around the image. The ToolTip also changes to the `alt` text of the `<area>` element. In parts of the image that are not designated as hot spots the status window goes blank and the ToolTip changes to the `alt` text of the image (you can see how we can handle a more complicated map such as a map of the US in the Chapter on Accessible Navigation).

```
<MAP name="banner">
    <AREA shape="rect" alt="UA Web Resources Homepage"
          coords="10,05 90,75" href=" … ">
    <AREA shape="rect" alt="UA Homepage" coords="95,05 360,35"
          href=" … " >
    <AREA shape="rect" alt="Search" coords="260,52 305,70"
          href=" … ">
    <AREA shape="rect" alt="Comments & Questions" coords="311,52 375,70"
          href=" … ">
    <AREA shape="rect" alt="Web Resources Homepage"
          coords="385,52 502,70" href=" … ">
    <AREA shape="rect" alt="UA Homepage" coords="515,52 572,70"
          href=" … ">
</MAP>
```

Assistive technology can cope with a correctly implemented image map just as well as it does with normal links. IBM Home Page Reader does an even better job; here is the way HPR begins reading the University of Arizona Web Resources image map:

HPR:
(Start of map with 6 items.)
(End of Map.)

Only the number of links in the map is announced, so as not to burden the listener when HPR is just reading the page. If you want to hear the actual hot spots, you just step through them with the arrow keys and this is the way they sound. (See "Accessible Navigation" in Chapter 5)

HPR:

(Start of map with 6 items.)

[UA Web Resources Homepage]

[UA Homepage]

[Search]

[Comments & Questions]

[Web Resources Homepage]

[UA Homepage]

(End of Map.)

---

*For a sighted person using HPR as an analytical tool to check their web sites for accessibility, it is convenient to get a hold of **all** the text including the links within image maps. This is done by moving focus to the text area and using CTRL+A to highlight the entire text view. HPR will then load all of the text and highlight it. Then, if desired, the entire text view can be copied to the clipboard (CTRL+C) and pasted into another application (CTRL+V). That is what was done here in order to display the links corresponding to the areas of the image map above.*

The textual value of the `alt` attribute is always displayed within square brackets, "[ ]." So-called meta-text, text that is generated by HPR and that does not appear on the page, is enclosed in parentheses, "( )," for example, "(End of Map.)"

Window-Eyes treats image map links with `alt` text just like any other kind of link. This makes sense since, in function, image map links are no different from any other kind of link and so should not be treated differently when spoken.

W-E:

Link UA Web Resources Homepage

Link UA Homepage

Link Search

Link Comments & Questions

Link Web Resources Homepage

Link UA Homepage

JAWS indicates that the links come from image map areas.

JFW:
Image map link UA Web Resources Homepage
Image map link UA Homepage
Image map link Search
Image map link Comments & Questions
Image map link Web Resources Homepage
Image map link UA Homepage

Note that with all three assistive technologies, the order of the hot spot links of an image map is determined by the order of the `<area>` elements in the `<map>`.

Style of Alternative Text

The choice of specific alternative text is a matter of style and judgment. For the six areas of the image map above, I would use `alt` text that is the same as that on the image, except where it makes sense to make it **shorter**. Here's a table comparing the `alt` text that the developers at University of Arizona used and what I would recommend instead:

Text in Image	`alt` text	My choice for `alt` text
Web Resources	UA Web Resources Home Page	Web resources
The University of Arizona	UA Home Page	U of A
Search	Search	Search
Comments	Comments & questions	Comments
Web Resources Home	Web Resources Home	Web Resources
UA Home	UA Home	U of A

The reason I prefer shorter `alt` text is that someone using a voice browser or a screen reader is going to have to sit and listen to all this. When a sighted person looks at the text on an image they have the ability to filter out the "visual noise" and focus on the main concept. It is true that this is still possible when you have to listen to the content, but it is more difficult.

I tend to avoid "home page" when identifying links. If the link says "The University or Arizona" or "IBM", I know it is going to the respective "home page" so "home page" is redundant.

Bearing in mind the importance of conciseness when considering `alt` text, it is not surprising that my preference is "U of A" over "University of Arizona". But why, you may ask, "U of A" over "UA"? That comes from my experience of screen readers occasionally *pronouncing* abbreviations like UA – or IBM for that matter – instead of spelling them out. If "UA" is pronounced, it truly fails in conveying the desired information. In this case it turns out that all three assistive technologies we are studying here spelled out "U A" rather than pronouncing it – probably because it is capitalized. However, since there are other voice browsers and assistive technologies available, it is best to adopt a safe approach.

Sometimes web designers prefer to see longer mouseover ToolTip text than the `alt` *text so that the mouse user gets more information than is on the image. To do this you keep the* `alt` *text the same as the image and put the longer text in the* `title` *attribute of the anchor element. This trick works with IE for links, but it does not work for the* `<area>` *elements.*

An Inaccessible Image Map

We talked about style in the last section. Unfortunately style isn't what we must take issue with on the Yahoo! home page, *http://www.yahoo.com:* here, we have to get right down to basics. There are only three images on this page, an image used as an image map with `alt="Yahoo"` and two advertisements – one with `alt="Click Here!"` and the other with `alt=""`.

The banner image looks like it contains text, *"Calendar"*, *"Messenger"*, *"Check Email"*, *"What's New"*, *"Personalize"*, and *"Help"*. The text under each image is made to look like a text link, whereas it is really part of the image. As such it doesn't work like a text link. Yahoo! could have decided to add `alt` text to the `<map>` element like this:

```
<map name=m>
    <area coords="0,0,52,52" href=r/c1 alt="Calendar">
    <area coords="53,0,121,52" href=r/p1 alt="Messenger">
    <area coords="122,0,191,52" href=r/m1 alt="Check Email">
    <area coords="441,0,510,52" href=r/wn alt="What's New">
    <area coords="511,0,579,52" href=r/i1 alt="Personalize">
    <area coords="580,0,637,52" href=r/hw alt="Help">
</map>
```

However at the time of publication the `<map>` element was coded without any `alt` text.

The Yahoo! page is designed with efficiency in mind. The web designers have tried to minimize the download time by reducing the number of characters on the page; however, the additional text (as above) that makes the navigation banner accessible only amounts to 186 bytes – less than 0.6 percent of the size of the page – increasing the download time by only about 5 hundredths of second even on a slow modem.

As it is, this is how Home Page Reader reads this navigation image map (grabbing the `href`, in the absence of any `alt` text):

HPR:
(Start of map with 6 items)
[Map: r/p1]
[Map: r/m1]
[Map: r/wn]
[Map: r/i1]
[Map: r/hw]
(End of Map.)

JAWS for Windows and Window-Eyes follow suit with JAWS prefacing each meaningless `href`, like `r/p1` with "image link" and Window-Eyes with the word "link."

Image Buttons

Image buttons are input elements with `type="image"`. The idea is to create something more interesting and eye catching than the standard push buttons. Here is a sample:

```
<INPUT type="image" src="images\search.gif" name="Search" height="23"
    width="64" value="Search" alt="Search">
```

Obviously the key again is `alt="Search"`. When screen readers encounter an image button, they treat it much like a push button (command button) and use the `alt` text instead of the value.

```
<INPUT type="submit" name="Search" value="Search">
```

Here is the way in which HPR speaks these two search buttons.

HPR:
[Search: Image Button.]
[Search: Submit Button.]

Notice that HPR informs the reader of the difference between an image button and the conventional text-based submit button, although, functionally, there is no difference. Window-Eyes and JAWS do not do this.

W-E:
Button Search
Button Search

JFW:
Search Button
Search Button

It is interesting to notice the difference in the ordering of the information presented. A strategy for communicating with speech synthesis is to rank the importance of the specific information and speak the most important first. To me, in this case, the most important information is the label, *"search"*. The fact that it is a button is secondary.

> As one tabs through active elements with a talking browser or a screen reader, the new item cancels the speaking of the previous one. As soon as you hear enough information to know you are not interested, you can tab again, and the speech of that item is stopped and the next one started. In this case, if you hear "button" first, you have to wait to hear "search" before you can move along. On the other hand, if you hear "search" first and are not interested in searching, you can move on right away. This observation can be applied to multiple word `alt` text, encouraging the placement of the "most important" words first.

Here is another image button, this time without alternative text. Here is the code for the button with some minor changes:

```
<input type=image width=21 value="Go" name="Go"
    src=" … images/G/01/v9/search-browse/go-button.gif" >
```

In the case of Window-Eyes and Home Page Reader, the careful listener might be able to guess the purpose of the image button because the image's source file is called `"go-button"`. However an `Alt="go"` attribute would make life so much easier. This is how HPR and the screen readers read the image button:

W-E:	Button images/G/01/v9/search-browse/go-button.gif
HPR:	[search-browse/go-button.gif: Image Button.]
JFW:	Go button

The announcement by JFW is surprising. Freedom Scientific in this case is picking up the `value` attribute of the image button – in this case "Go". The `value` attribute is used to set the initial value of things like textboxes and drop down-lists, but the `value` attribute is not required (or expected) for image buttons.

▶ Update Your Cart

This "*update your cart*" example from a major commercial site has neither a `value` attribute nor an `alt` attribute:

```
<input type="image"  width="120" height="20" border="0"
    src="… f/1055/979/5h/5h/compant.com/gresources/b4_update_cart.gif"
    id="AddAndGoToCart" name="AddAndGoToCart" >
```

Here is how HPR and the screen readers read this button, notice that JFW just announces "button":

HPR:	[gresources/b4_update_cart.gif: Image Button.]
W-E:	f/1055/979/5h/5h/compant.com/gresources/b4_update_cart.gif Button
JFW:	Button

Because many, if not most, active images on the web today do **not** have a text equivalent, users of screen readers have to try to find other ways to interpret them and these do not always produce comprehensible results. It is a discouraging and frustrating experience and it certainly does not make sense for business.

The simple change of adding `alt="go"` or `alt="Update Your Cart"` makes such a complete difference – the difference between gibberish and "smooth sailing".

A few screen reader users do find ingenious ways of coping with sites that lack the most basic accessibility considerations. However, they are only a small percentage of users who are visually impaired. If web designers make their sites accessible, all those potential customers can have an experience that is comfortable and supportive rather than frustrating and annoying.

Decorative or Formatting Images

In the sections above I have raised issues of judgment and style on the nature of the alternative text used for active images. Some of these are minor issues – for example whether to use two or three words. However, everyone agrees that for active images you always use words. When it comes to images used for decoration there are some more substantial differences of opinion.

So let's begin with one area where there is no disagreement: images used purely for formatting should have **null alt text**. What we are talking about here, are the single-pixel 1x1 "clear GIFs", with file names like `clear.gif`, `c.gif`, or `spacer.gif,` that are typically placed in otherwise empty table cells in order that those cells not appear empty to the browser. They ensure consistent formatting of layout tables in different browsers.

These spacer images should always have null `alt` text. This means using `alt=""`, two quotation marks and no space. Indeed there is no disagreement about the fact that formatting images should be treated this way, but some still continue to write `alt=  " "`, quote space quote.

What is wrong with quote space quote? Firstly, to a mathematician and logician, `null alt` text means `null alt` text – that is, *none*. Quote space quote is something; it is one space, where as quote-quote is nothing. Secondly, and confirming the first point, if you use `alt=" "` (quote space quote) for your image, Microsoft Internet Explorer will display the ToolTip, *[ ]*, whereas if you write `alt=""` it will not display anything.

An example of good practice could be found on the IBM home page on October 10, 2001. This used about 30 instances of `c.gif` in otherwise empty table cells, as follows:

```
<td >
    <img width="1" src="... c.gif" height="12" border="0" alt="">
</td>
```

The IBM site *(http://www.ibm.com)* has thirty occurrences of the spacer images, which you can check out by submitting it to WAVE *(http://www.temple.edu/inst_disabilities/piat/wave/)*. Wave inserts:

...everywhere it finds an image with null `alt` text.

There are some images other than spacers on the IBM site which also have null `alt` text. The small white right-facing arrows down the left side indicate list items, and similarly the black arrows at the bottom center serve the same function.

When special images are used instead of the bullets in bulleted lists – as in the IBM page – it is the author's decision whether to use `alt=""` or, say, `alt="bullet"` or `alt="item"`. Certainly you **do not** want to lengthen the `alt` text with words like "small right arrow," or "right facing arrow" because the information content of the graphic is at most "bullet" or "item" and it is just burdensome to have to listen to such descriptions over and over.

The IBM site chooses `alt=""` for all the graphical bullets, which is the way I would do it as well.

The right hand side of the IBM site also contains some images that have null `alt` text:

The horizontal lines between the main items are images (`dotted_rule_197pc.gif`) with `alt=""`. Again, an author might take the position that this image should have non-null `alt` text like, for example `alt="separator"` but I like `alt=""`.

There is another bullet-like indicator, a small white triangle on a blue background, next to NavCode™.

The IBM web developers choose `alt=""` here too. Again, this is a good choice.

There is one last issue that the IBM site demonstrates very well. Notice that near the top of the second screenshot there are three items, each of which has an image, followed by text, *"e-business on Demand,"* *"IBM e-business,"* and, *"Trials & betas."* Here is what Home Page Reader speaks for these three highlights:

HPR:
link: [e-business on demand.]
link: e-business on demand
link: The next utility: accessible, affordable and easy to use
link: [IBM e-business.]
link: IBM e-business
link: Infrastructure -- sooner, or later, it matters
link: [Software trials & betas.]
link: Trials and betas
link: Discover the latest
in IBM software

Notice the repetition of the links. First, the image has `alt` text (within the square brackets) "e-business on demand". Then there is the text, identical to the `alt` text of the image, which is also a link. Next, there is the descriptive text, saying where the link leads to. All three links have the same target, so effectively there are three links with the same target, and two with repeated text. How did this come about? An abbreviated fragment of the code will help to explain.

```
<tr>
<td …><a href=…><img src="… module_ebusiness.gif" alt="IBM e-business"></a></td>
<td …><a href=…><b>IBM e-business</b></a>
... </tr>
```

The best thing to do in a case like this is to combine the image with the text, all within one anchor tag, and then give the image `alt=""`. This is the only situation where an active image could have null `alt` text; namely if there is text there anyway. Basically the code should look like this:

```
<a href=…>
   <img src="... module_ebusiness.gif" alt="" ...>
   IBM e-business
</a>
```

This is a good idea, but it won't work on the IBM page because, as you can see from the original code above, the image and the text are in different table cells and the anchor element is not allowed to span table cells (or contain table data elements, `<td>`).

There are two possible solutions to this problem. You could change the formatting layout so that the image and the text are in the same table cell. In this way the anchor tag can include both the text and the image. Since there is some text in the anchor, using `alt=""` on the image is fine. Alternatively, remove the link from the image and simply use `alt=""`.

One practice that is remarkably common and should always be avoided is putting `alt=""` on the image which is a link, unless text is contained in the same anchor element.

Here is what a site "sounds" like with Home Page Reader when `alt=""` is placed on those redundant image links. (This is a LexisNexis Sign-in page *http://www.nexis.com/research*).

> **HPR:**
>
> link
>
> link What's new
>
> link
>
> link View a Demo
>
> link
>
> link Task Pages
>
> link
>
> link How to Subscribe

Listening to this you might guess that the occurrences of "link" were images without `alt` text and that they were the same as the subsequent text, but that is a risky guess.

> Never use null `alt` text on an image which is a link unless text explaining the target of the link is contained in the same anchor.

Images That Carry Lots of Information

The key to text equivalents for non-text content is to convey the information in the non-text element textually. It is easy (at least it should be easy) with image links and image map hot spots because the information of the image is where the link will go, like "*home*", "*products*", or, "*services*". It is also easy when images convey no information; just put `alt=""`! But sometimes there is more information in the image than the concise `alt` attribute should hold. A perfect example of this is the technology from CORDA Technologies, *http://www.corda.com*.

CORDA provides technology for producing charts and graphs as illustrated in the following screenshot:

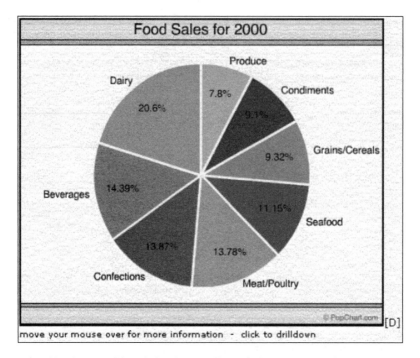

The `alt` text for this chart could and should say "Food Sales for 2000." But that is not conveying the information of the picture in any detail.

There are two mechanisms for providing textual equivalents for non-text content like charts and graphs. The first is the `longdesc` attribute of an image. The value of the `longdesc` (long description) attribute is a URI, a reference to another page or a file that contains a detailed description of the content of the image, which the CORDA technology will maintain as data changes and charts are updated.

```
<IMG src="chart22.gif" width="455" height="325"
     alt= "food sales for 2000" longdesc="sales2000.htm">
```

The problem with the `longdesc` attribute is that it is not widely supported by assistive technology. As a result, an alternative convention is suggested, using the **D-LINK**. The D-link, pictured in the screenshot above, is a link to a file or page which is the same as the `longdesc` value:

```
<IMG src="chart22.gif" width="455" height="325"
     alt= "food sales for 2000" longdesc="sales2000.htm">
<A href="sales2000.htm">D</A>
```

Here is a screenshot of the page returned after activating the D-link for the CORDA Food Sales chart:

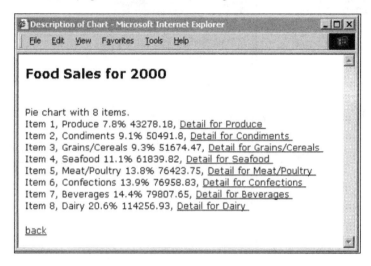

Not only is the data **equivalent** to the chart but the additional function of "drilling down" to get more detail is available here too. This is a perfect example of the kind of meaningful detailed description that can be provided either with the `longdesc` attribute or with the D-Link.

Here is another CORDA PopChart:

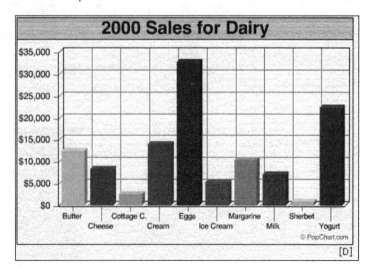

The corresponding long description opened from the D-link is shown on the right:

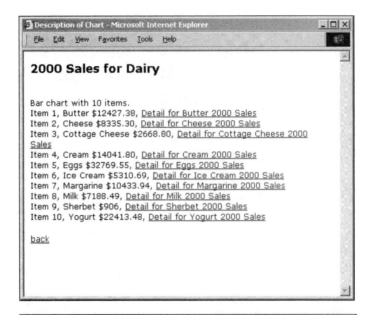

Long descriptions for images don't have to be files. Inline text can provide the description of an image. The following screenshot shows an image with a textual description of the image on the left:

Note that there is `alt` text, "Click for Large Photo," and though it is not a text equivalent, the in-line long description serves the purpose very well.

Summary for Images

- Every image (`<img>`), image map area (`<area>`), and image button should have a valid `alt` attribute. If you adopt this universal policy, you can easily test your site for images that might somehow slip through (testing will be covered in Chapter 7). If you allow some of your images to not have `alt` text, then this testing procedure is much more complicated and error prone.

- Every active image (image link, area, and image button) must have clear and succinct `alt` text that conveys the purpose of the active element.

- All images which are not active and do not convey information or are redundant should have `alt=""`, that is `null alt` text.

- If images contain information beyond what can be conveyed in a short `alt` attribute, use the long description attribute (`longdesc`) on the `<img>` element, a D-link, or in-line descriptions of the image that conveys the textual equivalent of the image.

I randomly picked ten of *PC Magazine's* Top 100 sites and analyzed them for missing alternative text. Here are the unpleasant results of this informal and unscientific survey.

Images *without* `alt` text			
Site	**Images**	**Image Map Hot Spots**	**Image buttons**
About: *http://www.about.com/*	44	n/a	n/a
Andale: *http://www.andale.com/*	26	23	2
Bizrate: *http://www.bizrate.com/*	17	n/a	n/a
Expert City: *http://www.expertcity.com/*	12	6	n/a
Lonely Planet: *http://www.lonelyplanet.com/*	7	n/a	1
Britannica: *http://www.britannica.com/*	96	n/a	n/a
HotBot: *http://www.hotbot.lycos.com/*	4	2	n/a
Schwab: *http://www.schwab.com/*	12	n/a	n/a
Backflip: *http://www.blackflip.com/*	0	n/a	n/a
MyPalm: *http://www.palm.com/*	31	n/a	n/a

Transcripts of Audio

More and more audio is becoming part of the user experience in the web. Most commonly streaming audio (RealAudio, QuickTime, Windows Media) provides access to news and events while wave files add sound to the user experience. If audio is decoration, sounds that the web author feels add to the experience of the site and do not carry information, then there is no need to add text equivalents for those sounds. Text equivalents are needed when audio includes spoken words, when the audio is in fact the message. To be accessible to people who are deaf or hearing-impaired, speeches or news reports need to have associated textual transcripts.

Although we applied it to the needs of users who are visually impaired, the Section 508 provision, §1194.22(a) is still the one that applies to audio files:

> §1194.22(a) A text equivalent for every non-text element shall be provided (for example, via "alt", "longdesc", or in element content).

The Web Accessibility Initiative Web Content Accessibility Guideline checkpoint 1.1 is still the applicable checkpoint:

> 1.1 Provide a text equivalent for every non-text element (for example, via "alt", "longdesc", or in element content). This includes: ... sounds (played with or without user interaction), stand-alone audio files, audio tracks of video, and video.

Checkpoint 4 of IBM's Web Accessability Guidelines addresses audio files along with multimedia:

> 4. Multimedia. Provide captions or transcripts of important audio content. Provide text or audio descriptions of important video content.

The part of the IBM checkpoint that is relevant to us here is the requirement for "transcripts of important audio content."

Compared with the subtleties of "text equivalents" for images and the judgment required to decide on how much text will be adequate, it is refreshing to talk about text equivalents for audio which are defined simply as transcripts.

There are many examples on the Web of sites that include transcripts with their audio content. One of them is the Bloomberg Politics site. Below is a screenshot of the site (*http://www.bloomberg.com/bbn/electiontrans.html*) where there are links to audio files for the broadcast (Listen) and links to transcripts (More...).

The *"Listen"* link is in fact an image and it has `alt` text, "listen..." The wording of both of these links could be improved for accessibility, because when they are taken out of context in a list of links they don't carry the information about the target of the link (see Chapter 5).

Color

Color may enhance the experience of visitors coming to a web site. It can be eye catching, add emphasis, or just add to the visual pleasure of the site. There are conditions, however, where the use of color will make your web site inaccessible to some people with disabilities, because some people are not able to distinguish colors.

Avoiding Use of Color Alone To Convey Information

In fact it is estimated that one in 20 visitors to your web site will have some form of color vision deficiency and may find your web site either difficult or impossible to use if you use color alone to convey information. Such people who are color-blind (achromatopsia) will have difficulty finding the required fields if they are coded in blue or red as is often the case.

Isn't this an issue for users of the Web who are blind? It shouldn't be a problem because screen readers could provide information about colors to their users. It is a problem because this color information is not available through the major screen readers or IBM's talking browser.

It is good to use color to convey information. The key is not to use color **alone**. Doing a fairly rapid survey, I would estimate that about one in ten sites do in fact use color to convey information.

The Section 508 provisions require that color not be the sole way information is conveyed (*http://www.access-board.gov/sec508/guide/1194.22.htm*).

> *§1194.22(c) Web pages shall be designed so that all information conveyed with color is also available without color, for example from context or markup.*

This is almost exactly the same wording as the Web Accessibility Initiative priority 1 checkpoint 2.1. (*http://www.w3.org/TR/WCAG10/full-checklist.html*):

> *2.1 Ensure that all information conveyed with color is also available without color, for example from context or markup.*

The IBM checkpoint (April, 2001, *http://www-3.ibm.com/able/wbchecklist12.html*) relating to color addresses the use of color alone to convey information but also includes a concern about adequate contrast:

> *12. Color & Contrast. Ensure that all information conveyed with color is also conveyed in the absence of color and that the contrast is sufficient in images.*

There are lots of ways that information, like required fields in forms, can be conveyed without (or in addition to) color.

Tell us who you are. (* indicates required fields)

Company:	
Salutation:	(please select)
* First name:	
* Last name:	
Job title:	(please select)
* Phone:	e.g., 415-555-1111
Web address:	http://
* E-mail:	

In the example above, the asterisk precedes the field label. This is by far the best method because this adaptation helps screen reader users too. With the asterisk placed before the prompt, that is the first thing heard, and an easy notice to the user that the field is required.

Contrast

In addition to the concern about using color alone to convey information, web designers need to be aware of the combinations of foreground and background colors used on their web page, especially in images. If the foreground and background are too close to the same hue, they may not provide sufficient contrast for people with different types of color deficits or for people who are using monochrome displays.

The reason images are especially important is that users with color deficits choose to use their own contrast setting in their browser. The easiest way to avoid this problem is to choose highly contrastive colors for the foreground and background.

Section 508 does not have a provision requiring contrast on web pages. IBM checkpoint number 12, which was cited in the previous section, recommends adequate contrast like the corresponding Web Accessibility Initiative Checkpoint 2.2:

> *2.2 Ensure that foreground and background color combinations provide sufficient contrast when viewed by someone having color deficits or when viewed on a black and white screen. [Priority 2 for images, Priority 3 for text].*

I have searched for a measure of contrast for the Web and have not found it. There is an excellent discussion of issues of contrast for people with vision loss at the Lighthouse site, *http://www.lighthouse.org/color_contrast.htm*. Images in the article illustrate effective contrast and ineffective contrast. A nice addition to the site would be a numeric "contrast" value computed from two RGB values, with recommendations of values for the least numeric contrast. This could be used during the design of images containing text and for compliance testing for contrast of normal text foreground and background colors.

A standard spreadsheet (Excel or Lotus 1-2-3, for example) can provide an example of good contrast. Try placing colors on cells and move the cell pointer across those cells. Alternatively, highlight text in a word processor and move the cursor into that text. The programmers who designed the spreadsheet program or word processor knew how to alter the cell pointer or cursor's color to contrast with the background color by using the complementary color. For an RGB color, with red, green, and blue values R, G, and B respectively, the complementary color can be calculated as being (255-R), (255-G), (255-B).

It is clear that good contrast occurs when two colors are close to complementary. "Closeness" can be calculated as if the R G B colors are points in three-dimensional space:

$$Distance = (\ (R_1 \text{-} R_2)^2 + (G_1 \text{-} G_2)^2 + (B_1 - B_2)^2\ )^{\frac{1}{2}}$$

One web site accessibility tool called InFocus from SSB Technologies (*http://www.ssbtechnologies.com*) includes a check for contrast that is proprietary but probably uses a calculation similar to this one. Such checking is possible for foreground and background colors specified in stylesheets or HTML code.

The most common cases of poor contrast, however, are in images of text and it would be nearly impossible to computationally check these, even if we agreed on a viable contrast number.

Creating Accessible Tables

HTML tables are widely used on the Web. However most are used for formatting purposes and relatively few are used for displaying data. It is these data tables that primarily concern us here for the purposes of accessibility. Before getting to data tables, let's briefly investigate how tables are used to format web pages and the consequences for people using text browsers or screen readers.

Formatting Tables and How Tables Linearize

Let's begin with a very simple basic table and understand how it is spoken with a screen reader or other assistive technology:

Cell 1 1	Cell 1 2
Cell 2 1	Cell 2 2

Here is the HTML code for this table:

```
<TABLE border="1">
  <TBODY>
    <TR>
      <TD>Cell 1 1</TD>
      <TD>Cell 1 2</TD>
    </TR>
    <TR>
      <TD>Cell 2 1</TD>
      <TD>Cell 2 2</TD>
    </TR>
  </TBODY>
</TABLE>
```

Home Page Reader starts with the first row, completely reads each cell there, and then proceeds to the second row, repeating that process.

HPR:
Cell 1 1
Cell 1 2
Cell 2 1
Cell 2 2

This method of reading the contents of a table is called "linearization." The way the reading (linearizing) is done is to start in the first row, first column (Cell 1 1), read the entire contents of that cell, then proceed to the next column going across the first row. When row 1 is complete, proceed to row 2 and so on.

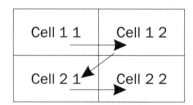

If there is a lot of information in any cell, all of it is read before proceeding to the next cell. This is a very important aspect of the linearization of tables, and it is different from the way screen readers worked just a few years ago. Today they take advantage of the HTML structure of the document. They used to "read the screen" so they would, in effect, speak the first line from each cell, then the second line from each cell and so on. Often this would make no sense whatsoever.

When the linearization process comes to a cell that includes a nested table then that table is to be completely linearized, before continuing on to the next cell. A rather typical layout table in the sample opposite illustrates the way tables are used for laying out content on the page:

This is a title cell		
Navigation link 1 Navigation link 2 Navigation link 3 Navigation link 4	Banner ad	Right Navigation 1 Right Navigation 2 Right Navigation 3
	Main content area with lots of text and content filling the center part of the window	

What is especially important here is that some of the cells "span" rows or columns. In the HTML code for this table you can see that the very first cell has `colspan="3"`. That means that the first cell goes across (spans) the entire table. Here is the HTML code not including alignment or color information:

```
<TABLE border="1">
   <TR>
      <TD colspan="3">This is a title cell</TD>
   </TR>
   <TR>
      <TD rowspan="2">
         Navigation link 1<BR>
         Navigation link 2<BR>
         Navigation link 3<BR>
         Navigation link 4
      </TD>
      <TD>Banner ad</TD>
      <TD rowspan="2" >
         Right Navigation 1<BR>
         Right Navigation 2<BR>
         Right Navigation 3
      </TD>
   </TR>
   <TR>
      <TD>Main content area with lots of text and<BR>
         content filling the center part of the <BR>
         window
      </TD>
   </TR>
</TABLE>
```

So this is really a table with three rows and three columns as pictured below:

Title (colspan #1)	Title (colspan #2)	Title (colspan #3)
Left Navigation (rowspan #1)	Banner	Right Navigation (rowspan #1)
Left Navigation (rowspan #2)	Content	Right Navigation (rowspan #2)

The three cells across the top are merged into one with `colspan=3`, while the lower **two** cells in the first and third columns are combined in a single cell with the attribute `rowspan="2"`. The top three cells are combined into one to give the title bar across the top of the page. The left navigation panel comprises the bottom two cells combined into one and similarly the right navigation panel arises from combining the last two cells of the last column.

The spanning of columns and rows affects the way tables are linearized or spoken. The basic rule is that everything in a cell (independent of its spanning properties) is read when the cell is first encountered.

In our hypothetical layout table, the complete title panel is read first. Then moving to the second row, the *entire* left navigation panel is read followed by the "Banner" and all of the right navigation. In the middle row, only the cell called "content" remains to be read, and this is read last.

HPR:
This is a title cell
Navigation link 1
Navigation link 2
Navigation link 3
Navigation link 4
Banner ad
Right Navigation 1
Right Navigation 2
Right Navigation 3
Main content area with lots of text and content filling the center part of the window

We are going to return to this example in Chapter 5 when we talk about accessible navigation. The formatting illustrated here raises a serious issue for access to a site. The main message of a page may be very hard to find. If you are listening to the page, chances are you want to hear that "main content." With layout like this it takes a long time before you get to hear the information you were looking for.

The Web Accessibility Initiative addresses table linearization in two priority 2 checkpoints of the Web Content Accessibility Guidelines. The first checkpoint cautions against the use of tables for layout, unless they linearize well:

> *5.3 Do not use tables for layout unless the table makes sense when linearized. Otherwise, if the table does not make sense, provide an alternative equivalent (which may be a linearized version). [Priority 2]*

The layout of our sample page above makes perfectly good sense, but it is inconvenient to the point of raising access issues. I suppose it may even be possible to create a layout table that does not make sense when linearized, but I have yet to see one and I don't know how to do it.

The second priority 2 checkpoint about layout tables from the WAI recommends the avoidance of structural markup inside a layout table:

> *5.4 If a table is used for layout, do not use any structural markup for the purpose of visual formatting. [Priority 2]*

In general it is important to use markup for its intended purpose, not to artificially create visual effects. For example it is a bad idea to use the `<blockquote>` element in order to create indenting. As tables are currently used for site layout, you should avoid using the `<th>` element to have text centered and bold. If you do, then the assistive technology will think the table is a data table, and try to deal with it accordingly.

The WCAG also has a further Priority 3 checkpoint related to our discussion of the way screen readers speak text on the web page:

> *10.3 Until user agents (including assistive technologies) render side-by-side text correctly, provide a linear text alternative (on the current page or some other) for **all** tables that lay out text in parallel, word-wrapped columns. [Priority 3]*

User agents, including assistive technologies, do in fact render side-by-side text correctly, so in my opinion, this checkpoint is moot.

Neither the Section 508 Rules on Web accessibility nor the IBM Web Accessibility Guidelines include provisions that specifically address layout tables because, apparently, these issues are interpreted as less pressing.

It is next to impossible to look at the source of a large commercial web page and determine what it will look like when it is linearized. The linearization algorithm that we have described, involving recursion as it does, is somewhat hard to apply even when you know the structure of your page. Fortunately there are readily available tools that let developers look at their linearized page.

Often the tabular structure for layout is part of the basic template used for development of the site. When this is the case, you can understand how your pages linearize just by looking at one of the pages.

Lynx (*http://lynx.browser.org/*) is a text-only browser that is popular in the Unix world and is available for Windows, OS/2, and VMS. It is shareware so you can download Lynx and try it yourself. Short of that, however, Delorie Software provides the Lynx Viewer (*http://www.delorie.com/web/lynxview.html*). Just browse to that site and submit the URL of a page you want to test. I ran the sample table at the beginning of this section through this Lynx Viewer and here is a screenshot of the result:

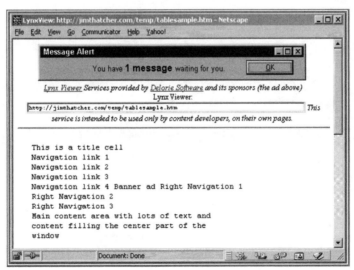

This text view of our table as seen by the Lynx Viewer is show overleaf. It is essentially identical to the HPR view that we saw previously.

IBM Home Page Reader provides a text view, which by definition linearizes all tables. There is a free trial of HPR available at *http://www.ibm.com/able/hpr.html*. When you use HPR to observe the linearized text view, you don't have to listen to the whole page; instead, bring up the web page and place the focus on the text view, either by clicking on that view or using *F6* to cycle to the text view.

When in the text view, use *CTRL+A* to mark (highlight) the text view. HPR will analyze the complete page and get all the text and mark it. Then use *CTRL+C* to copy the text view to the clipboard. You can then paste the view into your favorite text editor, for example Notepad, and analyze it there, or print it.

Another way to check out the linear version of your site is to use the Tablin tool (*http://www.w3.org/WAI/Resources/Tablin/*) from the Web Accessibility Initiative's Education and Outreach working group. Tablin is available in several formats including an online service and downloadable Java source.

Data Tables

Data tables are a different story. Data tables don't have to be made up of numeric data. They are made up of any kind of data that depends on the rows and columns to convey information. The accessibility issue is that information is lost when a data table is linearized. Consider this table of TV listings (*http://tvguide.com/listings*):

fantasysports.com

	7:00 PM	7:30 PM	8:00 PM	8:30 PM	
2 KTBC	Titus (Repeat)	Titus (Repeat)	Dark Angel (Repeat)		
3 KVUE	Who Wants to Be a Millionaire		Monday Night Football>>		
4 KXAN	Third Watch				
5 K-EYE	King of Queens	Yes, Dear	Everybody Loves Raymond	Becker	
8 NEWS8	News 8 Tonight>>				
9 KLRU	Antiques Roadshow (Repeat)		Masterpiece Theatre American Collection>>		
12 KNVA	7th Heaven		Angel		
13 KVC13	Judge Hatchett	Power of Attorney	Judge Joe Brown	Divorce Court	
14 MAX	<<Me, Myself & Irene	How to Make a Monster			
15 AMN	<<Austin Music Network>>				
20 KLRU 2	Newshour with Jim Lehrer		Religion & Ethics Newsweekly	Health Diary	
21 WGN	No One Cries Forever				
23 KBEJ	The Hughleys	One on One	The Parkers	Girlfriends	
24 QVC	PM Style				
25 HSN	NFL Shop		Discover Pearls		

By listening to the linearized version of this table you may, with difficulty, be able to tell what is playing on KVUE. You can listen to this page to hear the shows that follow KVUE and come before KXAN. Those are the ones playing on KVUE. But because of spanning cells, it is impossible to tell what time Monday Night Football is starting. Information is lost when the table is linearized.

Notice that if there were no column spans then technically you might be able to figure out the times of each show. In the example the third show heard after the station name would be the one that is showing at 8:00PM. But that is only technically true, as this is not a reasonable solution to the problem. Imagine searching for "Angel" with your screen reader and finding it. There you would be in the middle of the table. What time does it start? On which channel will it be aired? This is the central issue with the accessibility of data tables.

The advice for marking up tables in a way that will allow assistive technology to help the user decipher the information is divided into two parts: simple data tables and complex data tables. The example above is a complex table, and we will be returning to it later, but first let us look at the guidelines for simple data tables.

Simple Data Tables in the Guidelines

A data table is simple if it satisfies two conditions:

- The column headers for any given data cell is in the same column as the cell.

- The row headers for any given data cell is in the same row as the cell.

The Section 508 provisions require that row and column headers be identified with markup:

> §1194.22(g) Row and column headers shall be identified for data tables.

This provision is essentially the same as Checkpoint 5.1 from the Web Content Accessibility Guidelines:

> 5.1 For data tables, identify row and column headers.

The IBM Web Accessibility Guidelines follow suit but specify how to identify headers and how to deal with complex tables. We will discuss the complex tables shortly.

> 10. Table Headers. Use the TH element to mark up table heading cells. Use the headers attribute on cells of complex data tables.

These guidelines are all designed so that the assistive technology can provide information about tabular structure to people who use screen readers or talking browsers.

When you are listening to a page, the content is linearized and when tables are linearized, information is lost unless steps are taken to recover it. The intent of the guidelines is to allow a screen reader to recover the lost information and present it to the user. In particular the screen reader or talking browser needs to know which cells contain header or title information for any given data cell.

Table Reading with Assistive Technologies

In order to fully understand this "table problem", it is very helpful to listen to tables with a screen reader or talking browser. To test the recovery of the tabular information that is lost when the table is linearized, you have to listen to the cells of a table a cell-at-a-time, rather than just listening to a whole page.

Unfortunately, listening to tables is not the easiest task with these technologies. First you may have to make sure that the settings are correct, and then you have to read the table cells one at a time. It would be a case of information overload to always read out table headings when reading tables, since almost all tables are layout tables. Header information is not interesting or relevant for layout tables.

Here are the techniques needed to set up and use our three assistive technologies for reading table cells.

- **Window-Eyes:** Use *CTRL+SHIFT+H* to cycle through table heading speaking choices. Choose "Column or Row" to hear the row heading when the row changes and the column heading when the column changes.

  CTRL+ALT+TAB moves to the next table; *CTRL+ALT+SHIFT+TAB* moves to the previous table. Turn on table mode with *CTRL+PLUS*. Turn table mode off with *CTRL+MINUS*. When in table mode use *INS+ARROW* to move from cell to cell in the table.

- **HPR:** You must turn on reading of table headers in the programs settings. Go to *menu items*, then *Settings*, then *Miscellaneous*, and then check the two checkboxes, *Read Column Headers* and *Read Row Headers*. These are **not** checked by default.

  Switch to Table Jump Mode with *ALT+J* and then use the left and right arrow keys to jump from table to table. When you are ready to read a table, go into Table Reading Mode and then use all the arrow keys to move from cell to cell.

- **JFW:** You don't change modes to work with tables. Use *ALT+CTRL+ARROWS* to move around table cells.

Let's begin by seeing how these technologies read the cells of a simple data table, one with no specific markup indicating which cells are header cells. Here's a table which is apparently a performance chart for some mutual fund:

	1998	1999	2000	09-01
Fund	17.7	52.9	6.9	-9.6
+/- Cat	13.0	21.2	6.8	6.3
+/- Index	-10.9	31.9	16.0	10.8

Here is the HTML for this table. There is no specific code indicating headers beyond the fact that the headers are all in the first row and in the first column.

```
<TABLE border="1" bgcolor="#ffffcc" Width="60%">
   <TR>
      <TD width="20%"></TD>
      <TD width="10%">1998</TD>
      <TD width="10%">1999</TD>
      <TD width="10%">2000</TD>
      <TD width="10%">09-01</TD>
   </TR>
   <TR>
      <TD>Fund</TD>
      <TD>17.7</TD>
```

```
      <TD>52.9</TD>
      <TD>6.9</TD>
      <TD>-9.6</TD>
   </TR>
   <TR>
      <TD>+/- Cat</TD>
      <TD>13.0</TD>
      <TD>21.2</TD>
      <TD>6.8</TD>
      <TD>6.3</TD>
   </TR>
   <TR>
      <TD>+/- Index</TD>
      <TD>-10.9</TD>
      <TD>31.9</TD>
      <TD>16.0</TD>
      <TD>10.8</TD>
   </TR>
</TABLE>
```

All three assistive technologies treat this table in exactly the same way. When reading cells which are outside of the header rows and columns, that is, not in the first row or the first column, each technology speaks the heading information in the first row when the column changes and speaks the heading information in first column when the row changes.

The following table shows how all three assistive technologies read cells in the table. It is not enough to just indicate how a given cell is announced because the announcement depends on whether you arrive at the cell from the side or from above or below.

	To row 1 column 3	To row 2 column 2
Move from row 1 column 2	*1999 52.9*	*+/- Cat 13.0*
Move from row 2 column 3	*Fund 52.9*	*1998 13.0*

As soon as the headings are moved out of the first row or the first column this accessible rendering is lost to users of assistive technology. For a simple example of how the accessibility gets broken, let's look at what happens when a caption is added *as a* **cell** in the table. (We will discuss a better way to introduce captions, or headings, in a later section.)

Here is the code added at the top of the table. This so-called caption is centered and in bold style, but it is not designated as a heading <th>.

```
<TR>
   <TD colspan="5" align="center"><STRONG>Performance</STRONG></TD>
</TR>
```

The resulting table is shown below:

Performance				
	1998	1999	2000	09-01
Fund	17.7	52.9	6.9	-9.6
+/- Cat	13.0	21.2	6.8	6.3
+/- Index	-10.9	31.9	16.0	10.8

Window-Eyes and IBM Home Page Reader both think "Performance" is the information to be used as column headings including the cells containing the dates. Here is how they speak with this new table:

	To row 3 column 3	To row 4 column 2
Move from row 3 column 2	*Performance 52.9*	*+/- Cat 13.0*
Move from row 4 column 3	*Fund 52.9*	*Performance 13.0*

JFW, on the other hand, uses a heuristic whereby a row with spanned cells is assumed not to be heading information. This screen reader ignores the first row in this example and correctly uses the dates as headings.

Using the <th> Element and Scope Attribute

<th> is used to enclose data in a table that is intended to be a heading. The default implementation in a visual browser of the <th> element is to center the text and make it bold. It is both easy (and advisable) to use Cascading Style Sheets (CSS) to modify the presentation of the <th> element if this default is not what is desired.

In the figure below, the <th> element is used for all the cells of the first row and for the first column – all the headings, in other words.

Performance				
	1998	**1999**	**2000**	**09-01**
Fund	17.7	52.9	6.9	-9.6
+/- Cat	13.0	21.2	6.8	6.3
+/- Index	-10.9	31.9	16.0	10.8

Here is the new HTML, which you may wish to compare with what we used earlier:

```
<TABLE border="1" bgcolor="#ffffcc" Width="60%">
   <TR>
      <TD colspan="5" align="center"><STRONG>Performance</STRONG></TD>
   </TR>
   <TR>
      <TD width="20%"></TD>
      <TH width="10%">1998</TH>
      <TH width="10%">1999</TH>
      <TH width="10%">2000</TH>
      <TH width="10%">09-01</TH>
   </TR>
```

```
    <TR>
        <TH>Fund</TH>
        <TD>17.7</TD>
...
</TABLE>
```

The behavior of Home Page Reader is now exactly as it was before we added the performance cell to our table because the `<th>` elements help to identify the cells containing the headers. The two screen readers, however, ignore `<th>` and `scope` elements. The fact that JFW reads the table correctly is a matter of luck or good judgment on the part of its makers, as we noted earlier.

The `scope` attribute offers an alternative to the `<th>` element for specifying header information in an HTML Table. It has the advantage that the heading cells would not be formatted differently than the other data cells (not centered or bold). It is worth bearing in mind, however, that it is a more recent element that is only supported by the 4+ visual browsers, so employ it with caution if you are using this formatting data for reasons other than accessibility.

Here is our sample table marked up with `scope` instead of `<th>`:

```
<TBODY>
    <TR>
    <TR>
        <TD colspan="5" align="center"><STRONG>Performance</STRONG></TD>
    </TR>
        <TD width="20%"></TD>
        <TD width="10%" scope="col">1998</TD>
        <TD width="10%" scope="col">1999</TD>
        <TD width="10%" scope="col">2000</TD>
        <TD width="10%" scope="col">09-01</TD>
    </TR>
    <TR>
        <TD scope="row">Fund</TD>
        <TD>17.7</TD>
        <TD>52.9</TD>
        <TD>6.9</TD>
        ...
</Table>
```

Again, HPR uses this information to correctly identify the headers in this table, but the two screen readers ignore it. Once more, JAWS gets it right, but only because it ignores the spanned cell.

Here is a summary of the effects of `<th>` and `scope` markup on speaking simple data tables with assistive technologies.

HPR:

- If there is no `scope` or `<th>` markup, HPR will read headings from the first row and first column.

- If any table cell is designated as a heading with `scope` or `<th>`, then only the heading information specified by the scope or `<th>` will be announced. It is announced in rows to the right of or below the heading cells.

Window-Eyes:

- Window-Eyes always speaks heading information from row one and column one independent of the `scope` attribute and `<th>` element.

JFW:

- JAWS for Windows speaks heading information from the first row and column independent of the `scope` and `<th>` element.

- Sometimes JFW will choose an alternative adjacent row or column for headings if the first has spanned cells.

So, of these three assistive technologies, only HPR supports the simple table heading markup, `<th>` and `scope`. There is a simple reason for this: it takes development time for the screen readers to implement support for these constructs and the assistive technology companies have to ask how that effort will benefit their customers. Since there are almost no data tables out there on the Web that use these markup techniques, it follows there is no direct value in supporting these markup techniques to the screen reader customers.

However there is an indirect benefit that probably forms the basis for IBM's decision to support `<th>` and `scope`. As it comes into greater use, the needs of assistive technologies will raise in developer's minds the importance of using `<th>` and/or `scope` markup, so that assistive technologies can stop having to **guess** where the headings are, and can instead use the ones that the author has designated.

When HPR finds `<th>` or `scope` markup, it assumes that the author knew what they were doing and uses the headings specified in the markup.

Going back to our TV listings page, an ironic postscript to this issue of support for headers markup is that the cell containing the advertisement is marked as `<th>`. As a consequence HPR doesn't read the TV stations in column 1.

It is clear that with today's technology, it is best to identify table headers by placing them in the first row and first column, but to use `<th>` and/or `scope`, where appropriate, in the hope that future technologies will implement them.

> **Recommendation:** For simple data tables, identify row and column headers by placing them in column one and row one. In all cases use `<th>` or `scope` to identify which cells are row and/or column headers.

Let's now take a look at how assistive technologies cope with complex tables.

Complex Data Tables

There are lots of access problems with the table of TV listings at the beginning of this section. The problem relevant to this discussion is the fact that the advertisement for *fantasysports.com at* the top of the table is an image in a cell in the first row of the table, a cell that spans the entire table.

The `alt` text for the image is, disappointingly, "*click here*". Window-Eyes and Home Page Reader think "*click here*" is the column heading for all the columns and so announce "click here" when changing columns just as they announced "Performance" in the earlier example.

Here are the guidelines for tables that are complex, that is those which have "two or more logical levels of row or column headers" (the source of this wording is the WAI Web Content Accessibility Guidelines):

> **5.2** *For data tables that have two or more logical levels of row or column headers, use markup to associate data cells and header cells. [Priority 1]*

The Access Board again uses essentially the same language:

> *§1194.22(g) Markup shall be used to associate data cells and header cells for data tables that have two or more logical levels of row or column headers.*

We already saw the way the IBM Guideline 10 refers to complex tables:

> *10. Table Headers. Use the TH element to mark up table heading cells. Use the headers attribute on cells of complex data tables.*

I have looked high and low for a definition of "two or more logical levels" and the closest thing I have found is an example from the Web Accessibility Initiative techniques document for the Web Content Accessibility Guidelines, *http://www.w3.org/TR/WCAG10-HTML-TECHS/#identifying-table-rows-columns*.

	Meals	Hotels	Transport	subtotals
San Jose				
25-Aug-97	37.74	112.00	45.00	
26-Aug-97		27.28	112.00	45.00
subtotals	65.02	224.00	90.00	379.02
Seattle				
27-Aug-97	96.25	109.00	36.00	
28-Aug-97	35.00	109.00	36.00	
subtotals	131.25	218.00	72.00	421.25
Totals	196.27	442.00	162.00	800.27

I believe the idea behind this frequently used example is that there are "two logical levels of row headers". The heading "*subtotals*" is only useful if you also know whether the trip destination is San Jose or Seattle. The first logical level of row headers consists of "*San Jose, Seattle, and Totals*". The second level consist of the dates and subtotals under each city.

The crucial point in this kind of complex table is that heading information for the highlighted cell at row 5, column 2, with the value 65.02 cannot be determined from heading information in *its* row and column. That information, meals, subtotals, is relevant, for sure, but you need to know the city as well.

HTML 4.0 includes markup specifically designed to address this situation. It is robust in that, as required by both the 508 provision and the WCAG checkpoint, it associates heading information **with** the data cell. Each cell can have specific heading information associated with it.

The way it works is that each heading cell is assigned an ID, using the `id` attribute. Then the `headers` attribute is added to each data cell, and the value of the attribute is a space-delimited list of ID's of heading information. The highlighted cell has `headers="C5 R2 C2"` which would read `"subtotals Meals San Jose"`.

Here is the markup for half of the table above:

```
<TABLE border="1" bgcolor="#ffffcc">
  <CAPTION><STRONG>Travel Expense Report</STRONG></CAPTION>
    <TR>
      <TD></TD>
      <TH id="c2">Meals</TH>
      <TH id="c3">Hotels</TH>
      <TH id="c4">Transport</TH>
      <TD id="c5">subtotals</TD>
    </TR>
    <TR>
      <TH id="r2">San Jose</TH>
      <TD></TD><TD></TD><TD></TD><TD></TD>
    </TR>
    <TR>
      <TD id="r3" >25-Aug-97</TD>
      <TD headers="c2 r2 r3">37.74</TD>
      <TD headers="c3 r2 r3">112.00</TD>
      <TD headers="c4 r2 r3">45.00</TD>
      <TD></TD>
    </TR>
    <TR>
      <TD id="r4">26-Aug-97<TD>
      <TD headers="c2 r2 r4">27.28</TD>
      <TD headers="c3 r2 r4">112.00</TD>
      <TD headers="c4 r2 r4">45.00</TD>
    </TR>
    <TR>
      <TD id="r5">subtotals</TD>
      <TD headers="c2 r2 r5" bgcolor="#ffff00">65.02</TD>
      <TD headers="c3 r2 r5">224.00</TD>
      <TD headers="c4 r2 r5">90.00</TD>
      <TD headers="c5 r2 r5">379.02</TD>
    </TR>
    <TR>
      <TH id="r6" >Seattle</TH>
      <TD></TD><TD></TD><TD></TD><TD></TD>
    </TR>
    ...
</TABLE>
```

Window-Eyes does not support the `headers` attribute while both IBM Home Page Reader and JAWS for Windows do. Rather than speaking all the headers information at every cell, JFW and HPR speak the header cells that change as you move from one cell to another in the same way that they speak headers for simple data tables.

There is one difference between the JFW and HPR implementation of headers on tables. When JFW encounters a cell with no headers tag, it assumes the header information is located in the first row and first column while HPR assumes there is no header information.

Guidelines for Accessible Tables

Implementing accessible tables can be an expensive proposition, in terms of money and workload, but that expense can be totally avoided with careful design of data tables. In a table with 10 rows and 10 columns, a complex table requires all 100 cells to be specially coded. When the table is simple but the header positions are not in the first row or first column, there are about 20 specially coded cells. When the headers are in the first row and first column there don't have to be any specially coded cells.

- Identify row and column headers by placing them in the first row and first column.

- Use the table header element, `<th>`, for all header cells or, if the visual effects of `<th>` are not desired, use `scope="row"` or `scope="col"` on all header cells. This is essential if header information is not in the first row or first column.

- Use the `headers` attribute to explicitly associate header information with data cells. This is essential if the table is not simple, meaning if the header information for a data cell is **not** in the same row and the same column as that cell.

Avoiding Flicker

Rapid visual changes, flashes, or blinking objects on a web page can cause photosensitive epileptic seizures in susceptible individuals. This is particularly true when the flashing has a high intensity and is in the frequency range between 2 Hz and 55 Hz. All of our target guidelines contain some advice on avoiding flicker.

The Web Accessibility Initiative, Web Content Accessibility Guidelines caution web developers to avoid flicker so long as users have no control over flickering:

> 7.1 Until user agents allow users to control flickering, avoid causing the screen to flicker.

The two major browsers (Microsoft Internet Explorer and Netscape Navigator) permit users to stop animation in GIF's by pressing the escape key. Opera more effectively allows users to turn off animation by using the menu options, *File | Preferences*, there in the *Multimedia* section uncheck the checkbox labeled "*Enable Animation (GIF images).*"

> §1194.22(j) Pages shall be designed to avoid causing the screen to flicker with a frequency greater than 2 Hz and lower than 55 Hz.

The IBM Web Accessibility Guideline is not as specific as the Section 508 provision from the Access Board.

> 13. Blinking, Moving, or Flickering Content. Avoid causing content to blink, flicker, or move.

It may be helpful to have an idea of what the frequencies of concern are like. The flashing rate of my text cursor is just shy of 1 Hz, of course that doesn't help the reader very much! The caret blink rate (or cursor blink rate) in Windows 2000 is set in *Keyboard* settings from the *Control* panel. The blink rate varies from .4 Hz at the slowest setting to 3.1 Hz at the fastest; the middle setting is about .8 Hz.

There are other ways that web pages can be caused to have flicker. There is the `<blink>` element, which is not officially part of HTML 3.2 or 4.0 – as described on WebMonkey, *http://hotwired.lycos.com/webmonkey/teachingtool/blink.html*, *Authoring HTML Basics*. To quote:

> *Blink may well be the most irritating tag available, and not just because it's only supported by Netscape (that is, it doesn't work on IE).*

```
<blink>This is Blinking text</blink>
```

The frequency of the Netscape implementation of the `<blink>` element is around .8 Hz so it is not in the dangerous range specified by the Access Board. However, it cannot be controlled by the *ESC* key. Opera does not support it (good for them!).

Whereas IE5 does not implement the `<blink>` element and Netscape does, the situation is unfortunately reversed for the `<marquee>` element. Here's how the description begins from *neiljohan.com*'s advanced HTML techniques:

> *A pretty useless tag and like the dreaded <blink> tag it could get very annoying if overused (or even used at all). You can use it to scroll messages across the screen.*

> *(*http://www.neiljohan.com/html/advancedhtml.htm#Marquees*)*

In my opinion, this tag is even worse, both in annoyance value and in potential for causing accessibility issues. Admittedly, a simple application of the `<marquee>` is not too offensive:

```
<marquee>This text will scroll right to left quite slowly.</marquee>
```

However, attributes of the `<marquee>` element can be modified so that the text is jumping and moving well above the 2 Hz limit and the *ESC* key will not stop the movement.

In summary, don't use the `<blink>` or `<marquee>` elements because they are not valid HTML and because their effects cannot be controlled in the browsers that support them. Keep flashing frequencies of animated GIF's well below the 2 Hz limit or much better, avoid animated GIF's alltogether.

Bear in mind also that things which jump, flicker, and move about are a nightmare for people who use screen magnification or a magnifying glass and so can only see part of the screen at any one time.

Summary

Lets distill the message of this chapter into our own checklist of specific techniques for creating accessible content relating to text equivalents, use of color, accessible tables, and flicker rate.

- Every image must have a valid `alt` attribute. The `alt` attribute should convey the information or purpose of the image.

- When an image stands by itself as a link (inside an anchor) it must have a non-empty `alt` attribute giving a text equivalent for the corresponding picture that clearly specifies the purpose of the link.

- All images which are not active and which do not convey information should have `alt=""`, null `alt` text. That is `alt="quote quote"` with no spaces between.

- Avoid duplicate adjacent links. If both an image and text are links with the same `href`, enclose them both in the same anchor tag, and then place `alt=""` on the image. Inside a *BUTTON* element put `non-null` alt text on any image to the extent that the information conveyed by the image is not redundant.

- Each `INPUT` of type `image` must have `alt` text specifying the purpose of the button.

- Include `alt` text on every `<area>` of a `<map>` which clearly identifies the propose of the corresponding hot spot.

- Use the long description attribute (`longdesc`) to provide text equivalents for images like charts or graphs which carry more important information than can be conveyed with their short `alt` attribute.

- Include a readily available text transcript for each informational audio file.

- Whenever color carries information, make sure that other parts of the page convey the same information, for example, additional characters, images (with `alt` text), or font changes.

- Identify the row and column headers of every data table by **at least one** of the following methods:

- Place column headings in the first row and place row headings in the first column.

- Use the `scope` attribute on all heading cells specifying whether the heading labels a column or a row, `scope="col"` or `scope="row"`.

- Use the `TH` element for all heading cells.

- Assign an `id` to each heading cell and string of `id`'s as the `header` attribute for each data cell to say which are heading cells for that data cell.

- To obtain the widest possible coverage of assistive technology along with actual programmatic identification of headers, use positioning of the headings (10a) together with the `scope` attribute on heading cells (10b).

- Any of the alternatives, 10a through 10d, can be used alone or combined with others to make simple data tables accessible. **Simple** tables are ones in which the row headings for every data cell are in the same row as the cell and the column headings are in the same column as the cell.

- For **complex** tables in which headings for some data cells are not in the same row and/or column as the cell, you must use the `headers` attribute approach (7d).

- The frequency of flicker (image appearing and disappearing) in animated GIF's or other objects must be greater than 2 Hz or less than 55 Hz.

5

- Skipping over navigation links
- Creating accessible frames
- Accessible image maps
- Accessible links

Author: Jim Thatcher

Accessible Navigation

In the previous chapter we talked about creating accessible content; content that is compatible with assistive technologies, and that provides alternatives to non-text elements such as images and audio. We discussed how web pages can be programmed more effectively and designed to be easily accessible by people with disabilities. In this chapter we'll discuss the accessibility issues of getting around a given page, or navigating within the web site and on to other web pages. There are simple things that you, as a web author or web designer, can do that will make that process of navigation much easier for customers who are visiting your site, especially those with disabilities. There are important things that must be done if your page is going to comply with the Section 508 provisions for web accessibility or the Web Content Accessibility Guidelines from the Web Accessibility Initiative.

Actually the distinction between navigation and content is somewhat unrealistic. Several of the issues discussed in Chapter 4 also influence navigation. For example, if you don't provide text equivalents for images that are links, then people using screen readers or text browsers won't be able to navigate your site. Similarly, if you have not included `alt` text for image map hot spots (`<area>` tags) then navigation of your site is definitely broken for people who are blind.

Unrealistic though our distinction may be, here are the navigation topics we will develop in this chapter:

- Skipping over navigation links. Many of the issues of web accessibility have to do with making sure links, such as image links, image map hot spots, and descriptive link text are accessible. The first topic of this chapter, surprisingly, addresses the need to skip over those links you worked so hard to make accessible.

- Creating accessible frames. Although frames seem to be decreasing in popularity, they can help in making your site more accessible. The key to this, however, is that those frames have to be coded accessibly.

- Accessible image maps. We talked about image maps in the previous chapter. Here we address the issues of accessibility of different kinds of image maps, namely client-side image maps versus server-side image maps.

- How layout can affect navigation. The way tables are used in laying out a page dramatically affects the text version of a page. In fact, layout tables can actually be used to improve the accessibility of your page.

- Accessible links. The words you use as alternative text on image links or as the text content of an anchor tag is called the `link text`. The link text you use can have a major impact on your web page accessibility.

The chapter concludes with a summary of the dos and don'ts of accessible navigation.

Skip Over Navigation Links

In the previous chapter we used a layout table to illustrate linearization of layout, the process that happens when someone listens to a page, or views it in a text browser:

This is a title cell		
Navigation link 1 Navigation link 2 Navigation link 3 Navigation link 4	Banner ad	Right Navigation 1 Right Navigation 2 Right Navigation 3
	Main content area with lots of text and content filling the center part of the window	

As we saw the title is the first item of the text view, then the left navigation links, and then the banner, followed by the right navigation section. Finally, after everything else, the main content is the last part of the text view of the linearized page:

Home Page Reader
This is a title cell
Navigation link 1
Navigation link 2
Navigation link 3
Navigation link 4
Banner ad
Right Navigation 1
Right Navigation 2
Right Navigation 3
Main content area with lots of text and content filling the center part of the window

In this very simple mockup of a page the main content comprises a quarter of the page. A person who is listening to the page may have to wait through three quarters of the words, when what they really want is that main content.

It is easy for a sighted person to focus on the main content of the page because web designers use page layout and color to create a visual center, or focus, so that the process of finding the main content for a person who is sighted is intuitive. If you have to listen to the page instead, it can be very difficult. This is only the beginning of the problem. Usually a structure like that illustrated in the figure opposite is found on *every* page on the site and the only thing that changes from page to page is the main content. So on each page the problem of having to navigate through the navigation links in order to find the main content reoccurs.

Guidelines for Skipping Navigation

The Section 508 rule on web accessibility from the Access Board includes a provision to address this problem:

> *§1194.22(o) A method shall be provided that permits users to skip repetitive navigation links.*

The IBM Accessibility guidelines also advise a skip navigation link:

> *8. Skip to main content. Provide methods for skipping over navigation links to get to main content of page.*

The Web Accessibility Initiative does not specifically address skipping navigation, or skipping to main content, but there are two Priority 3 Web Content Accessibility Guidelines checkpoints that are clearly related to this issue that we will be discussing later.

We will look at three methods for providing skip navigation links, namely:

- Placing the link in normal text

- Creating a link as `alt` text on an image that doesn't carry information

- Using a text link with the same foreground and background colors

Link in Normal Text

One simple method that satisfies provision §1194.22(o) of the Section 508 standard, was first used by the American Council of the Blind (*http://www.acb.org*). The ACB site has a link at the top of the page in a small font with link text, *Skip Navigation Links*. The target of the link is a local anchor just above the main content:

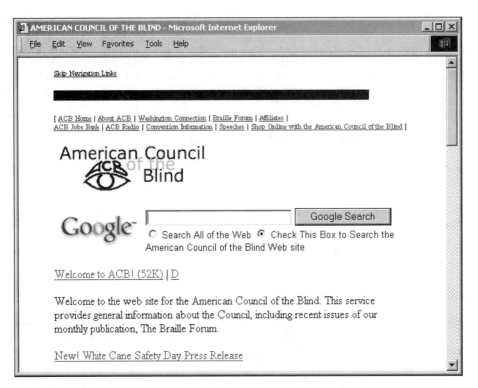

When a user who is visually impaired using a screen reader loads up the page, the first announcement is 'link skip navigation links'. If a user wants to listen to the navigation links, he or she just ignores this skip link like any other link. On a first visit to the page the user might indeed want to listen to those navigation links, but the presence of the skip link empowers the screen reader user with the choice.

The code for the 'skip link' at the top of the page looks like this:

```
<a href="#nonav"><font size="-2">Skip Navigation Links</font></a>
```

The ACB developers placed the defining anchor with `name="nonav"` on the American Council of the Blind logo image:

```
<a name="nonav">
    <img src="acob5.gif" alt="American Council of the Blind" …>
</a>
```

That means when the skip link is followed, the `alt` text for the logo, *American Council of the Blind* is the next item to be announced.

The definition of the local anchor does *not* have to have content. The code:

```
<a name="nonav"></a>
```

works just fine and could have been placed just before the *Welcome to ACB* link. This is a very important part of the skip navigation idea. The target anchor does *not* have to enclose any content either. As such it can easily be placed in the template to be used for all pages based on the template. This possibility is not generally understood.

The ACB site seems to take the words *skip navigation links* literally. Their skip link just skips over the two lines of text links at the top of the page and does not skip over the logo, or the search fields for the input area. I would code the target of the skip just before the main content starting with *Welcome* in the screenshot above. Remember that this anchor does not have to have content; it is just establishing a location in the document.

Link As alt Text On an Invisible Image

A good example of the need for, and implementation of, skip links is the CNN site shown below:

Notice that the CNN page shown overleaf has a top area, including a logo and some Netscape navigation links, in addition to navigation areas down the left and right sides of the page. The left navigation is site navigation (from CNN page to CNN page), while the *Top Stories* navigation on the right changes from day to day and is local to the area of the site (here, *Entertainment*). On this page the layout table structure is like that shown below:

This is a title cell		
Navigation link 1 Navigation link 2 Navigation link 3 Navigation link 4	Main content area with lots of text and content filling the center part of the window	Right Navigation 1 Right Navigation 2 Right Navigation 3

Only the top material and the left navigation are spoken before the main content, when the page has a structure like this. The right navigation is spoken after the main content. This format has changed from the structure of the CNN site of a year ago, where *everything* on the page preceded the main content in the text view.

An invisible GIF on the top right of the page is the skip navigation link. If you turn off images (this is done by going to the *Internet Options / Advanced* menu and checking the *Always expand ALT text for images* option, followed by unchecking the *Show pictures* option) in Internet Explorer the link appears far off to the right. Instead of turning off images you can view the source code and here is what you will find, first for the image link, then the local anchor.

```
<a href="#ContentArea">
    <img src="1.gif" … alt="Skip to main content" align="right">
</a>

<a name="ContentArea"></a>
```

This local anchor, `ContentArea`, is just after the *'Updated'* information and just before the *'Franzen: The author of the moment'* image. The anchor is in the template and above the content that changes hourly.

Let's summarize this method. At the top of the page, you place a link on an invisible image with `alt` text such as `"skip navigation"` or `"skip to main content"` and with an `href` that points to a local anchor with empty content just above the main content. This is a very practical method of providing a skip navigation link satisfying the Section 508 provision without changing the visual appearance of the page or site at all.

The same technique is used on many sites, including IBM whose home page (*http://www.ibm.com*) we saw in the previous chapter. Here is the IBM code for their skip navigation link. The IBM site uses the XHTML standard and so it is well formed. In other words, every tag must be closed, and if a tag has no content, for example the image and second anchor below, then it must have a forward slash (/) at the end of the tag:

```
<a href="#main">
    <img width="1" src="... c.gif" ...  alt="Skip to main content"/>
</a>

<a name="main"/>
```

Link with the Same Foreground and Background Colors

Another way of providing screen reader users an opportunity to skip navigation links is found at the FirstGov (*http://www.firstgov.gov*) portal site for the Federal Government. Here is a screenshot of the top of the FirstGov site:

The screenshot looks normal, except that there is an area of white at the top of the page that is a little larger than usual. If you were to listen to this page with IBM Home Page Reader this is what you would hear at the top:

Home Page Reader
Link: Skip to content.
Link: Skip to Government search.
Link: Skip to Departments and Agencies.
Link: Skip to Reference
Link: Skip to Customer Survey.
[FirstGov, your first click to the U. S. Government.]
Link: [Image of a U. S. flag.]
Link: FirstGov Home	Link: About us	Link: Help	Link: Site Map	

The first five links, starting with *Skip to content*, and ending with *Skip to Customer Survey* are not normally visible on the page. If however, the page is viewed with colors ignored it is a different picture. In IE, go to the *Tools | Internet Options | General* menu, click the *Accessibility...* button, and then check the *Ignore colors specified on Web pages* checkbox. Now you can set background color with the *colors...* button on the *Internet Options* dialog. With Netscape, use the *Edit | Preferences* menu item and in the *Preferences* dialog, choose the *Color* section and check *Always use my colors overriding document*. You must also uncheck *Use windows colors*. With those settings, here is what the FirstGov site looks like:

The skip links are like a hidden table of contents, with a link to each of the main content areas of the site. You can see how the links work by clicking them if they are visible, otherwise by hovering the links you can see where they point to in the status window of the browser. If you click *Skip to Government Search* the page will reposition with the search box at the top.

Here is the code for the FirstGov skip links:

```
<a href="#content">
  <font color="#ffffff" size="-6">Skip to content</font>
</a> 
<a href="#featured">
  <font color="#ffffff" size="-6">Skip to Government Search</font>
</a> 
...
<a href="#contact">
    <font color="#ffffff" size="-6">Skip to Departments & Agencies</font>
</a>
```

The `<font>` tag is used to set the color of the text the same (`#ffffff`) as the background color, making it invisible. The small font size makes the amount of white space at the top not visually burdensome.

Notice that a non-breaking space (` `) is used at the end of each anchor so that the links have at least one space separating them. Instead of the `<font>` tag the authors should have used Cascading Style Sheets (as discussed in Chapter 9) to describe the presentation of the page, as we will see in the next example. This is the home page of *http://www.ittatc.org*:

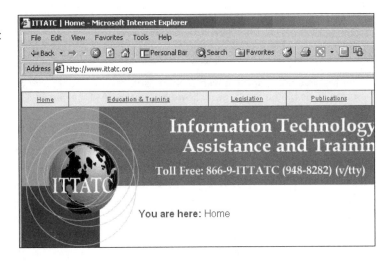

The Information Technology Technical Assistance and Training Center (ITTATC) is funded by the National Institute on Disability and Rehabilitation Research (NIDRR) of the Department of Education in support of Section 508.

This is part of a screenshot of the ITTATC homepage with IE configured to ignore colors and fonts specified on the page:

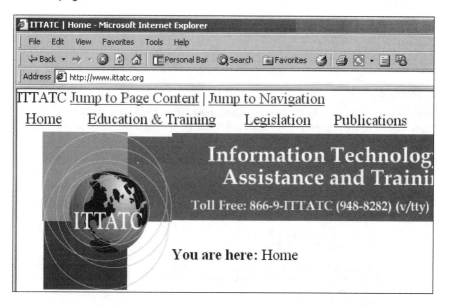

The web authors have placed skip navigation links at the top of the page just like the FirstGov site. They use a small font and the same background and foreground colors for the text. Here is one of the links:

```
<a href="#Content" class="InvisiLink" title="">Jump to Page Content</a>
```

The link has `class="InvisiLink"` in which the necessary font and color attributes are specified. Here is the style information for the class `A.InvisiLink` specifying the same foreground and background colors and small font size, 20% of normal.

```
A.InvisiLink
    { font-family: "Arial","Helvetica", sans-serif;
      font-size:20%;
      color:#FFFFFF;
      background-color:#FFFFFF;}
```

There is one additional accessibility feature of the ITTATC site, since the acronym ITTATC is defined there using the `<acronym>` tag of HTML 4.0.

```
<td width="100%" class="Invisible" bgcolor="#FFFFFF" colspan="6">
    <acronym title="Information Technology Technical Assistance and
                    Training Center">
    ITTATC
    </acronym>
```

121

Using this content that is hidden for people who look at the page, the site designers are complying with the Web Content Accessibility Guideline checkpoint 4.2 that requires that abbreviations and acronyms be expanded:

> *4.2 Specify the expansion of each abbreviation or acronym in a document where it first occurs. [Priority 3]*

I assume the reason for attaching the `<acronym>` element to an invisible table cell is that otherwise the ITTATC logo might be perceived as the first occurrence of the acronym ITTATC and there is no way to use the `<acronym>` element on the logo itself.

Combined Techniques

The last example of a skip navigation technique comes from the LexisNexis company and one of their research products (*http://www.lexis.com/research*). Below is part of a screenshot of the LexisNexis page:

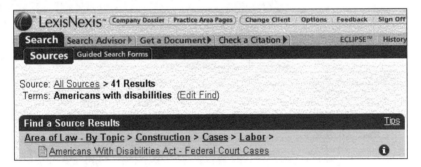

Notice that there are global navigation links across the very top of the page, *Company Dossier*, *Practice Area Pages*, etc., then there are navigation links that are specific to this particular LexisNexis research product, *Search*, *Search Advisor*, etc. Finally the results of a search are displayed beginning with *Source: All Sources > 41 Results*.

LexisNexis has one skip link attached to an invisible GIF at the top of the page. The link text in this case is *skip global navigation*, which is the `alt` text on a small GIF. That link takes the user to the local navigation links. The first of these is again an invisible link, which allows the user to jump to the beginning of the search results.

A user with a screen reader can follow two links to get to the main content of the page, or one link to use local navigation. One of the truly accessible aspects of this design is that it is treated in the same way throughout the site, and throughout other LexisNexis products.

Skipping Text Blocks with Assistive Technologies

Unfortunately there are only a few web sites that provide this simple accommodation to permit people who are blind to quickly get to the main content of the page. As is typically the case, the assistive technology developers recognize this problem and make valiant efforts to solve it in the screen readers or talking browsers.

Window-Eyes

Window-Eyes was the first screen reader to attempt to build in mechanisms for skipping over blocks of links, and has eight different commands for this purpose. By means of various key combinations, Window-Eyes permits jumping to the next (or previous) block of text. You can also jump to other, more specific points in the document, such as to the next form control, the next link, and the next block of normal inactive text. This last jump can be configured to specify how much text will be considered a block of normal text, so that a word or two, or a heading can be ignored. Settings for the number of characters (*Next Text Minimum Line Length*) and number of lines (*Next Text Consecutive Lines*) are in the Window-Eyes *Global | Verbosity | MSAA* dialog. Both of these values default to 1, meaning that in the default environment any single non-active word will be considered to be a block.

With the default settings, you need to use the *Next Text Jump* twice to get to the same place that the ACB *Skip Navigation* link targets. CNN requires six *next text jumps* to arrive at the main content targeted by CNN's skip link.

If the settings are changed to a minimum of 25 text characters and a minimum of two text lines, the *jump to next text* command actually does a *better* job than the skip navigation, landing just below the *Welcome to ACB (52K)* link on the first jump. The situation is similar for the CNN page where one jump takes the user to the area of the main story for the day.

IBM Home Page Reader

IBM Home Page Reader includes commands to jump to the next block of text or links similar to Window-Eyes. The idea, like Window-Eyes, is to skip over the groups of links. The problem is that there is some non-link text scattered amongst the links, and to add to the problem, HPR inserts meta text, such as *Internal frame 2: Untitled,* in its text view, which is then counted as non-link text. Similarly *Start of form 1* and *End of form 1* are both stops for this jump command. HPR uses three jumps for ACB and in the CNN case HPR uses twelve of its jumps to get to the main content.

JAWS for Windows

JAWS for Windows (JFW) has one command for jumping to the next block of non-link text compared to eight commands for navigating the page in Window-Eyes, and 2 with HPR. For this command, the JFW strategy is similar to that employed by Window-Eyes in providing a jump to next text block, which can be configured by the user. With JFW you can only configure the size (in characters) of the text block and the default is 25, not 1 as in the case of Window-Eyes.

In the case of the ACB site JFW stops at the *Search* form on the first jump. The second jump takes the user to the block of non-link text starting the main content. JAWS requires seven jumps to arrive at the main content of the CNN site. Similar to the behavior of Home Page Reader, three of the seven stops are meta text inserted by JAWS, in this case announcing the end of internal frames.

What we have here is a picture of the assistive technologies struggling to overcome a problem that causes frustration and disappointment amongst those users of the Web who are blind. All the navigation or following of links is to little avail if you can't find the information you need. That information is almost always obvious visually; it has to be because that is the way pages are designed.

As we have seen, some of the assistive technologies are very successful with the examples we tested, but with the authors not specifying the start of the main content, the process is surely prone to errors.

On the other hand the web designers could, at almost no cost, add a *skip to main content* link that would take a user who is blind to the content that the web designers deem to be the central point of the page, rather than relying on the heuristics incorporated into the assistive technology to find that point.

I say 'almost no cost'. It is terribly important to understand that. As we have seen above, the skip navigation link can be added to the template. Similarly the target of the skip link doesn't have to include that main content; it can be immediately above the main content so it too is part of the template and the same code is just copied for every page.

Web Accessibility Initiative Recommendations

The Web Content Accessibility Guidelines contain two Priority 3 checkpoints that pertain to the issue of skipping navigation. They seem to assume technology that is not yet supported by any browsers or screen readers that I know of, namely grouping and labeling links:

> *13.5 Provide navigation bars to highlight and give access to the navigation mechanism. [Priority 3]*

> *13.6 Group related links, identify the group (for user agents), and, until user agents do so, provide a way to bypass the group. [Priority 3]*

Checkpoint 13.6 seems to have a "skip these links" clause, assuming the author has grouped and identified the related links. What I see as the issue is skipping to the main content, which will skip over links that may or may not be related and may or may not be grouped.

From what we have seen while exploring how assistive technology can skip blocks of text, the main issue is not so much skipping groups of links, as it is skipping links and small text titles as typified by the CNN site.

Creating Accessible Frames

As we said in the introduction to this chapter, it is becoming harder and harder to find sites that use frames. However, as we shall see, sites that do use them, when coded correctly, can achieve access improvements, at least as good as those with a good skip navigation link.

The Access Board advises that frames be identifiable with titles:

> *§1194.22(i) Frames shall be titled with text that facilitates frame identification and navigation.*

The IBM guidelines follow suit:

> *9. Frames. Provide a title for each frame and frame page so that users can track frames by title.*

The wording of the Web Accessibility Initiative checkpoint is nearly the same as the Action Board's wording:

> *12.1 Title each frame to facilitate frame identification and navigation.*

So where are these 'titles' that the guidelines require? The problem with all of these guidelines is that the word 'title' in them is ambiguous.

Frame Site Example

Let's see how frames work, so as to help make the issues raised by the guidelines clearer. We will use an example frame site that duplicates the structure of the table we first saw in the *Skip over navigation links* section at the beginning of this chapter. Here is a screenshot of the frame site with background colors chosen so as to make the connection with the previous figure:

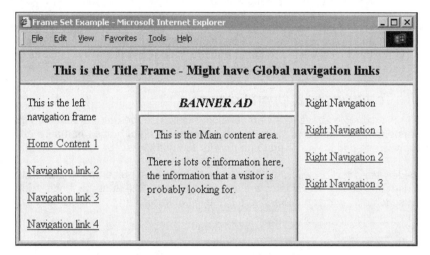

A frame page is actually a collection of pages displayed in separate windows (or frames) within the main window. The main page of a frame site is called the `frameset page` and it specifies the layout of the various pages (frames). What is appealing about this design is the fact that the different functions of various parts of the page are separated into different files, which can contribute to helpful navigation for everybody.

The example frame page above consists of 5 frames (a title frame, two navigation frames, a banner and the main content), corresponding to the cells of the table we saw earlier. Here is the code for this frame structure:

```
<frameset rows="40,*" >
    <frame src="Title.htm" noresize name="TopTitle"
           frameborder="yes" scrolling="no" title="Top Title">
    <frameset cols="150,*,150">
        <frame src="Left.htm" noresize name="LeftNavigation"
               frameborder="yes" scrolling="no" title="Left Navigation">
    <frameset rows="40,*" border="2">
        <frame src="Banner.htm" noresize name="BannerAd"
               frameborder="yes" scrolling="no" title="Banner Ad">
        <frame src="Content1.htm" noresize name="MainContent"
               frameborder="yes" scrolling="no" title="Main Content">
    </frameset>
    <frame src="Right.htm" noresize name="RightNavigation"
           frameborder="yes" scrolling="no" title="Right Navigation">
    </frameset>
<noframes>
```

Notice that in our example each <frame> is provided with both a title and a name attribute. The name attribute is used to programmatically interact with the frame and is the key to effectively using frames. Links need to specify a target frame in which the new page will open. In our previous example, when a link in the navigation frame opens up a page in the main content window, the navigation link has to specify maincontent as its target attribute:

```
<a href="Content2.htm" target="MainContent">Navigation link 2</a>
```

The beauty of this for all audiences is that, when this link is activated, *only* the new main content page is opened; the other frames, perhaps with lots of images, stay as they are. If you want to read the main content of our sample frame site, just open the main content frame. If you want to check out the navigation links, read the navigation frame. And when you decide to follow a navigation link, since the target frame is specified, assistive technology can automatically read the main content page where the page you requested will be displayed. This scenario is why frame navigation can, and should, be easy if it is designed correctly.

How Assistive Technologies Support Frames

As we saw in the example above, the web developer must use the name attribute as the target of links. This importance of the name attribute in the programming of frames naturally led developers of specialty browsers to use the name attribute to refer to the frames.

When the widely used text browser, Lynx, opens a frame site, it presents the user with a list of links to the various frame pages. The frames are identified by the name attribute if one exists; otherwise each frame is identified with a number. Here is the list of frames as Lynx sees our example above:

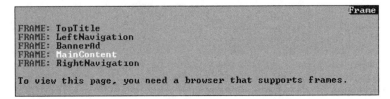

In the Lynx screenshot above, the current link is *MainContent*. If the Lynx user follows that link (using *RIGHT ARROW*) the main content page is opened:

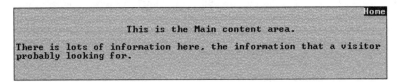

With a meaningful name attribute on every frame, the Lynx user can easily identify which frame to open. This Lynx view of the frame world captures the idea of frame browsing as a list of named HTML pages and their contents.

Remember that the name attribute must be only one word.

The situation is similar in the case of JAWS for Windows. However, when JAWS opens a frame page it begins reading frame content one frame at a time in the order seen in the Lynx view opposite, and which is explicit in the `<frameset>` page.

As a new frame is encountered JFW announces *Frame*, along with the value of the `name` attribute of the frame. The JFW user can also request a list of frames using the *INS+F9* command and the list looks very much like that seen in Lynx:

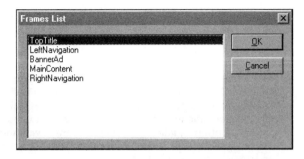

All the guidelines we saw in the *Creating Accessible Frames* section above require that frames be titled with text, and yet both Lynx and JAWS depend on the `name` attribute. Unsurprisingly, different assistive technologies do different things. Both Window-Eyes and Home Page Reader use the `<title>` elements on the actual frame pages in their lists. Note this is not the `title` attribute of the `<frame>` element, but rather the title given to the frame page. Very often frame pages do not have `<title>` elements because the developers of those pages don't see those titles in the title bar; they only see the title of the `<frameset>` page.

When IBM Home Page Reader encounters our sample frame site, it opens the first frame, announces the `<title>` element of the `<frameset>` page, which frame is being read, the `<title>` element of the frame page and finally reads the frame page content:

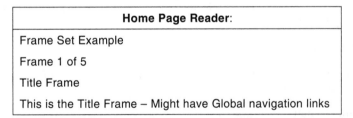

Home Page Reader:
Frame Set Example
Frame 1 of 5
Title Frame
This is the Title Frame – Might have Global navigation links

The HPR user, on hearing that a frame page has been encountered ('*Frame x of y*') can request a list of frames similar to that provided in Lynx and JFW. Here is the way IBM Home Page Reader lists the frames of our sample:

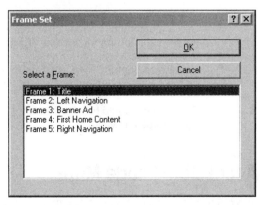

The fourth frame, for example, is the main content frame and has `MainContent` as its `name` attribute and `Main Content` as its `title` attribute.

> Note that spaces are allowed in the `title` attribute but not in the `name` attribute.

The `<title>` element of the page `Content1.htm` is `First Home Content`.

```
<title>First Home Content</title>
```

Home Page Reader is using the `<title>` elements of the frame pages to list the frames for selection. The title on individual frame pages is not shown in the title bar of the browser, and thus it is not clear to developers why these separate HTML pages (that are used for each frame) even need titles. It is common to find frame pages without titles, or indeed with unhelpful titles. If, for example, you have both navigation and content frames with the same title, this naturally enough does not help with navigation. Also, since the `name` attribute is seen as a programmatic tool, one often finds meaningless names such as:

> *FRAME: frame70890*
> *FRAME: frame70888*

At the time of writing, the assistive technologies with which we tested frames used either the value of the `name` attribute of the `<frame>` element, or the title of the frame page in order to identify the different pages in a framed site. None of the technologies used the `title` attribute of the `<frame>` element, which is the technique recommended by the Web Accessibility Initiative Techniques document for Checkpoint 12.1 (*http://www.w3.org/TR/WCAG10-HTML-TECHS/#frame-names*).

I have no doubt that some assistive technologies will start using the `title` attribute of the `<frame>` element since it is more appropriate for this task, and is recommended in the guidelines we listed in the beginning of this section.

Summary for Frames

Adding attributes to the `<frameset>` components is a very small task compared to the development of a framed site. Therefore there should be no difficulty ensuring that all `<frame>` elements have meaningful `title` *and* `name` attributes and that all frame pages have meaningful titles. If you do choose to use frames then:

- Use a meaningful single-word `name` attribute for each `<frame>`. It should explain the role of the frame in the frame set, like *Navigation* or *title*.

- Use a meaningful `title` attribute for each `<frame>` element that is essentially the same as the name. You might use `Main Content` for the title and `MainContent` for the name.

- Every page should have a meaningful `<title>` element. Make sure this is true for all frame pages as well.

Accessible Image Maps

We talked about client-side image maps in the previous chapter where the requirement of text equivalents for all image map hot spots was emphasized. These text equivalents are absolutely essential for accessibility.

The image on the right is a client-side image map from the United States Senate web site, *http://www.senate.gov/*:

The alt text on the image that creates the map is QUICK LIST. Here is the code that designates the image as a client-side image map:

```
<img src="sidebar.gif" alt="Quick List" ... usemap="#subnav">
```

There are two kinds of image maps, client-side and server-side. Client-side maps need to have a usemap attribute and *not* an ismap attribute. In this case, the usemap attribute points to a map called subnav that defines the areas of the image map that are hot spots. In the Senate example there are four areas:

```
<map name="subnav">
    <area shape="rect" coords="4,33,76,72" href=" … "
        alt="Committee Hearing Schedule">
    <area shape="rect" coords="5,78,88,117" href=" … "
        alt="Yesterday's Senate Floor Activity">
    <area shape="rect" coords="5,121,75,140" href=" … "
        alt="Senate Art">
    <area shape="rect" coords="5,143,59,172" href=" … "
        alt="Senate History">
</map>
```

The four image map areas have alt text that is exactly the same as the text in the image, which I think is perfect. The way that this client-side image map works is that each <area> specifies a region of the image in which a click will open a certain URL, namely the href of the <area>.

The shape and coord (coordinates) attributes define the region of each <area>. There are three possible shapes, rect for rectangle, circle, and poly for polygon. The coordinates are pixel coordinates measured from the top left of the image. For a rectangle the developer must specify the top-left and bottom-right corners. A circle is given by the center point and radius. A polygon is specified by a series of points corresponding to the corners of the polygon.

The image map is called **client-side** because the browser (the client) must figure out how to handle the result of a click on the image. Any time there is a click on the page, the client asks whether or not the coordinates of that click fell inside one of the regions specified as an <area> of a client-side map. If the click is in one of those regions, then the browser opens the corresponding URL, that is, the value of the href for that <area>. Client-side image maps like the one from the US Senate site are by far the most common to be found on the Web today.

Let's consider another image map, this time from *http://www.metrokc.gov/*:

It is fundamentally different from the previous Senate example. It is a server-side image map with the following (modified) code.

```
<a href=" ... ">
    <img src=" ... navbar.gif" border="0" ismap
        alt="King County Navigation Bar (text navigation at bottom)" >
</a>
```

Since this is a server-side map, there is no `usemap` attribute, instead the `ismap` attribute tells the client browser to send the coordinates that the user clicked directly to the server, to the value of the `href` in the anchor element. For any person who cannot use the mouse this is a fundamentally *inaccessible* form of navigation because it requires positioning the mouse on some part of a picture indicating a desired action. The Access Board recognized the problem with server-side maps and recommends having redundant text links if you do use a server-side map:

> *§1194.22(e) Redundant text links shall be provided for each active region of a server-side image map.*

Indeed the King County site has redundant text links at the bottom of the home page, and the `alt` text for the server-side map tells the user to find *text navigation at bottom*.

```
HPR:
[Server Side Map: King County Navigation Bar (text navigation at bottom).]
```

I can't see any reason why the King County site would use a server-side map for its main navigation, although, the equivalent text links at the bottom of the page make it accessible. The King County site, however, does not satisfy the second provision of the Section 508 rule on web accessibility:

> *§1194.22(f) Client-side image maps shall be provided instead of server-side image maps except where the regions cannot be defined with an available geometric shape.*

The Section 508 provisions are almost identical to Checkpoints 1.2 and 9.1 of the Web Content Accessibility Guidelines from the Web Accessibility Initiative:

> *1.2 Provide redundant text links for each active region of a server-side image map.*

> *9.1 Provide client-side image maps instead of server-side image maps except where the regions cannot be defined with an available geometric shape.*

The IBM Web Accessibility Guidelines recommend text equivalents for server-side maps, but without the restriction on the use of server-side maps, so the server-side map from King County complies with IBM checkpoint 2:

> *2. Image Maps. Use client-side image maps with alternative text for image map hot spots. If you use server-side maps, provide equivalent text links.*

There is nothing about the regions in the King County image map that would make them difficult to define with available geometric shapes; simple rectangles would work well. Surprisingly, the next image on the King Country web site is a client-side map:

So King County, Washington, has us baffled.

Client-side maps provide three shapes to describe regions, namely rectangles (`shape="rect"`), circles (`shape="circle"`) and polygons (`shape="poly"`). Effectively any shape can be described with a polygon or collection of polygons.

Here is a good example of a client-side image map with rather complex hot spots which are regions defined by polygons. It is Microsoft's Local District Information map at *http://www.microsoft.com/usa/map.asp*:

The code for the upper Midwest region of the map uses a polygon determined by about 45 points:

```
<area shape=poly
    coords="173,7,181,9,180,10,227,9,232,10,233,12,238,11,244,12,
      250,13,257,14,263,15,267,17,259,27,251,27,245,36,249,41,246,48,
      254,53,256,57,257,61,258,66,262,68,263,73,264,75,263,77,
      262,78,260,78,259,80,258,82,257,84,256,86,254,87,243,87,243,88,
      229,88,229,92,207,92,206,90,186,90,184,85,173,82,170,45,
      172,30,172,7,174,8"
    href=" ... "
    alt="Twin Cities: ND, MN, SD, NE, IA">
```

Since any reasonable region can be defined by one of the available geometric patterns of a client-side map, I have to conclude that there is no case where a server-side map is permitted under §1194.22(f).

There may be cases where a designer might want every pixel to be a hot spot. You might argue that there are too many regions in this case. But that is a different issue than the one raised by §1194.22(f). In fact, map sites use client-side maps for regions to zoom or re-center thus diminishing the load on their servers.

Summary for Image Maps

- If you want an image map, make it a client-side image map.

- Include meaningful `alt` text for every `<area>` of the `<map>`.

- If you must use a server-side map, please write to this author explaining a requirement for such, and also include equivalent text links on the page to all the hot spots of your server-side map.

What Else Would Help Navigation?

Most of us will navigate *within* a page intuitively. If you can see the page, you can visually move to the main content of the page and read the story, or indeed look across the top global navigation buttons to find the *Search* link or *Contact Us* link that you need. You look down the right column to find the other top stories or shopping specials. The process of finding those items is as much navigation as the process of moving from page to page. While reading the main content you may have to page down, or use the mouse to move down the page with the vertical scroll bar. Clearly layout is affecting your process of navigating the content of the page.

> This process is much more difficult if you are a partially sighted or unsighted user.

We have already seen one way in which we can aid such users, by using a skip navigation link in order to facilitate movement to the main story by someone using a screen reader. The hidden table of contents at the top of the FirstGov (*http://www.firstgov.gov*) site is a second approach.

We saw an alternative to the short table of contents in one of the LexisNexis products (*http://www.lexisnexis.com*). This site included a short chain of links on each page. The first invisible link said *Skip global navigation*, while the first link of the local navigation area (*Skip local navigation*) took us to the main content. In this case the link described more what was being skipped than where the link was going (*'skip to main content'*).

Programmers refer to techniques such as the skip navigation link as **hacks**, something that is unstructured, undocumented, and open to programmer whim and whimsy. The skip navigation link is not part of the underlying language, HTML. There are techniques that are part of HTML 4.01 that could help with in-page navigation but these are not widely used on web pages (if at all).

Headings

A very simple example of this is the use of headings, `<h1>`, `<h2>`, and so on, for heading level one, and heading level two. Many web sites have sections that are titled with text that looks like it is a heading, but are not using the heading tags at all. The FirstGov site has seven of these 'headings'. Such sites often use Cascading Style Sheets, or at least in-line style changes, so that they know that the 'style' of headings is completely under their control. They could use headings just as well as not, but unfortunately those same web developers and designers have no idea that using headings might help users who are visually impaired.

IBM Home Page Reader supports heading navigation, and simply pressing *ALT+1* takes you to heading reading mode. The right, left, and down arrow keys move to the next, previous, and current heading. Using this form of navigation would make it possible to navigate within a page more easily than the jump table used by FirstGov.

The other assistive technologies that we have discussed in this book do not support headings navigation at this time, probably because headings are almost never present in web pages today. If that were to change, and headings were widely used I am convinced that assistive technology would use some form of headings navigation to take advantage of the structure provided by the author.

Improving Page Navigation with Layout

We have seen how layout tables can make it very time consuming to find the main content in a page that is laid out like the one we saw at the beginning of the chapter. There are some simple tricks with layout tables that actually make it easier to find the main content with a screen reader or talking browser.

It is not clear why at least one column of navigation links is routinely placed on the left side of web pages. On *http://JimThatcher.com* I use a tabular structure like that shown below which places the navigation column on the right and the main content on the left:

This is a title cell	
Main content area with lots of text and content filling the left-hand part of the window	Right Navigation 1 Right Navigation 2 Right Navigation 3

With this layout, the main content follows the title in a text or linearized view of the page. There is no need to provide a skip navigation link in order to comply with the Section 508 Provision §1194.22(o). However, in this situation I do add a *skip to navigation links* link attached to an invisible GIF at the top of the page. This certainly is not required for compliance with any of the guidelines we are considering.

Another suggestion for using layout to enhance navigation is a layout table that I have not yet seen on any web page. It works on the basis that since tables are read a row at a time, if we can force the main content to be the only content in row 2, and force the navigation panels down to row 3, then the main content will read first.

The result of this idea is a three-column table in which the first title row spans all three columns, as shown in the sample below:

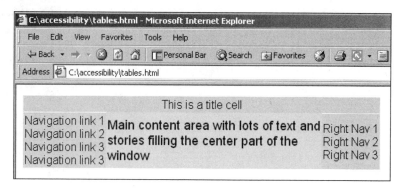

In the second row of this table the first and third cells are empty and the second cell spans *two* rows. The third row is then made up of the left and right navigation panels in the first and third table cells. With a page layout corresponding to the diagram above, the main content occurs immediately after the title, and before both navigation panels, in a text or linearized view. That means the main content would be spoken by a screen reader or talking browser right after the title information.

Here's the code for this table with spacing, padding, and color attributes omitted so that the important structure is clearer:

```
<table >
   <tr>
      <td colspan="3" >This is a title cell</td>
   </tr>
   <tr>
      <td></td> <!-- The empty cell on the left -->
      <td rowspan="2">
         Main content area with lots of text and<br>
         stories filling the center part of the <br>
         window</td>
      <td></td> <!-- The empty cell on the right -->
   </tr>
   <tr>
      <td align="top">Navigation link 1<br>
         Navigation link 2<br>
         Navigation link 3<br>
         Navigation link 3</td>
      <td align="top">Right Nav 1<br>
         Right Nav 2<br>
         Right Nav 3</td>
   </tr>
</table>
```

Accessible links

Some users of the web are so mouse-dependent that they may not be aware of the fact that you can *TAB* through all the active elements of a web page. As you do that, there is a dotted enclosing polygon called a `focus rectangle` that moves along highlighting the current link text inside. The example on the right from *http://JimThatcher.com* illustrates this:

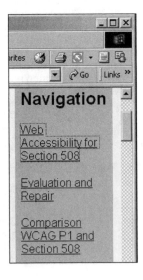

The text enclosed inside this focus rectangle is called the `link text`, which is the content of the anchor element <a>:

```
<a href="webcourse1.htm">Web Accessibility for Section 508</a>
```

As you navigate around the links of a page with the *TAB* key (and *SHIFT+TAB* to go backwards), you can use the *ENTER* key at any time to activate a link. This action corresponds to clicking on a link.

When you are listening to a page, the link text will be identified in one of a number of ways, but generally screen readers precede the text of a link with the word 'link'. Home Page reader has several options for indicating links. With the default settings HPR changes to a female voice on a link, alternatively you can set Home Page Reader to produce a sound alerting the user as the link is spoken, or you can set it to speak some meta text, (such as the word 'link'), before, or even after, the link.

The actual link text is important. What does it say? Is the link text clearly explaining what the link is pointing to? The Web Accessibility Initiative Priority 2 checkpoint 13.1 captures an important requirement:

13.1 Clearly identify the target of each link. [Priority 2]

You must be able to understand where a link will take you even if you read the link text out of the context of the page. As you tab from link to link, the focus rectangle highlights the link text. Whether you are using magnification, or whether you are focusing on the focus rectangle, or listening to the page, it is the link text that is important. The page excerpt below has a service to sell, but the targets of the links are not clearly identified:

Starting at $44.90 per month	$34.95 per month	$24.95 per month	$9.95 per month
Learn more.	Try it free or learn more.	Try it free or learn more.	Try it free or learn more.

With link text such as *Learn more* and *Try it free*, a disabled user is left asking himself, 'Learn more about what?' 'Try what free?' They need to be much more meaningful, such as *Learn more AccVerify* and *Try Bobby Worldwide for free.* The worst offender of course is *Click Here.* All of the assistive technologies that we have been discussing in these chapters can help users by generating a list of links. With JAWS *INS+F7* brings up the list, with HPR *CTRL+L* generates a list, the Window-Eyes command is *INS+TAB*. Here is their links list for a site that just does not understand the importance of identifying the target of links:

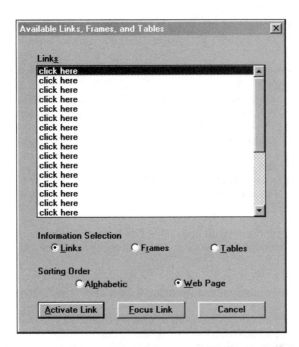

There are other, less crucial but still important, aspects of accessible link text. We mentioned above that links are read as 'links' by screen readers and talking browsers so there is no need to include the words 'link to' in the link text as is commonly done in `alt` text for image links.

Every image that is a link must have non-empty and meaningful `alt` text because when you *TAB* to a link there must be something there. When the link text is the `alt` text of an image it should convey the target of the link. Remember from the previous chapter that an image inside an anchor tag *may* have `null` `alt` text if text describing the nature of the link is also included within the *same* anchor.

Summary

In this chapter we looked at several ways of providing navigation that is accessible to users who depend on screen readers. We saw how a link at the top of the page that takes a user to the main content can be an extremely useful facility for users who are visually impaired, while hardly changing the appearance of the site to sighted users.

We also looked at how frames can help make a site more accessible if meaningful `title` and `name` attributes on the `<frame>` elements are used and `<title>` elements are included on the frame pages themselves.

Good page layout is another important factor that can increase a web site's accessibility. Strategies for improving navigation such as the use of heading tags (`<h1>`, `<h2>`, etc.) to indicate the main sections of your page, and laying the page out so that the main content is near the top when it is linearized, can make a site easier to use.

We also looked at how client-side image maps can provide an accessible form of site navigation, so long as you provide clear `alt` text on each `<area>` of the `<map>`, which clearly describes the target of the corresponding hot spot. Server-side images are fundamentally inaccessible, so redundant text links for all hot spots of the map should be provided whenever used.

All link text, whether it is visible on your page or the `alt` text on image links, must clearly tell the user the purpose of the link. Phrases like *Click Here* or *Learn More* are of little use to someone using an assistive technology. Not only that, but there is no need to preface link text with 'link to'; simply describe the target.

6

- Accessible HTML forms

- Accessible PDF forms

- Forms for people who are deaf

- Timed responses

Author: Jim Thatcher

Accessible Data Input

Increasingly ordinary businesses are adopting a web presence for sales and services to their customers. These businesses in the United States are required by the **Americans with Disabilities Act** (ADA) to make their physical bricks-and-mortar facilities accessible to people with disabilities. Many believe that the ADA also applies to the virtual world of the Internet as a "place of public accommodation", and that thus web services and sales must also be accessible.

The local bank has a web site where you can check your balances, make transactions, and fill out a loan application. Similarly if you own a mutual fund, you can probably open an online account where you can check the status of your funds and transfer assets from one fund to another.

However, the chances are that these shopping and financial sites are not tuned to the simple requirements of web accessibility. In particular these sites stress the importance of being able to interact with the web page, to enter data and submit information.

All of the issues about accessible content come into play when we think about how people with disabilities interact with a web page to input information, whether to fill out a survey, to purchase a software product, or to request information.

Is there convenient access to the form elements with the keyboard? Are there images that convey information about the form and do those images have clear text equivalents? Are image buttons in use and do those images include `alt` text? Is color being used to convey information? What is the redundant method conveying the same information?

There are some interesting new issues. Well, they are not completely new. When you can look at the screen, you can make associations easily like focusing on the main content of a page. In a similar way, when we input data into an online form, like name, address, telephone number, and so on, it is usually quite easy to understand what information goes where, what is required, and how to submit the results. If you are in trepidation about passing personal data across the Internet, then consider how your concern would be heightened if you weren't absolutely certain of which information goes where. If you cannot see the screen and rely on a screen reader, the task can be daunting at best. This is the principal issue to be discussed in this chapter.

Data Input Forms and the Guidelines

The Section 508 Standards for web accessibility are very clear on the point that data input should be accessible.

> *§1194.22(n) When electronic forms are designed to be completed online, the form shall allow people using assistive technology to access the information, field elements, and functionality required for completion and submission of the form, including all directions and cues.*

There is a fundamental difference between this provision of the Section 508 standards and some of the others, in that this one is far more general. §1194.22(a) says provide text equivalents for non-text elements and §1194.22(i) says provide titles for frames, but this simply says make forms accessible to people using assistive technology. The reason for providing text equivalents for non-text elements is to make those images accessible to people with disabilities, especially those using assistive technology. In the same way, the reason for providing titles (and names) for frames is to make it possible for people using assistive technology or text browsers to access the information in the frames. The Section 508 provisions for text equivalents and frame titles are very specific in suggesting what web developers should do in order to make their pages accessible to people using assistive technology. §1194.22(i) isn't. It is up to us!

The IBM guidelines for accessible web content are even more direct, and I might say, just as unhelpful as the Section 508 provision §1194.22(n):

> *7. Forms. Make forms accessible to assistive technology.*

Looking to the **Web Content Accessibility Guidelines** (**WCAG**) from the **Web Accessibility Initiative** (**WAI**) we find a different story. There are several checkpoints that directly address accessibility of electronic forms. That is, they address the question of what to do to make forms accessible.

It is surprising to me that these are only priority 2 checkpoints since, as we shall see in detail, the issues raised here are crucial for a person with a screen reader to access and deal with forms.

> *10.2 Until user agents support explicit associations between labels and form controls, for all form controls with implicitly associated labels, ensure that the label is properly positioned. [Priority 2]*

> *12.4 Associate labels explicitly with their controls. [Priority 2]*

The key to accessible forms is that the function of any form control element should be clear to a person using an assistive technology and they should be able to manipulate it easily. Knowing the intent of the input element is the purpose of WCAG Priority 2 checkpoints 10.2 and 12.4. The first checkpoint says position the prompt correctly. The second says that you should programmatically connect the prompt with the input control.

In a form you might have "*First Name*:" next to a text entry field, that is an <input> element of `type="text"`. The text, "*First Name*:" is what we will call the **prompt** or the **label** of the form element. Or, to take another example, the text "*Send literature*" next to a checkbox is the prompt for that checkbox. The prompt is thus the textual information that explains the purpose of the input control. Sometimes the prompt is included in the control, as in "*Cancel*" on a push button.

There is an interesting issue in Checkpoint 10.2. We will see how positioning labels or prompts is one very good way to ensure that screen readers interpret which text is labeling the form elements. I do advocate explicit association of labels with form controls, but since that requires significant development effort, explicit labeling should be used only when there is a decision not to position the prompts correctly.

We will reach the conclusion in this chapter that the best strategy is to position labels for form controls appropriately, or if that is not possible, then either place titles in the `<input>` elements that identify the purpose of the control, or explicitly and programmatically associate form controls with their labels.

There are other issues raised by the WAI. Priority 3 checkpoint 10.4 addresses an issue of screen readers not being able to find empty text input controls:

> *10.4 Until user agents handle empty controls correctly, include default, place-holding characters in edit boxes and text areas. [Priority 3]*

It used to be, when screen readers literally "read the screen", that they had difficulty detecting an input field that was blank. Now that screen readers use **Microsoft Active Accessibility** (**MSAA**) or the **Document Object Model** (**DOM**) of the browser, they do not have that problem anymore. The usefulness of Checkpoint 10.4 has passed.

The same is not true for Checkpoint 12.3, which is basically asking the information be grouped:

> *12.3 Divide large blocks of information into more manageable groups where natural and appropriate. [Priority 2]*

This is especially true for form elements, as we will discuss in the *<fieldset>*, *<legend>* and *Keyboard Interaction* section later in the chapter. The intent of Checkpoint 12.3 is clarified by the explanatory text from its guidelines document (*http://www.w3.org/TR/WCAG10/wai-pageauth.html*) below:

> *For example, in HTML, use OPTGROUP to group OPTION elements inside a SELECT; group form controls with FIELDSET and LEGEND; use nested lists where appropriate; use headings to structure documents, etc.*

HTML Forms

Forms consist of a number of possible input or interaction elements including the following:

- Push buttons `<INPUT type="button">` or `<INPUT type="submit">`

- Image buttons `<INPUT type="image">` and `<BUTTON>`

- Text entry fields `<INPUT type="text">` and areas `<TEXTAREA>`

- Radio buttons `<INPUT type="radio">`

- Checkboxes `<INPUT type="checkbox">`

- Select menus `<SELECT>`

Several of these can be collected in a `<form>` element along with other content including images and text. Usually `<form>` elements contain at least one *submit* button (`<BUTTON>` or `<INPUT type="submit">`).

How Do Forms Sound?

We will look at some HTML forms and understand how screen readers and IBM Home Page Reader deal with them. This will demonstrate the sources of accessibility problems and what can be done about them.

An Inaccessible Form

Let's first look at an awkwardly coded and inaccessible form below. The form is a simple form with a text entry field (`input, type="text"`), two radio buttons (`input, type="radio"`), a combo box or select menu (`select`), a text area (`textarea`), a checkbox (`input, type="checkbox"`), and finally two push buttons, one *submit* button (`input, type="submit"`) and one *reset* button (`input, type="reset"`):

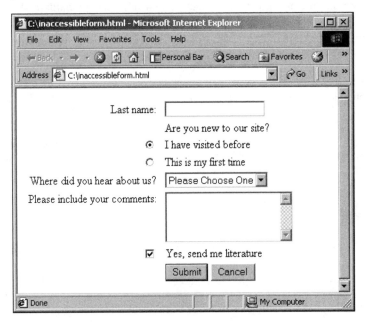

Although the form looks quite straightforward, the form elements do not speak well, and the whole form does not linearize correctly because it is laid out using a table with three columns and one row. The first cell itself contains a nested table as does the third. This layout is illustrated in the figure opposite:

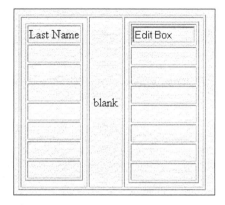

The nested table in the first cell has one column and eight rows containing all the prompts. The second cell is blank and the third cell contains a table with all the controls.

As we saw in Chapter 4, when a table is linearized, the data is extracted cell by cell, left to right and then top to bottom. So when a screen reader reads this form it starts by reading the first cell that contains all the prompts, followed by the empty middle cell, and then finally the third cell that contains a nested table with all the controls. This is a table that does not linearize well.

Screen readers try to identify the correct text prompts by looking in the table cell immediately to the left of the control. Here, in this inaccessible form, the prompt "*Last name*" for the edit field is in a completely different table from that of the `<input>` control so it is difficult for the screen readers to find these prompts. In forms mode, HPR finds *none* of the prompts, JAWS finds the prompt for the combo box (`Where did you hear about us?`) while, surprisingly, Window-Eyes succeeds with both edit fields and the combo box.

An Accessible Form

Let's now look at an accessible form that is constructed *without* using any markup specifically targeted at making it more accessible. There is specific markup in HTML 4.0 designed to address concerns of people with disabilities but we have not used this in this form. Instead, the prompts for each control were carefully placed in such a way that assistive technologies would easily find the information.

The form looks the same as the inaccessible form above:

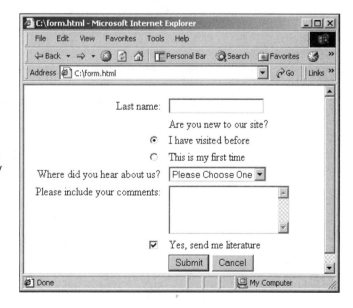

The HTML code for the form is straightforward. The layout is accomplished with a single table consisting of three columns and eight rows. The center column is blank and the first cell of that column has a non-breaking blank space, . This provides a space between the right-justified objects in the first column and the left-justified objects in column three.

The prompts are carefully placed. The prompts for text input fields and the select menu are positioned in the cells to the left of the control, whereas the prompts for radio buttons and the checkboxes are placed in the cells to the right of the input controls.

The buttons require no textual prompts since the text associated with the value attribute of the <input> element is the text that appears on the button and the assistive technology will know about it. Even if you forget to include a value attribute, the browsers and assistive technology still come to the rescue and just use type, submit, or reset as the identifying text.

Here is the code for our sample form:

```html
<form>
  <table border="0">
    <tr>
      <td width="50%" align="right">Last name:</td>
      <td> </td>
      <td><input size="20" type="text" name="name"></td>
    </tr>
    <tr>
      <td></td>
      <td></td>
      <td>Are you new to our site?</td>
    </tr>
    <tr>
      <td align="right"><input type="radio" checked name="visited"
          value="1"></td>
      <td></td>
      <td align="left" valign="top">I have visited before</td>
    </tr>
    <tr>
      <td align="right"><input type="radio" name="visited"
          value="0"></td>
      <td></td>
      <td align="left">This is my first time</td>
    </tr>
    <tr>
      <td align="right">Where did you hear about us?</td>
      <td></td>
      <td><select name="referral">
          <option value="0" selected>Please Choose One</option>
          <option value="1">From a TV show</option>
          <option value="2">On the Internet</option>
          <option value="7">It was a guess</option>
          <option value="3">Other</option>
          </select>
      </td>
    </tr>
    <tr>
      <td align="right" valign="top">Please include your comments:</td>
      <td></td>
      <td><textarea rows="4" cols="20" name="comments"></textarea></td>
    </tr>
```

```
    <tr>
      <td align="right"><input type="checkbox" checked
         name="literature" value="lit"></td>
      <td></td>
      <td>Yes, send me literature</td>
    </tr>
    <tr>
      <td></td>
      <td></td>
      <td><input type="submit" name="submit" value="Submit">
         <input type="reset" name="reset" value="Cancel"></td>
    </tr>
  </table>
</form>
```

It is always possible to simply listen to a page while using a screen reader or talking browser, and when encountering a `<form>` element, stop and handle it. Then you could read on to the next form control, stop, make an entry, and continue on. But it is rarely done that way.

Instead, when a user who is blind encounters a `<form>` element, either it is part of a form that they want to fill out, or not. If it is, then the most effective thing to do is to switch to "forms mode" and interact with the form. In "forms mode" the user moves from form element to form element with the TAB or some other key.

This is where the accessibility of the form is so very important. Besides knowing what kind of control it is (that is the easy part) the user needs to know what the prompt is. Landing on a text entry field, what do I type? Landing on a checkbox, what am I agreeing to?

Let's examine how our sample form sounds.

IBM Home Page Reader (HPR) has a "forms mode" which is called **Controls Reading Mode**. You turn on Controls Reading Mode with *Alt+O* or from the *Read* menu, select *Controls*. When in this mode, HPR does its best to try to figure out which text is the prompting information for any control.

You move forwards or backwards through the form with the right and left arrow keys. The down arrow repeats the current form item.

The display below shows the HPR response to seven successive arrow keys in Controls Reading Mode starting at the top of the page of our sample form. The word "*Text*" indicates an `<input>` element of `type="text"`, that is, a text entry field:

HPR (Controls Reading Mode)
1	*Last name: Text.*
2	*Are You New to Our Site? I have visited Before. Pressed.*
3	*This is my first time. Not Pressed.*
4	*Where did you hear about us? Start of select menu with 5 items.*
5	*Please include your comment. TextArea.*

Table continued on following page

HPR (Controls Reading Mode)	
6	*Please include your comments. Yes, send me literature. Checked.*
7	*Submit: Submit button.*
8	*Cancel: Reset button.*

The text in italics is spoken in a female voice which indicates the element is active in the sense that you can interact with it using the keyboard. Normal inactive text, for example "Start of select menu with 5 items" is spoken in the default male voice. The treatment of active elements by HPR is different when not in controls reading mode. For example, in item reading mode the prompt "*Last name*" is spoken in a male voice and only the edit field indicator "*text*" is indicated with a female voice.

> *There is only one error in what HPR reports to be a prompt. It seems that HPR considers the text "*Please include your comments:*" to be part of the prompt for the following checkbox as well as for the text area.*

A user who is blind with HPR would have no problem filling out this form even with that minor glitch. The same is true for someone using JAWS, which works without this glitch.

To turn on forms reading mode in JAWS, use the *Enter* key on a form element, the *Tab* and *Shift+Tab* keys to move you through the form. The text in italics this time is the JAWS help text spoken in a different voice from the default. That Help information can be turned off through a configuration option, but it is easy to ignore since it comes after the important information. Whereas HPR used the word "text" to indicate an `<input>` field of type text and "text area" for a `textarea`, JFW uses the word "edit" for both:

JAWS (Forms mode on)	
1	Last name: edit *Type in text.*
2	Are You New to Our Site? I have visited before. Radio button checked. *To change the selection press up or down arrow.*
3	Where did you hear about us? Combo Box. Please Choose one. *To change the selection please use the arrow keys.*
4	Please include your comments: edit *Type in text.*
5	Yes send me literature. Checkbox Checked. *To clear check mark press space bar.*
6	Submit button. *To activate press space bar.*
7	Cancel button. *To activate press space bar.*

In just the same way as in JAWS for Windows, turn on Forms mode in Window-Eyes using *Enter* when positioned on a form control. When in forms mode the *Tab* key moves from form control to form control; *Shift Tab* moves backwards. Window-Eyes users would also have no problem with our sample form. In this example Window-Eyes speaks all text in the default voice. Here is what Window-Eyes reports for the seven steps with the *Tab* key:

146

W-E (Forms mode)	
1	Edit box. Last name.
2	Radio button. Checked I have visited before.
3	Combo Box. Where did you hear about us? Please Choose one. One of 5.
4	Edit box. Please include your comments.
5	Checkbox. Checked Yes Send me literature.
6	Button. Submit.
7	Button. Cancel.

All three of the assistive technologies are completely successful presenting this form to their users, and no specialized markup is used.

The reason the assistive technologies are so successful with this form is that the prompts for the form controls are perfectly placed. If you always place the text information for text entry fields and combo boxes to the left of (or above) the control, screen readers will find it. If the prompt for a checkbox or radio button is to the right of the object, screen readers will find it.

Let's take a look at another example of an accessible form. This one, which is visually less attractive (in my opinion), has the same form elements and prompting text as the first two examples:

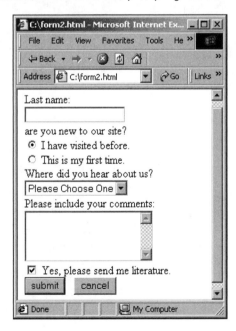

The code for the second example is very similar to the first, except that we used no layout table in this case. Each prompting piece of text and each text input element is placed on a separate line using <br> elements. The radio buttons and checkboxes are to the left of their labels (no <br> elements in that case). The coding is just about as simple as it could get:

```
<form>
  Last name:<br>
    <input size="20" type="text" name="name"><br>
  are you new to our site?<br>
    <input type="radio" checked name="visited" value="yes">
  I have visited before.<br>
    <input type="radio" name="visited" value="no">
  This is my first time.<br>
  Where did you hear about us?<br>
    <select name="referral">
      <option value="0" selected>Please Choose One</option>
      <option value="1">from a tv show</option>
      <option value="2">on the internet</option>
      <option value="7">it was a guess</option>
      <option value="3">other</option>
    </select><br>
  Please include your comments:<br>
    <textarea rows="4" cols="20" name="comments"></textarea><br>
    <input type="checkbox" checked name="literature" value="lit">
  Yes, please send me literature.<br>
    <input type="submit" name="submit" value="submit">
      <input type="reset" name="reset" value="cancel">
</form>
```

The results from reading this form in forms reading mode are similar to those from our first example form, but slightly better.

In each case the prompt that HPR detects is the intended one for the control:

HPR (Controls Reading Mode)	
1	*Last name: Text.*
2	*Are you new to our site? I have visited Before. Pressed.*
3	*This is my first time. Not Pressed.*
4	*Where did you hear about us? Start of select menu with 5 items.*
5	*Please include your comments: TextArea.*
6	*Yes, please send me literature. Checked.*
7	*Submit: Submit button.*
8	*Cancel: Reset button.*

JAWS for Windows is successful in exactly the same way. It makes no mistakes reading the controls of the form in our second example, because in each case the text that provides the information is properly placed; to the right of checkboxes and radio buttons and above the text entry controls or combo box:

JAWS (Forms mode on)	
1	Last name: edit *Type in text*
2	Are you new to our site? I have visited Before. Radio button checked. *To change the selection press up or down arrow.*
3	Where did you hear about us? Combo box. Please Choose one. *To change the selection please use the arrow keys.*
4	Please include your comments: edit *Type in text.*
5	Yes, please send me literature. Checkbox Checked. *To clear check mark press space bar.*
6	Submit button. *To activate press space bar.*
7	Cancel button. *To activate press space bar.*

Window-Eyes shows us exactly how they (the Window-Eyes developers) expect forms to be read. The correct prompt is picked up each time:

W-E (Forms mode)	
1	Edit box. Last name.
2	Radio button. Checked. I have visited before.
3	Combo Box. Where did you hear about us? Please Choose one. One of 5.
4	Edit box. Please include your comments.
5	Check Box. Checked. Yes. Please send me literature.
6	Button. Submit.
7	Button. Cancel.

The difference between our first accessible form and our second is that there is not even any table markup interfering with the prompts in the second. All three assistive technologies get it right because the prompts are correctly coded. So what is coded correctly? Without using markup specifically to associate prompts with controls, the answer is this:

- **Edit fields and select menus**: Place prompt to the left or above the control.

- **Checkboxes and radio buttons**: Place the prompt to the right of the control.

- **Buttons**: The prompt is part of the control, the `value` attribute.

> Any other placement will probably cause some screen reader or talking browser to give no information at all or the wrong information to its user.

There are two alternative methods of programmatically associating prompt text with form elements, so that screen readers can indicate to the user what information should be entered in the form:

- The `<label>` element which holds the text that goes with each form control

- The `title` attribute of the `<input>` element which clarifies the purpose of each `<input>`

The <label> Element

One way of making absolutely sure that screen readers associate the correct text prompts with each form control without relying on placement alone is to use the `<label>` element with the `for` attribute. Regardless of where the text prompts are on the page, you can assign them to specific form elements with the `<label>` element. The `<input>` element is given an `id`, and the prompt text is placed within a `<label>` element that has its `for` attribute set to the `id` of that input control:

```
<label for="maiden">Enter your mother's maiden name.</label>

<input type="text" name="mmn" id="maiden">
```

When the prompt is programmatically connected to the `<input>` element in this way, all the screen readers make the correct announcement.

Let's revisit the awkwardly coded and inaccessible form we saw at the beginning of this section. If the `<label>` element is used here to programmatically connect the prompt text with the form elements, all three assistive technologies read the correct prompts for each control. It is better to avoid coding a form like this one, however it illustrates how well the `<label>` element works, even in this worst-case situation:

```
<table border="0">
  <tr>
    <td>
      <table border="0">
        <tr><td height="30" valign="top" align="right">
          <label for="name">Last name:</label></td></tr>
        <tr><td height="30" valign="top" align="right">
          Are you new to our site?</td></tr>
        <tr><td height="30" valign="top" align="right">
          <label for="old">I have visited before.</label></td></tr>
        <tr><td height="30" valign="top" align="right">
          <label for="new">this is my first visit.</label></td></tr>
        <tr><td height="30" valign="top" align="right">
          <label for="refer">Where did you hear about us?</label></td></tr>
        <tr><td height="90" valign="top" align="right">
          <label for="comments">Please include you comments:</label></td></tr>
        <tr><td height="30" valign="top" align="right">
          <label for="lit">Yes, send me literature.</label></td></tr>
        <tr><td height="30" valign="top" align="right">
```

```
           </td></tr>
       </table></td>
    <td>
      <table border="0">
        <tr><td height="30" valign="top">
          <input size="20" type="text" id="name" name="name"></td></tr>
        <tr><td height="30"> </td></tr>
        <tr><td height="30" valign="top">
          <input type="radio" checked id="old" name="visit" value="1" ></td></tr>
        <tr><td height="30" valign="top">
          <input type="radio" id="new" name="visit" value="0"></td></tr>
        <tr><td height="30" valign="top">
          <select name="referral" id="refer">
            <option value="0" selected>Please Choose One</option>
            <option value="1">From a TV show</option>
            <option value="2">On the internet</option>
            <option value="7">It was a guess</option>
            <option value="3">Other</option></select></td></tr>
        <tr><td height="90" valign="top">
          <textarea rows="4" cols="20" id="comments" name="com"></textarea></td>
          </tr>
        <tr><td height="30" valign="top">
          <input type="checkbox" checked id="lit" name="lit" value="lit"></td>
          </tr>
        <tr><td height="30" valign="top">
           <input type="submit" name="submit" value="submit">
             <input type="reset" name="reset" value="cancel"></td>
          </tr>
      </table></td></tr></table>
```

The `<label>` element has a second format. It can be used as a container of both the text *and* the control and thus serve to implicitly connect the text to the control:

```
<label>
Phone Number<br>
<input type="text" name="phone">
</label>
```

With this code the text `Phone Number` is implicitly associated with the edit field with name `phone`.

There are very few situations where this implicit association between text and the input control would make sense. HTML requirements don't allow associations with the `<label>` element across cells of a layout table, for example. In particular the contents of the `<label>` element are restricted to character-level elements and text strings (%inline).

The natural association of text to the left of or on top of an edit box, or to the right of a checkbox, is picked up by assistive technology without the use of the `<label>` container and therefore the tag is not needed. In the example above, the prompt `Phone Number` would be found by a screen reader completely independently of the `<label>` element.

It is probably this analysis that has resulted in the fact that neither JFW nor Window-Eyes supports the implicit association of text with a form control with the `<label>` container, although HPR does support this construct.

151

Form Controls without Text Prompts

Placing the prompts right next to the input elements, or enclosing the prompts within the label element as we have discussed so far both require that prompts be available as text. However there are several situations in which there are no text prompts.

I was working with a client who had forms like the following where the "*Zip Code*" served as a prompt for two fields and "*Phone Number*" is followed by three input fields, similar to the screenshot shown below:

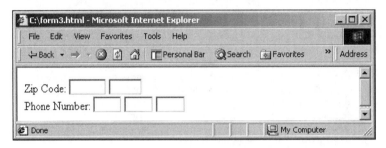

The problem is that the positioning of the form elements and the way they are presented carries information for people who can see, but not so for people using screen readers.

You might think that when you hear the second entry field without prompt, then that must be the "plus 4" of the zip code or the exchange for the phone. But that isn't the way it works for screen reader users. Many, if not most, form controls don't have properly positioned prompts and very few use the <label> element at all. When the screen reader user comes to a control for which no prompt is spoken, the natural instinct is to try to figure out what the prompt is by searching around for neighboring text.

The techniques we have discussed here won't work for this example. There is no text to position correctly, there is no text to enclose in the <label> element with the for attribute, so we need to get a bit more creative.

To solve this problem the client used invisible images similar to those used for skip navigation links in Chapter 5. The 1-pixel image would have alt text, say "plus four" in the Zip Code case, and "area code" "exchange" and "number" in the phone number example. Then these images are programmatically connected to the corresponding controls with the <label> element.

Let's look at one other common example of position or presentation conveying information in a form.

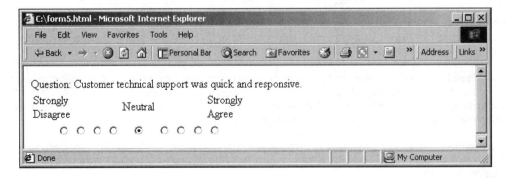

The form we see here is a natural for combining the `<label>` element and invisible images. A table is used as layout. It has two rows and nine columns. The second row contains the radio buttons. The first row has text in columns one, five, and nine. That text can be specified as the prompt for the first, fifth, and ninth radio buttons with the `<label>` element. That works well.

Then, add invisible images in columns two, three, four, six, seven, and eight, with appropriate `alt` text to convey the position in the array of radio buttons, and use the `<label>` with the `for` attribute, to associate the `alt` text with the corresponding radio button. Here's the idea:

```
Question: Customer technical support was quick and responsive.
<table border="0">
  <tr>
    <td><label for="q1m4">Strongly<br> Disagree</label></td>
    <td><label for="q1m3"><img src="c.gif" ... alt="disagree 3">
        </label></td>
    <td><label for="q1m2"><img src="c.gif" ... alt="disagree 2">
        </label></td>
    <td><label for="q1m1"><img src="c.gif" ... alt="disagree 1">
        </label></td>
    <td><label for="q10">Neutral</label></td>
    <td><label for="q1p1"><img src="c.gif" ... alt="agree 1">
        </label></td>
    <td><label for="q1p2"><img src="c.gif" ... alt="agree 2">
        </label></td>
    <td><label for="q1p3"><img src="c.gif" ... alt="agree 3">
        </label></td>
    <td><label for="q1p4">Strongly<br> Agree</label></td>
  </tr>
  <tr>
    <td align="right">
        <input type="radio" name="eval" value="1" id="q1m4"></td>
    <td><input type="radio" name="eval" value="2" id="q1m3"></td>
    <td><input type="radio" name="eval" value="3" id="q1m2"></td>
    <td><input type="radio" name="eval" value="4" id="q1m1"></td>
    <td align="center">
        <input type="radio" name="eval" value="4.5" checked id="q10">
    </td>
    <td><input type="radio" name="eval" value="5" id="q1p1"></td>
    <td><input type="radio" name="eval" value="7" id="q1p2"></td>
    <td><input type="radio" name="eval" value="7" id="q1p3"></td>
    <td><input type="radio" name="eval" value="8" id="q1p4"></td>
  </tr>
</table>
```

It certainly is a creative idea. Indeed, HPR picks up those invisible images as labels and reads them just as intended. But neither JAWS for Windows nor Window-Eyes speaks the `alt` text intended to label the radio buttons. *Why?* It is the real world of screen reader developers. Do very small images, especially those that are *not* links, *ever* carry information that is useful to the screen reader user? Not really! So screen readers can't afford to bother their users with this 'information' which almost always will not be 'information' at all. However there is another way.

The title Attribute of the input Element

The `title` attribute of the `<input>` element can be used to carry information about the form control, which can be accessed by screen readers to convey the purpose of the control to the user. As of the beginning of 2002 the current versions of Home Page Reader and JAWS for Windows have followed the lead of Window-Eyes and can now read the `title` attribute on `<input>` elements if it is present.

Let's revise the code of our last form to use the `title` attribute to give the prompt:

```
Question: Customer technical support was quick and responsive.
<table border="0">
  <tr>
    <td>Strongly<br>Disagree</td>
    <td></td><td></td><td></td>
    <td>Neutral</td>
    <td></td><td></td><td></td>
    <td>Strongly<br>Agree</td>
  </tr>
  <tr>
    <td><input type="radio" ... title="strongly disagree" ></td>
    <td><input type="radio" ... title="disagree 3"></td>
    <td><input type="radio" ... title="disagree 2"></td>
    <td><input type="radio" ... title="disagree 1"></td>
    <td><input type="radio" ... checked title="neutral"></td>
    <td><input type="radio" ... title="agree 1"></td>
    <td><input type="radio" ... title="agree 2"></td>
    <td><input type="radio" ... title="agree 3"></td>
    <td><input type="radio" ... title="strongly agree"></td>
  </tr>
</table>
```

There is a huge difference here between the amounts of accessibility coding required using the `<label>` element compared with the accessibility coding specific to the `title` attribute. For the `title` attribute all the coding is localized on the `<input>` elements. For the `<label>` coding, the prompting text has to be enclosed in the `<label>` container and the `id` of the `<input>` element must match the corresponding value of the `for` attribute. Generating the `id`s and making sure they match the corresponding prompts is a possible source of errors.

These reasons, and the fact that some form elements require that prompts be specified with text that is not visible, led me to urge the assistive technology vendors to support this option. The use of the `title` attribute on `input` elements is not, at this time, advocated by the Web Accessibility Initiative Guidelines, Version 1. I hope it will be a technique in the next version of the Web Content Accessibility Guidelines.

Let's look at the ways in which the assistive technologies read the controls in our form using `title` markup, beginning with HPR:

HPR (Controls reading mode, right arrow for each line):	
1	*Strongly Disagree. Not Pressed.*
2	*Disagree 3. Not Pressed.*
3	*Disagree 2. Not Pressed.*
4	*Disagree 1. Not Pressed.*
5	*Neutral. Pressed*
6	*Agree 1. Not Pressed*

HPR (Controls reading mode, right arrow for each line):	
7	*Agree 2. Not Pressed*
8	*Agree 3. Not Pressed*
9	*Strongly Agree. Not Pressed*

For both Window-Eyes and Jaws, the *Tab* key takes you to the center default checked radio button, `neutral`. Then moving with the arrow keys, the current radio button becomes checked. For this reason, all the reports show "radio button checked":

W-E (Forms Mode – Tab Key):	
1	Radio button checked. Strongly Disagree.
2	Radio button checked. Disagree 3.
3	Radio button checked. Disagree 2.
4	Radio button checked. Disagree 1.
5	Radio button checked. Neutral.

JAWS for Windows speaks the title correctly but also picks up the word "Agree" from the rightmost prompt, "Strongly Agree." This is probably an unwanted effect of looking for prompting text to the right of the radio button:

JFW (Forms Mode – Tab Key):	
1	Agree Strongly disagree radio button checked. *To change the selection press up or down arrow.*
2	Agree Disagree 3 radio button checked. *To change the selection press up or down arrow.*
3	Agree Disagree 2 radio button checked. *To change the selection press up or down arrow.*
4	Agree Disagree 1 radio button checked. *To change the selection press up or down arrow.*
5	Agree Neutral radio button checked. *To change the selection press up or down arrow.*

Grouping Form Controls for Clarity and Access

The purpose of the `<fieldset>` element is to group different parts of a form to simplify the process of filling it out, and clarify the intent of groups of controls. A form might consist of "contact information", "report the problem information", and "your hardware and software versions", and these separate parts of the form can be grouped together with the `<fieldset>` element and the name of the group appears in the `<legend>` element. In this way the group is visually highlighted.

The following figure shows the same form we saw earlier but with groups added to separate its parts. Because this is such a short form, this coding is certainly not necessary, but on longer forms, especially ones that are frequently used, this coding can make a difference in accessibility:

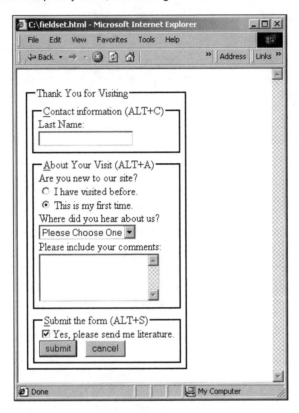

The `<fieldset>` and `<legend>` elements provide the grouping. The `accesskey` attribute is included in the `<legend>` element. This makes it possible (when using Internet Explorer) to jump to different groups with access keys, for example *Alt+C* for contact information and *Alt+A* for adding information about your visit.

Following the normal conventions, the access keys in this example are underlined. Screen readers won't announce simple underlining so in order for the access keys to be useful, users must be notified of their existence in some other way. The parenthetical access key (*Alt+C*) is added in each `<legend>` element for that purpose.

It is true that screen readers inform their users about accelerator keys in normal Windows menus. For example, for the "*File*" menu item, Window-Eyes says "F equals file pull down," JFW says "File alt f" while Home Page Reader says "File submenu press f." None of this identification is available for access keys as implemented on the Web.

Internet Explorer 5.0 and above implements the `<fieldset>`, `<legend>`, and `accesskey` accessibility features of HTML 4.0; Netscape Navigator 4.x does not support any of them, however Netscape 6 implements `<fieldset>` and `<legend>` but not accesskey.

Here is some of the code with `<fieldset>`, `<legend>`, and `accesskey` for our form:

```
<form>
  <table>
    <tr><td>
      <fieldset>
        <legend>Thank You for Visiting</legend>
        <fieldset>
          <legend accesskey="c"><u>C</u>ontact information (ALT+C)
          </legend>
          Last Name:<br>
          <input size="20" type="text" name="name"><br>
        </fieldset>
        <fieldset>
          <legend accesskey="a"><u>A</u>bout Your Visit (ALT+A)
          </legend>
          Are you new to our site?<br>
          <input type="radio" checked name="visited" value="yes">
          ...
          <textarea rows="4" cols="20" id="comments" name="comments">
          </textarea><br>
        </fieldset>
        <fieldset>
          <legend accesskey="s"><u>S</u>ubmit the form (ALT+S)
          </legend>
          <input type="checkbox" checked name="literature" value="lit">
          ...
        </fieldset>
      </fieldset>
    </td></tr>
  </table>
</form>
```

The access keys work very nicely in IE5. They position the focus on the first input element of the group. *Alt+S*, for *submit the form*, places focus on the checkbox. *Alt+C* for *contact information*, places focus on the text entry field.

If your access key conflicts with the accelerator keys on the Internet Explorer menu, like *Alt+F* for file or *Alt+H* for help, then the web application takes precedence and then for menu commands all users must use *Alt* by itself which puts focus on the menu, then *F* separately and similarly, *Alt* then *H*, instead of the key combinations.

IBM Home Page Reader seems to recognize the `<fieldset>` and `<legend>` tags and reports the contents of the `<legend>` when the first form element of the group is encountered. Here is the way HPR speaks the first controls of each group:

1	*Thank you for visiting. Contact information. Alt+C. Last name. Text.*
2	*About your visit. Alt+A. Are you new to our site? I have visited before. Pressed.*
3	*Submit the form. Alt+S. Yes, please send me literature. Checked.*

After working with this example I was checking a second situation where I thought the `<fieldset>` and `<legend>` elements might significantly help with access using HPR, but this time HPR *did not* speak the `<legend>` information. It turns out that we were just "lucky" with our example when HPR announced the `<legend>` information. When a simple break (`<br>`) is added between the ending `<legend>` tag (`</legend>`) and the text `Last Name` then HPR no longer announces the `<legend>` information.

Adding the break confirms that HPR does not support these accessibility features of HTML 4.0. This situation points to a big problem in evaluating how assistive technology works with new markup that was specifically added to HTML 4.0 for the purpose of increasing accessibility. In Chapter 4 we saw that one might conclude that all the assistive technologies supported `<th>` and `scope`, if a table marked up with them is correctly spoken. But in fact the reason for the correct speaking is placement of headings in the first row and first column, not the specialized accessibility markup.

Not only does HPR not support these tags, neither do Window-Eyes nor JAWS for Windows. Use of the `<fieldset>` and `<legend>` elements is valuable to improve clarity of a form; unfortunately, at this time, it doesn't help users with screen readers or talking browsers.

PDF Forms

You have probably seen content on the Web that at least appeared to be a form but it didn't have the look and feel of the forms we have been talking about so far.

The part of the form shown below from *http://www.irs.gov/* is all too familiar. This is a PDF document, specifically, *http://ftp.fedworld.gov/pub/irs-pdf/f1040.pdf*:

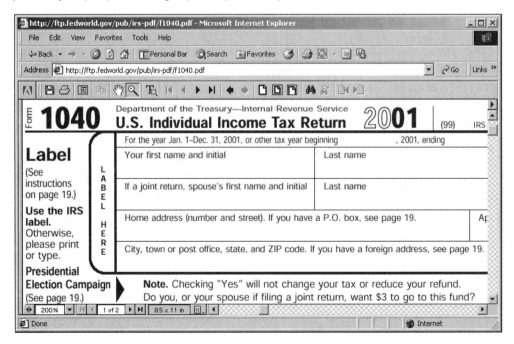

PDF stands for Portable Document Format from Adobe (*http://www.adobe.com*). The whole idea of PDF is to be able to share documents that will *look the same* when printed. The focus of PDF is presentation while accessibility must focus on content.

Many PDF documents are just images of printed pages, and thus are totally inaccessible. Up until recently even those that are not images were generally inaccessible.

Adobe (see *http://access.adobe.com/*) has made significant efforts to incorporate accessibility into its products. Now, with just the right combination of circumstances, it is possible for someone who is blind to access some PDF documents.

What do I mean by "the right combination of circumstances"? As with everything we have discussed about web accessibility, the author of the document has to take responsibility and design it with accessibility built in, that is, the document has to be prepared accessibly.

With Adobe Acrobat 5 it is possible to create **tagged forms** so that a screen reader can report the prompt for a form. The developer must go through the special effort to provide that access, though.

Here is a very small part of a form from a State of Connecticut web site:

I. **General Information**	
Date of Report: 12/23/2001	Date of Original IRB Approval:
Title of Project:	
Principal Investigator (or Major Advisor, if student project):	
Department/Agency/University:	
Address:	Department/Agency/University of Principal Investigator

Notice the 'ToolTip' text. This text results from holding the mouse pointer over the form field for the *Department/Agency/University*. This is the text that the developer has attached as a 'tag' to this form field and it is the information that is announced when listening to the form with JAWS for Windows. You will hear that prompt only if you are using Acrobat Reader Version 5 and the latest version of JAWS or Window-Eyes. Of course, you will also only hear that prompt if the developer has taken the extra effort to code it there.

It is possible to fill out the form because screen readers have specifically tailored their behavior to the special features of Adobe Acrobat Reader Version 5. I say "*possible*". As you work with a form and type into a text entry, the screen reader will speak each key as it is pressed. However, I could find no way to review what had been typed, whether character by character, word by word, or the whole entry.

I have not seen PDF forms that were intended to be completed on line, but I believe it is possible. Generally PDF documents are used for printing, filling out, signing, and mailing. If forms to be filled out on line do exist and they have been submitted, then I would say that even under optimal circumstances (tagged, Acrobat Reader Version 5), they only barely meet the section 508 provision at the beginning of this chapter because the functionality of being able to review entries is missing.

There is another provision of the Section 508 standards that applies to PDF forms:

§1194.22(m) When a web page requires that an applet, plug-in or other application be present on the client system to interpret page content, the page must provide a link to a plug-in or applet that complies with §1194.21(a) through (l).

Acrobat Reader is a plug-in and it is required when a page points to a PDF file (extension .pdf). §1194.22(m) requires, therefore, that the page provide a link to a plug-in that meets the Section 508 provisions for software accessibility.

The last of the software provisions, §1194.21(l), is one, like web provision §1194.22(n), that requires accessible forms:

§1194.21(l) When electronic forms are used, the form shall allow people using assistive technology to access the information, field elements, and functionality required for completion and submission of the form, including all directions and cues.

Accessibility of Forms for People Who Are Deaf

I have always thought of accessibility of the Web as being measured by how well people who have disabilities can use it. Yet, as is obvious, I stress blindness and how well people who are visually impaired using assistive technology can get the information or interact with a web site. The reason for that focus is because, in my opinion, ninety nine percent of the problems with web access are problems that directly affect people who are blind. The remaining one percent of the accessibility problems affects people with other disabilities.

If you are deaf or hearing impaired, you are going to miss out on an audio file or the audio portion of a multi media presentation, however at the moment the Internet is primarily a visual medium rather than an aural one. Also, if you can see the screen but you are deaf, then when an audio file begins to play, at least you know exactly what the problem is because Windows Media Player opened or the RealAudio player opened. But for the visually impaired, when `alt` text is missing from an image map or a form is not labeled correctly (accessibly), the confusion and frustration must be as difficult and annoying as not being able to get the information or interact with the form. Most importantly, there are vastly more examples of web content inaccessible to users who are visually impaired, compared to being inaccessible to those who are deaf.

Recently a recommendation was presented to the Web Content Accessibility Working Group of the WAI by Donald L. Moore. The idea being addressed by Mr. Moore is that when individuals who are deaf fill out a form including a telephone number, they have no way to explain that they can't use a regular telephone.

This is a case, not of accessibility of the web content, but the limitation of the web content to convey or request information that is important for people with disabilities, namely people who are deaf. Let's look at Mr. Moore's example form:

Banks require a telephone number for a loan application and some mutual fund companies require a telephone number when submitting a transfer request. These phone numbers can be critical and if the service provider does not know how to communicate with a deaf customer using a **Telecommunication Device for the Deaf** (**TDD**) then the transaction could end up aborted. Mr. Moore's suggestion is simple: add the information specifying the desired form of communication in the typical web form.

Timed Responses

There are situations where it is necessary or useful to require responses from a user of a web page or web application within a certain period of time. There is a provision in the Section 508 standards for web accessibility that requires special consideration for the fact that some people with disabilities might require more time to complete an action:

> §1194.22(p) When a timed response is required, the user shall be alerted and given sufficient time to indicate more time is required.

Exactly what kinds of situations require a timed response? An example is a certification test where each question must be answered within a specified time. Brainbench (*http://www.brainbench.com/*) offers certification exams and each question, on the test I examined, is allotted 180 seconds.

The technique for accomplishing this is a simple JavaScript that counts down the 180 seconds. In the test I took at the Brainbench site, the script gives a warning at 30 seconds, and submits the form and moves to the next question at 180 seconds.

161

I timed speaking an average question in one of those tests. It took 90 seconds with HPR speaking at its default rate. That rate is, granted, relatively slow for accomplished users, but a minute and a half is half the allotted time, and I found that it was often necessary to read and reread the multiple choice answers to decide on the correct one. In this example an alert is provided, but there is no provision for additional time.

The Brainbench alert at 30 seconds replaces an image heading the question:

Question

with another image:

30 Seconds!

neither of which have alternative text, making the accessibility issue even worse.

This problem is not restricted to people depending on screen readers. Someone with extremely low vision may be a slower-than-average reader. Just like the Brainbench test, a form on a page may timeout before the data input task is complete. Often when that happens, the data that has been entered is erased. The result is that someone with a disability who is slow to enter data cannot complete the form. That is why the Section 508 provision requires that additional time be allowed.

WCAG Version 1.0 does not have any item that specifically addresses the issue of timed responses. The Web Accessibility Initiative Guideline Working Group (*http://www.w3.org/wai/gl/*) is developing a second generation of those guidelines. The draft of the WCAG Version 2.0, at the time of this writing, does have a provision relating to timed responses:

> *Checkpoint 2.4 Either give users control over how long they can interact with content that requires a timed response, or give them as much time as possible.*

The numbering of this checkpoint may change, its wording will undoubtedly change and it could be deleted altogether before WCAG 2.0 becomes an official document of the W3C.

The message is essentially the same as the Section 508 provision. When timed responses are required, provide enough time for those who might take significantly more time than average.

But aren't there situations when the time required is essential to the task at hand? The Brainbench certification test is an example. With unlimited time one could research each question so time should be limited. I also understand that there are securities-trading situations that are extremely time sensitive, that a specified price is only available for a limited time.

When timing of the input or interaction is essential to the function of the page, the warning of a potential timeout must be clear and offered before the timing starts. If possible we should provide for adjustment of the time or provide contact information so that a user who needs more time can arrange to get it.

When people write about timed responses they often include automatic page refresh and page redirections. The *draft* of Version 2.0 of the WCAG, includes these phenomena as part of the definition of "timed response". Similarly, the National Institutes of Health 508 Web Tutorial, *http://oc.nci.nih.gov/web508/tutorial.html,* includes page refreshes and redirects as examples of timed responses.

It is true that automatic page refreshes or page redirections can be annoying and frustrating for people with disabilities. For example, some recent versions of screen readers, which are probably in wide use today, will start reading a web page from the top when it refreshes.

It is also true that page refreshes or page redirections involve timing, but these are not examples of the timed responses that the Section 508 web provision addresses. A timed response is when the web site user must complete a specified data interaction or task in a certain amount of time before the form contents are cleared, or the form is automatically submitted.

Form Design Checklist

To round off the chapter here is a quick reference checklist to creating accessible forms:

- Place prompts for text fields and combo boxes above or to the left of the control.

- Place prompts for checkboxes and radio buttons to the right of the control.

- If placement is anything except the two cases above, use the `<label>` element with the `for` attribute to explicitly associate the prompts with the controls.

- Instead of the `<label>` element, you can use the `title` attribute on each `<input>` element to specify its label or prompt.

- Use the `<fieldset>` and `<legend>` tags to structure complex forms so that they are clearer and simpler to understand.

- Structure your contact information form to specify a desired communication channel (like TDD, pager, e-mail, etc.) for people who are deaf.

- Avoid limiting the amount of time allowed for completing and submitting forms. If that is not possible, explain the timing restrictions and issue an accessible alert before the timeout.

Summary

In this chapter we looked at how to design forms that are accessible to disabled people. We saw how to design forms so that screen readers can identify the appropriate prompt text for each control on the form, and we also looked at various methods of programmatically associating prompt text with controls using the `<label>` element. However there are certain situations in which an `<input>` element would not have any prompt text associated with it and we saw how to handle such situations with the `<label>` element and also the `title` attribute of the `<input>` element, which offers a simpler solution.

PDF forms can be made more accessible by adding tags describing each field that are readable to screen readers. However there are some problems meeting all of the Section 508 standards with PDFs.

There are also some subtle problems faced by people who are hard of hearing that the designer should consider when designing forms.

7

- Section 508 testing

- Accessibility checking software

- Bobby

- LIFT

Author: Jim Thatcher

Testing for Section 508 Compliance

There is a rapidly changing and growing field of software tools that can be used to check for web accessibility. US federal agencies and corporations are spending millions of dollars on software tools that claim to test web sites for accessibility. We want to raise the question of what can and cannot be tested with these tools. Then we will examine two such software tools in some detail.

Any accessibility testing must be viewed as a process that combines automated software tools with human judgment. No tool yet exists that you can just run your site through in order to prove conclusively that it is accessible and complies with the Section 508 provisions, however much you are willing to pay. Furthermore, such a tool is unlikely to appear in the near future; so human judgment is still absolutely essential.

Having said that, software-testing tools can help you find out if your site is *not* accessible or does not comply with Section 508, by testing for the absence of valid required attributes.

This chapter is split into two main sections:

- In the first half we will discuss the Section 508 provisions and the extent to which you can rely on software tools to check your web content for accessibility, compared to how much you must rely on human evaluation. I will call these two parts of the job the "algorithmic" part and the "judgment" part. Algorithmic testing generally verifies that a valid element or attribute is present – like the `name` attribute or `<label>` element, for instance. Judgment comes in with questions such as whether or not the `alt` text used for a given image is appropriate.

- The second half of the chapter looks at two widely used software tools – **Bobby** and **LIFT**.

What Testing Is possible – Section 508 (Web)

We are going to look at each Section 508 provision in turn and discuss the algorithmic and human judgment aspects involved in testing for its compliance. This will be a fairly open-ended discussion. In the algorithmic section we will talk about what parts of the accessibility testing *could* feasibly be automated; we will not concentrate on any particular tool. The points labeled here as *judgment* calls are things that you, as experts, can evaluate and say whether or not a given page passes or fails.

Text Equivalents

> *§1194.22(a). A text equivalent for every non-text element shall be provided (for example, via "alt", "longdesc", or in element content).*

Algorithmic Testing

A computer program can verify the presence of `alt` attributes on elements where they are required, such as `<img>` and `<area>` and `<input>` tags with `type="image"`. However, the only such check that can be done is whether `alt` text is actually present and whether it consists of a text string. This, of course, includes the null string `alt=""`, which is never valid on an `INPUT` of type `image` or on any link where there is no text as part of the anchor, so software could be used to detect this.

Common errors or violations could also be detected, such as the use of filenames for `alt` text. Words like *'spacer'*, *'go'*, *'click'* or *'null'*, and `alt` text consisting of a single space are also suspicious, so software could highlight these for examination.

It would be possible for a software program to raise the question of whether or not a `longdesc` attribute belongs on an image for, say, images larger than a predetermined size. This doesn't seem very helpful to me, but many software tools do raise this question for any non-trivial image. Furthermore, the presence of certain file types should trigger questions about the existence of text equivalents. These include (but are certainly not limited to) the various media file types such as `.wav` `.ra`, `.rm` or `.ram` files.

Some suggest that the `alt` attribute for applets may be considered a text equivalent, but it is important to ensure that this is actually the case. For example, "Applet displays current stock prices," (as suggested by the Access Board *http://www.access-board.gov/sec508/guide/1194.22.htm#(a)*) is not actually an equivalent, since it does not enable the user to obtain the current stock prices. Some more imaginative way of presenting the equivalent data must be found, and this requires human judgment. All this is especially true because of the special provision for applets in the Section 508 Web Provision §1194.22(m), which we cover later.

Judgment

Judgment comes in when evaluating the *quality* of the text equivalents: that is, *"Does a text string serve as a textual equivalent to the non-text element?"* As I have said in earlier chapters, there is some disagreement about the finer details. For example, I would say that graphical "bullets" in front of items in a list should have `alt=""` while others would argue for `alt="bullet"`. However, the basic rules still apply and either one complies with §1194.22(a) regardless of which side of this particular argument you take.

The existence of text equivalents for audio and multimedia will also need to be determined by visual inspection. Whether or not a transcript of a speech (or other audio communication) is accurate, for instance, will have to be checked by having someone actually read through the text and checking that it does match the audio presentation.

As I mentioned above, if `alt` text or object content is used for applets or objects, that text must be compared with the applet or object for equivalence. Consider an applet that acts as a ticker application for displaying headlines, as an example. Content that says "applet displaying headlines" is merely a *description* of the applet and does not give the user an alternative means of interacting with the site. However, `alt` text which reads `"See http://www.newspaper.com/headlines for today's headlines"` is better, since at least it lets the user find the content that the applet displays.

Human judgment is also required in finding images that require long descriptions and/or D-links, like charts and graphs, as we discussed in Chapter 4.

Synchronized Multimedia

> *§1194.22(b) Equivalent alternatives for any multimedia presentation shall be synchronized with the presentation.*

Algorithmic

The existence of multimedia content can be detected by file extension in an anchor or OBJECT. For some multimedia formats (`.smi`, for example) it may be possible to determine algorithmically whether or not captioning is included, though this is beyond the scope of this book.

Judgment

It is not possible to determine the existence of captions for all media formats. Therefore, human evaluation is required just to determine whether the synchronized equivalents are present. Then there is the question of the accuracy of the captions. Is an audio description necessary and if it is necessary, then is what has been provided, as such, appropriate? These questions have to be answered to determine compliance with this provision of the Section 508 Rules on Web Accessibility.

Color Coding

> *§1194.22(c). Web pages shall be designed so that all information conveyed with color is also available without color, for example from context or markup.*

Algorithmic

Automated software could be used to check for color specifications in the stylesheet and corresponding elements in the web page – and deduce any color changes in the page that way. If there are no color changes through HTML or CSS on a web page then the page automatically complies with §1194.22(c) as far as *text* is concerned. However, images on the page could still be color-coded (images used as links, for instance). If the image color conveys important information, then it raises accessibility issues.

Moreover, if there *were* color changes in the page then it would be difficult to detect algorithmically whether information was being conveyed by color *alone*. For example, a simple search for 'color words' in a page's source code might well turn up phrases from the page content such as 'the books in green are available for checkout' – which might suggest non-compliance, but still requires a user-check.

Judgment

A general evaluation of the page is necessary to determine if information is conveyed by color alone. Most sources that discuss testing for this provision recommend that (human) testing is done by viewing the page in black and white. Personally, I think it is much easier to check for the use of color when color is available to the viewer.

Stylesheets

> §1194.22(d). Documents shall be organized so they are readable without requiring an associated stylesheet.

Algorithmic

If there are no stylesheets, `<STYLE>` elements or `style` attributes, then the page complies with §1194.22(d). If stylesheets are used but no CSS positioning is included, then colors could be analyzed for adequate contrast.

Judgment

Pages should be viewed using a browser with stylesheets turned off to determine whether or not the page is still readable. For example, is there important structural markup (headings, lists) simulated using stylesheets? Check (with Netscape or Opera) that the page makes sense when CSS positioning is turned off.

Server-Side Maps 1

> §1194.22(e). Redundant text links shall be provided for each active region of a server-side image map.

Algorithmic

If no server-side maps are present (`<img>` with the `ismap` attribute) then the page obviously passes this provision. If a server-side map is found (`ismap` attribute and no valid `usemap` attribute) then the question must be addressed as to whether or not redundant text links are available. A program could be written to click on every pixel of the map, record the new URL, and compare it with all `href` values on the page. That sort of overkill would be kind of silly, though!

Software can at least detect the presence of server-side maps and flag them up for subsequent human evaluation, however.

Judgment

If a server-side map is found then it must be evaluated for the availability of text links for all the active regions of the map, as we discussed in Chapter 4.

Server-Side Maps 2

§1194.22(f). Client-side image maps shall be provided instead of server-side image maps except where the regions cannot be defined with an available geometric shape.

Algorithmic

If there is no server-side map on the page then it obviously complies with §1194.22(f). If there is one, then see §1194.22(e).

Since all regions can actually be defined with polygons the page should fail if a server-side map is used. This is troubling since there are sites where a server-side map is used as a technique for addressing point §1194.22(o) – *"provide a method for skipping navigation links"*. All areas of the client-side map must have a valid `alt` attribute (§1194.22(a)). The `ismap` attribute should never be used on an `input` element with `type="image"` (an "image button").

Judgment

My interpretation of this provision is that the page does not comply with §1194.22(f) when a server-side map is found. The absence of a server-side map means that the page is compliant. Since this is an either/or requirement, no human judgment is required.

Table Headers

§1194.22(g). Row and column headers shall be identified for data tables.

Algorithmic

If a page has no tables at all, then this provision does not apply. I believe it is possible to devise sophisticated heuristic algorithms to separate data tables from layout tables with adequate certainty. Since almost all tables are layout tables, and since most web pages use these layout tables, it would be especially advantageous if software could successfully separate out tables that are data tables. There are lots of issues involved in achieving this. The use of images in cells would suggest a layout table, whereas uniformity of cell content suggests a data table, and so on. Once an accessibility checker has determined that a table is probably a data table, then the question of compliance simply comes down to whether or not row and column headers have been identified.

If there is no specialized heading markup (through use of the `scope` and `headers/id` attributes or the `<th>` element) then the question is, *are the headings in the first row and first column?* If they are, then I believe that this is adequate identification, since the major screen readers (JAWS and Window-Eyes) will announce them as headings by default. At the time of writing, only HPR uses markup to identify table headers.

There are two distinct cases. If the table contains entirely numeric data apart from for the headings (whose cells contain non-numeric text) a software checker might be able to detect them. If the headings *are* in the first row and column, in such a case one could reasonably conclude that the table complies with §1194.22(g). This probably applies to a significant proportion of the data tables on the Web. If, on the other hand, a table lacks headings markup and contains non-numeric data, it is difficult to imagine any technique for algorithmically determining whether or not row one and column one are headings.

The second case is one where specific headings markup has been used, including header cells, `<th>` and/or `scope` and `headers` attributes. I think it would be possible to algorithmically determine if all (or most) non-header cells have been marked up as such; for example, if you define a heading cell using `<th>` or a `scope` attribute, or by making it the target of a `headers` attribute. If every non-heading cell has associated with it a row heading cell and column heading cell, then the table compiles with this provision.

Judgment

No matter how sophisticated the algorithm to detect data tables is, every page must be checked for their presence because the heuristics cannot be guaranteed to find them in every case. Once a table is determined to be a data table, the validity of its headings specification must be verified by testing with an assistive technology, or by carefully examining the HTML source for headings markup.

Complex Tables

> *§1194.22(h). Markup shall be used to associate data cells and header cells for data tables that have two or more logical levels of row or column headers.*

Algorithmic

Although one could probably determine which tables on a site are data tables (albeit with some degree of uncertainty), I cannot imagine any way of algorithmically determining whether or not a given table is complex, in the sense that it has two or more logical levels of row or column headers. However, if all data cells in the table have valid `headers` attributes then it conforms to this provision – whether complex or not.

Judgment

Again, the situation is similar to that for the previous provision. Firstly, any page must be searched for data tables. When one is found it requires human judgment to determine whether or not there are two or more logical levels of row or column headers. If there is *at most* one row heading and *at most* one column heading for each data cell, and these are in the same row and column as the cell, respectively, then the table is not complex. Judgment is required to determine whether or not the headers markup required by this provision is adequate. This can be verified by human testing with assistive technology or careful analysis of the HTML code.

Frames

> *§1194.22(i). Frames shall be titled with text that facilitates frame identification and navigation.*

Algorithmic

Software can check whether the `<frame>` elements in a `<frameset>` have valid `name` and `title` attributes. Also it would be possible to test whether or not the actual initial frame pages have `<title>` elements. As we discussed in Chapter 5, to be adequately "titled" for the three major assistive technologies, all three of these components should be present, though technically the presence of an adequate `title` or `name` attribute or `title` element would comply with this provision.

Judgment

Human judgment will determine whether or not the frame titles and/or names are useful for the purposes of identification and navigation. For example, `name="frame10078"` and `name="frame10077"` are not useful ways of identifying a frame to show what its purpose is.

Flicker Rate

§1194.22(j). Pages shall be designed to avoid causing the screen to flicker with a frequency greater than 2 Hz and lower than 55 Hz.

Algorithmic

Software can detect whether or not there are technologies present on a web page that *might* cause flickering in the hazardous range. Java, Flash or JavaScript all qualify as potential culprits. Furthermore, any animated gif on the page could cause flickering. Animation and the frequency of frame transitions also could be detected algorithmically, but a frame rate in the hazardous range does not necessarily mean that the screen will be flickering at this rate: it is the change from light to dark that causes flickering.

Judgment

We must inspect any page that has potential 'flickering technology' on it, to check whether or not flickering is occurring. If so, we need to determine whether the frequency is in the range disallowed by this provision and rectify matters if this is the case.

Text-only Page

§1194.22(k). A text-only page, with equivalent information or functionality, shall be provided to make a web site comply with the provisions of this part, when compliance cannot be accomplished in any other way. The content of the text-only page shall be updated whenever the primary page changes.

Algorithmic

While it is possible to detect algorithmically some references to text-only pages, it is impossible to evaluate the equivalence of content or frequency of update of a text-only page. This provision mandates the use of a text-only page only in circumstances where compliance cannot be accomplished in any other way. The fact that a page cannot be made accessible in the first place is obviously not determinable algorithmically.

Judgment

There are two parts to evaluating a web page for compliance with this provision. Firstly, is it really impossible to make the page accessible in any other way? Secondly (having determined that this is the case), is there a text-only page readily available and, if so, is it accessible? Does it meet all the other Section 508 provisions for web access and does the text-only version offer equivalent functionality and information to the original? Finally, is it kept up to date with the same frequency as the original page? These are all difficult questions to answer, making this one of the most daunting of the 508 provisions for compliance testing.

Scripting

§1194.22(l). When pages utilize scripting languages to display content, or to create interface elements, the information provided by the script shall be identified with functional text that can be read by assistive technology.

Algorithmic

If a page uses scripts to modify attributes for visual effect then this is fine, from an accessibility standpoint, since it does not affect the user's ability to interact with the site. In some cases this could be determined with a software accessibility checker since, in principle, an algorithm could be devised to check if the 'fly-over submenu' links are available on the page opened by the main menu item link. However, this is a pretty complex task: it is, in effect, one program trying to evaluate another.

Judgment

The criterion here should simply be whether someone using assistive technology can handle the page and its interactions. This requires testing using the screen readers or a talking browser like HPR. Without access to assistive technology you can evaluate items such as fly-over menus, by testing whether there are alternative text links for all submenu links readily available – that is, is the enhancement provided by the script simply visual?

Applets and Plug-Ins

§1194.22(m). When a web page requires that an applet, plug-ins, or other application be present on the client system to interpret page content, the page must provide a link to a plug-in or applet that complies with §1194.22(a) through (l).

Algorithmic

A software accessibility checker can detect whether or not applets, plug-ins or other applications are required to interact with a page, or are embedded into that page.

Judgment

Human involvement is required in determining whether or not a link is present to open or obtain the plug-in, applet, or application, and whether or not that plug-in, applet, or application meets the Section 508 Software standards §1194.21 (a)–(l).

Online Forms

§1194.22(n). When electronic forms are designed to be completed online, the form shall allow people using assistive technology to access the information, field elements, and functionality required for completion and submission of the form, including all directions and cues.

Algorithmic

The following test can be algorithmically performed on every non-button `<input>` element, `<textarea>` and `<select>` menu. Check to see that at least one of the following holds true for every input element that is not a button:

- The prompt is immediately above or to the left of an`<input>` of type `text`, a `<select>` menu or a `<textarea>` with no intervening HTML other than `BR`. The prompt should also be immediately to the right of a checkbox or radio button.

- The prompt is included in the `<input>` of type `text`, `<textarea>` or `<select>` menu.

- The prompt is specified with the `<label>` element.

- The prompt is specified with a valid `title` attribute of the `<input>` element, `<select>` menu, or `<textarea>`.

In addition, `<input>` elements of type `image` must have a valid `alt` attribute.

Judgment

Human judgment comes in verifying that the prompts are appropriate. Keyboard access should be checked as well.

Skip Navigation

§1194.22(o). A method shall be provided that permits users to skip repetitive navigation links.

Algorithmic

If there were a reliable algorithm to determine the position of the main content, and what to skip over, then screen reader developers would include that in their products, and so no 'skip navigation link' would be needed! In fact screen readers are beginning to include jumps like this, but they are still heuristic and quite likely to miss the mark. If there is at least one large block of links (greater than, say, four) at the top of the linearized page, then software could check if there is a link to a local anchor that skips over those links. If there is, then the page complies with this provision. The page probably also complies if there is no 'large block' of links at the top of the linearized page. The page also complies with this provision if it uses frames that comply with 1194.22(i), and which separate main content from navigation.

Judgment

Examine the page to determine whether there is a 'main content' area and use assistive technology to verify that a 'skip navigation link' works in taking the user from the top of the page to the beginning of the main content.

Timed Responses

§1194.22(p). When a timed response is required, the user shall be alerted and given sufficient time to indicate more time is required.

Algorithmic

If there are no forms, or if forms are present and there is no scripting, then there are no timed responses. There may be heuristics to help decide if a timed response is required, but it is difficult to imagine an algorithm that could further decide whether or not sufficient time has been allowed.

Judgment

Check all form submissions to determine if timed responses are required and if it is possible to request more time if they are.

Accessibility Checking Software

Now let us continue to the second half of the chapter: actually working with some examples of accessibility software. While there are a number of software tools available when checking for accessibility, we will study two of the more commonly used ones, Bobby and LIFT.

Bobby from CAST

Bobby is made by **CAST**, the **Center for Applied Special Technology** (*http://www.cast.org*). It is the most well-known accessibility checker and has been around longest. It was first released in September 1996 and up until the end of 2001 it was free. In December 2001 a new version was announced called **Bobby WorldWide** (Version 3.3). This downloadable accessibility checker costs US$99.00 for a single user license. There are also site and server licenses available at considerably greater cost.

The Web-Based Trial Version of Bobby

You can visit the Bobby site at *http://www.cast.org/bobby* and use Bobby to test individual live web pages at a time. This will apply either Bobby's 508 rules, or the WAI guideline rules, Priorities 1, 2, *and* 3. We will illustrate this trial using the 508 rules.

Some further refinement is possible using the *Advanced Options* link. Especially useful among these is the ability to split the Web Accessibility Initiative guidelines into three groups: Priority 1 (WAI Conformance Level "A"), Priority 1 and 2 (WAI Conformance Level "Double-A"), and finally all three priorities (WAI Conformance Level "Triple-A").

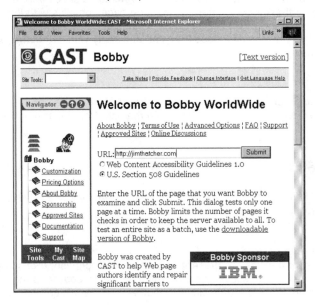

To analyze a given URL you simply type it into the textbox on the site. In the screenshot opposite I have entered my own web site's home page *http://JimThatcher.com*.

The Bobby Report

After the page is submitted, Bobby generates the report. This is an interesting and well-structured document that is divided into three main parts:

- The status, or summary

- The original page marked up with issues

- The list of problems or questions

Status

The first part of the report describes the overall status of the evaluation. It will return one of two logos:

	If *no* non-compliance issues are found, then the Bobby Approved Logo is offered, subject to the site owner completing an examination of the list of "manual checks" – which are either triggered by some specific content on the page or are always required.
	If non-compliance issues are detected, like missing `alt` text, the user is warned with a grayed approval icon, indicating that repair is required.

The status returned in the case of my home page is as follows:

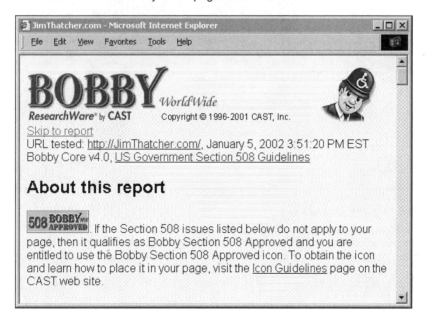

The Annotated Page

The second part of the Bobby report is the annotated page – a display of the original page with icons located at all places where potential problems exist. Two icons are used:

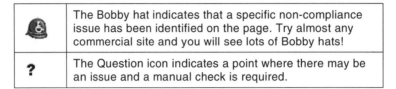	The Bobby hat indicates that a specific non-compliance issue has been identified on the page. Try almost any commercial site and you will see lots of Bobby hats!
?	The Question icon indicates a point where there may be an issue and a manual check is required.

The Bobby hat and question mark icons are shown for WCAG priority 1 issues and for all 508 issues. They are not displayed for WCAG priority 2 and 3 problems in order to keep screen-clutter down to a manageable level.

If the user clicks on either icon, focus is taken to the item in the accessibility errors list (the third section of the report). This describes the problem or question in greater detail. This is a very helpful feature, and is available only in the web trial version. It is not available with the downloadable product. The following screenshot shows *JimThatcher.com* marked up by Bobby.

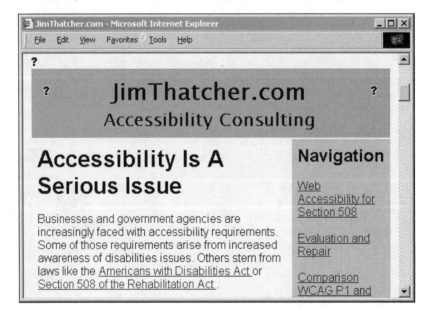

Accessibility Errors and Questions

The last section of the report lists all the potential problem areas, in three sections. Firstly, it shows the non-compliance issues Bobby actually detected; secondly, the manual checks triggered by some content of the page; and finally the manual checks that are always included in the report.

Opposite is a screenshot of the list of user checks triggered by *JimThatcher.com*:

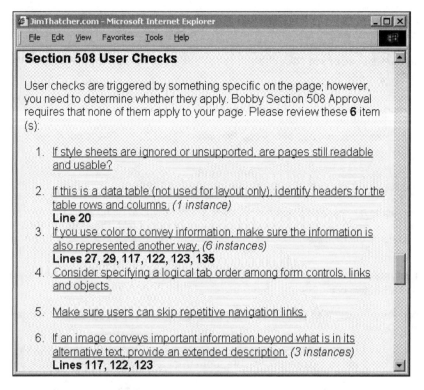

Issues Raised in the Evaluation

For most accessibility tools the details of the algorithms used in their rules are not public. Bobby, however, was developed by the Evaluation and Repair working group – a team who have worked with the W3C Web Accessibility initiative. Bobby's algorithms for the WAI checkpoints are those in *'Techniques For Accessibility Evaluation And Repair Tools,'* W3C Working Draft at *http://www.w3.org/WAI/ER/IG/ert/.*

Here is the list of issues and triggers for the *JimThatcher.com* site. With each issue raised, I have indicated in advance whether or not the same issue was raised by LIFT Online (as we'll see in the LIFT Online *'Issues raised in the evaluation'* section):

1. If stylesheets are ignored or unsupported, are pages still readable and usable?

Trigger: use of stylesheets. Provision: §1194.22(d). Also raised by LIFT Online.

2. If this is a data table (not used for layout only), identify headers for the table rows and columns.

Trigger: any TABLE. *Provision: §1194.22(g). Also raised by LIFT Online.*

3. If you use color to convey information, make sure the information is also represented another way.

Trigger: any image, or text color change, in the document. Provision: §1194.22(c). Also raised by LIFT Online.

4. Consider specifying a logical tab order among form controls, links, and objects.

Trigger: Links, form controls, or objects. Provision: §1194.22(n). This is not raised by LIFT Online.

5. Make sure users can skip repetitive navigation links.

Trigger: some number and placement of links. There seems to be no analysis of links that are available, nor positioning of the links relative to blocks of text. Provision: §1194.22(o). Also raised by LIFT Online.

6. If an image conveys important information beyond what is in its alternative text, provide an extended description.

Trigger: image larger than (at least) one pixel square. Provision: §1194.22(a). Also raised by LIFT Online.

7. If you can't make a page accessible, construct an alternative accessible version.

Trigger: none. Provision: §1194.22(k). Not raised by LIFT Online.

8. If a timed process is about to expire, give the user notification and a chance to extend the timeout.

Trigger: none. Provision: §1194.22(p). Not raised by LIFT Online.

The last two user checks are always included.

Personally, I am ambivalent about the advice in point 4. Since there is no FORM element on *JimThatcher.com* it seems gratuitous to raise this issue based on §1194.22(n). The logical tab order is not a requirement of form accessibility and is thus not really relevant to Section 508. However, if a link, control or object is not assigned a tabindex, then the tab order can become very strange. At this time IBM Home Page Reader does not support tabindex, but both Window-Eyes and JAWS work with Internet Explorer, which does. You can exclude this rule when you check your site using Bobby's customization feature.

Bobby's Help Information

Each item in the list of errors or questions that requires a manual check is a link that opens the Help document for that issue. These documents are very complete and highly accurate. They have code examples in common and each item includes the rationale for the provision and a reference to the source in the Section 508 and/or WAI documents.

Customization of Bobby

In both the trial on the Web and the full product there are options to use 508 rules, the Web Accessibility A, Double-A, or Triple-A rule sets, and, most importantly, an option to select which rules are to be applied by choosing *Custom* in the *Preferences* dialog:

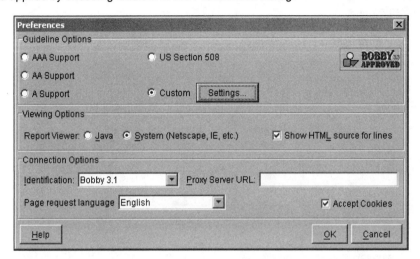

After selecting *Custom* a complete list of rules is available for selection. As you can see in the following figure, the rules are identified as being part of WCAG or Section 508, and in the former case, the priority of the checkpoint:

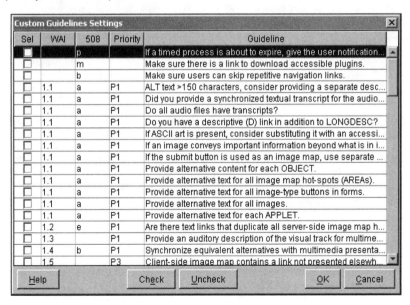

After a user is familiar with the warnings and user checks, they may not want the reports cluttered with the same reminders over and over again. If this is the case, they can select only those specific rules (there are 94 altogether) that can actually be tested by the tool. These are the rules labeled as 'full support' in earlier versions of Bobby. The rule selection interface is very compact and efficient with good information relating the rule designation (right-hand column) with the priority level and the Section 508 reference.

The Full Bobby Product

The downloadable Bobby product is a program written in Java offered for several platforms including Windows, Unix/Linux, and Solaris. There is also a generic version without any operating system specifics. The following screenshot shows the Bobby user interface having evaluated *JimThatcher.com* after the 508 rules have been chosen in the preferences (*Prefs*) dialog.

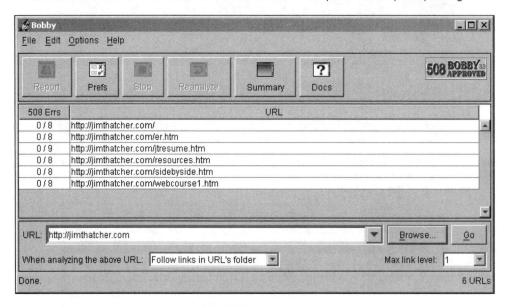

Under the heading *508 Errs* is a pair of numbers, x/y, where x is the number of errors detected and y is the number of user checks that are required; two user checks are always required for the 508 rule set. Any URL in the list of analyzed URLs can be activated to bring up the report for that page. The summary report collects together all the errors and warnings for pages that have been analyzed into one HTML document. The report first lists the issues then, for each one, the specific offending pages. The clicking on the issues will lead to the Help documents, while the URL of the offending page will open the actual page.

Trial vs. Full Version of Bobby

Important differences between the trial version of Bobby WorldWide on the Web and the full product are as follows:

- The full product will follow links and analyzing pages to particular depths – in the same folder or the same domain – without limit. This setting is conveniently placed next to the *edit* field for the URL to be analyzed.

- The "coverage" can be further tailored, so that the user can select which specific rules are applied.

- The downloadable Bobby can be used for local pages or sites, which are not live, and supports firewall proxies.

- With Bobby WorldWide the report can be made available as an XML document for custom analysis and recording.

LIFT from UsableNet

LIFT is a core semantic analysis technology that is packaged in several forms by **UsableNet** depending on the tester's needs. A web-based trial is available at the UsableNet home page *http://www.UsableNet.com*, where the tool will evaluate up to five pages, starting at a specified URL (although you can repeat this process with as many URLs as you want).

LIFT started life as a usability analyzer – first released in April 2000. It then naturally moved on to include accessibility during the following year. The incarnation of the LIFT technology that we will check out here is LIFT Online, which is a subscription-based service that costs US$249 initially, with (at the time of writing) an annual renewal fee of US$100. With LIFT Online you can run nearly unlimited tests on unlimited URLs. For any URL, the number of pages is limited to 1000, and you can schedule tests to be run periodically.

Other variations include **LIFT OnSite** (also US$249), a software-based version for the Mac OS that can be used to test local web content and sites that are under development. UsableNet has also teamed up with Macromedia to create **LIFT for Macromedia Dreamweaver** (US$249), another tool aimed at working with sites that are under development. LIFT for Macromedia Dreamweaver is available for the Mac and for Windows. Finally, **LIFT for Macromedia Dreamweaver Pro Suite** (US$349) is the next level up and includes the features of LIFT Online for scheduled testing and analysis of live sites.

LIFT Online Web-Based Trial

Unlike Bobby, the trial of LIFT Online is *not* a full function trial, in that the analysis is performed against a relatively small subset of the LIFT rule set. The resulting reports are the same, however.

To use the trial, enter a URL on the UsableNet home page along with your e-mail address (as shown in the above figure). You will then be informed by e-mail when the analysis is ready. The e-mail contains a link to the online results page. Notice that the input form requests a *Site Type*. UsableNet keeps statistics on the results of their evaluation and these statistics are available for your examination at *http://www.UsableNet.com/wui/wui_index.html*. The following figure is a partial screenshot of the LIFT OnLine Web trial result page for *http://jimthatcher.com*:

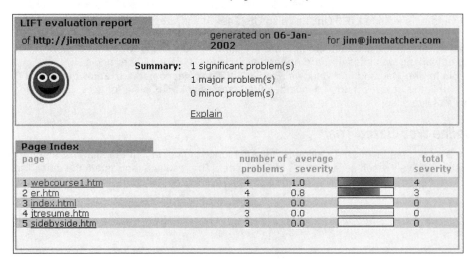

This main results page (the *Page Index*) lists all the URLs analyzed with a summary of the results found. Notice that pages are sorted by a *severity* measure. The listing also includes the number of problems reported on each page.

Results from LIFT Online (Full Product)

With the full LIFT Online product you can follow links on the *Index* page to examine page after page. The navigation scheme is simple and effective. In the screenshot below, we can see that the results of the trial of *http://jimthatcher.com* list 8 problems for `index.html`. Using the free trial version we saw just 3 because of the reduced rule set used by the free product.

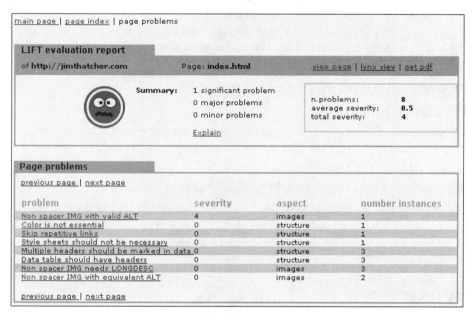

The details section lists the problems as links. If you follow any one of those links it leads to a comprehensive document explaining the problem, its source and resolution. If the problem is triggered by something specific on the page, then the document will quote the offending HTML source code. When examining a Help page, there are links to go to the next problem, back to *Page Problems* or all the way back to the *Page Index*.

Issues Raised

These correspond to the list in the *'Issues raised in the evaluation'* section for Bobby. Remember that I can't be sure of what exactly is triggering any given rule, unless the tool specifies the HTML.

Non-spacer img with valid alt.

Trigger: an image with invalid `alt` text. Provision: §1194.22(a). Not raised by Bobby. This requests a user check whether or not some existing `alt` text is in fact valid `alt` text. As discussed in the 'Text Equivalents' section above, there are certain examples of "suspicious" `alt` text and this is one of those. The trigger is an image with the word "New" and a file name `new.gif`. It is suspicious that the file name and the `alt` text are the same.

Color is not essential.

Trigger: Use of color. Provision: §1194.22(c). Also raised by Bobby.

Skip repetitive links.

Trigger: Links. Provision: §1194.22(o). Also raised by Bobby. Like Bobby, there seems to be no analysis of links that are available for positioning of text and links.

Stylesheets should not be necessary.

Trigger: Use of stylesheets. Provision: §1194.22(d). Also raised by Bobby.

Multiple headers should be marked in data tables.

Trigger: the `TABLE` *element. Provision: §1194.22(h). Not raised by Bobby. The tables on the page in question are layout tables. Raising this issue here indicates that LIFT was actually searching for data tables, so the algorithm it uses to do so is obviously quite limited. The explanation is not very good either, because headers markup, which is needed for §1194.22(h), is not mentioned in the documentation.*

Data table should have headers.

Trigger: `TABLE`*. Provision: §1194.22(g). Not raised by Bobby. See previous item. The* `headers` *attribute is mentioned here.*

Non-spacer IMG needs LONGDESC.

Trigger: non-trivial image. Provision: §1194.22(a). Also raised by Bobby.

Non-spacer IMG with equivalent ALT.

Trigger: non-trivial image. Provision: §1194.22(a). Not raised by Bobby. This rule is requiring the user to check that the valid `alt` *text is in fact equivalent; in other words that the text and the image convey the same information.*

LIFT Help Documentation

The documentation is remarkably complete. For example the link, *Non spacer IMG with valid ALT*, yields two pages of detailed explanation consisting of *Description*, *Explanation*, and *Remedies*. There is the subsection *Learn More* in the explanation, which includes many links to sources like Web Accessibility Initiative discussion list archives, J. Nielsen's Alert boxes and Section 508 guides, and this is something I have not seen in other tools. Another unique feature is the form at the bottom of the page that requests input from users on the value or importance of a particular rule.

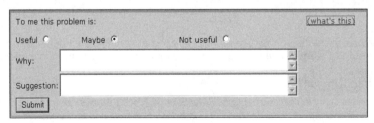

The comments collected this way are available for public scrutiny and are used by the UsableNet developers to further refine their product.

I have two issues with this otherwise excellent material. First the font size is way too small at about seven point. Second, the specific (HTML) instances or triggers for each problem are listed at the bottom of the documentation page. This is irritating to those who have used the product for some time, since you have to scroll through the Help file to find the details of the problem.

LIFT Online Customization

With the subscription purchase price of US$249, the owner is given password access to a server interface where URLs are submitted for analysis and where user preferences are set. The interface is quite similar to the free trial:

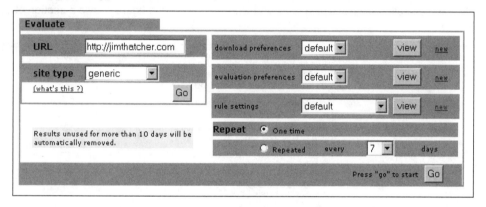

The area of the form for submitting the URL is the same as in the trial. The big difference is in the *preferences* section.

UsableNet has default settings for download preferences (how deeply it will follow links, max file size, etc.) and evaluation preferences (generally these are usability settings, like time to wait before a link is deemed broken, maximum number of characters in alt text, etc.). The *View* button opens a page containing your current preference settings. For the *Rule* preferences the *View* button opens the rules settings file indicated in the combo box. So you can view the default rule settings, the 508-Accessibility rule settings, etc.

If you follow the "*new*" link for any of these preferences groups, you are presented with a form in which you can make your own choices and then save your settings with a name. When you do that, the name you chose will appear in the select menu of the corresponding preferences dialog (you may need to refresh the main page).

The download preferences and evaluation preferences are mostly quite technical. Depending on circumstances, two items users will definitely want to change are the maximum number of pages and maximum depth of link chains. These settings are in the *Download* preferences. Remember that the related settings for Bobby are provided next to where you enter the URL of the site to be evaluated, and I feel that this is an advantage of using Bobby in comparison.

The crucial area in the preferences is the choice of rule sets. LIFT Online provides predefined rule sets called *default*, *accessibility*, *navigation*, and *508-accessibility*. Notice that the combo box in the above figure shows these rule sets and one imaginatively named Testing010802 (which I created). There are a total of 104 rules.

The `default` set consists of all rules that are not specifically to do with accessibility; these are UsableNet's usability rules. The `navigation` set consists of all rules from the default set to do with links and paths. The `accessibility` set contains all the rules labeled with the prefix `S508`, which are supposed to correspond to W3C Web Content Accessibility Priority 1 checkpoints. The *508 accessibility* rule set is the same, minus the natural language items (Checkpoint 14.1 from the Web Accessibility Initiative – *"use clear and consistent language"*, and Checkpoint 4.1 – *"identify the natural language of the document"*).

These are good rule sets, but they are not very faithful to either Section 508 or to WCAG Priority 1. As examples, the *"skip navigation"* rule (`S508 SkipRepetitiveLinks`) is included in the WCAG set, where it shouldn't be, and the rule that checks for JavaScript (`S508 NoJavascriptLinks`) is included in the 508 set, and shouldn't be. The whole point of this section of the user interface is that you can choose your own set of rules. Choose the *"new"* link and you will be offered a form for enabling and disabling exactly which rules you want. The following figure shows a section of that form:

NotValidRelativeLinks	The rule checks if the page contains relative links (URLs that don't specify protocol and server) that are not valid because they correspond to absolute link whose path starts with '../'. This rule generates major problems (severity = 3).	0 ▾	☑
NotUniqueBody	The rule checks if the page contains two or more <BODY> tags. (severity = 3).	0 ▾	☑
S508 nspIMGwValidALT	The rule implements WAI checkpoint 1.1 "Provide a text equivalent for every non-text element (e.g., via alt, longdesc, or in element content)" (guideline 1 of W3C/WAI corresponding to rule 1194.22(a) of the 508 standard). More specifically it implements checkpoint 1.1 of the W3C/WAI evaluation and repair document . This rule is a UsableNet extension that does not consider *spacer* images, that is those having one of their sizes equal to 1 or if their URL contains the words "spacer" or "bullet". The rule checks if images embedded in the page that are not used for decorative purposes only have a *valid* alternative description as an ALT attribute.	0 ▾	☐

Each rule has a name (the left-hand column), then a detailed description in the center followed by a combo box and a checkbox. The latter enables (or disables) the rule. With the combo box you can specify a weight between –3 and +3 but the purpose of that setting has escaped me to this point.

Comparison of LIFT Online and Bobby

These two tools come from very different backgrounds. Bobby is from CAST, the Center of Applied Special Technology, which is a not-for-profit organization, founded in 1984 and dedicated to *'expanding educational opportunities for individuals with disabilities through the development and innovative uses of technology.'* They have been involved with the disabilities community and the task of accessibility for a long time.

The people from CAST working on Bobby have also been involved with the Web Accessibility Initiative from the beginning. One result of this cooperation and interaction is that Bobby's rules are more faithful to the technical aspects of all levels of the Web Content Accessibility Guidelines from WAI. This is a very important characteristic because, in my view, one of the most important roles for accessibility evaluation tools is that they educate their users. If the wrong message is given, then the tool is failing in its educational role. Neither of these tools has serious flaws in this regard, but Bobby does do a better job of presenting the WCAG checkpoints and interpreting the Section 508 provisions.

LIFT, on the other hand, derives from UsableNet and that company's interest in usability. Their technology includes many interesting rules (54 to be precise) that are oriented towards general usability rather than accessibility. These include checking for broken links, checking for invalid MARQUEE elements, or for analyzing download times. The LIFT developers are not quite as close to the accessibility community, resulting in some minor misinterpretations on their part.

Rules that are not part of 508 (like *"clear and simple language"*, WCAG checkpoint 14.1) are labeled as 508 rules and they were included in the 508 default rule set (though that seems now to have been corrected). Besides the very useful usability rules, there is another up-side to the UsableNet focus on usability: LIFT Online has a very usable reporting interface – with the exception of the very small typeface! Every reporting page has a natural set of navigation links, next, previous, back to the previous level, and back to the top, to mention a few.

Contrast this with Bobby's reporting interface. Whether working from the main Bobby window or from the summary report, when you move to a report window for a specific page or to help information, the only return is with the browser's *Back* button. Another troublesome aspect of this reporting user interface is that each page report is opened in a new window, and often that new window does not receive focus.

While talking about usability here, it is only fair to mention again how inconvenient it is to modify the settings for depth of search in LIFT Online compared with Bobby. This is a change that I make frequently. Recall that Bobby's depth on analysis settings are next to the field where the URL is entered, while you must open, modify, and save a Settings file for LIFT Online to accomplish the same result.

One last comment about the rules. At the beginning of this chapter, I tried to emphasize that it was one thing to have software check for valid attributes, like valid `alt` text, but quite another – and a matter for judgment – to decide whether or not the `alt` text carries the same information as the image. LIFT Online takes that issue to the rules, having pairs of rules, one that checks for the valid attribute and a second that is raised as a user check when the attribute is valid, asking whether or not the `alt` text is equivalent. Bobby does not have this second set of rules. I would disable all these rules for my own work but it is interesting to have them show up.

Other Accessibility Testing Tools

I chose two tools to discuss here. As I said at the beginning of the chapter, the number of tools is growing. Some New and Emerging Technologies will be covered in Chapter 12. I am doing a more in-depth review of software accessibility evaluation and repair tools for the Information Technology Technical Assistance and Training Center (ITTATC) and that review should be available around May, 2002, at the ITTATC site (*http://www.ittatc.org*) and on my site, (*http://JimThatcher.com*). Here is a list of some other evaluation and repair software:

- AccessEnable by RetroAccess (*http://www.retroaccess.com*). (US$49.95 and up)

- AccVerify and AccRepair by HiSoftware (*http://www.hisoftware.com*). (US$495 - US$995 Repair)

- PageScreamer by Crunchy Technologies (*http://www.crunchy.com*) (US$2495; plug-ins available for Front Page, ColdFusion, HomeSite and Jrun Studio, $49.95).

- SSB Technologies InFocus evaluation and repair (*http://ssbtechnologies.com*). (US$899)

- A-Prompt from University of Toronto (*http://aprompt.snow.utoronto.ca/*). (Free)

These together with other versions of LIFT and Bobby will be included in the evaluation for ITTATC.

Summary

As we said at the beginning of this chapter, there is a growing number of sophisticated software tools designed to facilitate checking web content for accessibility. The basic products range in price from $50 to over $2500. According to the lists of customers on the suppliers' web sites, it is clear that federal agencies and corporations are buying into the idea of using these tools to test their sites for accessibility.

These tools are inherently limited in what they can do. All aspects of web accessibility require some human evaluation and the best that can be asked of these tools is that they facilitate the human evaluation process.

The two tools we studied carefully were developed from very different backgrounds. Bobby has a strong connection to the Web Accessibility Initiative and supports the Web Content Accessibility Guidelines in great detail. In contrast, LIFT Online, has a strong usability orientation and the tool can be very useful for addressing usability issues beyond Section 508 web accessibility.

8

Accessibility of authoring tools:

- Dreamweaver
- FrontPage
- GoLive
- HomeSite
- BBEdit

Author: Paul Bohman

Web Development Tools and Accessibility

It may be comforting to web developers to hear that they are not the only ones at fault for all of the accessibility problems on the Internet. The burden of accessibility is shared between web developers, those who design user agents, those who design assistive technologies, those who devise guidelines and standards (for example, the W3C, governments), and those who design authoring tools (for example, HTML editors). This chapter examines the current state of accessibility in modern authoring tools.

In recognition of the important role that authoring tools play in the accessibility of the final web content produced through them, the W3C formed a workgroup to formulate guidelines that software developers could implement in their authoring tools. Version 1.0 of the Authoring Tool Accessibility Guidelines was formally published on February 3, 2000. Since that time, the US Access Board has published standards for the Acquisition of Electronic and Information Technology under Section 508 of the Rehabilitation Act, which requires the US Federal government to purchase the most accessible electronic and information technology products available, including web authoring tools. The combination of these two milestones has spurred authoring tool developers to include more accessibility features in their products.

In general though, authoring tools are still in a state of transition. Some manufacturers have implemented a significant proportion of the guidelines, but none of them have fully realized their potential in this realm. Some tools seem to have ignored accessibility issues entirely. This chapter examines several authoring tools with respect to two criteria:

- conformance to the W3C authoring tool guidelines

- pitfalls to avoid

Before delving into the details of each software product, web developers should be aware of a few key points:

- Any tool can be used by an accessibility-savvy author to produce accessible content, as long as the tool preserves the designer's markup.

- Authoring tools cannot make the end result accessible; they can only assist the author to do so. Tools can guide, prompt, assist, instruct, and check for accessibility, but there is no substitute for a designer's good accessibility design skills.

- The most accessibility-advanced authoring tool can still produce inaccessible content if the designer uses the tool ignorantly or unwisely.

These three points do not negate the role or importance of accessibility-minded authoring tools. Indeed, such tools have enormous potential for transforming the Web into a truly universal medium. Rather, these points merely emphasize that no matter what tool is used and how much assistance it offers, it is still the designer's responsibility to ensure that the final result meets accessibility standards. In this sense, accountability rests squarely on the shoulders of the web developer.

It must also be noted that the accessibility potential of any particular authoring tool can be expanded by using an external accessibility validator to test the content produced by the tool. Tools such as Bobby, the WAVE, A-Prompt, InFocus, AccVerify, PageScreamer, LIFT, and others can be used to check the accessibility status of existing web content. A web developer could conceivably work with almost any authoring tool — even in an accessibility-unfriendly one — and then check the results with one of the external validators. The validator would then flag the objectively verifiable errors, allowing the developer to correct them. Although such a system wouldn't be foolproof (since automated validators are unable to accurately assess the subjective elements in the web content), it allows Web developers to work with their preferred authoring tools. A major limitation to any of these validators is that they are designed to assess and fix existing web content. Authoring tools, on the other hand, can be designed to reduce or prevent the occurrence of accessibility errors while the content is still being created. This is the unique role and potential strength of accessibility-minded authoring tools.

Defining Accessibility for Authoring Tools

In terms of accessibility, authoring tools should do two things:

- Permit, support, and encourage the creation of accessible content

- Allow authors with disabilities to use the tool

The first 6 of the W3C's Authoring Tool Accessibility Guidelines (*http://www.w3.org/TR/ATAG10/*) deal with the creation of accessible content, and the last guideline deals with the tool's accessibility to authors with disabilities as shown in the table opposite:

ATAG Guidelines 1.0	
1	Support accessible authoring practices
2	Generate standard markup
3	Support the creation of accessible content (Guide the author to produce accessible content)
4	Provide ways of checking and correcting inaccessible content
5	Integrate accessibility solutions into the overall "look and feel"
6	Promote accessibility in Help and documentation
7	Ensure that the authoring tool is accessible to authors with disabilities

Support accessible authoring practices

Authoring tools should preserve any accessibility information added by the author in the markup. Any markup which is automatically generated by the tool should conform to existing accessibility guidelines.

Generate standard markup

Browsers have been programmed to be very forgiving of sloppy, inaccurate, or incomplete HTML markup. Unfortunately, this has allowed web developers to produce documents that do not meet any published standards. Most pages on the Web today fail miserably when parsed through markup validators such as the W3C's online markup validator (*http://validator.w3.org*). While this may seem harmless on the surface, it is often the users of assistive technologies who suffer the consequences of lazy or ignorant web developers. Assistive technologies often depend on the accuracy of the markup in order to present the content faithfully to the user. Poorly-coded web content can sometimes be frustratingly difficult – perhaps even impossible – to comprehend when accessed through assistive technologies.

Valid markup begins with a DOCTYPE declaration at the beginning of the document. The DOCTYPE declaration provides a standard against which to compare the document's markup. The idea is to then write markup which conforms to the declared DOCTYPE.

> *By including a DOCTYPE, you make it possible to create markup that validates to a standard. Having valid markup increases the chance that your pages will be rendered consistently and correctly across browsers, platforms, and assistive technologies. In some cases, nonstandard markup is totally inaccessible to people who depend on assistive technologies. There are three basic DOCTYPES for HTML/XHTML: strict, transitional, and frameset. The frameset DOCTYPE is reserved for frameset documents. The transitional DOCTYPES allow authors to use some deprecated (outdated) tags, such as <font>, <b>, <i>, and <center>. The strict DOCTYPES allow only current, non-deprecated tags.*

Support the creation of accessible content (Guide the author to produce accessible content)

Authoring tools should prompt the user to include markup and attributes which increase the accessibility of the content.

Provide ways of checking and correcting inaccessible content.

Once content and markuphave been entered into the document, the author should be able to verify that no accessibility errors were introduced. If the tool finds any errors, it should flag them and allow the author to correct them.

Integrate accessibility solutions into the overall "look and feel"

If the accessibility features of a tool are hidden or unintuitive, they will rarely be used.

Promote accessibility in help and documentation

The accessibility features of the tool should be well documented, and this documentation should be integrated with the rest of the documentation for the software.

Ensure that the authoring tool is accessible to authors with disabilities

The software should conform to operating system conventions for accessibility, allowing assistive technologies to access the features and functionality of the program.

WYSIWYG Markup Editors

In this chapter, we'll take a look at three WYSIWYG editors: Dreamweaver, FrontPage, and GoLive, and at two text-based editors: BBEdit and HomeSite. I have rated each of these editors in terms of their compliance with the WAI Authoring Tool Guidelines, version 1.0, where four stars is the highest rating. Admitedly, my ratings are subjective – they're just my opinion – but I explain my rationale after each rating that I give.

Before looking at the individual authoring tools, we ought to identify some issues and pitfalls which many of them have in common.

Content Linearization

Content linearization refers to the literal reading order of the content when all of the markup tags are removed. Despite all of the layout tables, CSS positioning, or any other formatting elements, screen readers read the content as if none of the markup were there at all. Under certain circumstances, which we'll discuss below, the visual layout can differ substantially from the underlying order of the content in the markup. This means that screen readers may read the content out of order, possibly rendering it incomprehensible. In web authoring tools, there are three common instances in which content linearization can become a major issue: in layout tables, CSS layout, and image map hot spots.

Layout Tables

Although tables were not meant to perform the function of visual layout, most web designers use tables for just that purpose. As long as the content makes sense when all of the table tags are removed, there is little to worry about. However, if the visual order differs from the linearized order, this can cause serious problems for screen readers. For example, in the table layout opposite, where each box represents a table cell, the visual users will read "*It could happen to YOU*!" Screen reader users, however, will hear the words in the order that they appear in the markup. In this case, they will hear "TO happen It could YOU". It's important to double-check the reading order of layout table cells.

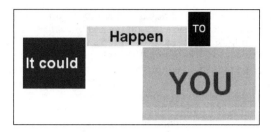

Below is the markup for the above table (note: I have simplified it somewhat, removing font and background styles). Notice the literal order of the actual content. This is the order in which screen readers will read it.

```
<table width="50%" border="0">
  <tr>
      <td width="29%"> </td>
      <td colspan="2"> </td>
      <td rowspan="3" width="9%">
        <div>TO</td>
      <td width="21%"> </td>
  </tr>
  <tr>
      <td width="29%" ></td>
      <td colspan="2" rowspan="2">
        <div>Happen</td>
      <td width="21%" rowspan="2"> </td>
  </tr>
  <tr>
      <td rowspan="2">
        <div>It could</td>
  </tr>
  <tr>
      <td width="24%"> </td>
      <td colspan="3" rowspan="2" size="7">YOU</td>
  </tr>
  <tr>
      <td width="29%"> </td>
      <td width="24%"> </td>
  </tr>
</table>
```

The WAVE online validator, available at *http://www.temple.edu/inst_disabilities/piat/wave/*, provides a method of checking the reading order of table cells, no matter which authoring tool was used to create them.

CSS Layout

Some of the WYSIWIG authoring tools allow the author to use CSS styles and attributes to create layout effects on a page. Most of these effects are achieved through the use of absolute-positioned div tags. Both Dreamweaver and GoLive, for example, have this capability. Dreamweaver refers to them as "layers" and GoLive calls them "Floating Text Boxes". Although the W3C recommends the use of CSS, rather than tables, for layout, there are certain pitfalls to be aware of with the CSS layout utilities in authoring tools.

Absolute Units. First of all, anything that has an absolute height or width has the potential to cause problems for people with low vision who must enlarge the viewing area. If, for example, the user enlarges the font size within Internet Explorer or Netscape, the text will become bigger even though the surrounding `div` element does not. In small `div` elements, this may cause unusual line breaks in the text and may even cause individual words to wrap from one line to another. In some cases, the text is eclipsed by other `div` elements, or overlaps with text elsewhere on the page. Any of these scenarios reduces the readability of the document. One remedy for this problem is to designate percentages rather than pixels for width and position. In the Dreamweaver screenshot below, you can see that the left (*L*) and top (*T*) positions of the `div` element are absolute (at *99px* from the left of the window and *457* pixels from the top), and that the width (*W*) is a percentage (*200%*), although in this case, the height (*H*) remains absolute (*16* pixels):

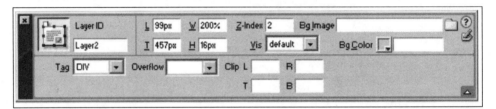

Reading Order. Both Dreamweaver and GoLive allow the `div` elements to be visually rearranged to any location within the document. Such flexibility can produce great visual results, but can wreak havoc for the person using a screen reader. As with table cells, screen readers ignore the visual layout of the content, reading it instead in a linearized format. Often, the visual layout and the markup reading order do not match. This means that the screen reader user may hear the contents of different `div` elements read in a completely nonsensical order, especially if the web designer uses a WYSIWYG tool's interface to rearrange the layers once they are created. The same problem occurs when portions of a web page are contained within absolute-positioned `div` elements and other portions are not. The screen reader user may hear the copyright information read first, followed by a navigational menu item, a paragraph of text, then another menu item, followed by another paragraph of text which is not related to the first one, and so on. It can be difficult or impossible to comprehend the content of pages when the linear reading order does not match the visual reading order.

Tab Order. Absolute-positioned `div` elements affect the tab order of a document in the same way that they affect the reading order. If there are links, form elements, or other elements which receive the focus of the keyboard when tabbing through the page, the default tab order is determined by the order of the elements in the markup. In a worse-case scenario, someone using only a keyboard to navigate may get lost or become disoriented while trying to navigate to a particular link on the page. It is also worth mentioning that, due to a bug in the Netscape software, documents become completely inaccessible by keyboard in Netscape browsers when absolute-positioned `div` elements are present.

The document opposite was created in a WYSIWYG tool using absolute-positioned `div` elements. Each `div` element is labeled in the order that it was created. Without changing the order of the `div` elements in the markup itself, this is also the order that screen readers will read the layers:

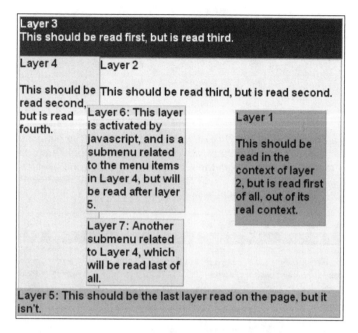

Here is the markup for the visual layout above (note: I have omitted the CSS positioning details and JavaScript for the sake of simplicity).

```
<div style="div1">
<p>Layer 1</p>
<p>This should be read in the context of layer 2, but is read first of all, out of
its real context.</p>
<div>
<div style="div2">
<p>Layer 2</p>
<p>This should be read third, but is read second.</p>
<div>
<div style="div3">
     <p>Layer 3</p>
<p>This should be read first, but is read third.</p>
<div>
<div style="div4">
     <p>Layer 4</p>
<p>This should be read second, but is read fourth.</p>
<div>
<div style="div5">
     <p>Layer 5</p>
<p>This should be the last layer read on the page, but it isn't.</p>
<div>
<div style="div6">
     <p>Layer 6</p>
<p>This layer is activated by javascript, and is a submenu item related to the
menu items in Layer 4, but will be read after layer 5.</p>
<div>
```

```
<div style="div7">
    <p>Layer 7</p>
<p>Another submenu related to Layer 4, which will be read last of all.</p>
<div>
<div style="div1">
<div>
```

Image Map Hot Spots

Image maps pose a problem similar to that of absolute-positioned `div` elements. The tab order of the image hot spots is dependent upon the order in which the hot spots are created. If the hot spots are created in an order which differs from the logical viewing order, the user will see the focus jump erratically from one hot spot to another. The screenshot below illustrates how the order in the markup may not correspond to the logical viewing order:

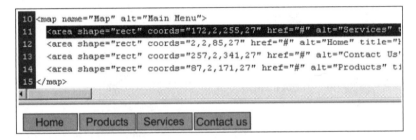

DHTML

Some authoring tools boast powerful DHTML capabilities. Unfortunately, this hybrid of HTML and JavaScript can cause problems for individuals with disabilities.

Keyboard Accessibility. The most likely pitfall of DHTML behaviors is that keyboard-dependent users and those using screen readers will not be able to access the content. Although most modern screen readers access web content via JavaScript-enabled mainstream web browsers, (for example, Internet Explorer), if the DHTML depends on the use of a mouse, the content will be inaccessible to those who cannot use them. JavaScript event handlers such as `onMouseOver` cannot be activated by the keyboard. Pop-up or dropdown DHTML menus which depend on this action will never be read by the screen reader, even if it is capable of reading the JavaScript, because such menus will never be activated at all without the use of a mouse. DHTML "Drag and drop" funtionality on a web page is another mouse-centric accessibility problem, with no easy solution. Sometimes the only solution is to provide an equivalent page with comparable content.

Dynamic Content. If the content or appearance of one part of the document can change based upon the user's actions in another part of the document, the screen reader user is unlikely to know that any change has taken place. This technique is sometimes used with form elements, where the user's input in the first form element determines the contents of the next form element, and so on until the user completes the form. Visual users will probably see the change immediately, but users who are blind do not have the benefit of visual feedback, and so may be unaware that any change occurred. Often, links are scripted to perform a function on the same page, rather than taking the user to a different page. It can be disorienting when users who are visually impaired click on a link and nothing seems to happen. They expect a link to take them to a different page, rather than call a JavaScript function which takes them nowhere.

Seizures. If the DHTML causes areas of the page to flicker or blink, the page may induce a seizure or nausea in some individuals.

Distractibility. Some individuals with attention deficit disorders, learning disorders, or cognitive disorders can become easily distracted by moving or dynamic content.

No JavaScript. Lastly, not every person with a disability can or chooses to use JavaScript-enabled browsers. Sometimes, the best browser for an individual is one that can only read the HTML elements of web pages. For these individuals, JavaScripted content will never be accessible. The only solution in this case is to provide comparable content in a `<noscript>` tag, or in another easily accessible page.

JavaScript-Activated Form-Based Menus

Different authoring tools have different names for forms with this type of functionality. Dreamweaver calls them "Jump Menus" and GoLive calls them "URL Pop-ups". The JavaScript causes the page to automatically jump to predetermined destinations when the end user selects an option from the drop-down menu, thus bypassing the need to click on a *submit* button. These jump menus can be convenient for individuals using a mouse, but terribly frustrating for someone using a keyboard. The jump menu behaves quite differently for users who navigate with only a keyboard. Rather than allowing the user to scroll down the list of options, the JavaScript causes the page to immediately jump to the first item that the user scrolls through when using the arrow keys on a keyboard. If there are 10 items on a list, the user will likely not be able to select the third, fourth, or fifth item, because the page will have already jumped to the first or second item in the list. Some operating systems have keyboard shortcuts that allow the user to scroll through the list without being forced to jump to the item which receives the focus first, but these shortcuts are so obscure that it would be unfair to assume that users know them.

Self-Refreshing Pages

Some tools have pre-packaged JavaScript code which causes the page to refresh itself at an author-specified interval. Pages that automatically refresh or that redirect to other pages can disorient users who are blind, and can sometimes render the pages unusable to them. When a page refreshes, screen readers begin reading the page from the top again. In some cases, the screen reader never reaches important sections of these self-refreshing web pages before the pages refresh once again. If at all possible, it is best to avoid self-refreshing web pages.

Multimedia Objects

None of the authoring tools mentioned in this chapter have any built-in utilities to make multimedia objects more accessible.

- **Videos** should have synchronized captioning and/or transcripts. A free, external tool, called MAGpie, can aid authors in providing captions for video content (*http://ncam.wgbh.org/webaccess/magpie/*). We will be seeing more of this tool in Chapter 12.

- **Flash and Shockwave** objects need accessible alternatives. Flash is completely inaccessible to most screen readers, although Macromedia just recently announced that Flash MX has utilities to make Flash content accessible to users of the Window-Eyes screen reader. Even so, it is still necessary to provide an alternative format for any Flash content to account for those using other technologies. Perhaps this will become less of a necessity over time as other screen readers add Flash compatibility. One important consideration is that, just as with HTML pages, there is no guarantee that Flash objects will be accessible, even if they can be made accessible. It will likely be quite some time before authors of Flash content catch the accessibility spirit, since they have been unable to create accessible Flash content for so long. We will be illustrating ways in which Flash content can be made accessible in Chapter 10.

- **Audio** elements need transcripts.

- **PDF** files can be made accessible to users of JAWS and WindowEyes, but not through any markup editor. Authors can only do so by using the utilities in the full commercial version of Adobe Acrobat. Just as with Flash, even though the possibility of accessible PDF files exists, a more inclusive approach is to provide HTML/XHTML versions along with the PDF version.

- **Other plug-ins** will generally require that the author provide an accessible version in HTML/XHTML format.

Overconfidence in the Accessibilty Features of the Authoring Tool

One of the most dangerous pitfalls of any authoring tool, especially those with built-in accessibility features, is the danger of overconfidence in the tool's accessibility features. Web authoring tools generally cannot create captioned video for the deaf, nor provide multimedia transcripts for the deaf-blind. Authoring tools cannot test the usability of the site, nor ensure that there are sufficient illustrations for those with learning disabilities, or that the illustrations are good enough to serve their purpose. Much is still left up to the designer, and this is where the final responsibility will always lie.

Now that we've covered some of the important general principles, let's take a look at some specific authoring tools.

Dreamweaver

Macromedia's Dreamweaver has become a staple in the web development community. As with most other authoring tool products, early versions of Dreamweaver did not focus on accessibility issues at all. Since that time, Macromedia has made a public commitment to the principles of accessibility, and has begun to revise its products accordingly. At the time of the writing this chapter, Dreamweaver MX was in beta development. This version shows the most promise of any Dreamweaver product yet, from an accessibility standpoint. Let's now look at how well Dreamweaver and Dreamweaver MX conform to the seven authoring tool guidelines.

Supporting Accessible Authoring

Guideline 1: Support accessible authoring practices.

One of the strengths of Dreamweaver is that the software preserves any markup created by the author in the Code View, thus allowing designers to include accessibility features which cannot be created through Dreamweaver's WYSIWYG interface. In this sense, it is always possible to create accessible web content with Dreamweaver. Until Dreamweaver MX, however, you could not input any accessibility-specific tags or attributes through the WYSIWIG interface, except for the image `alt` attribute. All of the accessibility markup had to be done in the Code View.

The user can customize Dreamweaver's code rewriting behavior through the Preferences dialog box: Edit | Preferences | Code Rewriting.

Rating (out of 4 stars):	
Dreamweaver 4.0:	☆ ☆ ☆
Dreamweaver MX	☆ ☆ ☆ ⯪

Generating Standard Markup

Guideline 2: Generate standard markup.

Nearly all of the markup which Dreamweaver produces is standards-compliant by default. The most notable exception is that the default template in versions 1.0 through 4.0 does not include a DOCTYPE declaration. The default DOCTYPE in Dreamweaver MX is HTML 4.0 Transitional, with the option to set XTHML 1.0 Transitional as the default (*Preferences | New Document*). In all versions 1.0 through 4.0, you can manually type in a DOCTYPE statement on each page individually, but a more efficient method would be to edit the default document template to include the DOCTYPE of your choice. Under a default installation of Dreamweaver 4.0 in Windows, the template is found at *C:\Program Files\Macromedia\Dreamweaver 4\Configuration\Templates*. You can edit the template within Dreamweaver itself and then save it. Each new document thereafter will include the your edits. Another option is to install a free Dreamweaver extension called "Super HTML–XHTML DTD" (available through the Macromedia web site at *http://www.macromedia.com/exchange/dreamweaver/*) developed by Digital Media Dreamwarrior, which allows the author to specify different DOCTYPEs for each document. The extension includes HTML and XHTML DOCTYPEs, along with options for encoding, xmlns and lang attributes.

Dreamweaver MX has a built-in HTML/XHTML validator which produces a report of markup errors which you can then correct.

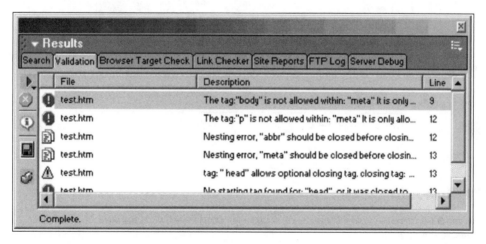

You also have the option of having all invalid markup highlighted in the Code View (*View | Code View Options | Highlight Invalid HTML*). In all previous versions of Dreamweaver, the markup can still be validated using the W3C's free online validator at *http://validator.w3.org*.

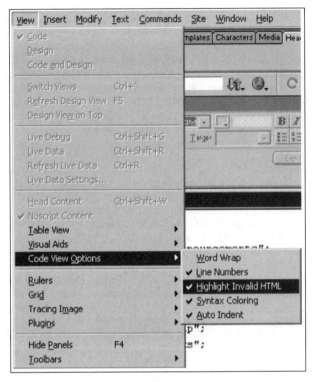

Rating (out of 4 stars):	
Dreamweaver 4.0:	☆ ☆ ☆
Dreamweaver MX:	☆ ☆ ☆ ☆

Creating Accessible Content

Guideline 3: Support the creation of accessible content. (Guide the author to produce accessible content.)

Macromedia has added an array of accessibility features to the latest version of Dreamweaver which guide the user in producing accessible content. You can activate a feature which prompts you to input accessibility information for form elements, frames, objects, images, and tables (*Edit / Preferences / Accessibility*):

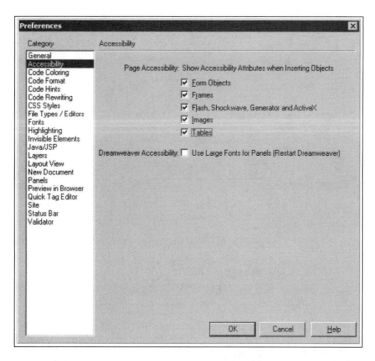

When this feature is activated, context-appropriate dialog boxes pop up, in which you can add such things as alternative text for images, labels for form elements, titles for frames, row or column headers for tables, and so on.

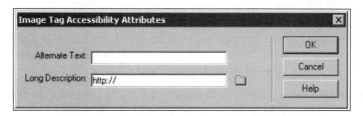

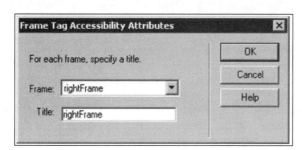

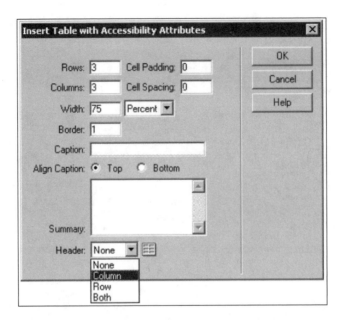

These dialog boxes help you to remember to input important accessibility tags and attributes. It is unfortunate that these settings (in the beta version) are not activated by default. The author must manually activate them through the preferences dialog box.

The accessibility status of Dreamweaver 4.0 is much less impressive than the newer version. Dreamweaver 4.0 was not built to guide the author to produce accessible content. Its accessibility features are few and unimpressive. Nearly all accessibility-related markup must be typed directly in the Code View, and cannot be created through the WYSIWYG interface (Design View).

Fortunately, the program preserves intact any accessible markup which you hand-code, but since the majority of accessibility features must be hand-coded, this reduces Dreamweaver 4.0 to little more than a plain text editor where accessibility is concerned. The only important accessibility feature available through the WYSIWYG interface is the image properties palette (see screenshot below), through which you can add `alt` attributes to image tags. Other features indirectly linked to accessibility which are readily available through this WYSIWYG interface include the CSS editor (*Window / CSS Styles*), relative font sizes (*Text / Size Change*), and abbreviation and acronym tags (*Text / Style*).

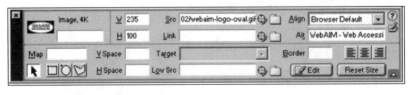

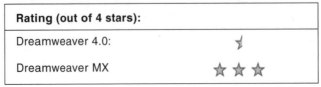

Rating (out of 4 stars):	
Dreamweaver 4.0:	½
Dreamweaver MX	★ ★ ★

Assessing and Repairing Content

Guideline 4: Provide ways of checking and correcting inaccessible content.

Dreamweaver 4.0 does not ship with any built-in method of checking or correcting accessible content. However, you can install certain Dreamweaver extensions which perform this function within Dreamweaver. In my evaluation of the Dreamweaver MX beta, it was unclear whether Dreamweaver MX would ship with a built-in accessibility validator, although some of the documentation suggested that it would.

The "Check Page for Accessibility" Extension.

The developers at Macromedia were among the first to create an accessibility extension for Dreamweaver. This extension parses a web page and generates an HTML report of any errors which it catches. It is like a "Bobby lite", and is of questionable value, since nearly every other accessibility checker, including Bobby, is superior to Macromedia's.

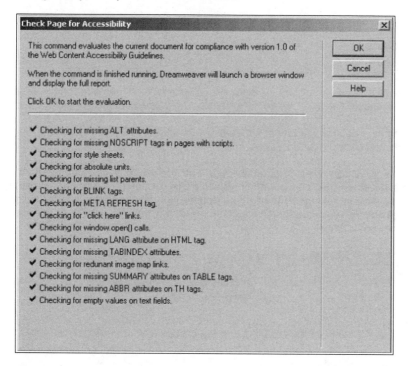

The "Section 508 Accessibility Suite" extension.

The developers at *UsableNet.com* created this accessibility validator, which adds an "*Accessibility*" item to Dreamweaver's main menu.

The extension operates in two basic modes. In the "*Evaluate and Fix*" mode, the extension parses the file, flags potential problem areas, and highlights those areas in the document's markup. You can then alter the markup in the Code View.

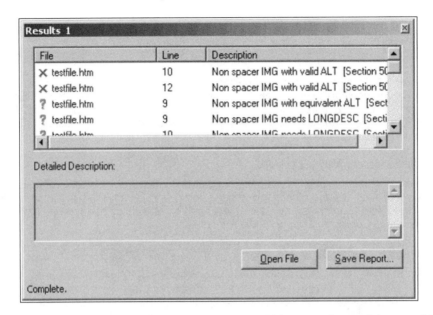

The 508 Accessibility Suite allows the author to specify which types of potential accessibility errors the extension should flag.

In addition to accessibility validation, it can also validate the HTML and produce reports on the design notes and checkout status of each file.

The 508 Accessibility Suite also has an **Explain and Fix mode**. This can be particularly useful to those who are just learning about web accessibility. This mode provides brief explanations as to why a certain area was flagged up on the web page. Although the extension will not automatically correct any of the errors, the explanations give a context within which you can make informed choices about any necessary corrections.

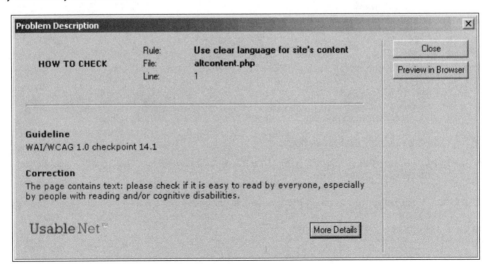

The "Accessible Image" extension

This simple extension replaces the default "*Insert image*" dialog box with one that prompts the author to add a "*Short Text Description*" (`alt` attribute) or the "*Location of Longer Description*" (`longdesc` attribute). Only users of Dreamweaver 4.0 should consider installing this extension since this functionality is already built into Dreamweaver MX. This increases the visibility of the need for an `alt attribute`, but does not force you to include one. If you leave the `alt` attribute blank, the extension automatically inserts a `null alt` attribute (`alt=""`). This is unfortunate, because a `null alt attribute` is usually insufficient to describe images, especially if they are used as links. With a `null alt` attribute in place, most accessibility validators will not flag the `null alt` attribute as an error even if it is inappropriate. They have no way of knowing if the `alt` attribute has been intentionally left blank or if it was an accident. This can deceive web developers into believing they have created accessible web content, when, in fact, they have not. Nevertheless, if the author diligently types in `alt` attributes when inserting images, this extension may be of value.

A `null alt` attribute can be appropriate under some circumstances, for example, if the image is a spacer GIF or a meaningless decorative graphic.

Rating (out of 4 stars):	
Dreamweaver 4.0:	Zero
Dreamweaver MX	Not Rated

Integrated Accessibility Solutions

Guideline 5: Integrate accessibility solutions into the overall "look and feel".

In the latest version of Dreamweaver, the developers have done a good job of integrating the accessibility features into the main interface of the software. The main drawback is that, as mentioned earlier, the accessibility features are not activated upon installation. You have to activate them manually. Most of the third-party accessibility extensions integrate quite well into the overall look and feel of the software as well.

Rating (out of 4 stars):	
Dreamweaver 4.0	N/A
Dreamweaver MX	☆ ☆ ☆

Promoting Accessibility

Guideline 6. Promote accessibility in help and documentation.

Rating (out of 4 stars):	
Dreamweaver 4.0	Zero
Dreamweaver MX	☆ ☆ ⸱

Although the beta version used in preparing this chapter did not have complete documentation, there were already numerous references to the program's new accessibility features. Dreamweaver 4.0 contains no accessibility documentation. The explanations and Help in the 508 Accessibility Suite extension are quite good, especially in the "Explain and Fix" mode.

Accessibility of the Tool

Guideline 7: Ensure that the authoring tool is accessible to authors with disabilities.

Keyboard-Dependent Users

Dreamweaver is largely keyboard-accessible, but has some deficiencies. Significantly, tables and layers, once created, cannot be accessed in the Design View without the use of a mouse. They can be accessed and modified through the Code View, however. DHTML timelines and behaviors are likewise inaccessible without a mouse in the Design View. The HTML reference guide, Assets, Templates, Library, and some of the other separate windows have some keyboard-accessible elements, none of which can be activated without first using a mouse. In some cases, some of this functionality can be accessed through the main menu system, which is keyboard-accessible, but other parts are entirely mouse-dependent. In short, among individuals who cannot use a mouse, those who feel comfortable manipulating the markup in the Code View will be most successful.

Visually Impaired Users

Dreamweaver 4.0 is quite accessible to full-featured screen readers such as JAWS and Window-Eyes. At the time of this writing, however, there were still some unresolved issues with JAWS 4.01 and Windows 2000, in which JAWS would read the menu items but not the author's input into either the Design View or the Code View. Macromedia claimed to be working with the software engineers at Freedom Scientific to resolve this problem. Except for this version and platform issue, nearly all of the program's features are available through Dreamweaver's main menu system, including the Design View and the Code View, although the visual cues in the Design View (such as the dotted line around form elements) are lost to screen reader users. Also, the keyboard accessibility deficiencies mentioned above will be of concern to the blind, since most cannot effectively use a mouse.

Rating (out of 4 stars):	
Dreamweaver 4.0	☆ ☆ ⯨
Dreamweaver MX	☆ ☆ ⯨

Pitfalls To Avoid in Dreamweaver

Pitfall 1. – Layers

Dreamweaver allows the user to create absolute-positioned `div` elements on a page, using CSS attributes for background color and other style attributes. Dreamweaver refers to these `div` elements as "layers" because you can arrange them so that they appear to be visually stacked on top of each other. The main pitfalls of these absolute-positioned `div` elements, as mentioned previously in this chapter are:

- The use of absolute units which may be difficult for those who enlarge the font

- The fact that the content may not linearize correctly, causing inconsistencies in the reading order for screen readers and the tab order for those who do not use a mouse

The default "layer" tag is `div`, *but Dreamweaver allows the author to specify* `<span>`, `<layer>`, *or* `<ilayer>` *tags instead.*

Pitfall 2: DHTML Behaviors and Timelines

As mentioned previously in this chapter, DHTML can cause problems for those who do not have JavaScript enabled, for those who cannot use a mouse, and for screen reader users who may become disoriented when content changes. Dreamweaver has some built-in behaviors which can be inserted into the markup. Whenever any of these behaviors are used to convey important content, it is imperative that you do the following:

- **Include a** `<noscript>` **tag** with any relevant content, links, or explanations.

- **Ensure that the page is still keyboard-accessible**. If the DHTML is not keyboard-accessible, then an accessible alternative must be provided. Oft-times this is accomplished by creating a text link which provides the same functionality either on the same page or a subsequent page.

Dreamweaver Timelines can be used to animate page content in many ways, making it move, appear, disappear, and morph into other forms. Screen reader users will likely be oblivious to most of this. Their screen readers cannot tell them what is happening visually on the page. If the animations are important to comprehending the page content, some alternative must be provided. If the timelines cause fast movements, authors run the risk of inducing seizures, or, even more likely, of frustrating those who do not have the neuromuscular control and cannot move quickly enough to use the page.

Pitfall 3: Shockwave/Flash Objects, Flash Text, and Flash Buttons

Dreamweaver has built-in support for the creation of simple Flash text and Flash navigation buttons (available from the "*common*" tab of the Objects palette in Dreamweaver 4.0, and from the "*Media*" tab in Dreamweaver MX). You can also use the Dreamweaver menu to easily insert externally-created Flash objects into the eb page. Notwithstanding the release of Flash MX, which claims to allow the creation of content compatible with some screen readers, Flash objects of any kind are potentially problematic for screen reader users and for those who cannot use a mouse. Macromedia has not announced screen reader support for Shockwave.

Alternatives. For simple Flash and Shockwave objects, it may be sufficient to provide a text alternative in the page itself. For complex objects, it is usually necessary to provide an alternative page with equivalent content and functionality.

Keyboard accessibility. Both Flash and Shockwave objects can be programmed to be keyboard-accessible within themselves, but keyboard users will find that Flash objects allow the user to tab into them, but once they are in the Flash object, they cannot tab out of them. Users become stuck in the Flash or Shockwave object. Anything after these objects, then, becomes unnavigable.

Pitfall #4: Miscellaneous Images without alt Attributes

Even in Dreamweaver MX with the accessibility options enabled, there are instances in which Dreamweaver does not prompt the author to include an `alt` attribute with images. This occurs with the "rollover image" feature, the "image placeholder" feature, and "navigation bar".

FrontPage

Microsoft's FrontPage has been a popular web development tool, especially among non-programmers. Its interface is reminiscent of a word processor, and most of its features are relatively easy to learn. Although early versions of FrontPage were not very disability-friendly, recent versions have improved in this area, allowing authors to create disability-accessible content.

Supporting Accessible Authoring

Guideline 1. Support accessible authoring practices.

Early versions of FrontPage had a reputation of altering the source code against the designer's wishes. Fortunately, more recent versions preserve your hand-coded markup, including any accessibility enhancements. Authors who feel comfortable working directly with the markup will be able to use FrontPage to create accessible content.

On the down side, the pre-coded templates included with FrontPage do not reflect accessible design practices. Designers will need to edit the templates in order to comply with accessibility guidelines.

Rating (out of 4 stars):
☆ ☆ ⸰

Generating Standard Markup

Guideline 2. Generate standard markup.

The default HTML page template does not include a `DOCTYPE` statement, so the author must type one in the markup, or else modify the default template to include a `DOCTYPE`. Under a routine installation in Windows, the default template can be found at:

C:\Program Files\Microsoft Office XP\Templates\1033\Pages\normal.tem.

Once this template is modified, all new files will include these modifications. There is no built-in method of validating the markup, but external utilities, such as the W3C validator (*http://validator.w3.org*) can be used.

A significant weakness of FrontPage 2002 is its lack of support for XHTML. You can hand-code XHTML-style markup without risk of having FrontPage altering it, but FrontPage itself cannot generate XHTML. In fact, a search through the Help file (using the trusty Office Assistant animated paper clip) resulted in no search results.

Another significant issue is Microsoft's implementation of VML (Vector Markup Language), invented by a group of programmers mostly from Microsoft, with input from programmers at Hewlett-Packard, Macromedia, Autodesk Inc., and Visio Corporation. This group submitted their proposal to the W3C for consideration in 1998, but the W3C has since turned its attention to another language instead: SVG, or Scaleable Vector Graphics, which was formally released as a W3C recommendation in 2001. The W3C never did endorse VML as a standard. In fact, Microsoft's Internet Explorer is the only browser capable of displaying VML, and FrontPage is the only major web authoring tool supporting its creation. One of the dangers in FrontPage's use of VML is that most users will not realize that they are generating VML when they enter into drawing mode. Designers will not realize that they are creating content which cannot be interpreted by assistive technologies. More specifically, FrontPage generates two versions of the graphics. The first version, for Internet Explorer, is created in VML. The second version, for every other browser, generates some simple alternative graphics in GIF format. As it turns out, the alternative version is the only one that can be made accessible to screen readers, which is unfortunate, since most screen readers work best with Internet Explorer.

Rating (out of 4 stars):
☆ ☆

Creating Accessible Content

> *Guideline 3: Support the creation of accessible content. (Guide the author to produce accessible content.)*

Most of the disability-related markup can be added through the WYSIWYG interface, but none of it is prominently-placed or in any way suggestive of the idea of disability access. For example, it is possible to add an `alt` attribute to an image, but FrontPage does not prompt you to do so when the image is inserted. After the image is in place, you have to right click on the image, select *Picture Properties*, then select the *General* tab, then go to *Alternative Representations* then add the `alt` text to the input labeled *Text*. This process is too complex and obscure for such a basic accessibility function.

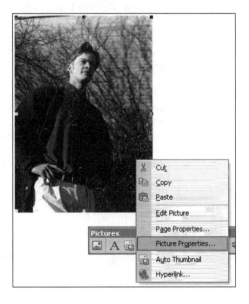

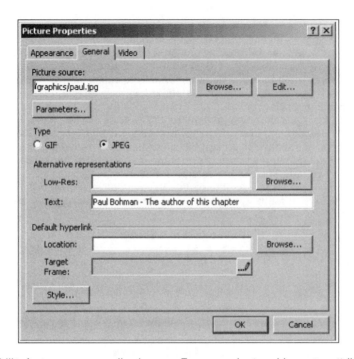

Other accessibility features are equally obscure. For example, to add an `alt` attribute to the VML graphics created in FrontPage, you have to right-click on the shape, then choose either *Format Autoshape* or *Autoshape* (the actual menu name differs depending on the type of item selected), then click on the *Web* tab, then add text in the *Alternative Text* input area.

> *It seems strange that Microsoft would create a tab called "Web" since the whole purpose of using FrontPage is to create Web content. The tab title is ambiguous, at best.*

It must be noted that the `alt` attribute for VML content in Internet Explorer will not be read by most screen readers, since VML is not supported. In all other browsers, where the VML image is replaced with a GIF image, the `alt` attribute is applied properly and will work with screen readers.

FrontPage allows authors to add `<label>` and `<fieldset>` tags to **forms**, although there is no indication that these are features that may be helpful to individuals with disabilities. To add a `<fieldset>` tag, select *Insert | Form | Group Box*. Adding a label is a bit more involved. You have to first create a form element (for example, an input, textbox, radio, checkbox tag), then type the text of the label next to the form element, then select both the form element and the text so that both are highlighted. At this point, you have to select *Insert | Form | Label* from the main menu. You can also specify the **tab order** of form elements by right-clicking on them, then selecting the *Properties* menu item, and entering a number in the *Tab order* field.

You can also create table header rows and columns, but there is no way within the WYSIWIG to associate the cells with their headers. To designate header rows or columns, highlight the appropriate headers, right-click, then select *cell properties*. Check the checkbox under *Layout* entitled *Header cell*. You have to go into the markup to add `scope`, `axis`, or `headers` attributes to cells.

`alt` attributes for image map hot spots can be added at the same time that the hot spot is created. After designating the hot spot area, a dialog box will appear in which you can select the link destination. In the upper right-hand corner is a button labeled *Screen Tip* which brings up another dialog box in which to enter the `alt` text. Care must be taken to ensure that the keyboard tab order through the image map is logical. The tab order reflects the literal order in which the `<area>` tags appear in the markup. If necessary, you can rearrange the order of the `<area>` tags in the markup to ensure a logical tab order and screen reading order.

There is no way to add a title to frames in the WYSIWYG. You have to do this by hand by selecting the "*Frames Page HTML*" tab from the bottom left of the WYSIWYG interface, then typing in the frame titles:

You can add no-frames content by selecting the *No Frames* tab from the same area.

Rating (out of 4 stars):
☆ ☆ ☆

Assessing and Repairing Content

Guideline 4: Provide ways of checking and correcting inaccessible content.

There is no built-in utility to check for or correct inaccessible content, but HiSoftware has created a free, downloadable validator, called **AccVerify SE** for FrontPage, available at: *http://www.hisoftware.com/msacc/index.html.*This is the "lite" version of their commercial products AccVerify and AccRepair for FrontPage. AccVerify SE is similar to UsableNet's 508 Accessibility Suite for Dreamweaver, except that AccVerify SE does not highlight the errors within the document itself; it merely produces a report of the errors and the line numbers on which they occur. AccVerify SE can be customized to check for conformance to either the W3C guidelines 1.0 or to Section 508 standards. As shown below, you can also choose which specific types of errors to display in the report:

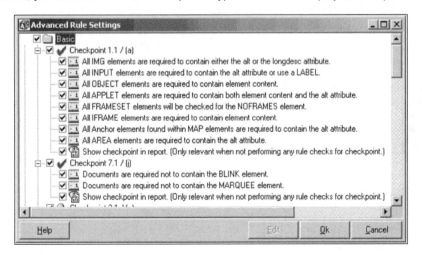

When AccVerify SE for FrontPage is installed, an extra "*Custom*" menu item appears, through which the author can access the validation features in AccVerify SE.

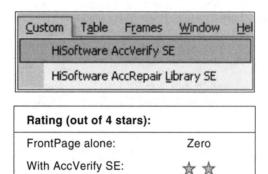

Rating (out of 4 stars):	
FrontPage alone:	Zero
With AccVerify SE:	☆ ☆

Integrated Accessibility Solutions

Guideline 5: Integrate accessibility solutions into the overall "look and feel".

Even though many accessibility features have been incorporated into FrontPage, Microsoft did not make a strong attempt to make accessibility features readily available or identifiable. In one sense, it could be said that the accessibility features are so well integrated that they essentially disappear. This contrasts with the approach in Dreamweaver XP, in which the dialog boxes are explicitly labeled to explain their relation to disability access (for example *Image Tag Accessibility Attributes*). However, the average FrontPage user will have no idea which features are related to disability access because the methods to reach those features and the titles given to them are too obscure.

Rating (out of 4 stars):
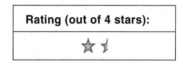

Promoting Accessibility

Guideline 6. Promote accessibility in Help and documentation.

On a positive note, it is encouraging to see that one of the most prominent Help topics on the Help main menu is "*Accessibility for people with disabilities.*" Despite this prominence, the Help files are not extensive, leaving the author to search elsewhere for more detailed information. Still, some information is provided for FrontPage users with disabilities, as well as for those who are trying to create web content which is accessible to people with disabilities. A search for the terms "disability" or "accessibility" yields a few results, including keyboard shortcuts, "*how to make accessible Office documents*", and generic information about accessibility in general.

Accessibility features in FrontPage

Keyboard shortcuts

<u>View all Keyboard shortcuts</u>

▶ Show or hide shortcut keys in ScreenTips

Size options

▶ Increase the size of toolbar buttons

▶ Change the width of a drop-down list box on a toolbar

▶ Scroll and zoom by using the Microsoft IntelliMouse or other pointing device

Toolbar and menu options

▶ Add a button to a toolbar

▶ Create a custom toolbar

▶ Group related buttons and menus on a toolbar

Color and sound options

▶ Change the color of text using the toolbar

▶ Turn sounds on or off for buttons, menus, and other screen elements

Rating (out of 4 stars):

Accessibility of the Tool

Guideline 7. Ensure that the authoring tool is accessible to authors with disabilities.

FrontPage is almost entirely keyboard-accessible. Screen readers can access the content well, although at the time of this writing, there were problems with FrontPage when used on Windows 2000 with Jaws 4.01 that still had not been resolved.

Rating (out of 4 stars):

Pitfalls To Avoid in FrontPage

Pitfall 1: Web Components

Many of FrontPage's Web Components (available from the main menu at *Insert / Web Components*) produce content which is not disability-accessible:

- **Dynamic Effects / Hover Button**. The buttons produced by FrontPage are Java applets which screen readers cannot access.

- ***Dynamic Effects / Banner Ad Manager***. This feature is also powered by Java, which will be problematic for screen readers.

- **Spreadsheets and charts**. All of these web components draw upon Microsoft technologies, which will create problems for anyone without Microsoft Office and Internet Explorer. These components are not entirely keyboard-accessible, and, in fact, they trap the keyboard focus, much the same way as Flash does, so that users cannot tab on to links or other objects elsewhere on the page.

- **Photo Gallery**. FrontPage does not prompt the user to enter `alt` attributes for the photo gallery images, although there is a place to add text "captions" and "descriptions" which will be inserted directly below the images.

- **MSN, MSNBC, Expedia, bCentral Components**. Many of these components are not disability-friendly. For example, the news headlines are presented as one image with a simple `alt` attribute (for example, "*View Technology Headlines at MSNBC*") even though visual users will be able to read the top three headlines. The weather forecast has accessible text, but it is dependent upon JavaScript and has several images without `alt` attributes. The text link to the Expedia maps is accessible, but the Expedia site and maps are not.

Pitfall 2: Drawing tools

- **Lines and shapes**, which FrontPage creates in VML for Internet Explorer and GIF format for all other browsers, can have `alt` attributes, but the `alt` attributes do not show up in Internet Explorer and cannot be accessed by screen readers.

- **Textboxes** are accessible in IE, because they contain true text, but will not be accessible in other browsers without an `alt` attribute because the whole object is turned into an image. To add an `alt` attribute to textboxes, right-click on the textbox, select *Format Text Box* then click on the *Web* tab and type in the text. The text in the `alt` attribute should be identical to the text in the text box. However, if a great amount of text is placed in the textbox, the appropriate accessibility fix would be to provide a short `alt` attribute and then also provide a link to another page with the full text, via a `longdesc` attribute or a "*D*" link, both of which must be added manually as we saw in Chapter 4.

- **Content Linearization**. FrontPage allows the author to move the objects created with the drawing tools to different visual locations in the document. Sometimes the resulting visual order will be radically different from the order in which the objects appear in the markup itself. To remedy this you have to enter into the markup and, if necessary, rearrange the literal markup order of the objects until they make sense within the context of the page.

- **WordArt**. All of the WordArt created in FrontPage is rendered as VML in Internet Explorer and as a GIF image in everything else. This means that the WordArt will be completely inaccessible to screen readers in Internet Explorer since the `alt` attribute is not rendered in Internet Explorer. FrontPage automatically creates `alt` text for the WordArt – which is rendered in all non-Internet Explorer browsers – based upon the text inside the WordArt itself. Unfortunately, the `alt` text may not be updated if the author changes the WordArt text after creating it. To update the `alt` attribute, right-click on the WordArt, select *Format WordArt*, select the *Web* tab, then add the `alt` text.

GoLive

Adobe GoLive is another powerful web authoring tool. It has a history of Mac-centric design which can still be felt, even in the Windows version. A few accessibility-related features have been added to GoLive 6.0, though there is still much room for improvement. GoLive 5.0 was not created with web accessibility in mind, but can be enhanced through the use of external validators, such as SSB Technologies' InSight LE, a software add-on which Adobe promotes on its web site (http://www.adobe.com/).

Supporting Accessible Authoring

Guideline 1: Support accessible authoring practices

Since it preserves any changes to the markup implemented by the author, GoLive can be used to successfully create accessible Web content. Some of the features in GoLive insert markup which is problematic with regard to accessibility. A discussion of these features can be found in the GoLive Pitfalls sections later in this chapter.

Rating (out of 4 stars):	
GoLive 5.0:	★ ★ ⯪
GoLive 6.0:	★ ★ ⯪

Generating Standard Markup

Guideline 2. Generate standard markup.

Most of the wizards, dialog boxes, and drag-on controls create standard markup. The default template for new documents in GoLive 6.0 is HTML 4 Transitional. You can also create XHTML documents by selecting *File / New Special / XHTML* Page. GoLive 5.0 does not include a `DOCTYPE` declaration. You can add one manually, or create a new file to use as the default template. To specify the default template file, select *Edit / Preferences / General*, then check the *New Document* box and browse the hard drive for your new template.

Rating (out of 4 stars):	
GoLive 5.0:	★ ★ ★
GoLive 6.0:	★ ★ ★ ★

Creating Accessible Content

Guideline 3: Support the creation of accessible content. (Guide the author to produce accessible content.)

Some accessibility features have been incorporated into GoLive 5.0, but most are not easily identifiable as such. It is not likely that average GoLive users will feel that the application is supporting them or guiding them in any way to make the content accessible.

- The most basic of accessibility features – the ability to add an `alt` attribute – is available in the *Inspector* palette. Within GoLive 6.0, `alt` text can also be added for rollover images, but, for some reason, alt attributes must be added in the Source View within GoLive 5.0.

- The Forms pallette provides a way to insert both `<label>` and `<fieldset>` tags, though no indication is given that these features are in any way related to disability access.

- As far as tables are concerned, it is possible to designate rows or columns as headers (by selecting the *Headers Style* checkbox in the *Inspector* palette), but there is no built-in method to associate the cells with their corresponding headers.

- Authors can add `alt` text for Java applets via the *Alt* tab in the *Inspector* palette.

- No method is given to input frame titles or noframes content through the WYSIWYG.

Rating (out of 4 stars):	
GoLive 5.0	★★
GoLive 6.0:	★★

Assessing and Repairing Content

Guideline 4: Provide ways of checking and correcting inaccessible content.

With the release of GoLive 6.0, Adobe has included a built-in utility to check for accessibility. Although this utility does check for some of the most important accessibility criteria (for example missing `alt` attributes, missing frame titles/noframes content), too many other features are left out. The built-in validator does not repair pages, nor does it highlight the errors.

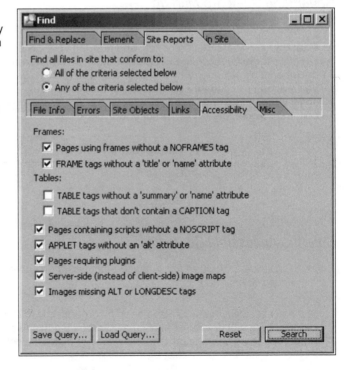

It provides a list of pages which fail the specified criteria, but it doesn't specify which errors caused the page to fail or how to fix it. Perhaps this is better than nothing, but authors will likely find other validators much more useful.

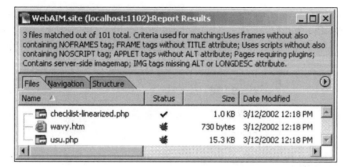

There is no built-in method of checking for or correcting inaccessible content in GoLive 5.0, but Adobe provides a link to a free download of InSight LE, by SSB Technologies. The information on the Adobe web site gives the impression that InSight LE was made specifically to work with GoLive, but it can check the accessibility of any page created by any authoring tool. In fact, it can even check pages on the Web. This tool parses files and then specifies and highlights the accessibility errors. InSight LE cannot correct the errors, but SSB Technologies (*http://www.ssbtechnologies.com*) makes a commercial product (InFocus) for this purpose.

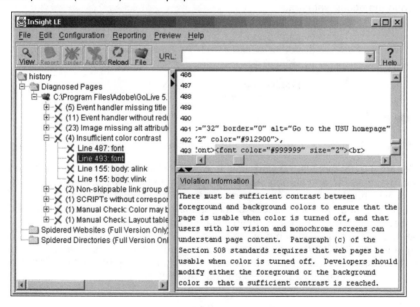

Rating (out of 4 stars):	
GoLive 5.0	Zero
GoLive 6.0	★★
With InSight LE:	★★★

Integrated Accessibility Solutions

Guideline 5: Integrate accessibility solutions into the overall "look and feel".

Although there are only a handful of accessibility features in GoLive, the ones that are present are well-integrated into the interface. The `alt` attribute edit field, form `<label>` tag, and table header checkbox are examples of features available from the palettes in the regular interface. The main drawback is that these features are not always labelled as accessibility-related.

Rating (out of 4 stars):	
GoLive 5.0:	★★★
GoLive 6.0:	★★★

Promoting Accessibility

Guideline 6: Promote accessibility in Help and documentation.

Adobe GoLive 6.0 contains very little documentation related to disability access. The most helpful information is found in the help pages under "Accessibility features of Help". The help pages themselves are in HTML format, and this document explains some of the accessible-design tactics that were used in designing the help files. GoLive 5.0 Contains no disability or access-related information in the documentation.

Rating (out of 4 stars):	
GoLive 5.0	Zero
GoLive 6.0:	★★

Accessibility of the Tool

Guideline 7: Ensure that the authoring tool is accessible to authors with disabilities.

Neither GoLive 6.0 nor GoLive 5.0 were built to be disability-accessible. Although the main menus are keyboard-accessible and screen-reader-compatible, most of the program's features exist only in the palettes, which are completely mouse-dependent. People who are unable to use a mouse, and those who depend upon screen readers to access the program will be unable to take advantage of a great number of GoLive's features. It would still be possible for them to enter into the Source view to create the document, or to add some of the basic HTML tags and attributes (such as font size and headings) in the WYSIWYG through the main menus, but there is little incentive to use GoLive in such a limited fashion. GoLive's strength lies in the features available in the palettes of its graphical user interface, rather than in its plain text editing capabilities.

Rating (out of 4 stars):	
GoLive 5.0:	★

Pitfalls To Avoid in GoLive

Pitfall 1: Layout Grid and Layout Textboxes

The layout grid allows authors to work with layout tables, allowing authors to reposition them, alter them and move them around at will. GoLive allows you to easily rearrange, expand, collapse, add, or subtract layout tables. Used wisely, this can be a powerful layout tool. Used indiscriminately, this tool is likely to create over complex complex table layouts, even when simple layouts would suffice. As mentioned earlier, such layouts can cause serious problems for screen readers. Here is the same example from the previous discussion about layout tables, this time created in GoLive's layout grid:

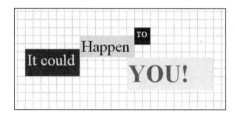

As before, the visual user will read "*It could Happen TO YOU!*", but the screen reader user will hear "TO Happen It could YOU!"

Text-Based Markup Editors

Text-based editors generally do not fall into the same traps as WYSIWYG editors. Although some text-based editors offer quite sophisticated text and markup editing, fewer come with pre-fabricated markup or content. This leaves nearly all of the work to the web designer. In some ways this can be an advantage. The web designer does not have to correct as many accessibility errors introduced by the tool. On the other hand, if the designer unaware or ignorant of accessibility princples, it is less likely that he will incorporate them into the design.

The task of rating these editors is complicated by the fact that, in comparison to the WYSIWYG editors, they automate much less of the authoring process. Some text editors have certain automated features, but it is probably unfair to compare WYSIWYG editors and text-based editors as equals. Their purposes are different, so the ratings I have included here are meant to be consistent within their respective category, rather than directly compared across categories.

HomeSite

HomeSite is one of the more popular text-based web editors for Windows. The designers of HomeSite have taken the initiative to add accessibility functionality in some ways superior to its WYSIWYG cousins.

Supporting Accessible Authoring

Guideline 1: Support accessible authoring practices.

As with the other software products analyzed here, HomeSite preserves all of the markup created by the author. The software provides the user with a way to enter in many accessibility-related tags and attributes, though it is up to the designer to actually enter them in.

Rating (out of 4 stars):

Generating Standard Markup

Guideline 2: Generate standard markup.

All of the markup generated by HomeSite conforms to some standard of HTML or XHTML, although the tool still allows you to insert markup which does not match the designated DOCTYPE. This is both a benefit and a potential pitfall. Web designer's don't want the tool to change their markup, but perhaps the tool could warn them when they are inserting markup which is inappropriate for the DOCTYPE.

HomeSite allows you to select a default template, with its corresponding DOCTYPE. The markup can be validated against its DOCTYPE by selecting *Tools / Validate Current Document* or *Validate Current Tag*.

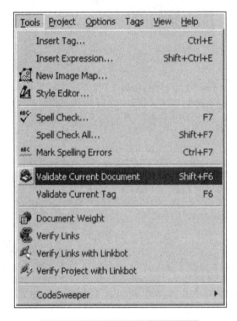

Rating (out of 4 stars):

Creating Accessible Content

Guideline 3: Support the creation of accessible content. (Guide the author to produce accessible content.)

HomeSite is one of the better tools in this area. Not only does the software provide a place for you to input the appropriate accessibility markup but each accessibility feature is labeled either with a separate "*Accessibility*" tab or with a corresponding label.

The image tag editor even places a star next to the alt attribute, giving the web designer a subtle hint that this is an important attribute.

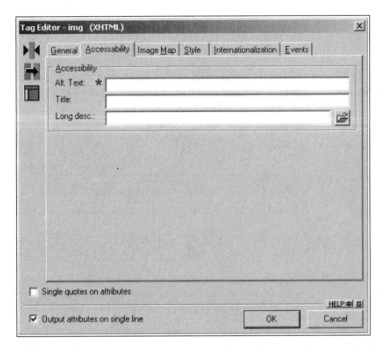

You can designate `headers` or `scope` attributes for table cells, which can greatly increase the accessibility of data tables to screen reader users. Web designers should always associate the cells of data tables with their corresponding headers. The same should not be done for layout tables, however, because that could potentially confuse screen reader users, causing them to think that they are in a data table when they are not.

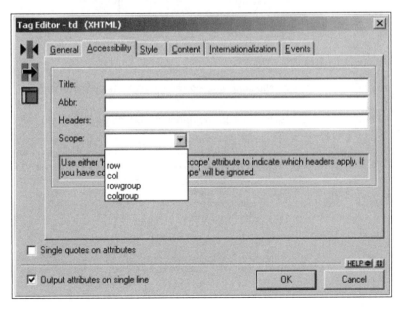

I consider the accessibility features of HomeSite to be among the strongest of its competitors, but there are a few areas that could use some improvement. For example, in the frame dialog box, there is a place to enter the frame title (and even a `longdesc` attribute in XHTML), but there is no prompt to enter `noframes` content. The `noframes` content can be added elsewhere, but it would be helpful if it were mentioned in the dialog box somewhere. Also, the frames wizard does not prompt you for any accessibility features, even though this information can be added later.

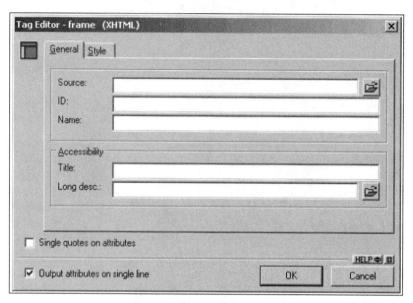

Rating (out of 4 stars):
☆☆☆⯪

Assessing and Repairing Content

Guideline 4: Provide ways of checking and correcting inaccessible content.

There is no built-in method to check for or correct inaccessible content. Authors will need to use external utilities for this purpose.

Rating (out of 4 stars):
Zero

Promoting Accessibility

Guideline 6: Promote accessibility in Help and documentation.

The help files include tips for designers with disabilities using HomeSite as an authoring tool. Information about "making web sites accessible to visitors who are visually impaired" is also available from the help files, although it is very limited in scope and there does not seem to be any significant mention of other types of disabilities.

Rating (out of 4 stars):

Accessibility of the Tool

Guideline 7: Ensure that the authoring tool is accessible to authors with disabilities.

HomeSite is keyboard-accessible and works with screen readers, but has one particularly annoying quirk, in that screen readers read the file name of a graphic—apparently part of the user interface—before every line of text in the markup. The repetition of the file name of this graphic is not an absolute barrier to accessibility, but is certainly an avoidable annoyance that will hopefully be eliminated in future versions.

Rating (out of 4 stars):

BBEdit

One of the most popular text-based markup editors for the Macintosh platform is BBEdit.

Supporting Accessible Authoring

Guideline 1: Support accessible authoring practices.

BBEdit allows you to do anything you please in the markup. All of the authors edits are preserved.

Rating (out of 4 stars):

Generating Standard Markup

Guideline 2: Generate standard markup.

When creating a new document, you can insert one of several DOCTYPEs, including XHTML. The default new page has no markup in it at all though. When using BBEdit, the quality of the markup is completely in the hands of the author. Once the document is created, you can check the final result using BBEdit's built-in document syntax validator, which produces a report of all of the errors and their line numbers. There is no "on-the-fly" validation of the code, though. It might be helpful to have the option of being alerted when markup errors are introduced.

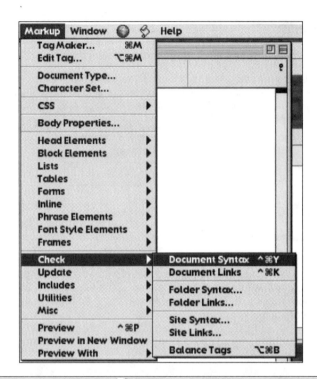

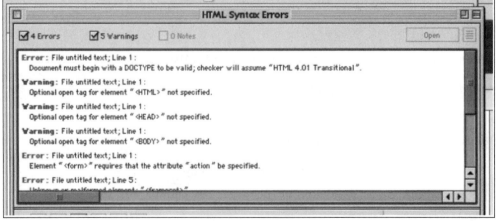

Rating (out of 4 stars):
☆☆☆

Creating Accessible Content

Guideline 3: Support the creation of accessible content. (Guide the author to produce accessible content)

One of the strengths of BBEdit is that it has a built-in method for nearly all of the HTML and XHTML tags and attributes in the specification, including many accessibility-specific tags:

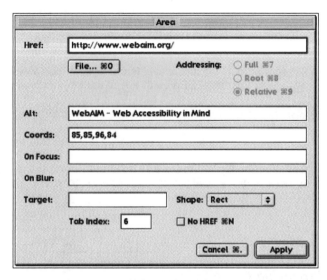

If there is a weakness in this area, it is that the accessibility features are not labled as such. There is nothing in the interface to indicate to the web designer that any of the features will benefit people with disabilities.

Notice the `axis`, `abbr`, `headers`, and `scope` attributes for the `<th>` tag in this dialog box:

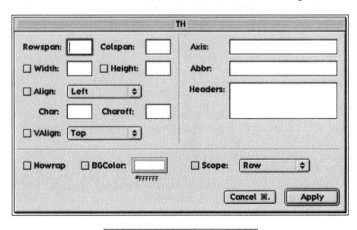

Rating (out of 4 stars):
★★★

Assessing and Repairing Content

Guideline 4. Provide ways of checking and correcting inaccessible content.

Rating (out of 4 stars):
Zero

There is no built-in functionality to check for or correct innaccessible content. However, you may wish to supplement BBEdit with any of the free or commercial utilities available for this purpose.

Integrated Accessibility Solutions

Guideline 5: Integrate accessibility solutions into the overall "look and feel".

The accessibility features are all integrated well into the software's interface. It still could be helpful to label all of the disability-related features, for easier identification.

Rating (out of 4 stars):

Promoting Accessibility

Guideline 6: Promote accessibility in help and documentation.

There is no mention of disabilities or accessibility in the help or documentation.

Rating (out of 4 stars):
Zero

Summary

This chapter has taken a look at some accessibility challenges of authoring tools in general, as well as those of a few specific authoring tools. Let's review some of the key principles.

- Authors are responsible for making the content accessible.

- Any tool can be used by an accessibility-savvy designer to produce accessible content, as long as the tool preserves the author's markup.

- Authoring tools cannot make the end result accessible; they can only assist the author to do so. Tools can guide, prompt, assist, instruct and check for accessibility, but there is no substitute for an author's good accessible design skills.

- The most accessibility-advanced authoring tool can still produce inaccessible content if the author uses the tool ignorantly or unwisely.

- In terms of accessibility, authoring tools should do two things:

- Permit, support, and encourage the creation of accessible content

- Allow authors with disabilities to use the tool.

- **Pay attention to content linearization**. Content linearization can affect the reading order and the tab order. Common areas where problem may occur include:

- Layout tables

- CSS layout

- Image map hot spots

- Be very careful with JavaScript and DHTML. Specifically, pay attention to:

- **Keyboard accessibility.** Make sure the functionality does not require a mouse, or provide a redundant keyboard-accessible alternative.

- **Dynamic content.** Users of screen readers may not be aware that the content has changed in other parts of the document.

- **Flicker.** Blinking or flashing content can cause seizures.

- **Distraction**. Moving or dynamic content can be distracting.

- **No Javascript.** Not everyone is able to use JavaScript-enabled technologies, and some people choose to disable JavaScript in order to avoid potential accessibility problems.

- External or add-on utilities can supplement the authoring tool's accessibility features, including:

- Accessibility validators

- Markup validators

- Multimedia accessibility tools

- Don't become overconfident in a tool's accessibility features.

9

- CSS basics

- CSS1 and CSS2 specifications

- Techniques for separating content and presentation

- Testing and validation

Author: Sarah Swierenga

Separating Content from Presentation

The purpose of this chapter is to address the issue of separating informational content from visual presentation. The first principle of design – *Form follows function* – is the golden rule that should be followed at all times whether it is designing a house, a coffee pot, or a web site. Many web design professionals begin the designing work by thinking in terms of how something will look rather than how it will work. The framework of any product must be thoroughly thought out and constructed before designing its outward presentation. The lack of understanding of this basic concept is the reason numerous web sites are difficult to use and are not easily accessible. Many of these designers, and the companies who commissioned them, have viewed the web initiative as something akin to advertising. While one can draw parallels between beautifully laid-out brochures or television commercials and effective web sites, there are some distinct differences. Hard-copy brochures and television commercials remain static once they have been published. Web sites, however, will render differently, depending on hardware configurations, user preference settings, and browser technologies, unless the pages are completely specified by the designer. Even then, there will be more variability than you would have in a brochure or television commercial. The web site must be constructed with this variability in mind.

Much of the importance of a well-designed web site lies behind the scenes. The structure, content, and framework of a web site must be in place before a designer considers the esthetics of the final presentation. The structure and framework deal with the page layout and flow of function, respectively. The page content would be concerned with the information that the user is trying to access through the user interface. The documents that make up a web site are more along the lines of an interactive tool than a passive marketing message. Distinguishing the structure and framework of a web site from its content provides improved accessibility, manageability, and portability.

One way to define and properly construct a document framework is to create a complete outline of the information to be presented and then define the structural hierarchy, that is, chapter, section, and paragraph. A designer who designs for accessibility should have a deep understanding of the content and how it is structured before considering the many ways in which it will be effectively presented.

After finalizing the content blueprint, the designer creates a basic framework or "skeleton" by determining the structural makeup for the content. In this way, designers create an effective and flexible framework that can transfer to many types of user agents or display devices. Although additional work would be needed to translate a design for a computer screen to a small-screen device, the priority of the informational content, functionality, and navigation would have already been analyzed, which should speed up the design process.

There are many methods a designer can use to help ensure the separation of content from presentation. Listed below are topics that will be discussed in this chapter:

> Using stylesheets for consistency across your web site
>
> Allowing user-override of styles if they cannot read your font size or colors
>
> Controlling fonts in such a way that users with disabilities can still read the text
>
> Formatting and positioning text without misusing HTML table tags
>
> Working with lists that can be recognized by screen reader technologies
>
> Designating colors that have good contrast for readability
>
> Using aural stylesheets to enhance the experience of the web site
>
> Designing for various media types, for example, computer screens, speech synthesizers, or Braille devices
>
> Designing pages that are readable without stylesheets in case the assistive technology does not support them
>
> Validating stylesheets for accessibility

After an overview of stylesheet fundamentals, stylesheet issues related to accessibility will be discussed in more detail. In general, well-designed stylesheets allow screen readers to interpret the web site structure and render it properly. Even though many designers are reluctant to use stylesheets because of browser support concerns and their experience using table elements for layout, more and more designers are incorporating stylesheets because they do offer significant advantages even beyond those for accessibility.

> Stylesheets give the user "global" control over the site. A master stylesheet or even a series of stylesheets allow all of the visual changes to be created or modified in one place for the entire site. This control saves designers a lot of time over the life cycle of a site.
>
> CSS stylesheets also allow users to override author styles when needed. Allowing users to adjust colors, font sizes, backgrounds, and spacing can mean the difference between a completely unusable site and a flexible, usable site that meets the user's needs.
>
> Stylesheets allow for precise positioning of information. Instead of relying on tables or transparent spacer images to create visual presentations, designers can use style properties to position, and even overlap, elements on the page.
>
> CSS also supports aural presentation of web pages and media types. Taking the extra time to code for this method of presentation can significantly enhance user experiences with your site. When browsers star to support aural stylesheets, more designers will take advantage of them.

Using media types, HTML documents can be presented on accessible devices, such as Braille readers and speech synthesizers. This flexibility will become increasingly important as small-screen devices become more prevalent as well.

CSS will eventually become a necessity because the web is moving in this direction. When XML becomes the primary language for web authoring, pages will not display properly without some kind of stylesheet. Additionally, the W3C has begun "deprecating," or declaring obsolete, elements such as `<font>`, `<center>`, `<menu>`, and `<u>`, and attributes, for example, `align`, `size`, `bgcolor`, `height`, `width`, and `nowrap`. While it is likely that the deprecated elements and attributes will be supported for some time, sooner or later it will happen. Designers are encouraged to be progressive and forward thinking for these reasons.

Once you start using stylesheets on a regular basis, you will discover that they are a more effecient means of designing the visual presentation of your site.

CSS Basics

Cascading stylesheets (CSS) are a mechanism for specifying style (for example., fonts, size, color, boldness, and spacing) in HTML documents without affecting the HTML markup used for structuring the pages. Stylesheets can be used to describe how information will appear on the screen or how it will look when printed. Users also might create a customized stylesheet to adjust the display of the page for their particular needs. Adding style to web pages is necessary to create attractive, effective web sites, but the method in which this visual treatment is added has implications for how well assistive technology can interpret the pages. For example, if designers use the standard headings (`<h1>` − `<h6>`) rather than creating their own fonts to mimic the settings, then screen reader users can listen to the headers to understand the content or context of the document, instead of having to listen to entire document to obtain that information. In other cases, users need to turn off stylesheets altogether because the layout may be too confusing due to a cognitive impairment, or because the assistive technology they use does not support stylesheets.

The key for designing accessible stylesheets is to ensure that pages do not depend entirely on stylesheet code. Indeed, Section 508 states:

"Documents shall be organized so they are readable without requiring an associated stylesheet" (§ 1194.22 (d)).

Stylesheets, then, can be used to enhance the presentation of the pages, but should not be used as the only means of describing the fundamental organization of the information on the pages. Web site designers must first think about the desired structure of the document before dealing with how the document will be presented to the user.

Fundamental Syntax

Although most designers are already familiar with the basic syntax used in stylesheets, this section provides a brief overview for those who need it. Stylesheets are made up of rules that apply to an HTML document. Rules are statements about one stylistic aspect of one or more elements. An example of a rule would be:

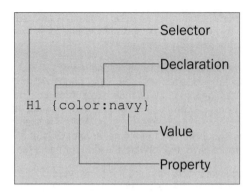

Rules consists of two parts:

- Selector – the part before the left curly brace

- Declaration – the part within the curly brace

In the example above, `H1` is the selector, while `color: navy` is the declaration. The selector is the link between the HTML document and the style, and specifies what elements are affected by the declaration. The declaration is where you define what the effect will be. Going deeper into the syntax, the declaration has two subparts: property and value. The property is the characteristic that something possesses, for example, "`color`" in the example above. The value, then, is a precise specification of the property, for example., "`navy`" in our example. More than one rule can be used for each selector, for example:

```
font-family: Verdana; Arial, font-style: normal; color: navy
```

Methods of Adding CSS Styles To Pages

Style can be included in an HTML document in the following ways:

> By embedding stylesheets using the `<style>` element directly on an individual HTML document.

> Linking and importing stylesheets using the `<link>` element or the @ import rule.

> Inserting an inline style using the `<style>` attribute, which adds style directly to an individual element on the HTML document.

Embedded Stylesheets

With this method of adding CSS styles to an HTML page, the `<style>` element should be included inside the `<head>` element. The `<style>` element is a container element within which individual style rules are nested. Note that the `type` attribute must be included in the `<style>` element's start tag. An example showing how the `<style>` element is used for specifying font weight and color would be:

```
<STYLE type="text/css">
<!--
H1, H2 { color: red; font-weight: bold; }
-->
</STYLE>
```

Linking and Importing Stylesheets

By linking or importing an external stylesheet, the designer can control the presentation of the whole web site from one or more stylesheets. By linking or importing an external stylesheet, designers can control the presentation of the whole web site from a single external stylesheet, rather than having to alter each page individually. Designers can also present the same information in different ways by associating different stylesheets. Note that embedded styles have precedence over linked or imported styles. Additionally, imported styles have precedence over linked styles. Examples of linking to or importing from an external stylesheet would be:

```
Linking method: <LINK rel="stylesheet" type="text/css" href="sitestyle.css">

Import method: @import { url("sitestyle.css"); }
```

Inline Styles

This method should only be used when the designer needs to specify a particular format in one place in the document, generally to override the default display or element style. An example would be:

```
<P style="font-weight: bold">
```

If you find yourself repeating the same inline style several times within a document, then you should consider creating a non-inline style rule to handle the styling. One way of doing this is to use a CLASS selector. A class selector lets you assign style to elements that are included within a particular class. For example, the same bold style that was just described could be specified as:

```
p.special {font-weight: bold; }
```

Specify the class selector by using a period followed by the name of the class. When you do this, all <p> elements that contain a class="special" attribute will be displayed in bold, for example:

```
<P class="special">This paragraph would display in bold.</P>
```

W3C Working Group – CSS1 and CSS2 Specifications

The World Wide Web Consortium (W3C) Working Group on Cascading Stylesheets and Formatting Properties has produced two very detailed stylesheet specifications, CSS1 and CSS2. The W3C Working Group published these standards to give authors the necessary information they need to use stylesheets effectively to create accessible documents.

CSS1 was first issued in December 1996, and covers common style properties. The specification defines font properties (font-family, font-style, font-variant, font-weight, and font), color and background properties, text properties (spacing, alignment, and indenting), box properties (margins, padding, border, width, height, float, and clear), and classification properties (display, whitespace, and list styles). The rules for resolving conflicts between different stylesheets are also defined.

CSS2, issued in May 1998, builds on CSS1. CSS2 encompasses all of the CSS1 properties and adds several more, including content positioning, downloadable fonts, table layout, features for internationalization, automatic counters and numbering, aural stylesheets, and some properties related to the user interface (cursors, user preferences for color and fonts, and dynamic outlines). CSS2 also supports media-specific stylesheets that enable authors to customize the presentation of their documents in visual browsers, aural devices, printers, Braille devices, and handheld devices.

> *The two specifications can be found at http://www.w3.org/TR/REC-CSS1 and http://www.w3.org/TR/REC-CSS2.*

Appendix A of the CSS2 specification provides a sample stylesheet that would be a good starting point for creating your default stylesheet. CSS2 Appendix B provides a Property Index in a summary table format that may be very helpful.

> *Note that the CSS1 and CSS2 specifications are not fully implemented by any browsers at this time. However, you should still include stylesheets on your site because most of CSS1 has been implemented in the later versions of the browsers.*

Browser Dependencies

Older browsers either do not support CSS at all or support it inconsistently. HTML is really the only option for these kinds of browsers. Netscape 4.0 and lower and Internet Explorer 4.0 and lower would be examples of problematic browsers. Internet Explorer 5.5 and higher, Netscape 6.0 and higher, and Opera 5.x are included in the list of browsers that support CSS. Note that, in general, HTML browsers ignore attributes that they do not support, and they render the content of unsupported elements. A list of CSS-enhanced browsers can be found on the W3C web site: *http://www.w3.org/Style/CSS/#LieBos1999.*

Specific Techniques for Separating Content from Presentation

This section will offer recommended approaches for designing accessible stylesheets based on the WAI work, as well as alternative approaches used by web designers who have spent considerable energy attempting to make reasonable tradeoffs because of limitations in the browser technologies. Until most browsers support CSS consistently, content developers will continue to create documents that mix supported features of CSS with some presentation features of HTML. These documents may well be accessible in many of the latest versions of the browsers, but they would not meet several of the WCAG checkpoints. The web designer, then, must ensure that the CSS transforms gracefully, if documents use HTML presentation features instead of CSS.

Use of Stylesheets for Consistency

In order to create a style of presentation that is consistent across pages (WCAG Checkpoint 14.3), designers should use a minimal number of stylesheets. It is more efficient to organize the many styles that may be necessary for a large web site in one document, especially if there are multiple designers involved over time. Identical styles that may have been created for a different part of the site would be more easily identified, and consequently merged, if all styles were placed in the same stylesheet document and it's easier to make changes in one place and have them reflected throughout the site. However, if designers must use more than one stylesheet, they should use the same CLASS name for the same concept in all of the stylesheets. Make sure that you clearly document the chain of the stylesheets. By doing so, the information will appear more consistent across the site for users.

Another way to create more consistent web sites is to use linked stylesheets, rather than embedded styles. Inline stylesheets should be avoided, if possible, because they affect individual elements on a page. The impact on other pages in other parts of the web site may not be considered, and therefore, inline stylesheets are more risky. It is possible that an inline style for one element may be used in a contradictory fashion in another part of the site by one of the other designers.

To read more on this subject see Chisholm, Wendy, Vanderheiden, Gregg, & Jacobs, Ian. HTML Techniques for Web Content Accessibility Guidelines 1.0. Worldwide Web Consortium (Massachusetts Institute of Technology, Institut National de Recherche en Informatique et en Automatique, Keio University). (http://www.w3.org/TR/WCAG10-HTML-TECHS/)

User Override of Styles

CSS2 allows users to override designer stylesheets. Allowing user stylesheets is important to users who cannot perceive a page with the author's chosen fonts and color. CSS enables users to view documents with their own preferred fonts, colors, etc., by specifying them using a user stylesheet. Remember that users are not going to go to the trouble of getting and setting up their own stylesheet unless they really need it. Using CSS also helps designers avoid deprecated features of W3C technologies (Checkpoint 11.2). As described earlier, a deprecated element or attribute is one that users are discouraged from using, since the same or better results can now be produced using stylesheets alone. Deprecated elements may be declared obsolete in future versions of HTML and XHTML. An obsolete element or attribute should not be used, as current or future browsers are not required to support it (although most deprecated elements and attributes will probably be supported in HTML for quite some time).

To override a rule in the author's stylesheet, a '! important' can be placed in the user's stylesheet. This is important for users who need large font sizes, or require certain contrasts. For example, the following rule overrides an author rule, and specifies a large font size for paragraph text:

```
P { font-size: 36pt ! important; }
```

Fonts

Stylesheets enable designers to have precise control over font size, color, and style. The following CSS2 properties can be used to control font information: font, font-family, font-size, font-size-adjust, font-stretch, font-style, font-variant, and font-weight instead of the following deprecated font elements and attributes in HTML: <font>, <basefont>, font, and size. Some designers have used images to represent text in a particular font when they are uncertain of the availability of the font on the client's machine. This technique is popular because if you do not specify the size of the font in absolute format, then the user sizes will affect the design and alignment on the page. However, CSS offers an excellent alternative to get the visual presentation that you want without having to set absolute font sizes or having images that may also increase download times and page size. You could even develop a stylesheet tailored specifically for screen readers using the same content, and then offer it as an option in a small transparent image at the top of the page.

Font Sizes

In standard HTML, designers typically use the deprecated <font> element. The <font> element allows only seven different font sizes, and only four (sizes 4, 5, 6, and 7) correspond to font sizes that are larger than the normal font size. The advantage of using stylesheets for font sizing is that you can set an unlimited range of font sizes. Use relative measurements, such as em, percentages (%), rather than absolute measurements, such as point sizes, in (inches), cm (centimeters), mm (millimeters), or pc (picas) (WCAG checkpoint 3.4) when you set the font size. The em and percentage units work identically. They both set the font size relative to the parent element's font size — not relative to the current element's font size. Thus, a setting of one em specifies a font size that is equal to the parent element's font size.

Examples that specifies relative font sizes instead of absolute font sizes would be:

```
P { font-size: 1em; } <!--Default proportional text font for the browser-->
P { font-size: 100%; }
```

To double these default sizes you would use the following code:

```
P { font-size: 2em; }
P { font-size: 200%; }
```

Another option for setting font sizes is to use the pixel (px) unit. With this unit, a measurement of 1px should correspond on a computer screen to one screen pixel. The advantage of using pixels for setting font sizes is that they scale relative to the screen resolution in exactly the same way as any other text. An example that specifies font sizes in pixels would be:

```
P { font-size: 16px; } for the default, and P { font-size: 32px; } to double the
font size.
```

Most CSS experts recommend using ems (or percentages) instead of pixels when setting font sizes because relative measurements allow your font sizes to scale relative to whatever default style is set in operating system configuration settings, the browser preferences, or a user stylesheet. The major concern, however, is that older browsers have problems with em measurements. For instance, Internet Explorer 3 interprets one em as one pixel, rendering the page unreadable. Netscape Navigator 4 meanwhile has "inheritance" problems. Child elements inherit the specified font-size, rather than the computed font-size. Because of problems like these, many web designers resort to using pixels and absolute font sizes to guarantee that the information fits within the intended layout of the page. Others advocate not setting font sizes at all. If you allow the browser or user to determine the appropriate size of the different HTML elements, then many accessibility problems can be avoided.

Font Weight and Font Style

Font weights and font styles can be achieved using stylesheet properties. The font-weight properties that are supported by the browsers are normal (or the numeric value of 400) and bold (numeric value of 700). Other weights are "bolder" and "lighter," as well as numeric values (100, 200, 200, 500, 600, 800, and 900), but they have various levels of browser support. The only comparable numerical weights across browsers are that a weight of 400 or less will display the text in a normal weight font, and a weight of 700 or 800 will look bolder. Bold and normal, then, are the recommended font weight settings.

Font styles have the values of normal, italic, and oblique. An italic value indicates that the browser will classify the font as an italic font, while the oblique value will specify a font that will be classified as an oblique font. Oblique means that the letters were slanted versions of the normal roman typeface, rather than created separately from the roman typeface like the italic font was originally.

Example using both font weight and font style properties:

```
<H2 style="font-weight: bold; font-style: italic">This is the original
Montanaboat, accept only the best.</H2>
```

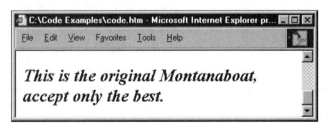

Font Family

Font family refers to either a specific font family, such as Times New Roman, Verdana, or Courier, or to a generic font family, such as serif, sans-serif, or monospace. If a font is not available on a local system, it cannot be displayed. Always specify a generic font for browsers that may not support newer fonts by including a list of fonts in priority order (most preferred font listed first). For example:

```
H1 { font-family: geneva, verdana, arial, sans-serif; }
```

If no font is specified, then the default text will be displayed instead.

Default Headings

HTML has default headings that should be used for structuring textual information. Designers can modify these basic headings using stylesheet rules. The list below gives the default HTML characteristics of the H1-H6 headings.

```
H1 -- 24 pt, bold
H2 -- 18 pt, bold
H3 -- 16 pt, bold
H4 -- 14 pt, bold
H5 -- 13 pt, bold
H6 -- 12 pt, bold
```

A common way to modify the default headings is font size. The client may well have given font size requirements for the site, and modifying the default settings in one place would allow the whole page to scale accordingly.

```
<STYLE type="text/css">
<!--
H2 { color: red; font-size: 2em; font-weight: bold; }
H3 { color: navy; font-size: 1.5em; font-style: italic; }
-->
</STYLE>

<H2>Montanaboat.com</H2>
<H3>River boats with the toughness of epoxy and the beauty of wood.</H3>
```

In this example the color, font size, font weight, and font style have all been modified using CSS properties, and the revised styling would appear across the entire page. If this code were in an external stylesheet, then the whole site could be easily changed.

Text Formatting and Positioning

One of the major advantages of using CSS instead of HTML markup for layout tables is that CSS allows precise control over spacing, alignment, and positioning. Designers can avoid "tag misuse" – the practice of using an inappropriate structural element because it gives the desired stylistic effects. Block quotes and tables have been popular elements for positioning items for visual effects, particularly for indentation and alignment. However, when specialized browsing software such as a speech synthesizer encounters elements that are misused in this way, the results can be unintelligible to the user.

Layout Tables

Tables are supposed to be used for displaying tabular data, and they should not be used for presentation (WCAG Checkpoint 5.4). However, most designers rely on HTML table markup to create the "layout tables," or a visual layout of the page. Tables used to lay out pages where cell text wraps pose problems for older screen readers that do not interpret the source HTML or browsers that do not allow navigation of individual table cells. These older screen readers will read across the page, reading sentences on the same row from different columns as one sentence. Another significant problem with using layout tables is that the pages need to be readable when the content is linearized.

Using the positioning properties of CSS2, content may be displayed at any position on the user's screen. The order in which items appear on a screen may be different than the order they are found in the source document for that page. The example below demonstrates the problem very clearly. The following source code generates the two-column visual table shown in the screenshot.

```
<HTML>
<HEAD><STYLE type="text/css"><!--
  .menu1 { position: absolute; top: 3em; left: 0em;
           margin: 0px; font-family: sans-serif;
           font-size: 120%; color: blue; background-color: white; }
  .menu2 { position: absolute; top: 3em; left: 10em;
           margin: 0px; font-family: sans-serif;
           font-size: 120%; color: blue; background-color: white; }
  .item1 { position: absolute; top: 7em; left: 0em; margin: 0px; }
  .item2 { position: absolute; top: 8em; left: 0em; margin: 0px; }
  .item3 { position: absolute; top: 7em; left: 12em; margin: 0px; }
  .item4 { position: absolute; top: 8em; left: 12em; margin: 0px; }
  #box { position: absolute; top: 5em; left: 5em; }
--></STYLE></HEAD>
<BODY>
<DIV class="box">
  <SPAN class="menu1">Wooden Boats</SPAN>
  <SPAN class="menu2">New Line</SPAN>
  <SPAN class="item1">16' Oregon Dory</SPAN>
  <SPAN class="item2">16' Viking rowboat</SPAN>
  <SPAN class="item3">Wide bottom 15'</SPAN>
  <SPAN class="item4">Standard Rogue River 14'</SPAN>
</DIV>
</BODY>
</HTML>
```

The screen below shows what the page looks like with CSS enabled:

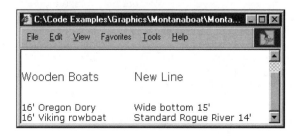

When the stylesheet is turned on, the text appears in two columns. The wooden boats information appears below the "*Wooden Boats*" column heading, while the new boats information is correctly listed under the "*New Line*" column heading. However, when the stylesheet is turned off, all of the structure contained in the content is lost, and the text appears as one sentence, "Wooden Boats New Line 16' Oregon Dory 16' Viking rowboat Wide Bottom 15' Standard Rogue River 14'." The words appear in the order in which they were written in the source. The screenshot below shows the garbled data:

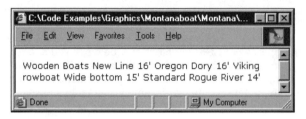

To fix this positioning problem, you can reorder the list of items in the source code. Since the positioning is described in the stylesheet, the visual presentation won't be adversely affected when the stylesheet is turned back on. In the previous code example, simply moving the `menu2` row down in the list corrects the reading order if the stylesheet is turned off:

```
<DIV class="box">
   <SPAN class="menu1">Wooden Boats</SPAN>
   <SPAN class="item1">16' Oregon Dory</SPAN>
   <SPAN class="item2">16' Viking rowboat</SPAN>
   <SPAN class="menu2">New Line</SPAN>
   <SPAN class="item3">Wide bottom 15'</SPAN>
   <SPAN class="item4">Standard Rogue River 14'</SPAN>
</DIV>
```

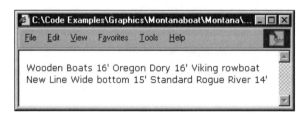

Indentation

Designers commonly use the `<blockquote>` element or transparent images for positioning page information. Even though the `<blockquote>` element may cause indented text in some browsers, it is designed to identify a quotation, not create a visual presentation effect (WCAG Checkpoint 3.7). `<blockquote>` elements used for indentation cause confusion for users and search robots alike, which expect the element to be used to mark up block quotations. Similarly, designers sometimes use 1-pixel invisible images (specified with the `alt=""` property) to position content. However, indentation can be achieved more efficiently using stylesheet properties. You can use the `text-indent` property to create the appropriate spacing.

The following example shows three lines of indented text, the first uses the `<blockquote>` element, the second uses an invisible spacer image and the third uses the `text-indent` property. Notice how the `<blockquote>` element indents the text, but adjusts margins on both sides of the page for each line. The transparent image indents the text correctly (only text in the first line is indented), but the third sentence creates the appropriate spacing using the `text-indent` property in a stylesheet to indent the paragraph without adding unnecessary images to the site:

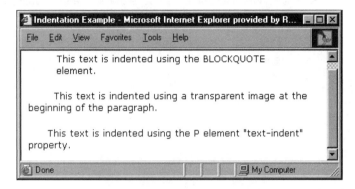

This is the line of code that indents the text using the `P` element:

```
P { text-indent: 2em; }
```

Another way to indent text is to use a `class` selector that resets the alignment for paragraphs included in the class:

```
p.indent { text-indent: 2em; }
```

PRE and Non-Breaking Space Elements

Finally, the `PRE` and non-breaking space (` `) elements have been used inappropriately by web designers – not because they should have been using CSS for visual layout, but because they really were trying to display tabular data. These elements should not be used to create a tabular layout of the text. The designer should use the `<table>` element instead, so that assistive technologies recognize it as a table.

Lists

Lists are very popular on web sites, especially bulleted lists. The most common use for a bulleted list is to present lists of hypertext links. In HTML, list items should be marked up as `<ul>` (Unordered List or bulleted list), `<ol>` (Ordered List or numbered list), or `<dl>` (Definition List or glossary list) elements, along with the `<li>` (List Item) element. As with the other HTML structural elements discussed above, the HTML list elements should only be used for creating lists, not for formatting effects such as indentation (WCAG Checkpoint 3.6).

Providing additional information about the list gives contextual clues for lists that are nested, and are easier for non-visual users to navigate. Nested lists that do not indicate the specific nest level for each item may be confusing for non-visual users. Unordered lists should include a text description before or after the list item. For ordered lists, using compound numbers are more helpful for providing additional context, for example, 1, 1.1, 1.2, 1.2.1, 1.3, 2, 2.1. The example below demonstrates how you could create an unordered list using the `list-style-position` property to neatly organize the nested list items. The sentence above the list clearly identifies the nature of the items in the list.

```
<HTML>
<TITLE>Unordered List Example</TITLE>
<STYLE>
<!--
.outside {list-style-position: outside; }
.inside {list-style-position: inside; }
-->
</STYLE>
<BODY>
The following list describes features of Montanaboat river boats:

<UL>
  <LI class="outside">Ash/Fir Oars</LI>
    <LI class="inside">sleeves</LI>
    <LI class="inside">tips</LI>
    <LI class="inside">bronze 5/8" oarlocks</LI>
    <LI class="inside">nylon bushing</LI>
  <LI class="outside">25 lb. anchor; nylon &amp; stainless steel ballbearing
    pulleys, 50ft. of 1/2"rope</LI>
  <LI class="outside">3 swivel seats adjust for flyfishing or pulling plugs</LI>
  <LI class="outside">Marine ply hull</LI>
    <LI class="inside">sides 3/8"</LI>
    <LI class="inside">bottom 11/8" thick</LI>
    <LI class="inside">hardwood trim</LI>
  <LI class="outside">Bow eye, drain plug, unobstructed non-skid floor</LI>
  <LI class="outside">Level  front floor on wide model</LI>
  <LI class="outside">Lower dry storage deck in bow</LI>
  <LI class="outside">Power: longshaft outboard to 8 hp</LI>
  <LI class="outside">Seat heights fit dry boxes and coolers</LI>
  <LI class="outside">Slick graphite bottom glides over rocks ramps</LI>
  <LI class="outside">Choice of color. Lifetime Guarantee</LI></UL>
</BODY>
</HTML>
```

Here is what this code looks like on a standard browser:

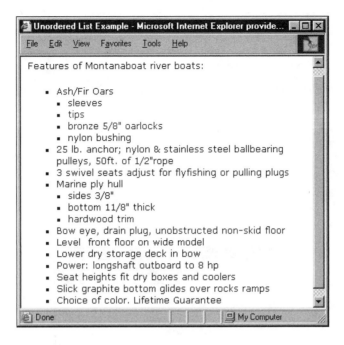

Color

The WCAG checkpoint 2.2 recommends that the foreground and background color combinations provide sufficient contrast when viewed by someone having color deficits or when viewed on a black and white screen. In HTML 4 and XHTML 1, all of the elements and attributes that designers have become accustomed to using have been deprecated in favor of using styles to achieve the same or better results.

The color property is used to set the text (or foreground) color. When you set a foreground color, you should also set a background color, since you have no way of knowing whether the user has set a background color in their browser preferences or personal stylesheet that may not contrast sufficiently with the color you've chosen.

The CSS properties for color include "color" for foreground color, background-color for background colors, border-color and outline-color for border colors. For link colors designers should refer to the :link, :visited, and :active pseudo-classes.

Here is an example in which we set all the heading text blue and link text purple using a stylesheet:

```
<HTML>
<TITLE>Color Example</TITLE>

<STYLE>
<!--
H2 { font-size: 1.5em; color: blue; }
A { font-family: Verdana, Arial, san-serif; font-size: 1.1em; color: purple; }
-->
</STYLE>
```

```
<BODY>
<H2>Related Links</H2>
<A href="http://www.woodenboat.com">WoodenBoat Publications</A> <BR />
<A href="http://www.riverstouch.com">The River's Touch</A> <BR />
<A href="http://www.glaciertoyellowstone.com">Montana Fly Fishing</A> <BR />
<A href="http://www.flyshop.com">Fly Fisherman On-Line</A> <BR />
<A href="http://www.greatlodge.com">GreatLodge</A> <BR />
<A href="http://www.worldwaters.com">WorldWaters</A> <BR />
<A href="http://www.databoat.com">DataBoat</A> <BR />
<A href="http://www.kingfisherflyshop.com">The Kingfisher</A> <BR />
<A href="http://www.flyfish.com">The Flyfishing Resource Guide</A>
</BODY>
</HTML>
```

And here is the output:

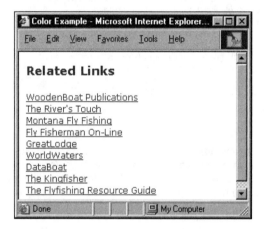

Aural Stylesheets

Aural stylesheets enable voice-rendered documents that combine speech synthesis and "auditory icons". According to the W3C's CSS2 specification on aural stylesheets, the advantage of using aural stylesheets is that the original structure of the document can be preserved. Unfortunately, aural stylesheets are supported by very few browsers. Emacspeak 15.0, is a speech interface that fully supports aural stylesheets. More information is available at this web site: *http://www.cs.cornell.edu/Info/People/raman/emacspeak/emacspeak.html*.

It is more effective for the person visiting the site to hear a well-programmed aural stylesheet than to convert the document to plain text and then use a screen reader to vocalize the text. Stylesheet properties for aural presentation may be used together with visual properties, called mixed media, or as an aural alternative to visual presentation. CSS2 supports aural stylesheets and the designer can specify how a document will sound when rendered as speech. The aural properties provide information to non-sighted users and voice-browser users much in the same way as fonts provide visual information. Indeed, when they are fully supported they will be valuable to a range of users, for example, greeting a visitor using a voice upon their arrival or for those who want directions while they are driving.

The way that aural stylesheets work is that the designer sets up the page such that it consists of a three-dimensional space, or sound surrounds, and a temporal space to specify sounds before, during, and after other sounds. Several properties are identified in the CSS2 specification, including volume, speak, pause, cue, play-during, azimuth, elevation, speech-rate, voice-family, pitch, pitch-range, speech-punctuation, speech-numeral, and speech-header. Detailed information can be found in the CSS2 specification, which can be found at: *http://www.w3.org/TR/REC-CSS2/aural.html.*

The following example demonstrates how to set up an aural stylesheet to read H1-H3 headings in a rich (bright) female voice with an average pitch (around 210 Hz), while H4-H6 headings would be read in an average soft male voice. Paragraphs with class Sydney would be read in a child's voice that seems to come from the left side; paragraphs of class Louis will be read in a child's voice from the right side, and paragraphs of class Robert would quickly spell out text one letter at a time (useful for acronyms and abbreviations) in a male voice with a pause after each word.

```
H1, H2, H3
{ voice-family: female;
richness: 90;
pitch: medium;
pitch-range: 60;
}
H4, H5, H6 {
voice-family: male;
volume: soft;
}
p.sydney  {   voice-family: child; azimuth: left;  }
p.louis  {   voice-family: child; azimuth: right;  }
p.robert  {   voice-family: male; speak: spell-out; pause-after: 250ms; speech-
rate: fast;  }
```

The ability to spatially organize information using auditory means is a powerful tool for designers. As browser technologies advance, then aural stylesheets will significantly enhance the experience of non-sighted users and voice-browser users.

Media Types

Media types allow authors and users to design stylesheets that will cause documents to render more appropriately on certain target devices, such as handhelds, Braille devices, speech synthesizers, computer screens, and the printed page. Some stylesheet properties are only available for specific media, such as the `speech-rate` attribute for aural media types. Stylesheets can also be used to specify how a document will look on a computer screen versus a printed version of the same page. Often designers have to create two separate versions of the page, because the version of the web page does not print well or it includes a lot of extraneous information that does not need to be included in the printout.

One way to specify media dependencies for stylesheets is to specify the target device with `@media` rule in the stylesheet. The `@media` rule in the `<style>` element is used to specify the target medium or media (separated by commas) in which the document is to be presented or displayed. The default media is "screen" (referring to a nonpaged computer display). The example shows how a different media could be specified for computer screen and paged printed documents:

```
<HEAD>
<TITLE>Montana Boat Home Page</TITLE>
<STYLE type="text/css">
<!--
@media screen {
BODY {background-color: #ccccff; color: #333399;
     font-family: verdana, arial, san-serif;
     margin-top: 30px; bottom-margin: 30px;
     margin-left: 30px; margin-right: 30px; }

H1 { font-family: geneva, verdana, arial, san-serif; }
}

@media print {
     BODY { font-family: helvetica, times new roman, serif; margin: 10px; }
     H1 { font-family: helvetica, times new roman, serif; text-align: center; }
}
-->
</STYLE>
</HEAD>
```

Otherwise you can use the @import at-rule to import an external stylesheet. The code example demonstrates how to use this rule to access an external aural stylesheet:

```
<HEAD>
<TITLE>Montana Boat Home Page</TITLE>
<STYLE type="text/css">
<!--
@import url ("../montanaboatvoice.css") aural;
-->
</STYLE>
</HEAD>
```

Another way to specify the media type is to use the `media` attribute. The following example shows how this could be done by placing `media="screen"` and `media="print"` in the `<style>` element:

```
<HEAD>
<TITLE>Montana Boat Home Page</TITLE>
<STYLE type="text/css" media="screen">
<!--
BODY {background-color: #ccccff; color: #333399;
     font-family: verdana, arial, san-serif;
     margin-top: 30px; bottom-margin: 30px;
     margin-left: 30px; margin-right: 30px; }
H1 { font-family: geneva, verdana, arial, san-serif; }
-->
</STYLE>

<STYLE type="text/css" media="print">
<!--
BODY { font-family: helvetica, times new roman, serif; margin: 10px; }
H1 { font-family: helvetica, times new roman, serif; text-align: center; }
-->
```

```
</STYLE>
</HEAD>

<BODY>
<H1>Montanaboat.com</H1>
<P>
This is the original Montanaboat, accept only the best.
<BR />
<BR />
The Montanaboat has been used by guides throughout the world.
<BR />
Time tested and fish approved!
<BR />
Call 406 721-7604 now to get your order in!
</P>
</BODY>
```

In this example, several different fonts were specified. The first screenshot shows how the page would display on a computer screen:

And the second screenshot shows how the printed document would look:

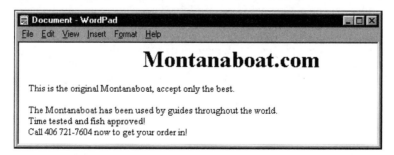

Finally, the media type can be specified within the document language. For example, you could link to an external stylesheet using the `<link>` element with a `media` attribute:

```
<LINK rel="stylesheet" href="montanaboat.css" type="text/css" media="print,
embossed">
```

The full CSS2 specification for media types can be found at: *http://www.w3.org/TR/REC-CSS2/medial.html.*

Using @media or @import rules can reduce download times by allowing browsers to ignore inapplicable rules.

Recognized Media Types

The HTML 4.0 specification refers to a variety of media attributes. These media attribute descriptors are the values reflect the target devices for which they are relevant.

Media attribute	Target device description
all	All devices
aural	Speech synthesizers
braille	Braille tactile feedback devices
embossed	Paged braille printers
handheld	Small-screen devices, for example, PDAs or cell phones
print	Paged printed documents
projection	Projected presentations, for example, projectors or print to transparencies
screen	Color computer screens
tty	Teletypes, terminals, or portable devices with fixed-pitch displays
tv	Television-type devices

Designing Pages That Are Readable Without Stylesheets

Since Section 508 requires that pages be readable if the stylesheet is turned off altogether, designers must remain cognizant of how the page will render when the stylesheets are removed. Organizing pages in a consistent, logical manner would help to ensure that the page would be readable without stylesheets. Grouping similar information, placing the most important information at or near the top, grouping global navigational links, placing menu-type items horizontally below the global links, using a left-to-right design orientation for English language content, and so on, would make linearized versions of the page much more understandable. If designers use these kinds of design principles for layout and organization, the pages may not be as visually complex as most web sites, but functionally they will be more usable. If you are not able for one reason or another to keep the design of the page simple, then you may want to consider making a text-only version of the page as recommended in WCAG Checkpoint 10.3.

Reading Pages with CSS Turned Off

CSS can be turned off by renaming the external style, turning off the styling using browser features, or commenting out the style element code. Even though the newer browsers allow users to turn off formatting such as font style, font sizes, and colors, this does not really ensure that style is not being rendered altogether.

To completely disable stylesheets, designers using stylesheet files can rename the file to a different extension than .css. The next step depends on the browser because there are significant differences between the way Internet Explorer and Netscape address stylesheets.

In Internet Explorer, no specific procedure exists to turn the stylesheet off altogether, so designers need to rename the .css file and create a "nostyle.css" empty stylesheet. In addition, in Internet Explorer 5 and higher, use the Accessibility button on the *Tools | Internet Options* menu to access the accessibility features. Check the three boxes at the Accessibility Dialog to ignore colors, font styles, and font sizes. Also, uncheck the box to "*Format documents using my stylesheet*", or check it and specify an empty stylesheet.

> *To create an empty stylesheet merely use Notepad to create a file, and save it as something like "nostyle.css". Then specify that file and correct path in the Accessibility dialog box.*

In Netscape, use the *Edit | Preferences | Advanced* menu, and then uncheck *Enable stylesheets*. Make sure that you clear the cache before you start working with the pages again.

The Lynx Browser

The Lynx browser gives designers a good idea about how a text version of the page would be rendered. It is best to download the Lynx browser to your machine, and run the application locally, if possible, especially for sites that are located inside firewalls. However, the Lynx Viewer, which can be found at *http://www.delorie.com/web/lynxview.html*, gives a reasonable approximation, offering a quick way to view pages through a text-mode web browser.

Montanaboat.com

We'll now take a detailed look at our case study, *montanaboat.com*. The *montanaboat.com* home page is shown below in Internet Explorer 5.5 and part of the code that generated it. The page includes a visual table, a tabular data table, and an unordered list that will be used to demonstrate how the Lynx browser creates a text version of the page:

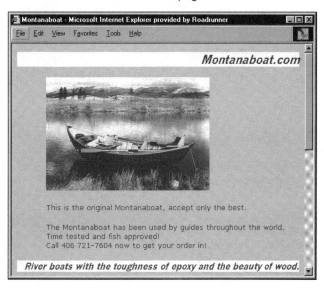

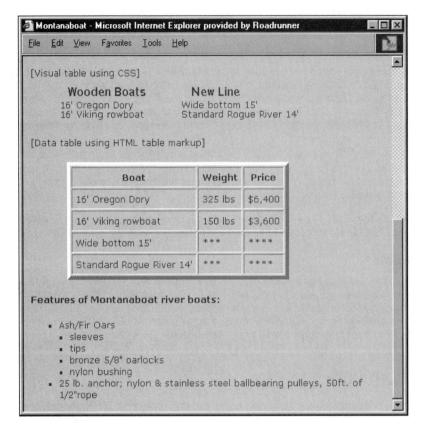

Here is the HTML source code for *montanaboat.com*:

```
<HTML>
<HEAD>
<TITLE>Montanaboat</TITLE>
<STYLE TYPE="text/css" MEDIA="screen">
BODY { background-color: #ccccff; color: #333399; }
H1 { text-align: right; font: bold italic 160% sans-serif;
     color: #333399; background-color: white; }
H2 { text-align: right; font: bold italic 120% sans-serif;
     color: #333399;  background-color: white; }
H4 { text-align: left; font-weight: bold;
    background-color: #ccccff; color: #333399; }
.special { text-align: justify;  margin-left: 4em;}
.menu1 { position: absolute; top: 28em; left: 4em;
         margin: 0px; font-family: sans-serif; font-weight: bold;
         font-size: 120%; color: #333399; background-color: #ccccff; }
.menu2 { position: absolute; top: 28em; left: 15em;
         margin: 0px; font-family: sans-serif; font-weight: bold;
         font-size: 120%; color: #333399; background-color: #ccccff; }
.item1 { position: absolute; top: 35em; left: 4em; margin: 0px; }
.item2 { position: absolute; top: 36em; left: 4em; margin: 0px; }
.item3 { position: absolute; top: 35em; left: 17em; margin: 0px; }
```

```
  .item4 { position: absolute; top: 36em; left: 17em; margin: 0px; }
  .outside {list-style-position: outside; }
  .inside {list-style-position: inside; }
  </STYLE>
  </HEAD>

  <BODY>
  <H1>Montanaboat.com</H1>
  <P class="special">
  <img SRC="images/stuboatsm.jpg" height="200" width="297" alt="Wide Bottom Drift
  Boat">
  <P class="special">
  This is the original Montanaboat, accept only the best.
  <P class="special">
  The Montanaboat has been used by guides throughout the world.
  <BR />
  Time tested and fish approved!
  <BR />
  Call 406 721-7604 now to get your order in!
  <H2>River boats with the toughness of epoxy and the beauty of wood.</H2>
  [Visual table using CSS]
  <BR />
  <DIV class="box">
    <SPAN class="menu1">Wooden Boats</SPAN>
    <SPAN class="item1">16' Oregon Dory</SPAN>
    <SPAN class="item2">16' Viking rowboat</SPAN>
    <SPAN class="menu2">New Line</SPAN>
    <SPAN class="item3">Wide bottom 15'</SPAN>
    <SPAN class="item4">Standard Rogue River 14'</SPAN>
  </DIV>
  <BR /><BR /><BR /><BR /><BR />

  [Data table using HTML table markup]
  <P class=special>
  <TABLE border=5 cellpadding=5 cellpadding=5>
  <TR><TH>Boat</TH><TH>Weight</TH><TH>Price</TH></TR>
  <TR><TD>16' Oregon Dory</TD><TD>325 lbs</TD><TD>$6,400</TD></TR>
  <TR><TD>16' Viking rowboat</TD><TD>150 lbs</TD><TD>$3,600</TD></TR>
  <TR><TD>Wide bottom 15'</TD><TD>***</TD><TD>****</TD></TR>
  <TR><TD>Standard Rogue River 14'</TD><TD>***</TD><TD>****</TD></TR>
  </TABLE>
  <P>
  <H4>Features of Montanaboat river boats:</H4>
  <UL>
    <LI class="outside">Ash/Fir Oars</LI>
      <LI class="inside">sleeves</LI>
      <LI class="inside">tips</LI>
      <LI class="inside">bronze 5/8" oarlocks</LI>
      <LI class="inside">nylon bushing</LI>
    <LI class="outside">25 lb. anchor; nylon &amp; stainless steel ballbearing
      pulleys, 50ft. of 1/2"rope</LI>
  <!--The rest of the HTML has been removed for space consideration--> <HTML>
```

To see what our page looks like with CSS turned off, we can use the Lynx Viewer. We simply enter the URL for the *montanaboat.com* page, and submit the page using the *View Page* button:

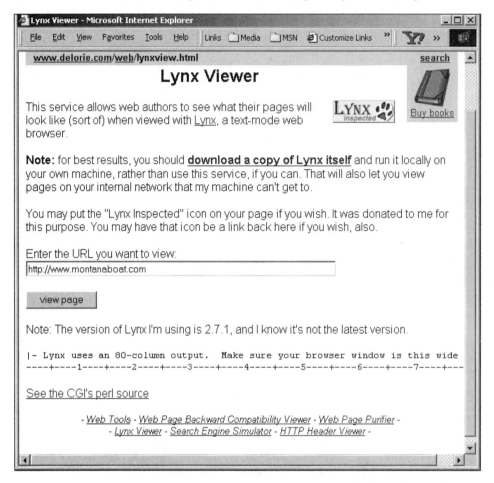

The output of the Lynx Viewer displays the entire page in a linearized fashion. The linearization issue that was described in the *display tables* section earlier in this chapter (see also Chapter 4 for more detail) is demonstrated again in the text-based Lynx Viewer. Using the Lynx Viewer is similar to turning CSS stylesheets off, since Lynx does not recognize stylesheets. In this particular example, the information in the visual table was designed using style elements, and it renders correctly when linearized:

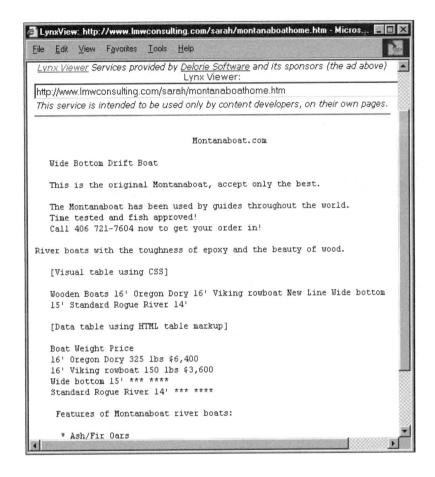

Testing & Validation

After spending a considerable amount of time working on a web site, designers would be wise to run their stylesheets through a CSS validation tool. It is a fast way to ensure that errors are caught before the site is published. CSS validation tools are very easy to use, and they serve as a form of proofreading. Common errors include forgetting to specify measuring units (for example, ems, pixels, percentages, etc.) and using regular parentheses instead of curly braces or using a colon instead of a semicolon. Validating stylesheets can also help ensure that designers are following best practices when creating the stylesheets. Remember that you need to validate your HTML files in addition to validating the CSS files, since you want to ensure that you don't have any errors in the HTML code as well. (The W3C site, *http://www.w3.org/*, has a link to an HTML validator.)

Validation for CSS accessibility compliance involves two steps. The first step is to make sure that the HTML page is Section 508 compliant, that is, readable without any stylesheets (as we described in the previous section). After making sure that the pages are rendering correctly without CSS, then designers should use a CSS validation tool to check the validity of the CSS code. Two main tools that exist for validating stylesheets: The W3C CSS Validation Service and the CSSCheck/CSSCheckup tools which we'll take a look at now.

W3C CSS Validation Service

To use the W3C CSS Validator, just go to the W3C's home page at *http://www.w3.org/* and click on the CSS Validator link in the sidebar menu. Three different methods are available for validating the CSS information:

entering a URL

pasting the stylesheet elements into a text area in the tool

uploading a stylesheet source file

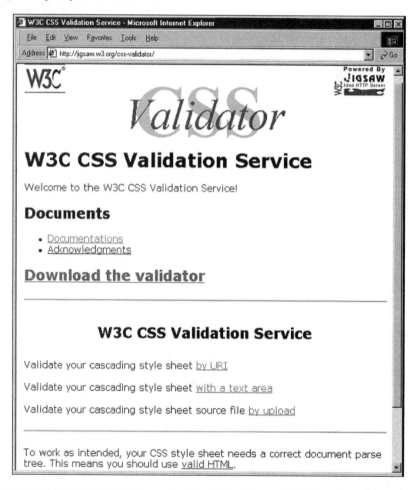

©1995 Worldwide Web Consortium (Massachusetts Institute of Technology, Institut National de Recherche en Informatique et en Automatique, Keio University. Full copyright available at: http://jigsaw.w3.org/css-validator/COPYRIGHT.html).

To use the first method, designers must transfer the CSS file to the web. As shown in the screenshot below, the next step is to specify the web address of the source file to be validated. Note that if the file cannot be accessed over the Web (outside of a firewall, for example), then designers cannot use this option.

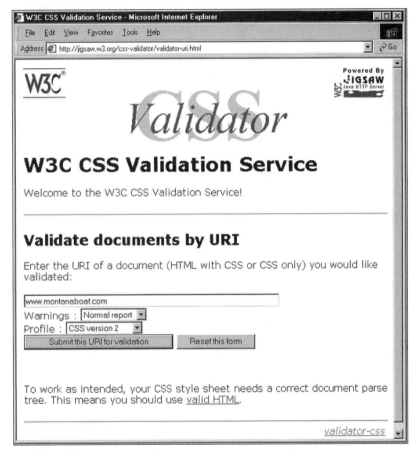

©1995 Worldwide Web Consortium (Massachusetts Institute of Technology, Institut National de Recherche en Informatique et en Automatique, Keio University. Full copyright available at: *http://jigsaw.w3.org/css-validator/COPYRIGHT.html*).

The second method of validating the CSS involves copying the stylesheet into the text area of the page. To use this method, only paste the style rules themselves into the text area – do not include the `<style>` begin and end tags or the comment tags.

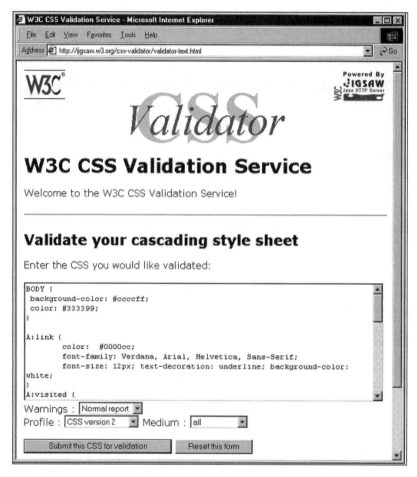

©1995 Worldwide Web Consortium (Massachusetts Institute of Technology, Institut National de Recherche en Informatique et en Automatique, Keio University. Full copyright available at: *http://jigsaw.w3.org/css-validator/COPYRIGHT.html*).

The third method allows designers to upload a standalone CSS stylesheet that has a .css extension. If your styles are embedded, rather than linked or imported, then copy and paste the style code into a separate blank text file and then save it as the upload file:

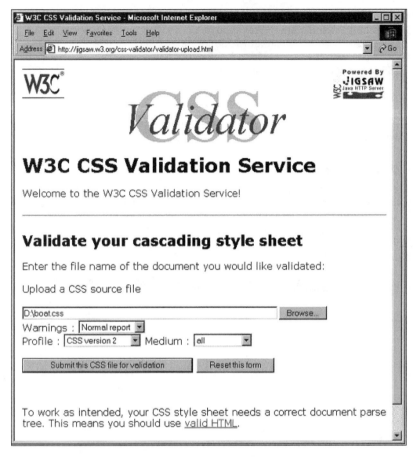

©1995 Worldwide Web Consortium (Massachusetts Institute of Technology, Institut National de Recherche en Informatique et en Automatique, Keio University. Full copyright available at: *http://jigsaw.w3.org/css-validator/COPYRIGHT.html*).

Validation Options

All three methods have additional features available for validating the stylesheet code at different levels. The *Warnings* list menu allows designers to set the level of warnings to be reported. "*All*" is the highest level, while "*No warning*" returns errors, but no warnings. The default is "*Normal report*", which is sufficient in most cases. The report that the tool generates may include both warnings and errors. Warnings generally refer to best practices for designing stylesheets. For example, you'll get a warning if you just specify a foreground color without also specifying a background color because a user might have created a stylesheet that specifies both foreground and background colors, and your foreground color might be the same or similar to the user-specified custom background color. The result would be that your text would be difficult to read. Errors, however, are mistakes that need to be fixed, for example, using regular parentheses instead of curly braces. The stylesheet will not work properly if the errors are not corrected.

The *Profiles* list allows designers to set the level of CSS support to be validated. Again, the default setting, CSS version 2, is sufficient. If you choose the second option, CSS version 1, any CSS2 properties or selectors in your stylesheet will generate errors. The other options are "*No special profile*", and "*Mobile*", with the latter testing for conformance to the W3C's CSS Mobile Profile, a subset of CSS2 that is tailored for mobile devices, such as cell phones or other wireless devices.

When using either of the last two validation methods (text area method or upload the CSS source file), the *Medium* option allows designers to specify the stylesheet's target medium. The default, "*All*", is the recommended option. The other options enable designers to select a specific target medium for which to test the stylesheet.

W3C Validation Example

When the *montanaboats.com* web site was initially validated using the W3C CSS Validation tool, the report identified three errors and one warning. The CSS Validation tool evaluated the syntax for every line of the CSS code for typos and incorrect use of semi-colons, colons, curly braces, etc. It also assessed whether there were any property/value mismatches. The errors uncovered on the example page included using a colon when a semi-colon should have been used in the <body> element, and a missing colon in the menu code. The following report was produced:

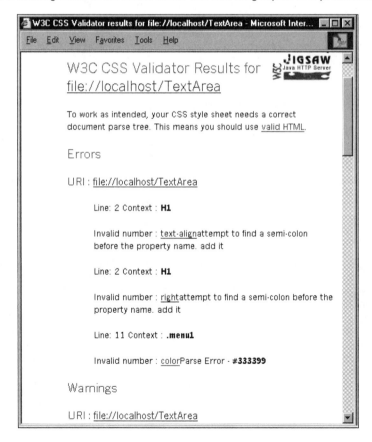

©1995 Worldwide Web Consortium (Massachusetts Institute of Technology, Institut National de Recherche en Informatique et en Automatique, Keio University. Full copyright available at: *http://jigsaw.w3.org/css-validator/COPYRIGHT.html*).

After the stylesheet was corrected, the validation tool gave a message indicating that the stylesheet found no errors. The W3C provides designers with the code to include the icon on the page to show that it has been programmed using valid CSS code. The following screenshot displays the approval page for *montanaboat.com*:

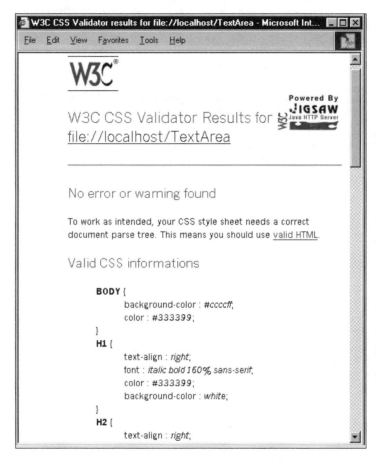

©1995 Worldwide Web Consortium (Massachusetts Institute of Technology, Institut National de Recherche en Informatique et en Automatique, Keio University. Full copyright available at: *http://jigsaw.w3.org/css-validator/COPYRIGHT.html*).

CSSCheck

The Web Design Group has created two tools to validate CSS code. The first tool, CSSCheck, which can be found at *http://www.htmlhelp.com/tools/csscheck/*, allows designers to enter the URL of a CSS, or enter a stylesheet directly into the text area on the page. CSSCheckUp (*http://www.htmlhelp.com/tools/csscheck/upload.html*) is a related tool that allows designers to check files on the computer by uploading them. Note that unlike the W3C CSS Validation Service, designers cannot just specify the URL of an HTML file containing a stylesheet. The following screenshots show the CSSCheck tool and the CSSCheckUp tool:

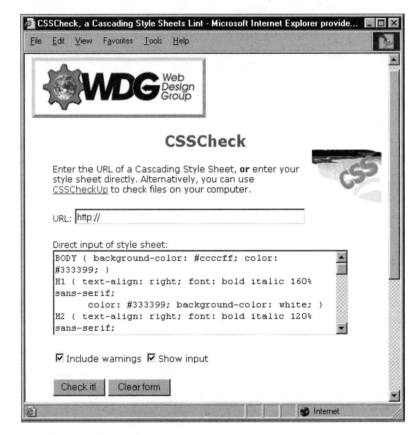

WWG CSSCheck validation tool. ©1997-99 Liam Quinn.

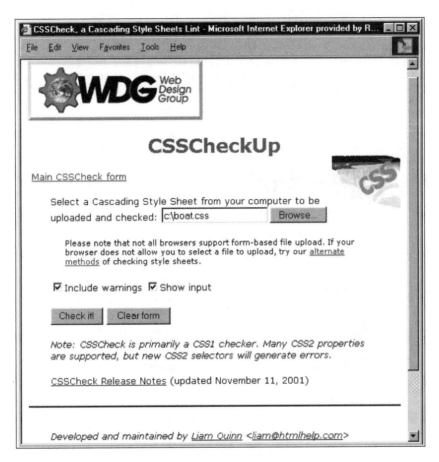

©1997-99 Liam Quinn.

DG CSSCheckUp Example

Using the WDG CSSCheckUp tool to validate the *montanaboat.com* web stylesheet demonstrates that the WDG CSSCheckUp tool is more rigorous than the W3C CSS Validation Service, usually producing more warnings. See the screenshot overleaf for the validation results of the original version of the *montanaboat.com* CSS source file.

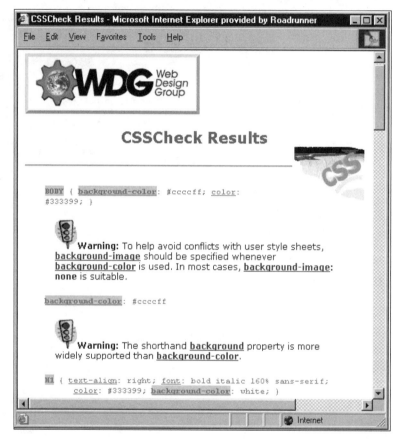

©1997-99 Liam Quinn.

Similar to the W3C CSS Validation Service, when the CSS stylesheet was corrected, an approval page displayed.

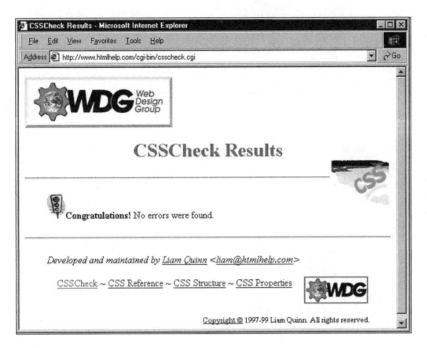

©1997-99 Liam Quinn.

Repair Tools

Validators usually report what problems were found, and maybe even give examples to help solve them, but they do not allow designers to repair the code interactively. The WAI Evaluation and Repair Working Group (http://www.w3.org/WAI/ER/) are working to develop a suite of tools that will help designers to identify issues and to solve them interactively as well.

Summary

This chapter described how designers could use stylesheets to separate the content of the page from the visual presentation aspects. Practical examples were used to demonstrate how to use stylesheets to make your web sites more usable and accessible for all users, not just disabled users. Although learning to use stylesheets may involve some practice, they are worth the extra effort to create elegant, flexible, and progressive web sites.

10

- Making flash content accessible

- Flash Player 6

- Flash MX

Author: Bob Regan

Accessibility and Macromedia Flash

Rich media plays an increasingly important role in the web as it matures and spills over the traditional boundaries of HTML and text markup. First there was music, video and animation, and the web started to look different from a word processed document. Next, there came interactivity, and the web started to behave differently from a word processing document. As developers and the technologies have matured, the line between a web page and an application has become increasingly blurred.

From an accessibility standpoint, rich media presents some unique challenges for accessible design. Often, designers anticipate that users will visually scan a page quickly and often in several places at once. However, a screen reader user concentrates on one piece of content at a time, as it is read aloud. If there is one mantra of accessible rich media, it is to keep it simple, but at the same time, rich media offers some tools and techniques that are not available in plain old HTML.

With the advent of Macromedia Flash MX, designers are able to create content that works with assistive technologies in ways that were not previously possible. In this chapter, we look at the tools and techniques available that can be used to make Flash accessible.

Flash Player 6

Flash Player 6 is the first rich media player to make web content available to screen readers, using Microsoft® Active Accessibility® (MSAA) to serve as a bridge between Flash Player 6 and assistive technologies such as Window-Eyes. Adopting MSAA makes it easier for other vendors of screen readers and assistive technologies to integrate support for Flash Player 6.

Flash Player 6 also makes available Flash content generated in previous versions of Flash. Text elements and buttons in Flash movies created in Flash 4 and 5 will be made available to screen readers, without modification. This means that the majority of Flash content available today will be significantly more accessible using Flash Player 6. The Flash player is available free from *http://www.macromedia.com/*.

Flash MX

The screen reader environment poses new challenges for many designers and developers. While providing text equivalents may now be simple, knowing what to say isn't always quite so easy. Just as designers and developers are mindful of the user experience in a browser or standalone environment, it is important to consider how users of assistive technologies such as screen readers will interact with Flash content.

Flash MX allows us to meet all of the design requirements set forth in Section 508. Features that are built into the product today – such as support for Microsoft Active Accessibility (MSAA), content magnification, mouse-free navigation, sound synchronization, and custom color palettes – can help us to deliver accessible web content through rich media.

In general, there are four key issues for designers and developers of Macromedia Flash content:

- Text Equivalents

- Animated Elements

- Buttons and Forms

- Tab Order

These issues will be looked at in the sections below.

Text Equivalents

To help create accessible Flash content, a new *Accessibility* panel has been added to Flash MX, which allows text equivalents to be specified for elements of Flash movies, and provides control over how assistive technologies handle these elements. Shown opposite, the Accessibility panel allows designers and developers to specify a brief descriptive text equivalent in the *Name* field. A longer text equivalent, if needed, can be placed in the *Description* field. This makes it very easy to specify what a screen reader will speak as it encounters individual elements of a movie.

Using Microsoft Active Accessibility (MSAA), Flash Player 6 exposes Flash content to the screen reader. Text contained within a Flash movie is exposed by default; however, graphic elements are not exposed automatically. As in HTML, graphic elements require a text equivalent that is read by the screen reader in place of the image. In Flash MX, you can easily assign text equivalents for elements in Flash content. In most cases, the biggest challenge for designers and developers is deciding when to use text equivalents and what they should say.

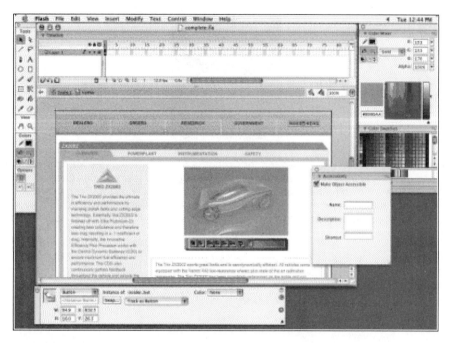

Next, we will look at how Flash Player 6 handles text equivalents, how you go about adding text equivalents to elements of a Flash movie, and we will review the accessible elements available in Flash MX.

Text in Flash Player 6

By default, Macromedia Flash Player 6 exposes all text elements to the screen reader user; designers and developers do not need make any modifications. For example, the simple Flash banner below was created by adding text to the stage (the proper name for the Flash working environment).

Keep in mind that not all assistive technologies handle MSAA data in the same way. There may be slight differences from one tool to another and from one screen reader to another. A screen reader might read this banner as "Trio Motor Company." Text is read by default; therefore, the designer/developer would not need to make any changes to this movie in order to make it accessible to screen readers.

Adding Text Equivalents in Flash MX

Now let's look at another example that will require a text equivalent. In the example overleaf, the Flash MX logo is displayed. The letter 'f' in the logo is not actually text, but a graphic that is part of the design as a whole.

Since the letter 'f' is not text, a screen reader cannot read it. Moreover, the letter 'f' alone does not provide enough information about the banner for screen reader users. In this case a text equivalent should be provided. To add a text equivalent, use the Accessibility panel. First, make sure the logo is selected. Before adding a text equivalent to this item, the object must be saved as a symbol in the library. Since text equivalents are not supported for graphic symbols, save the object as a movie symbol or a button.

To bring the Accessibility panel to the front, press *F9*.

Notice the two fields titled *Name* and *Description*. In general terms, the *Name* field is used for shorter text equivalents and the *Description* field is used for longer ones, paralleling the use of the `alt` and `longdesc` attributes in HTML.

Deciding on the proper text equivalent is not always easy. In most cases, it is wise to consider the purpose of the image rather than giving it a merely literal description. In the example above, a description may read, "Dark rectangle with letter f in red." This may not be particularly helpful information to a screen reader user. By contrast, the phrase "Flash MX" might be a more meaningful equivalent for the logo.

In this case a description would not likely be necessary. Descriptions are best used in cases where the text equivalent needs to be longer than about 50 characters. One thing to keep in mind is that the description is generally read following the name. If the content does not flow when the two are read together, you may choose not to use a name, rather a description of the object.

Accessible Elements of a Flash Movie

By default, Flash MX is able to make text, input text fields, buttons, movie clips, and even entire movies accessible. While text elements do not require modification, other elements do (for example, by adding a text equivalent as discussed above, or even hiding elements from assistive technologies).

In the previous example, the logo has a letter 'f' inside of a dark rectangle. If the letter were a text element, it would be read after the name of the logo. In this case, the screen reader would likely read, "Macromedia Flash MX, F."

To prevent this, we will select the logo and decheck the *Make Child Objects Accessible* option, as seen below. This action tells the screen reader not to look inside of the Flash logo for other elements. This time, the screen reader would read, "Macromedia Flash MX".

Understanding when not to make an object or child objects accessible can be a complex issue. It is not always necessary or helpful to make all elements of a movie accessible, for example an animation of an electric car engine running, a screenshot of which can be seen here:

Since the relationships displayed here are inherently visual, it will not be helpful to provide names for the parts of the engine. Instead, we can provide a single text equivalent for the entire animation that describes what is being displayed. In the *Accessibility* panel, we shall deselect all elements on the stage. As before, the *Make Child Objects Accessible* option is deselected, and a description for the animation is entered, to be displayed, and/or read out by a screen reader.

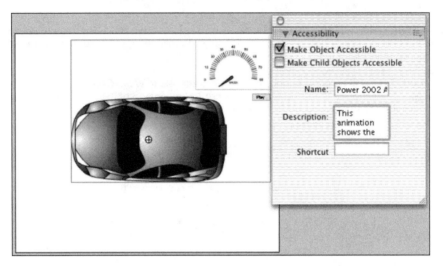

Animated Events

A second general issue for Flash designers and developers is the use of animated elements. Screen readers are designed to work best with web content that changes based on user commands like a mouse click or a button press that causes a new page to load, whereas Flash content operates on an entirely different model.

Macromedia Flash movies may change constantly without requiring the page to refresh; consequently designers and developers should be mindful of how a Flash movie will work with a screen reader. Flash MX provides a powerful set of tools for creating animations and interactive content and applications; however, most assistive technologies are not designed with these types of animations in mind. This section covers how Flash MX allows optimization of accessibility when creating animation:

- Understanding how assistive technologies handle animation

- Providing text equivalents for entire movies

- Animation and buttons

Understanding How Assistive Technologies Handle Animation

When a screen reader encounters a piece of Flash content, the screen reader loads the current state of the movie and notifies the user. With the Window-Eyes screen reader for example, the user hears, "Loading...load done." Once a piece of content has been read, the screen reader moves on to read other parts of the Flash content and the rest of the page.

A basic feature of Flash content is that it may change over time. As the content changes, Flash Player 6 sends a signal to the screen reader notifying it that there has been a change. When the screen reader receives this notification, it automatically returns to the top of the page and begins reading it again.

The following example illustrates the serious implications of Flash animations created without consideration for users of screen readers. A poorly designed logo with spinning letters placed at the top of the page might loop constantly through a few frames. When Flash Player encounters this banner, it will send repeated notifications to the screen reader of changes in the content, and the screen reader will continually return to the top of the page. This problem can seriously erode the user experience for screen reader users.

To address this specific issue, Macromedia worked with GW Micro to create a "Halt Flash events" keystroke (*Alt-Shift-M*) for the Window-Eyes screen reader. This keystroke allows a screen reader user to suspend Flash notifications on the page. Pressing the keystroke again allows the user to resume Flash notifications.

Providing Text Equivalents for Entire Movies

A better solution for the handling of animation is simply to hide the animation from assistive technologies. Flash MX allows designers and developers to assign a text equivalent for an entire movie or for a collection of objects within a movie. Designers and developers might choose to provide a text equivalent for Flash content for one of two reasons:

1. Animations are often used to illustrate visual relationships among elements on the screen. Adding text equivalents to the individual elements may not provide a sufficient description of the relationships among the elements, for example in an animation of the solar system, we might add text equivalents to the planets; however, these text equivalents would not convey information about how the planets move in relation to one another. A text equivalent for the entire movie could provide a better description of this relationship.

2. Text equivalents may be used to hide animated content from the screen reader. In the example of a rotating banner ad, a single text equivalent for the entire ad would convey the content of the advertisement to the user and prevent the screen reader from constantly returning to the top of the page.

Animation and Buttons

Developers of accessible Flash content should refrain from using animated movie clips or other animations within button symbols in Flash MX. The use of such animations makes it difficult for screen readers and other assistive technologies to work with buttons.

Buttons and Forms

A third important use of Flash MX is creating interactive applications that allow users to click, drag, and enter data into the movie. Making an application accessible means enabling users not only to access the content, but to operate the controls as well.

This section will discuss the following accessibility issues related to the use of buttons and form objects in Macromedia Flash MX:

- Buttons and Forms in Flash Player 6

- Auto-labeling in Flash MX

- Using the down state in buttons

- Notes on keyboard shortcuts

- Creating accessible forms

Buttons and Forms in Macromedia Flash Player 6

By default, the Flash Player makes buttons available to assistive technology. With a screen reader, the sample button below would be read as follows. First, the word 'button' is read to provide a cue to the user that there is an action associated with this element. Next, the text equivalent is read to the user – in this case, the word 'Home'. Finally, the user may activate this button by pressing *Enter* on the keyboard.

As with buttons, screen reader users are also notified of form fields. In the example below, the screen reader might read, "Electronic Registration. Edit Box: Name. Edit Box: Address. Button: Send."

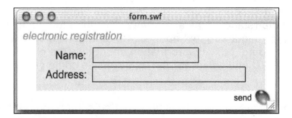

Auto-Labeling in Flash MX

In both of the examples above, the name and description do not have to be specified in the *Accessibility* panel. Flash MX uses its auto-labeling feature to generate the labels automatically. It looks for a text label placed on top of, inside, or near a button or text field. When the Flash Player discovers an arrangement like this, it assumes that the text object is a label for the button or text field.

In some cases, it may be desirable to specify a text equivalent that is different from the text label. This may be appropriate when using a short text label, or when the label is split up or placed away from the button or form object.

In the example below, notice that the name fields are grouped visually. Putting the word *name* at the top implies that the labels *first* and *last* signify "first name" and "last name." Using assistive technology, this relationship may not be obvious. To clarify these labels, the text equivalents "first name" and "last name" can be specified using the *Accessibility* panel.

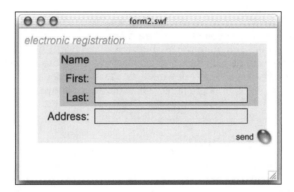

In this case, the text labels should be hidden from the assistive technology. Assistive technologies might otherwise read the text label and the text equivalent to say, "Name. First. Edit Box: First Name." If we convert the text objects to a movie symbol and then deselect the *Make Object Accessible* option, the assistive technology would read only the text equivalent. It would then read, "Edit Box: First Name."

Using the Down State in Buttons

In Flash MX, we are able to create buttons with animation and scripting to build complex interactions; however, screen readers and other assistive technologies generally work best with buttons that are relatively simple.

One common technique is to place text and graphics in the down state of a button in Flash MX. When the button is pressed, the text and graphics are revealed. The Flash Player does not expose the contents of the down state, except for a single text element. Navigational cues, menu bars, and other content are not made available using this technique.

Another common technique among Flash designers and developers is the use of invisible buttons placed over a background with text. This practice is discouraged for accessibility purposes, because the Flash Player notices only buttons that have content; thus invisible buttons are not made available to assistive technologies.

Notes on Keyboard Shortcuts

The keyboard shortcut field on the *Accessibility* panel allows us to add keystrokes to individual buttons and form elements. To provide a keyboard shortcut, ActionScript must be used to detect keypresses by the user during movie playback. Keyboard shortcut functionality can vary depending on the assistive technology and software used.

For keyboard shortcuts the following conventions are recommended:

- Spell out key-names, such as *Ctrl* or *Alt*

- Use capital letters for alphabetic characters

- Use a plus sign (+) between key names, with no spaces – for example, *Ctrl+A*

Creating Accessible Forms

Flash MX allows designers and developers to create accessible forms to build dynamic web applications. The simple form components, such as input text, radio buttons, checkboxes, and component buttons, work with assistive technologies; however, more complex objects like the scroll bar, the combo box, and the list box do not work with assistive technologies. Macromedia plans to distribute accessible versions of these objects in the future, but they are not available as of the launch of Flash MX.

ActionScript and Accessibility

The fourth issue is the control of tab order in Flash content – we need to consider how screen readers will move through the contents of a Flash movie. The order in which screen readers perceive Macromedia Flash content may be controlled through careful placement on the stage or through the use of ActionScript, the scripting language of Flash.

Specifying a Tab Order Via ActionScript

When designing accessible Flash content, it is important to remember that many users of assistive technology use the keyboard alone to navigate through web content. As such, it is important that when a Flash project is being developed, it should provide alternative navigation methods for assistive technology. In many cases a user may simply navigate through content by hitting the *Tab* key on their keyboard. However, the default tab order (otherwise known as the tab index) may not reflect the visual layout of your Flash movie.

In the example below, two sets of buttons are presented visually as a row and a column. In cases where the designer would like the column of buttons to be read before the row, a tab order would need to be specified. This custom tab order for content within a Flash movie may be specified using ActionScript.

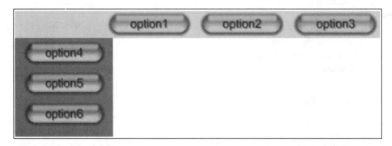

Tab order can be assigned to dynamic text objects, buttons, movie clips, and input text fields. To assign tab order to a static text object, you must first convert it to a dynamic text object. Next, each instance of the item on the stage must be given a name, different from the symbol name.

The instance name may be assigned on the *Property Inspector* (see the highlighted section below). It is important that instance names be assigned for each button, as well as for the dynamic text within that button.

Once this is done it's simply a matter of assigning a number to the `tabIndex` property. At the root level of the movie, the ActionScript code below is entered. In the first line, note that `myOption1` refers to the instance name of the button and `text` refers to the instance name for the dynamic text within the button. It is acceptable for all of the dynamic text elements to use the same instance name, since they exist within separate buttons:

```
_root.myOption1.text.tabIndex = 1;
_root.myOption2.text.tabIndex = 2;
_root.myOption3.text.tabIndex = 3;
_root.myOption4.text.tabIndex = 4;
_root.myOption5.text.tabIndex = 5;
_root.myOption6.text.tabIndex = 6;
```

Please make a note of the following exception however: if you provide a custom tab order for a given frame in your movie, and you do not specify a tab position for one or more of the accessible objects in that frame, the Flash Player will disregard your custom tab order when users are using a screen reader. It is important to realize that providing a complete tab order for all accessible objects requires assigning tab indexes to dynamic text objects and movie clips, even when these objects are not tab stops (they never receive the input focus).

Screen Reader Detection

You can sometimes improve the accessibility of your Flash content by altering the behavior of your movie when a screen reader is present. ActionScript provides a way to make this check: the function `Accessibility.isActive()` will return `true` when a screen reader is present, and `false` otherwise.

Consider the following example. In an e-commerce application built in Flash MX, there is a panel that rotates periodically among several product offers. This panel updates spontaneously every minute or so. This is less than ideal for screen reader users since the content may change before they have finished reading the page. In some cases, this will cause the screen reader to return to the top of the page each time a user nears the bottom of the content.

To deal with this problem, there are at least two solutions. We could use the *Accessibility* panel to hide the rotating content or its child elements. The disadvantage to this strategy is that the screen reader users would not know the content was there or would get a general text equivalent. A better option would be to skip the rotation of product offers when a screen reader is present – that is, when `Accessibility.isActive()` returns `true`.

There is a caveat to the use of `Accessibility.isActive()`. The communication between a screen reader and the Flash Player is asynchronous – that is, there is a small, variable real-time delay between when the Flash Player starts up and when a screen reader first contacts the Flash Player. This means that if you call `Accessibility.isActive()` early in the lifetime of a movie, you may get an answer of `false` even though a screen reader is present.

One way you can deal with this limitation is to call `Accessibility.isActive()` any time you need to make a decision regarding accessibility, instead of calling it just once at the beginning of your movie and using it to choose between two major modes. Another way to deal with this is simply to introduce a delay of one to two seconds at the beginning of your movie. It should be quite rare for a screen reader to take longer than two seconds to contact the Flash Player.

> Note that `Accessibility.isActive()` is not the same thing as
> `System.capabilities.hasAccessibility`. `Accessibility.isActive()` reports
> whether a screen reader is currently present, whereas
> `System.capabilities.hasAccessibility` simply reports whether the current
> Flash player supports screen readers.

Assigning Dynamic Accessibility Properties Using ActionScript

Flash provides developers with the ability to create dynamic content, such as movie clips that change based on user interaction, or text that may provide users with a targeted response based on their input. In each and all of these situations, it is important to consider users of assistive technology. This is an advanced technique that may require careful testing to ensure success.

Through the *Accessibility* panel, Flash MX already allows developers to provide a name and description of graphic elements and movie clips to better clarify what may be important to a user who may be unable to see key visual elements. For example: a movie clip of a car may need to be provided with the name, "red car", and a description, "An animation of a red car speeding away." This would be entered into the *Accessibility* panel. However, if this movie clip were dynamic and the contents of the movie clip changed, the clip's Accessibility properties would need to be updated as well to provide an accurate description of this new image. This update can be made via ActionScript. The following technique is a workaround developed for this purpose. Developers may find it works in individual circumstances, with varying results, so testing the effectiveness of this strategy in each case is extremely important to ensure it works with assistive technology.

The following example duplicates a MovieClip and then shrinks the duplicate clip to half the size of the original. In this example, the height and width of the movie clip may be meaningful in demonstrating some kind of statistical relationship between the two. For example, a larger picture of a red car might indicate a lower gas mileage. Because the size relationships between the two clips may not be obvious to users who are blind, a description of the second clip is needed to make this known. Using the `_accProps` object, this information can be assigned via ActionScript.

```
_root.myRedCar.duplicateMovieClip("myRedCar2");
_root.myRedCar2._width = _root.myRedCar._width /2;
_root.myRedCar2._height = _root.myRedCar._height /2;

_root.myNewClip.accessibilityName = "Second Red Car";
_root.myNewClip.accessibilityDescription = "This second red car is smaller than
the
                                        first.";
```

```
_root.myRedCar.duplicateMovieClip("myRedCar2");
_root.myRedCar2._width = _root.myRedCar._width / 2;
_root.myRedCar2._height = _root.myRedCar._height / 2;

_root.myRedCar._accProps = new Object();
_root.myRedCar2._accProps.name = "Second Red Car";
_root.myRedCar2._accProps.description = "This second car is smaller than the
                                         first.";
```

Notice in the last two lines of code, the name for the duplicate clip is assigned as `Second Red Car` and the description is assigned as `This second red car is smaller than the first`. This information is then made available to the screen reader.

The properties of the `_accProps` object mirror the controls in the *Accessibility* panel of Flash MX, although the property names do not match exactly. Here is the correspondence:

String properties:

Name in *Accessibility* panel	Name in `_accProps` object
Name	name
Description	description
Shortcut	shortcut

Boolean properties (sense inverted from the checkboxes in the Accessibility panel):

Name in *Accessibility* panel	Name in `_accProps` object
Make Object Accessible	silent
Make Child Objects Accessible	forceSimple
Auto Label	noAutoLabeling

Note that the various kinds of accessible objects – dynamic text objects, buttons, movie clips, and input text fields – have different combinations of the above properties applicable to them. You can see which of the properties apply by selecting an object of the appropriate type on the Stage and seeing which controls are present in the *Accessibility* panel. These same sets of properties apply in the `_accProps` object. Setting properties that aren't applicable, such as `forceSimple` for a button, has no effect.

Also note that for any particular object, you cannot use both the *Accessibility* panel and the `_accProps` object – make sure to use only one of the two. Also note that assignments to the properties of the `_accProps` object are only effective at the time that an object is first created; changing these properties later in the object's lifetime will have no effect.

Summary

Designing accessible content requires designers and developers to pay attention to the user experience. Since many Flash MX designers and developers are not familiar with the capabilities of screen readers and other assistive technologies, this section provides several hints to keep in mind while creating content in Flash MX. These hints are not intended to be a complete list or to serve as design guidelines for accessibility in Flash MX; rather, they are intended to provide helpful information to designers and developers striving to create accessible content in Flash MX.

Be sure to visit the Macromedia Accessibility Resource Center for up-to-date information on Macromedia Flash MX and other Macromedia products (*http://www.macromedia.com/macromedia/accessibility/*).

Accessibility Hints

The following are some practical suggestions for optimizing the accessibility of your Flash content:

- Provide text equivalents for graphic elements in Flash MX. Provide names for graphic icons. Add text equivalents for gesturing animations that highlight an area of the page. When you use a feature like "Break Apart" for text, be sure to provide a name or description.

- Consider visual relationships among elements when adding text equivalents. Think about whether it is better to provide a name for each element in a movie or whether the name should reflect a group of elements. For example, with an animation of the solar system, it might be more meaningful to say, "animation of solar system," rather than "Mercury, Venus, Earth," and so on.

- Try to avoid animating the text, buttons, and input text fields in your movie. Each time a Macromedia Flash movie updates, the screen reader receives a command to return to the top of the page. In the case of the Window-Eyes screen reader from GW Micro, the user will hear, "Loading page...load done" each time the screen reader returns to the top of the page. If you keep text, buttons, and other objects stable, you reduce the chance of causing a screen reader to emit extra "chatter" that may annoy users. For the same reason, try to avoid the use of looping movies.

- Remember that sound is a very important medium for most screen reader users. Consider how the sounds in your movie, if any, will interact with the text spoken aloud by screen readers. If you have a lot of loud sound, it may be difficult for a screen reader user to hear what the screen reader is saying. On the other hand, some quieter or well-placed sound can greatly enhance the experience.

- When creating interactive movies, make sure that users can navigate through your movie effectively using only the keyboard. Keep in mind that users can operate simple buttons and forms with the same keystrokes as in other applications. If you are using ActionScript to capture keystrokes, be sure to test the application in a screen reader. Different screen readers may process input from the keyboard differently.

- Try not to present information in your movie that remains on the screen for only a short time. Screen readers may have a difficult time keeping up with quick changes (for example, scenes that change every three seconds) in Flash movies. You can resolve this type of problem by adding `Next` buttons that control scene movement, or by including the full string of all of your text as a description for your entire movie.

11

- Integration of accessibility into enterprise
- Accessibility Organization
- Integration strategy

Author: Mark Urban

Implementing Accessibility in Enterprise

One of the best ways for any enterprise to successfully implement an accessibility solution is for there to be some sort of group or organization that will handle and support accessibility issues. The details of how this is done will differ depending on the type of enterprise. Certainly there will be differences in the way this is implemented in non-profit organizations, governmental entities, for profit businesses, and educational institutions. Larger enterprises will have different issues from middle sized and smaller organizations. There are, however, important similarities and this chapter will describe and highlight the important basics of implementing a web-based accessibility solution. We will look at the development of a model accessibility organization that could be set up within any enterprise of moderate to large size. The principles here are also useful for smaller enterprises even if they may not have the need or the resources to set up an Accessibility Organization. While this chapter is geared towards web accessibility, this process could also be used to implement other accessibility solutions, such as enterprise-wide standards for assistive and adaptive technology, or employment practices related to disability.

Model Accessibility Organization (AO)

It is important to understand why an AO or similar organization or group should exist in the first place. In any enterprise it is important to have consistency in policies and implementation technologies that will be used by employees and the public alike. Inconsistent policies lead to confusion amongst those who must implement them, and confusion amongst those who must use them. One of the main purposes of the AO will be to see that policies and the attendant technologies used to implement them are deployed in a consistent manner.

A **model accessibility organization** within a larger enterprise must have certain qualities. One of the most important is the ability to cut across departmental lines within an enterprise to maximize knowledge and awareness of accessibility itself. Its ultimate goal should be to build a group of qualified people within the company who can manage and oversee accessibility projects, rather than overseeing them itself. To that end, the AO should be a resource within the enterprise, not a controlling organization. Its management should be carefully structured and its members should have a mix of characteristics directly related to their role in implementing accessible web technology. The membership should mostly be drawn from departments that will use it, being mostly field personnel working on implementing accessible web technology. Most should only work in the group part-time, having their primary responsibilities in their departments, as their understanding of departmental needs may be invaluable in achieving successful integration of accessibility into your web technology. They should also have a commitment to implementing accessibility. There are several important concerns that must be addressed both from a management standpoint and from the standpoint of the accessible web technology itself, and we will examine these more closely as we go along.

Even though it is not a controlling organization per se, there must be an enforcement mechanism to ensure that accessibility standards and processes are implemented consistently. Let's now look at this AO from a number of different angles, using some of the questions that might be asked along the way as prompts. We'll discuss:

- The makeup of the AO

- AO functions

- The integration of AO strategy

Makeup of the AO

The AO should consist of members of stakeholder departments and internal experts in the field of web accessibility. As mentioned before, very few of the members of the AO should be full-time workers in the AO. Only a small number are needed to run the AO administrative functions. Most should be drawn from the departments that will be affected by the implementation of accessibility in web technology. All should be enthusiastic supporters of web accessibility and all should be committed to efficient and effective implementation. The AO will bring consistency of implementation to any enterprise, large or small; this is important to reduce confusion and to keep implementation efficient and cost effective. It is recommended that the AO not be just a working group, but have the authority and mandate to implement accessibility standards and policies throughout the enterprise. Just as an enterprise has certain standards in other areas so should it have accessibility standards that must be used.

All the AO members should be working towards the same goal and be personally and professionally committed to it. In other words, members must have great integrity in the way they pursue the goal of web accessibility.

The following diagram shows how an AO might be structured:

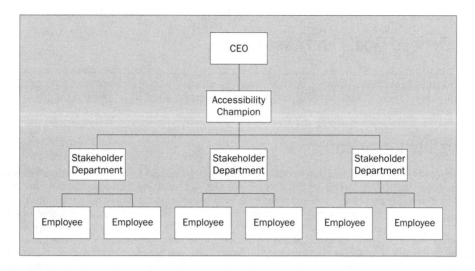

Lending Authority to Implementation

One of the most important factors in implementing accessibility is seeing to it that the organization charged with this implementation has the necessary authority to implement change, to match this responsibility. This organization must be able to set standards, make decisions on the tools needed and lay out the processes to be followed. Without such authority, the implementation of accessible web technology will be difficult if not impossible.

In addition the AO must also have authority to:

- Bring various groups together to discuss accessibility and discover, define, and articulate accessibility-related issues of concern to both the whole enterprise and to its individual parts.

- Use both the "carrot" and the "stick". It must be able to reward innovation, and discourage non-productive actions to ensure proper implementation of accessibility within the entire enterprise.

- Arbitrate disputes and settle misunderstandings about accessibility within and between departments. On occasion it will need to make decisions on issues that cannot be decided any other way.

Clear and Focused Scope

Defining the scope of the AO is critical to its success. Its scope must be narrow and well-defined to keep the organization small and compact. This will also help to keep the workload of its members from becoming too large to handle.

A clear and focused scope will also keep the organization from becoming bogged down in a morass of side issues not directly related to accessibility. The departments using the AO better handle these issues.

Clearly Defined Goals and Mission

The goals and mission of the AO should be clear and simple, helping members to understand clearly what is expected of them. This will keep the group on target for achieving its goals. For the initial implementation of accessibility, clear timelines must be set with checkpoints for the organization's goals.

Accessibility Champion

As shown in the previous figure the Accessibility Champion should have direct communication with the CEO or whoever is in charge of the enterprise. The Accessibility Champion is the person who must lead this effort and give it the initial focus and needed impetus. More than that, the Champion must see that the group stays focused, gets the resources it needs and has the authority necessary to accomplish its mission. The Champion must also be the one who makes sure that upper management understands the general issues, and that they are well enough informed about the progress of the AO. The Champion is also the person who will ultimately be responsible for the implementation and enforcement of the accessibility standards and policies that are the mission of the AO. In short they must be the person who leads.

Management

Below are some important concerns that the AO will have to deal with in order to be effective.

- Empowerment from the highest level

- Providing assistance and consulting services

- Commitment from upper management for implementation

- Choosing a web accessiblity Champion

- Implementation from the "bottom up"

- Pushing issues, by the Champion

- Overseeing of various aspects of the AO's operations and how they interface with the enterprise

- Positive and negative consequences involved with implementation of accessibility standards and methods within the enterprise (rewards and punishments)

The AO presented here is a model, and the factors above are only examples of the issues that it must deal with.

The AO must have empowerment from the highest levels of an enterprise. It must be able to assist or consult on all related projects. The upper management of your enterprise will need to make a commitment to implementing web accessibility. It must make this commitment publicly and provide financial backing for the AO. It is preferable for this empowerment and commitment to come from the head of your organization, such as the chancellor of a university, or the CEO of a corporation. It must be in place or there will be no effective implementation of accessibility in an enterprise of any size.

A good example of the types of organizations that have made such a commitment can be seen in the three letters sent to President Clinton by technology executives and research university presidents. These letters committed the organizations to various aspects of accessibility in general, but the principle is the same. The letters can be seen at:

http://www.icdri.org/digital_divide_summary_page.htm.

> *Although these letters were sent as a commitment to an initiative under the Clinton Administration, the group that initiated the commitment is still operating under the Bush administration and every indication is that the Bush Administration is heavily committed to disability issues in general and web accessibility in particular.*

After the head of your organization has committed to making your web technology accessible, a web accessibility "Champion" should be chosen, or should volunteer. This would be a member of upper management who is familiar with web accessibility issues, is in favor of their implementation, and has enough authority and prestige to ensure that everything that needs to be done, is done.

A bottom-up approach is fine for implementation and training about accessibility, but for this to succeed and to be implemented in an efficient and effective manner, there has to be at least one member of upper management who can "push" solutions when needed. They must have a good grounding in this area and they must believe in what they are doing. This is the role of the accessibility champion. The champion is the one who must be the driving force and should be responsible for forming the AO and choosing the people that will oversee the various aspects of the AO's operations.

It is unfortunate, but true, that if there are no consequences for non-compliance within organizational policy, low levels of compliance will generally follow. Negative consequences are necessary in order that standards are followed. On the positive side, it is just as important to reward meaningfully the efforts of those who do make the effort to implement web accessibility. The AO must be empowered to use both types of consequence as tools to implement web accessibility throughout the enterprise efficiently.

An Ad Hoc Approach Is Not Sufficient

In many enterprises that consider accessibility, the common approach is to create a project that will add accessibility to existing services, or offer accessibility on an ad hoc or as needed basis – addressing accessibility only when persons with disabilities raise issues. There are at least two dangers in this approach:

1. Adding accessibility to existing products and services is expensive, requiring accessibility personnel to understand the product or service and to develop a specific accessibility interface, often reinventing or re-engineering the product or service in the process.

2. The law, policy, and technical aspects of accessibility are often focused into a small team, who, due to attrition, illness, or competition, can disappear leaving no resource base for the enterprises.

It is important to understand some of the reasons for avoiding an ad hoc approach to web accessibility.

The US federal government, in looking at this problem, also realized that an ad hoc approach would not be effective in resolving some of the issues on an enterprise basis. The US Department of Justice, in a report to the federal agencies, stressed the need for a broad-based architectural approach:

> *"Data provided by the agencies suggest that the majority of agencies continue to handle IT accessibility issues exclusively on an "ad hoc" or "as needed" basis, instead of integrating accessibility into the development and procurement of their mainstream IT products (sic). Many IT officials hold the mistaken belief that persons with disabilities can always be accommodated upon request by using widely available assistive technology devices (e.g., screen readers, screen enlargers, volume control apparatuses, pointing devices that serve as alternatives to a computer mouse, voice recognition software, etc.) in conjunction with mainstream technology applications. Indeed, the goal of Section 508 is to ensure that the agency will always be able to provide reasonable accommodations. Without adequate planning, however, the possibility of providing an accommodation to a person with a disability may be foreclosed. Use of an "ad hoc" or "as needed" approach to IT accessibility will result in barriers for persons with disabilities. A much better approach is to integrate accessibility reviews into the earliest stages of design, development, and procurement of IT. Once an accessible IT architecture is established, then and only then can persons with disabilities be successfully accommodated on an "as needed" basis."*
>
> *Excerpt from the April 2000 Report of the US Attorney General "Information Technology and People with Disabilities: The Current State of Federal Accessibility," Section II, General Findings and Recommendations, p. 7, at* http://www.usdoj.gov/crt/508/report/intro.htm.

The point is, of course, that if you take the ad hoc approach your web-based architecture may require so much retrofitting that it will be unusable to a large degree. Designing from the beginning and using good planning can avoid this trap. It can also save an enormous amount of money. Retrofitting anything is expensive and it should be avoided whenever possible.

AO Functions

A collection of the tangible work of the AO should be stored and available to all members of the enterprise for their use and as a way to make existing solutions to problems available so that those in the enterprise charged with implementing accessibility can use previous solutions to solve existing problems where possible. This is known as the **Knowledge Base**.

The AO has a **Public Affairs** function which deal with all public dealings of members of the enterprise and the outside world. This ensures a consistent approach and message dealing with accessibility being delivered by members of the enterprise to the outside world. This will include conference presentations, press briefings and other public statements and presentations dealing with the enterprise's stance or position on accessibility.

The AO should also have a **Government Affairs** function which handles all government dealings that link the enterprise and accessibility to government, policy, legislative, legal, or regulatory matters. All activities of members of the enterprise and standards-setting bodies dealing with accessibility will be covered by the **Standards** function of the AO.

The **Assistance** function manages the assistance that the AO offers and gives to other organizations within the enterprise on accessibility matters. It will be linked to the knowledge base in so far as it will utilize what is stored in the knowledge base to help render assistance to the enterprise's organizations and members.

These functions are shown in the diagram below:

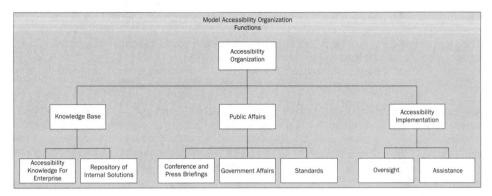

Accessibility

Implementation of accessible web-based technology involves many factors:

- Awareness of Accessibility issues is crucial to the success of the accessibility implementation program

- Properly implemented training programs can help to raise the awareness amongst those charged with using and implementing web-based technology

- The knowledge base should contain both internal and external solutions to accessibility

A good understanding of these factors will help in implementing accessibility in any organization in an effective and efficient manner.

Awareness

Awareness of accessibility issues may be the single greatest challenge that has to be faced in implementing accessibility in any enterprise. The AO must make education and raising accessibility awareness top priorities. On its own, this can solve many of the accessibility issues in your enterprise and go a long way towards making its web sites accessible to people with disabilities. Awareness is very low amongst those who have not had any reason to implement accessibility in web-based technology. Many people do not even realise that there is an issue.

Raising the awareness of web accessibility issues amongst those who have to implement these techniques can be used to the advantage of all. The very act of educating those who will be responsible for making the web technology accessible will alleviate many problems. If properly trained, many people who work with web-based technologies not only start to work to the required accessibility standards, but also go on to develop new and innovative accessibility techniques. Their solutions can be propagated throughout the enterprise and their success can be used to encourage others to be equally creative in their approach to accessibility issues.

Training

Training should be closely focused to give personnel not only a good grounding in the technical aspects of web accessibility, but also a clear understanding of the laws involved and how they can be applied to their work. Depending on their level, they will need different depths of accessiblity awareness. Higher-level managers should only need to know enough to understand the issues. This should be the first level of training, which everyone involved will need. As you move deeper into the various departmental roles, training will have to be provided in greater detail on a need-to-know basis.

Training should be done both with live instructors and with online training, for example EASI (*http://www.easi.cc/*), and the course developed by Jim Thatcher (*http://www.jimthatcher.com/webcourse1.htm* for ITTATC (*http://www.ittatc.org/*) and the efforts of NETg (*http://www.netg.com/*) to make online learning courses accessible.

Instructors can give the initial coursework, answer questions, and get personnel started with accessibility training. The remainder of the training can be done using online distance learning techniques, as provided by EASI (*http://www.easi.cc/*). Externally developed online coursework can be considered both for basic and advanced courses. There are a number of online courses available in web accessibility. Using these resources can save your enterprise considerable time and money whilst giving staff a good grounding in accessible web design. This can be supplemented with a good textbook that will also serve as a reference manual (such as this book for example).

If the distance-learning site is set up properly, it can also be used for reference and reviews. It should not be the only option; rather it should be set up with the idea that those who are implementing web accessibility in your enterprise will use it as a reference work. Large enterprises can set up distance learning centers that can actually save them money, because employees attending courses will have to travel less and the travel expenses and time away from the job will be reduced. Other organizations may have to find companies such as NETg (*http://www.netg.com/*) that are working to build accessible learning products.

Knowledge Base

The AO should have a knowledge base, that is, an accessible collection of practices (internal & external) that can be queried by members of the enterprise who need assistance with accessibility issues. This knowledge base should serve as the central hub for people looking for solutions and a way of collecting new ideas and implementation methods. Employees should be encouraged to use the solutions stored in this repository, and also to contribute new ones. These new solutions can be propagated through this central repository to the rest of the enterprise. Those who develop new and usable solutions to accessibility issues should be rewarded to encourage others to do the same. Along with these internally developed solutions and resources, existing external standards and information on possible solutions should also be stored in the knowledge base for dissemination throughout the whole enterprise.

It should be easy to get to. If it isn't, the simple fact is that it will be unused. It is therefore very important to ensure that it is designed well. Part of the feedback mechanism should be set up so people can easily enter information that would be appropriate to the knowledge base and increase the information it holds for dissemination to the organization. This information should be easy to submit, and easy to extract. It should be checked and formatted before it actually reaches the knowledge base, but this should not affect the ease of submission.

This method should be known throughout the enterprise and copies of the procedure should be placed to constantly remind people of its existence. Reminders of this procedure can be included in company newsletters, e-mails, and internal articles.

Feedback

One of the functions of the AO should be to encourage the sharing of solutions within the enterprise. It should also encourage the sharing of common issues and problems. The feedback mechanisms should allow the expression of problems that are perceived in the implementation of the standards set up by the AO. This will allow problems to aired, investigated, and resolved quickly.

A feedback process must be developed so that the AO can work to improve its methods. Changes may be made both in procedures for implementing accessibility into new areas in the enterprise and existing processes, already in use.

The ability to give feedback will promote a legitimate sense of ownership of accessibility processes and standards in the enterprise. Feedback will also provide critical information on what is happening in the field, where processes are being used. The importance of this cannot be overemphasized. If the AO uses it to help in decisions on improvements, and does this in an honest way by giving credit to providers, then the trust between the AO and the various field departments will continue to grow. This will lead to better feedback and better processes.

It is also useful to use a consistent look and feel for both internal and external sites, to provide your best chance of getting as much customer feedback as possible. A "customer" can be any person who needs access to the services you provide. This might be another division or group within your enterprise, or it could be a student, another organization, or a consumer. Having a consistent "look and feel" to both external and internal services gives employees a sense of the type of environment that the customers are using. This gives them an opportunity to provide continuing feedback on accessibility, without customer complaints being the only measure. This is important, because in electronic services, customers rarely complain about a cumbersome or inaccessible interface – they just leave.

Focus Groups

Human factors and usability of your web pages are important to ease of use of the web sites built for customers, both internal and external. Focus groups can help your organization to understand the needs of users, and usability studies during the development of your web pages and web sites can increase your customer satisfaction ratings.

Information on how to develop the usability studies can be found on Jakob Nielsen's site, *http://www.useit.com/*, as well as in his two excellent books, *Usability Engineering* (Neilsen, Morgan Kaufmann, ISBN 0125184069) and *Designing Web Usability* (Nielsen, New Riders, ISBN 1056205810x). These works will give you a good idea of what to do to set up focus groups and some of the factors involved in building usable web pages. Usability is critical, no matter how many accessibility features a page has: if it is not usable, then it is not accessible.

Focus groups and usability studies can help you achieve good usable pages that meet the needs of your customers. In the long run this will be cheaper and more cost-effective for both the enterprise and the customer.

Quality Assurance

Whilst feedback is one method of ensuring that accessibility initiatives constantly improve, the AO also needs to implement more formal procedures for monitoring and assessing the quality of web accessibility initiatives in the enterprise.

The AO and its member organizations should set department-specific milestones that quantify accessibility. Those people responsible for implementing and managing the work necessary to reach each milestone should be involved in setting what should be accomplished by when. This will give you the best chance of success. These should be set up as a regular set of checkpoints that are used to implement web-based projects within the enterprise and become a standard project management tool for implementing web-based solutions.

A Subject Matter Expert should audit quality and expenditure when each milestone is reached. This information should be recorded and made available for future reference in the knowledge base. These reports should also be integrated with larger periodic reviews to make sure that a good overall picture of the progress of the enterprise is produced on top of the snapshot at each milestone.

Periodic Objective Reviews

A Subject Matter Expert or experts in accessibility should conduct annual reviews of enterprise web accessibility. These should be done within a set framework or clearly delineated set of checklists, standards, and milestones that have been set up by the AO for the entire enterprise.

This review should be able to clearly show where each portion of the organization has arrived in achieving web accessiblity, as well as giving a good idea of where the entire enterprise is in achieving this goal. This can be integrated with the quality reviews and used to display the overall progress of the enterprise, as well as giving individual departments within the enterprise a good idea of what progress they are making towards the goal of making their web technology accessible to people with disabilities. These can be placed in the AO knowledge base so the entire enterprise will have access to them.

Your enterprise may want to consider using an outside service for this assessment, such as TecAcces (*http://www.tecaccess.net*) or a consultant such as Jim Thatcher (*http://www.jimthatcher.com/*). This reduces the chance of the assessment being influenced by internal politics and pressures.

Technological Monitoring

There must be a consistent way to determine if the company-wide standards are being followed. These can be in the form of checklists, accessibility analysis and or repair tools, or a combination of these things. Depending on the size of the enterprise, and the number and type of web pages, there will have to be a suite of methods to determine if standards are being met. Whatever they are, the method should be consistent across the enterprise.

Support

Having support personnel devoted to web accessibility is not recommended, unless your organization is huge. It is suggested that much of this support can be done by electronic means. A well laid out set of web pages addressing the major concerns of the organization can assist greatly in supporting your organization's support needs for accessible web design. A good feedback mechanism can help keep the electronic support up to date, and can help identify new problems your enterprise is facing. It is very important to answer the feedback, in a timely and accurate manner so people know that you are indeed supporting them and that they can indeed count on help.

To enable the talents of people with disabilities to be utilized most effectively in an enterprise, a clear infrastructure for support and integration of assistive technology is essential. Ideally, the following questions should be asked and answered:

Standard Configuration and Support for Assistive Systems

Standard configurations and software support help you define service options with the specific vendors you need. Specifying operating systems for computers and specific browsers for use with internal documents can go a long way in reducing cost for supporting internal web accessiblity.

Web documents and sites for external or public consumption are another matter. They should be coded to be used by the largest audience possible, not only those with disabilities, but also those with diverse browsers and devices.

Outsourced v. Internal Support

It is best to have internal support for applications and external support for hardware, purchased software, and integration issues. You know your applications best, so you should support them. The vendors should support the hardware and the software, except where they are integrated into your operations. Where the two meet, when the software and hardware your enterprise uses interfaces with your localized web-based applications and development, your personnel should supply support.

For generalized support of the hardware and software used in the web-based applications in your enterprise, you should rely on vendor support. They know the product the best and you have probably already paid for the support anyway.

Support for systems and applications for people with disabilities should be formalized. Often the problems experienced by users of adaptive systems can be resolved once, and the solutions applied throughout the enterprise. A model assistive technology support structure could follow this pattern:

1. The user in need of help calls into internal support

2. Support checks for standard browser and assistive technology issues

3. Support checks with knowledge base for known problems and solutions.

4. If necessary, the problem is escalated to outside vendor support

5. The solution is implemented to solve the user's problem

6. Solutions are entered into the knowledge base

Making Sure Your Knowledge Base Is Accessible and Usable

The AO should be available to resolve issues as they arise. It should be a base of publicly available knowledge and resources as well as a collection of internal standards, resources, and solutions to web accessibility issues.

Coordinating Your Procurement Process To Make Sure Web-Based Technology Is Accessible.

Accessible technology systems are often destabilized by changes in "standard" PC components, such as CPUs, video cards, sound cards, and monitors. Procurement departments within an organization should have members on the AO to prevent inaccessible systems from being introduced into the enterprise.

Support Checklist

The questions below can help you determine the best way to set up your support systems to deal with accessibility issues related to web-based technology. Honest answers to these questions can identify problem areas and help to build processes to deal with support issues related to accessibility.

1. Do you have standard configurations and support for assistive systems?

2. Will you have outsourced or internal assistive technology support?

3. Is your knowledge base accessible by support personnel?

4. Is Procurement of Web-Based Technology coordinated with the AO?

Decision Making

There may be web-based services that you simply cannot make accessible. It may simply be too expensive to make a service accessible immediately and an economically viable alternative will have to be found until these web-based services can be made accessible.

Legal and Policy Matters

The AO should have at least one legal expert on staff, but the heart of the legal contribution should be a section of the knowledge base devoted to the laws, regulations, and policies that apply to web accessibility in the enterprise. These should be explained clearly with examples illustrating the relationships to the enterprise's web activities. The legal and policy information should be reviewed by legal experts and then placed in the knowledge base. Legal experts should periodically review this information to be sure that it remains correct and accurate. Laws change, and the knowledge base should reflect these changes. For more information on the current state of legal and policy issues related to accessibility see Chapters 2 and 13.

The main job of the legal expert should be to deal with exceptions, and to make sure the knowledge base is usable and understandable to both attorneys and non-legal personnel. Legal and policy issues of any consequence should always be dealt with by the department that handles these issues for the entire enterprise or locally for the department involved, depending on how an organization is structured.

Governmental Communications

It is critical that the AO and the Legal department maintain strict control over the dissemination of governmental communications that could affect the future of the entire enterprise. All such communications should be routed through the AO. This is critical to both the health of the AO and the enterprise in general.

Standards

Standards are the framework upon which an organization will be able to base its solutions to accessiblity issues. Most organizations will deal with two types of standards, external and internal:

External

These have a national or international scope. Standards bodies with representatives from many areas of expertise, companies, and other organizations develop them. These bodies meet, discuss, and decide upon standards for web accessibility, developing rules that are designed to promote web accessibility.

World Wide Web Consortium (W3C)

The main standards body that deals with web accessiblity is the W3C. They have several sets of standards designed to improve the accessibility of web sites. They are currently detailed at *http://www.w3.org/WAI/* and are divided into three distinct sets of standards:

- Web Content Accessiblity Guidelines (WCAG) (*http://www.w3.org/TR/WCAG10/*). These are the most often quoted standards and deal with the authoring of web pages.

- User Agent Accessibility Guidelines (UAAG) (*http://www.w3.org/TR/UAAG10/*). These deal with browser type issues and seek to solve accessibility problems in the browser rather than putting all of the onus on the web author.

- Authoring Tool Accessiblity Guidelines. (ATAG) (*http://www.w3.org/TR/ATAG10/*) These are designed to deal with accessibility issues concerning authoring tools and makes sure that they are designed to help web authors implement accessible web based technology on their pages and sites.

These standards are being developed as part of an international effort started in 1997 by the W3C. The original effort was started, in part, with money provided by several large corporations and the US Government. Its goal is to ensure that web technology would produce output that would be usable by people with disabilities, using assistive and adaptive technology, and that these people would not be excluded from the Web.

As a result of these efforts, the three sets of guidelines above emerged as the de facto standards in the area of web accessibility.

The set of guidelines cited the most often is the WCAG or Web Content Accessibility Guidelines. Prior to the development of these guidelines, the only real guidelines were those authored by Cynthia Waddell, the co-author of this book. She wrote them when she was the ADA coordinator of the City of San Jose and they were in used extensively to assist the development of the W3C WCAG.

Section 508 of the Rehabilitation Act

Another excellent example of the external standards is the set of guidelines that were developed in response to the passing of Section 508 of the Rehabilitation Act by the US Congress in 1998. These standards were developed to make it clear how Electronic and Information Technology purchased by the US Government after a certain date, has to be accessible to people with disabilities. They do address web-based technology and did set standards for how this technology must be implemented by the US Government. These standards can be found at *http://www.section508.gov/final_summary.html*. There is additional information at *http://www.section508.gov/About508.htm*.

Other Standards

IBM have also developed web accessibility guidelines that can be implemented (*http://www-3.ibm.com/able/accessweb.html*). Depending on your location and the organization in which you work, these may or may not be the standards you use. However, there will be some external standards to which you should or possibly must adhere. Part of the function of the AO will be to identify these standards and make them both available and understandable to the staff.

Internal

These standards should consist of a number of things:

- A manual, which addresses the consistency of style on the web site and should have accessibility built into the guidelines and standards that authors use to produce accessible web sites. This is usually known as a Style Guide.

- Software that will be used by the enterprise to produce web sites. There may be several types of software and can help ensure consistency of results across the enterprise if used properly in conjunction with a style guide. These software packages should meet the needs of developers and be able to produce accessible web sites. This should also reduce training costs, as a limited number of software packages will have to be supported.

Internal standards must be developed carefully with the input of the people who will actually be doing the work. This is critical to the success of the program. The people in the field who are building the web sites, and who will have to use the software daily, are the ones who should have the main input into what tools will be chosen. A good example of integrating accessibility standards is the North Carolina State Architecture (*http://irm.state.nc.us/techarch/chaps/chap13.htm*).

A standard that is not applied is no standard at all. Your internal standards must not only be applied on a consistent basis, they must be applicable to the situations that exist within the organization. If the standards are not realistically chosen they will not be applied. If they are not applicable to the web technology that your organization is using, they cannot be applied. If they are not enforced they will not be used.

The Style Guide should be developed using the experience of your developers and institute accessibility standards. It should reflect best practices that have been developed both internally and externally, and should be tailored to fit the specific situations that your developers are likely to encounter.

This ensures that the developers feel they are being listened to, that their expertise is being respected, and that the best tools are chosen to accomplish the tasks at hand. The people who are going to use the Guide will have ownership of it. This will ensure that it gets used and that new knowledge, acquired by experience, will be integrated into the document.

The best way for developers to address accessibility whilst dealing with your customer needs, is for it to be incorporated in the design phase of planning. The basic set of web site design rules set down in the Style Guide will cover such things as spelling, colors used, copyright and trademark issues, navigation issues. Accessibility should be dealt with both specifically in a separate section and in everything in the Style Guide that is appropriate. For example, in the section on image use and presentation, `alt` text should be a requirement; they should also be dealt with in the section on accessibility.

A style guide can contain the rules for accessibility as well as all the other rules for how you will produce web sites both internally and externally. It can relieve developers of many onerous tasks and decisions, and can make their job a good deal easier. They will not have to worry about many details of the web site and can concentrate on the building of its infrastructure and content. The Style Guide can mandate the types of templates that are used and provide samples of pages and templates that meet the guidelines that the Style Guide demands.

AT&T built a good example of a style guide for their public web site (*http://www.att.com/style/*). In the long run this could save your organization much time and effort. Time is money, so the use of a well-written style guide can save your organization a good deal of both.

Another important consideration for internal standards is that project personnel should be informed of the functional requirements of accessibility, not their implementation. Don't tell people how to do things, rather what needs to be done. Personnel must be educated to the fact that most standards do not give specific details of how to achieve a desired functionality.

This allows developers to exercise creativity in implementing the desired functionality in any particular situation. Where possible the AO should not only encourage creative solutions to problems but also collect these solutions and make them available to all through the knowledge base.

Tools

The choice of software tools should be reviewed on a regular basis, and there should be a process for constantly receiving input from the users so that everyone can benefit from their experience. These experiences should be collected in a form that will be available to everyone.

There must also be a process to allow people in the field to give input on and test new tools that will be used to produce accessible web sites.

It is important to note that these tools must address a wide range of skill levels in the actual mechanics of web site development. There are many people working on web sites who are quite familiar with the coding techniques involved, but there might also be a large number who only understand using editors that do the coding for them.

The tools and techniques chosen and the training developed will have to meet the needs of both groups. They should be reviewed regularly to ensure that they are appropriate for the tasks they are being used for and that they are the most effective technology for the job. The frequency of this review will depend on the overall structure of the enterprise and the way the AO has been organized. In the author's opinion this should be no less than twice a year.

Enforcement and Reward

The standards that are in effect and have been developed by your organizations must be enforced, otherwise there is no reason to have them. The procedures for enforcing these standards must be decided upon by the AO and must be enforced by the Accessibility Champion with the knowledge and consent of the Chief Executive of your organization.

In cases where people have done an outstanding job of implementing accessiblity in web sites, there should be a procedure for giving them meaningful, public praise. The public part of this could be giving them a plaque, or some other form of public recognition, in front of the entire organization, and the tangible part of the reward could be money, trips, promotions, stock, vacation time, or some other way of showing that the organization recognizes and values their contributions to the accessiblity effort.

Public Representation

The AO should represent the parent organization in public affairs related to accessibility such as the following:

Press Briefings

Since the AO will be the single most concentrated area of accessibility expertise in the enterprise, its members should be the ones facing the public and representing the enterprise to the accessibility community. This will present a unified front to the public and prevent misunderstandings about your organization's web accessibility policies in the wider arena.

Standards Bodies

The AO can represent the entire enterprise in standards groups. This will serve the needs of everyone. Even if there are members of the organization that are on standards bodies and are not formally members of the AO, they should be listed as associated with it and should co-ordinate their activities with it to keep everyone informed and to be sure a united front is presented. The best way to ensure that people are committed to this goal is to make sure that the AO helps to finance these activities.

Standards committees can be difficult to work with, and it takes a certain type of person to be effective within them. This person must be able to work within the standards process, and to collect and integrate all of the concerns of the member organizations. They must then be able be sure that these concerns are addressed by the standards committee, as well as fairly representing your organizations interests and accessibility issues. Not an easy job, it takes a great deal of patience and skill.

Conferences

The AO should maintain a list of appropriate conferences and who is attending them. They can assist the personnel who are making presentations with the resources they will require, both financial and research. This will ensure that the AO knows who is going where and that all who attend conferences are committed to the goals of the AO. Too often employees are denied the opportunity to attend conferences and make contributions because of lack of resources in their organization or lack of interest by their management. This can be damaging to both the employee and the enterprise. The AO can help by supplying the needed financial and other resources and can help both the enterprise and the employee at the same time.

Integration Strategy Overview

In this section, we'll overview the process you might go through when setting up your own AO, including:

- An initial assessment of the accessibility of your organization's web- based technology

- Using an assessment questionnaire to help determine what, if any, accessibility issues exist in your organization

- Building an implementation checklist that will help you implement accessible web based technology in your enterprise

- Reviewing all of your web-based technology to see where accessibility issues exist

Initial Assessment (Where are You?)

An initial assessment must be done. If you do not know where you are, then you will never figure out how to get where you want to be. The initial assessment provides a starting point from which you can gauge how long it will take to achieve the goals you have set, and how much resource is required. The most effective way to begin accessibility integration is to make an objective analysis of the current situation in your organization. An honest and thorough assessment, along with a detailed, time-limited plan for remediation, can help an organization meet its accessibility needs in a cohesive, cost effective way. Although some organizations may have the resources to do accessibility analysis internally, one of the most effective methods is to have an independent assessment. In the US at least there are several organizations that do this sort of assessment. They are centered on Section 508 Compliance at the moment but can also do usability and accessiblity assessments. This rules out the possibility of political forces (internal and external) or subjective attachments and conceptions skewing the assessment. An assessment should, at least, involve answers to the following questions:

Assessment Questionnaire

- Do senior policy makers understand what accessibility is, and what it means?

- What departments and personnel within your organization are responsible for Legal Compliance? Is compliance handled by legal and policy personnel in each department or on an enterprise-wide basis from one centralized authority?

- Do your IT managers (Department heads/MIS directors/Webmasters) understand electronic & information technology accessibility issues?

- Have you adopted an architecture and web design standard for accessibility (W3C/WAI, Section 508, etc.)?

- Did you include all organizational stakeholders in their development?

- Do you have training and technical support available for those who do not understand the practical implementation of that standard?

- Is the standard applied throughout your organization?

- Do you have a phased, cost-effective approach to limit undue burdens?

- Do your e-commerce/e-government sites have a consistent, accessible interface?

- Do your customers have alternatives to e-commerce/e-government services?

- How will you evaluate your progress towards accessibility? (Checklists, checkpoints, timelines, assessment tools, etc.)

- Are your web-based documents and databases accessible? (Public and internal)

Once the questions are answered, then the organization should put together a document that summarizes the strengths and weaknesses of the entire organization with regard to web accessibility and what needs to be done to improve the weak areas and how the strengths can be used to improve the weaker areas. This document should be used as the basis for the overall accessibility implementation plan. Part of this document should be a checklist such as the one suggested below:

Implementation Checklist

It is not realistic to suppose that you can simply convert every single web page overnight and make it accessible. A phased approach is the most workable and realistic approach. The following are suggested steps for implementing such a phased approach in your organization. There should be a project manager assigned to phase in the work and monitor its progress. This will keep the team focused and on target.

- Decide upon a standard or set of guidelines that will be used for web accessibility. This can be internally developed or an existing external standard or set of guidelines, but will be implemented internally.

- Announce the standard to the entire organization.

- Announce support and training for the standard.

- Set a date beyond which all new web-based technology must be accessible according to the standard you have chosen.

- Have organizational members of the AO analyze their web-based systems to determine which technology will be changing first, since this will have to be accessible.

- Determine if any critical web-based technology must be made accessible.

- Determine if any critical web-based technology cannot be made accessible.

- Set up a schedule to replace critical systems that cannot be made accessible with accessible technology.

- Have each member department in the AO present a plan phasing in accessible web technology.

- Make sure all support systems are in place, including technical support and training.

- Begin the phased-in approach so members of the AO are ready by launch date.

- Monitor the progress and supply help where needed or requested.

Web Technology Review

When conducting a review of your existing web technologies themselves, you should ensure that you include the following:

- Web Portals

- Web Pages

- Internal Documents

- Telecommunications web-based devices such as cell phones

- Desktop Applications using web-based technology.

- All other web-based documents and services

All devices and services that are going to use web-based technology must be accessible to your disabled employees and to the public if that is appropriate. These products and services may need testing with a wide range of access devices, and in cases such as web-based kiosks, they should be made accessible to people with disabilities wherever possible.

Implementation Plan

When looking at the costs associated with retrofitting existing inaccessible technology, it becomes apparent that the implementation plan should stress implementing accessibility as part of new development, procurement, and use of electronic and information technology. This "forward accessibility" focus will maximize the resources within the enterprise by making accessibility simply part of the natural development of the organization. This plan will have to deal with both retrofitting old web material, and seeing that standards are developed to make sure that all new web based projects are implemented in an accessible manner.

Once this plan is in place, you can then start to monitor against it using the feedback and quality assurance procedures included in the functions of the AO.

Handover To AO

Accessibility, if being handled by a project team, should be handed off to the AO upon completion of the initial integration. The AO should meet no less than quarterly to ensure enterprise-wide accessibility. If that is not sufficient to allow efficient implementation of the AO's mission and objectives, then it should meet more frequently. Between the meetings, information should be gathered so that progress reports and agenda items can be brought to the AO for action.

If properly handled, and the initial integration is complete, the requirements for keeping web-based products and services accessible should be no more onerous than making sure any other required design features are included in the next site redesign. It is a simple matter of raising awareness and keeping a good set of requirements available to designers, developers, and those who must implement the technology.

Summary

When considering web accessibility in any organization, it is essential to do so by coordinating all its resources. Without this "holistic" view, accessibility can be both expensive and difficult. Additionally, there is danger of creating pockets of inaccessible web-based technologies within the enterprise. By having management and field personnel participation in accessibility integration, an understanding of the needs of people with disabilities can be disseminated throughout the enterprise, creating an environment that allows the largest number of people to be as productive as their talents permit. By having the personnel who are actually developing and implementing solutions as ongoing participants in the implementation process, you will get commitment from the people who know the most about the technology being used by your enterprise.

The following steps can be used to successfully implement accessibility issues in your organization:

- Get commitment from the Top Manager

- Get an Accessiblity Champion to head the AO with authority to implement accessible web design

- Clearly lay out the purpose of your AO and its goals and scope

- Recruit the AO membership from the people doing the work and the people managing them

- Lay out your accessibility plan

- Set your specific goals and timeline

- Begin your implementation

- Monitor your progress

- Make any necessary corrections

- Provide feedback mechanisms

- Create a central resource for ongoing use

- Meet with field personnel on a regular basis to monitor progress, introduce new technologies, and collect internal methodologies and reward progress

A final note: the US federal government has developed standards for accessible web technologies. Organizations interested in accessibility would do well to note the standards that come from these discussions. Although non-federal agencies, private organizations, and others outside of US Federal jurisdiction are not subject to federal accessibility regulations, there are other laws, which may mandate accessibility for employees and areas of public accommodation, such as the Internet. Even in instances where these laws do not directly apply, the regulations and standards that are being set up are bound to have a great influence in many places. Therefore, it is a good idea to keep informed what these regulations and standards are and how they are being applied in the technical venue. Further information is contained in Chapter 13 in which these legal and policy issues are discussed in detail.

12

- Data-Centric technologies

- Web page specific technologies

- Assessment and repair tools

- Custom presentation

Author: Michael Burks

Emerging Technologies

New technologies are constantly emerging on the Web. Some of these are helpful in increasing overall accessibility of web pages and some are not. Some need to be retrofitted and some must simply be used with care.

These technologies do not necessarily have to be inaccessible to people with disabilities. If implemented by those who understand accessibility, these technologies used to enhance the accessibility of a web site. A technology that is inaccessible to people with a particular disability, may actually improve accessibility for those with disabilities of another type.

An example of this is the animated presentations on certain web sites. While they may be inaccessible to those who are blind or who have vision impairments, for those who are visually oriented, or who find images helpful (people with dyslexia, for example) this type of presentation can be very effective in delivering a message or concept.

Whenever possible, the content should not be delivered in only one medium, and provision should be made for the user to convert the means of presentation into one that they can use. A lot of accessibility techniques are about presenting the same information in more than one way; using several different media empowers the user to choose whichever is more suitable.

In this chapter we will be looking at:

- Data-centric technologies such as XML and other languages derived from it

- Web page-specific technologies

- Various multimedia technologies

- Assessment and repair tools for assessing how accessible a site is and improving it

- Device independence

- Biometrics

- Problems associated with emerging technologies

We will explore these new technologies and how they can improve the accessibility of web sites and make them usable by the largest number of people possible. This will help reach a wider audience as laid out in the principles of Universal Design, which can be viewed at *http://www.design.ncsu.edu/cud/univ_design/princ_overview.htm*.

Data-Centric Technologies

We will begin by looking at data-centric technologies that are focused on organizing and manipulating data, and presentation and management of the content. Perhaps one of the most important new technology is Extensible Markup Language (XML), a very powerful and flexible language used for describing data.

XML

Extensible Markup Language (**XML**) was developed after it was realized that HTML had some shortcomings that were limiting the effectiveness of the Web. While HTML is very good at describing how web pages should be presented to the user, it cannot describe the content itself. This is where XML comes in. XML can describe content, and is a particularly powerful tool for separating content from presentation.

XML was brought into the limelight at the W3C Conference in June of 1997 in Santa Clara, California. Ironically, it was the same conference at which the W3C announced the Web Accessibility Initiative (WAI). The two are not totally unrelated, in fact, XML developers have been aware of accessibility issues from the very beginning. XML as an emerging technology can help you develop accessible web sites and tools to address accessibility issues.

Let's have a quick look at a basic structure of an XML document. The following example illustrates how a simple XML document might contain information about customers:

```xml
<?xml version="1.0"?>
<customers>
  <customer>
    <firstNname>John</firstName>
    <secondName>Smith</secondName>
    <email>JohnSmith@nowhere.com</email>
  </customer>
  <customer>
    <firstName>Jane</firstName>
    <secondName>Smith</secondName>
    <email>JaneSmith@nowhere.com</email>
  </customer>
</customers>
```

The first line of our example is the XML declaration which defines this as an XML document and is a requirement for validity. In XML you can create your own tag names to describe your content appropriately. However there are some rules about element naming: element names cannot begin with "xml" or contain any punctuation except the underscore, and element names are case sensitive. The first element after the XML declaration is known as the **root element** and contains the entire document except the XML declaration. In our example document this is the `<customers>` element.

XML is stricter than HTML, every opening tag must have a corresponding closing tag, and each tag must be properly nested. XML also requires that all attribute values be enclosed in quotation marks. When a document satisfies all these rules then it is **well-formed**, and a well-formed document that contains a root element and the XML declaration is **valid**. The following construct will not be accepted by an XML parser:

```
<customer>
    <firstName>John<secondName>Smith</firstName></secondName>
</customer>
```

It is not well-formed because the elements are not nested correctly. Additionally, to make this valid, we would have to add an XML declaration at the top of the document.

XML allows us to create our own element attributes. For instance, our previous example could have been written like this:

```
<?xml version="1.0"?>
<customers>
    <customer firstName="John" secondName="Smith" email="JohnSmith@nowhere.com">
    </customer>
    <customer firstName="Jane" secondName="Smith" email="JaneSmith@nowhere.com">
    </customer>
</customers>
```

Not only does the flexibility of XML make it a powerful tool for describing any information, but also further specialized markup languages can be derived from it for specific purposes. We will be looking at several languages that are subsets of XML later in this chapter.

> *For a quick summary of XML, see http://www.w3.org/XML/1999/XML-in-10-points. For a more in-depth look, try http://www.w3.org/XML/ and also Beginning XML* (David Hunter et al., Wrox press, *1861005598*).

An important language that is derived from XML is XHTML, which is HTML redefined as a subset of XML, thus it is HTML that adheres to the strict rules of XML.

XHTML

A lot of HTML on the Web is badly written so browsers have extra functionality built into them to handle bad markup. However, other devices, or user-agents, not all of which have the processing power to handle this bad markup, are now accessing the Web. The W3C and developers of XML recognized that there would need to be a way to gracefully migrate from HTML to XML and version 1.0 of XHTML (Extensible Hypertext Markup Language) was developed which fills this need (*http://www.w3.org/TR/xhtml1/*). It is a reformulation of HTML 4 as an XML 1.0 application. It may well replace HTML in the future. Like all XML-derived languages, it requires documents to be well-formed and valid, adhering to the strict syntax of XML that was mentioned earlier.

Despite this, it takes little effort to convert HTML pages into XHTML.

> *There is a good tutorial on XHTML that can assist with this at*
> http://hotwired.lycos.com/webmonkey/00/50/index2a.html?tw=authoring. *You may also like to read the section on "Differences with HTML4" at*
> http://www.w3.org/TR/xhtml1/#diffs, *it explains some of the specifics of what must be done to convert HTML4 to XHTML.*

There are guidelines to help make sure that, if you do make web pages in XHTML, they will work with browsers that are currently available. These can be found at:
http://www.w3.org/TR/xhtml1/#guidelines

> *You can find an XHTML Tutorial at:*
> *http://hotwired.lycos.com/webmonkey/00/50/index2a.html?tw=authoring* and the XHTML 1.0 Specification can be found here:*http://www.w3.org/TR/xhtml1/*. See also *Beginning XHTML (Frank Boumphrey et al., Wrox press,1861003439)*

XSL

Extensible Stylesheet Language (**XSL**) is a rule-based language that allows you to write rules to select particular elements of a markup document for manipulation. As long as your markup document is XML-rule-compliant, you can apply an **Extensible Stylesheet Language Transformation** (**XSLT**) to it containing the rules you have written. With XSLT you can select any element or group of elements and perform such modifications as applying styles, duplication, or changing them into other elements, and a new markup document will be created from the result. XSLT uses another part of XSL, **XPath,** to manipulate XML documents. XPath treats the markup document like a hierarchical tree, or Document Object Model, and selects elements via paths, for example the `<firstName>` element in our example above is accessed as `customers\customer\firstName`.

So XSL is very useful for accessibility – it allows you to take your data and present it in any way you want, whether it is simply changing it into XML for further data manipulation, WML (Wireless Markup Language) for display on a WAP phone, HTML with big fonts for people with visual impairment, or even VoiceXML, or specific media for a Braille display.

We have already mentioned two parts of XSL, however, there is a third – **XSL Formatting Objects** (**XSL-FO**), which describes how a document should be formatted, and is mainly of use when a strictly controlled data format is required, for example, when you want a document to have a very specific look when printed.

XSL is a complex subject and definitely warrants further research – the XSL Specification is located at:*http://www.w3.org/Style/XSL/,* and the XSLT Specification is at *http://www.w3.org/TR/xslt.* For a good description of XSL see *http://www.xml.com/pub/a/2000/08/holman/index.html* and *http://xml.coverpages.org/xsl.html* Accessibility Advantages.

The flexibility of XML implies that it can be used in an accessible way, but there is much scope for incorrect usage. Therefore, there are detailed XML accessibility guidelines that explain the correct way of using XML. Since it is a meta-language, the accessibility features in XML are also available in any languages derived from it. The foremost of these is that XML is geared towards separating content from presentation, and has facilities to help transform documents from one type of XML vocabulary to another.

The XML Accessibility Guidelines can be found at http://www.w3.org/TR/xag.html.

The requirements of XML are stringent, as discussed above, and in the XML Accessibility Guidelines. This stringency means that pages will not render or work if they are not constructed in the proper manner. This ensures that many accessibility features are not optional and have to be used.

Using the Technology – Tools

XML is often used in conjunction with other tools and there are a large number of tools on the market. Since XML has been used to create new languages, and allowing you to define your own markup language, the possibilities are only limited by the developer's creativity and imagination. It is, and will be, the basis for many new languages and has already been used in many new and innovative ways, both on and off the Web.

*XML.org (*http://www.xml.org/) *includes information on XML tools, as well as news, papers, conferences, and many other XML-related resources.*

We have had a brief look at emerging data-centric technologies. There are also some emerging technologies that work specifically with the web page itself.

Web Page-Specific Technologies

Some technologies work with web pages as units, or manifest as objects on the page and can be used to make many features of a web page accessible not just to people with disabilities, but also to whatever device the user may be using to access a page. While some of them are not confined to the web page and can have implications across the web site, in the author's opinion they are more attuned to the web pages themselves, so they are discussed under this heading.

Java

Java is a programming language developed by Sun Microsystems (*http://java.sun.com/*). It is a powerful tool that can bring many exciting and useful things to a web page. Until recently it presented many accessibility problems and alternative content was often required.

Accessibility Features

The Accessibility Application Programming Interface (API) for Java (*http://java.sun.com/products/jfc/jaccess-1.2.2/doc/guide.html*) was designed to make Java applets accessible to people with disabilities. It is an interface designed to let Java interact with the assistive technology that people with disabilities may be using.

Using the Technology – Tools

Developers who use the Accessibility API and the other accessibility features of Java can produce products that are accessible to a wide range of devices. Java is increasingly being used to program things other than computers, such as mobile phones and handheld devices, so the importance of the accessibility Java programs is increasing. A full list of Java products and APIs can be obtained from *http://java.sun.com/products/*.

Multimedia

Multimedia is the technique of presenting information in more than one media form, such as simultaneous audio and visual presentations or tactile formats. It also refers to presenting information on a web site in more than one format.

People without disabilities can also benefit from having information in different formats. People have different learning styles and presenting information in multiple formats can help your visitors to remember and understand your content better.

The difficulty of multimedia comes when information is presented in a media format that is not accessible to people with certain disabilities. Unless that information can be presented in or converted to other formats, your content will be inaccessible.

The new technologies discussed here offer a wider range of features and flexibility in presenting the same information in different ways. Some of them offer performance enhancements as well and help separate content from presentation.

Scalable Vector Graphics (SVG)

SVG (*http://www.w3.org/Graphics/SVG/*) is a subset of XML that is used to produce graphics for web pages. This multimedia application seeks to address many of the issues inherent to the use of graphics, sound, and other forms of multimedia. It can be used to produce both animated and unanimated graphics.

Accessibility Features

Since SVG is an XML-based language it has a number of accessibility features. Some are inherited from XML itself, and some are derived from the vector graphics model. These graphics are scaleable with little or no loss of resolution, which is clearly helpful to users who have vision impairments and can only see larger images.

SVG also provides innovative ways of providing alternative representations. By the use of these features, excellent alternative content can be attached to graphics and users who are unable to see the graphic for whatever reason can have good textual representation of what the graphic depicts. SVG graphics can also be animated.

A more detailed explanation of the accessibility features of SVG can be found in the Accessibility Features of SVG, August 7, 2000 (http://www.w3.org/TR/SVG-access/).

Using the Technology – Tools

SVG is being used on web sites now, and there are a number of tools to help with producing what web designers need. These tools can be found in a number of places but the best listing at the moment is at W3C Scalable Vector Graphics Page (*http://www.w3.org/Graphics/SVG/Overview.htm8*). There are also a number of books being published on the subject such as *SVG Essentials* (J. David Eisenberg, O'Reilly, 0596002238)
This is a good indication that the technology is being used and that it will continue to develop.

The scalability and alternative representation features offer excellent advantages to people using assistive technology and adaptive devices. Additionally, because SVG is based on text files, web designers can include descriptive text that is accessible to screen readers.

A simple text editor and knowledge of SVG is the minimum needed to produce SVG graphics. However, software manufacturers are producing a number of tools and some of them are listed on the SVG Spot Tool page at *http://www.svg-spot.com/tools/*.

Let's look at a simple example of an SVG document:

```
<?xml version="1.0"?>
<svg width="200" height="220" xmlns="http://www.w3.org/2000/svg">
  <g style="stroke:blue;stroke-width:3; fill:pink" >
    <title>Some shapes</title>
    <desc>A circle and a rectangle</desc>
    <circle cx="60"  cy="60" r="50" />
    <rect x="3o" y="130" width="150" height="75" rx="10" ry="20"/>
  </g>
</svg>
```

Here is the output this produces:

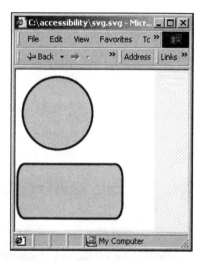

This can be scaled up by right-clicking and selecting the *zoom in* option without any loss in image quality:

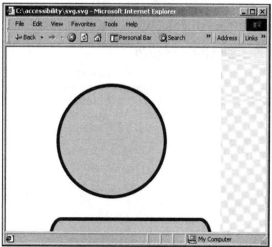

The first line of code is the XML declaration which is required to make the document valid XML. You will notice also a <g> element that acts as a container for similar graphics. Here we can define attributes that are common to all the elements contained within the <g> element. Notice the <title> and <desc> elements which contain a textual description of the graphic so that it can be accessed by screen readers or other assistive technologies. Standard shapes such as rectangles, circles, polygons, ellipses, and also lines are all predefined in the SVG standard.

The major problem with SVG is that it is not widely used at the moment because it requires a viewer plug-in to be installed on the browser and most users don't have this. As the technology develops, future browsers will probably support SVG without the need for a separate plug-in, and this is expected to increase the popularity of SVG graphics.

There is a list of free viewers at: *http://www.w3.org/Graphics/SVG/SVG-Implementations.htm8#viewer*. This list includes SVG editors and tools that will convert other graphics formats to SVG as well.

There are some interesting examples of SVG graphics on the Adobe web site. To take a look at them you will need to follow the following steps:

- If you haven't got an SVG viewer installed on your browser you can download a free version at: *http://www.adobe.com/svg/viewer/install/main.html*

- After having installed the viewer you will be able to see the demonstrations on *http://www.adobe.com/svg/demos/main.html*

The demonstrations above illustrate how SVG can be used in several different ways.

Synchronized Multimedia Integration Language (SMIL)

SMIL(pronounced "smile") is an XML application that is used to produce interactive audiovisual presentations over the Web. It is used to define the timings of multimedia presentations, so the web designer could use it to specify exactly when a particular sound should occur, for instance. It simplifies the production of presentations that are rich in multimedia and can integrate such things as streaming video and audio with any other media type. Most often this is text, but any media type is possible (see *http://www.w3.org/AudioVideo/*).

Accessibility and SMIL

A good example of how SMIL can be used to help increase the accessibility of a presentation is the Media Access Generator, MAGpie, developed by the National Center for Accessible Media (NCAM). This tool allows the user to captions a number of different types of multimedia formats. Using MAGpie, web designers can create caption and subtitles, or describe the content in audio format. MAGpie can work with three multimedia formats: QuickTime from Apple, Synchronized Multimedia Integration Language (SMIL) from the W3C, and Microsoft's Synchronized Accessible Media Interchange (SAMI).

- The MAGpie web site is *http://ncam.wgbh.org/webaccess/magpie/*.

- The instructions on how to download and install MAGpie are located at: *http://ncam.wgbh.org/webaccess/magpie/*. It is free and straightforward to use.

- MAGpie comes with an integrated help center, and help is also available online at: *http://ncam.wgbh.org/webaccess/magpie/webhelp/index.html*. This tutorial offers detailed instructions on how to create captions and audio descriptions of files.

Using the Technology – Tools

SMIL can be used to insert captioning into multimedia and do other things that will increase the accessibility of multimedia presentations on the Web. The tools that have been built to accomplish this are powerful and many are quite easy to use. It should be noted here that captioning video presentations is considered by many teachers to be a great aid to their non-disabled students. It helps present the material in a second way and often reinforces what students are learning. People who do not speak your language very well may also benefit from seeing the written version of the presentation presented at the same time. If you are considering whether to use captioning in a video presentation, then be aware that many people will benefit from it, not just those who have disabilities.

Captioning is a skill in itself. It usually involves having to create a shortened or summarized version of any dialog if the captions are to run at the same time as the dialog, as with subtitles. Subtitles and basic captioning can be quite different, particularly in the way that captioning can just be a re-iteration of the main points without the context. The MAGpie tutorial (*http://ncam.wgbh.org/webaccess/magpie/webhelp/index.html*) mentioned above contains some excellent lessons in captioning.

If you would like to learn how to use this technology, you can try any of the following tutorials:

- Synchronized Multimedia On The Web By Larry Bouthillier: (*http://www.webtechniques.com/archives/1998/09/bouthillier/*)

- The Helio SMIL Tutorial: (*http://www.helio.org/products/smil/tutorial/*)

- Learn SMIL with a SMIL: (*http://www.empirenet.com/~joseram/index.html*)

Assessment and Repair Tools

There are many new assessment and repair tools on the market today. These tools help to find accessibility errors and some of them help to repair them. They are quite useful and can save a great deal of time on large web sites. This is a relatively new development and still cannot assess every type of technology or technique used on web sites. Nonetheless assessment and repair tools are a valuable addition to the tools that webmasters and web developers have at their disposal. They can help increase the efficiency of assessing web pages and can help repair many basic problems.

As we saw in Chapter 7, these tools cannot replace human judgment. The user is still required to understand accessibility techniques and must still be required to understand how to fix the problems. Automated tools are going to make mistakes and their users must have a good enough grounding in the basics behind the tools to understand what they are trying to do.

Having made this statement it is clear that these tools are quite valuable in situations where there are many pages to retrofit, and there is a great deal to fix on each page. They can also assist a designer by analyzing the prototypes and helping to determine the problems that may exist with the new site or page.

Many of the tools can be downloaded. Some of the downloads are free versions and some of them are demo versions. Most will give you a chance to see if the product is useful to you in your situation as we will see later on in the chapter.

Human Judgment

No matter what tools you use, it will still be necessary to use human judgment to figure out if a web page is accessible. So the user will need a thorough understanding of the causes of problems with web page accessibility. For example assessment tools can tell you if there is some `alt` text missing, but cannot tell you if the alternative representation makes sense and will be of any use to those for whom it is intended.

These tools are just that – tools. They help make the job easier and improve the efficiency of those who are using them. They do not replace the human being any more than an electric saw replaces a carpenter or cabinetmaker.

This is a limitation of the technology, not the tool. There are only certain things the currently available tools can assess and repair, and this must always be taken into account. It is probably safe to say that these tools will always be slightly behind the emerging technology itself, so there will always be a need for an expert to make the final determination of the accessibility of a site or page.

> *To help you understand the type of human judgments that could be necessary, please look at Some Human Judgments Required for Section 508 Evaluations by Dr. Len Kasday (http://astro.temple.edu/~kasday/talks/wave508/judge.html).*

Free Assessment and Repair Tools

The first tools to appear were free. One was Bobby by CAST (*http://www.cast.org*), a non-profit educational organization, and the other was The WAVE written by the late Dr. Len Kasday.

Bobby

For many years Bobby was the major assessment tool used to determine the accessibility of web sites (*http://www.cast.org/bobby/*). Bobby is a very useful tool that was initially given out free of charge. It also allows you to test files that are not on the Internet, so it is very useful for developing internal applications.

As we saw in Chapter 7, the tool has been enhanced – it can now check for W3C WAI WCAG compliance as well as Section 508 compliance. The online version can be configured for either Section 508 or W3C WCAG Guidelines and is fully functional. The current online version can be used free of charge, however the downloadable version must be purchased. This product is fully reviewed in Chapter 7.

The WAVE

The WAVE was developed by Temple University Institute on Disabilities. It has a number of excellent features that are not included with other assessment tools (*http://www.temple.edu/inst_disabilities/piat/wave/*). It shows which images have the `alt` attribute tags missing and it also shows the order in which a screen reader will read a page. A new version is being developed to address Section 508 issues.

A-Prompt

The Trace Center and the University of Toronto developed A-prompt
(*http://aprompt.snow.utoronto.ca/*). It acts as both a repair and assessment tool that can be used
with files that are not on the Internet. It does not at this time address Section 508 issues directly but
does use the W3C WCAG to measure the accessibility of a site.

Some Purchased Assessment and Repair Tools

As we saw in Chapter 7, several tools have appeared on the market that can be purchased. Most of
these appeared in response to US Section 508 and its requirement to make web pages accessible to
people with disabilities.

HiSoftware

AccVerify and AccRepair are tools developed by HiSoftware Inc
(*http://www.hisoftware.com/access/*). They will verify that a page is Section 508-compliant, and
meets WCAG standards. AccRepair can repair the page if needed. They are available as both a
standalone product and as add-ons to Microsoft FrontPage. They also have an Application
Programming Interface (API) that will allow developers to integrate these products into their web site
publishing or testing processes (*http://www.hisoftware.com/access/30APISDK.html*).

LIFT

LIFT from UsableNet (*http://www.UsableNet.com*) comes in a variety of versions and can be used on
both the MAC and Windows platforms. There are versions for Macromedia Dreamweaver and there
is a demo version that has a limited functionality. This product is extensively reviewed in Chapter 7

Page Screamer

Page Screamer was developed by Crunchy Technologies to address US Section 508 issues. It has a
number of different versions and plug-ins. Some of these can run standalone and some are
associated with other products. Some will do repairs and some will simply provide assessments and
recommendations (*http://www.crunchy.com/news/crnews/indexpr1.html*). There are also tools in the
suite that will work with server-based architecture. There are plug-ins that will work with Microsoft
FrontPage, Cold Fusion Studio, JRun Studio, and HomeSite, and there is also a management tool
called PageScreamer Central.

SSB Technologies

SSB Technologies (*http://www.ssbtechnologies.com/*) developed their assessment and repair tool,
InFocus, to specifically address US Section 508 issues. The tool was developed in Java and is not only
able to assess a web site for Section 508 violations, but is also accessible so that disabled webmasters
and technical people are able to use it. Some human intervention is required to accomplish repairs.

Tools That Are Attached To Specific Products

Some assessment and repair add-ons for specific products, such as Macromedia's Dreamweaver
and Microsoft's FrontPage, are available. In many cases they are free but offer only a limited amount
of functionality. While some of these tools have been around for a while, they are all relatively new,
and the idea of attaching them to an HTML editor as a validator is recent. These tools can be quite
useful but, once again, human judgment is required to ensure that the site is actually accessible.

Assessment Tools

This table is a summary of the assessment tools mentioned in this section:

Assessment Tools					
Tool	Produced By	Free	Download	Usable on the Internet	Comments
AccVerify	HiSoftware	No	Yes	Yes	There is a version available as a plug-in for Microsoft FrontPage and an API for integration into web publishing and testing processes.
Bobby	CAST	No, see Comments	Yes	Yes	The online version of Bobby is free, but CAST now charges for the downloadable version.
InSight	SSB Technologies Inc.	No	Yes	Yes	There is a version available as a plug-in for the Adobe Golive product.
PageScreamer	Crunchy Technologies Inc.	No, see Comments	Yes	Yes	There are plug-ins that will work with Microsoft FrontPage, Cold Fusion Studio, JRun Studio and HomeSite. The product comes in a regular as well as an enterprise version. There is also a management tool available
The WAVE	Temple University Institute on Disabilities	Yes	No	No	A new version is under development to address Section 508 Issues.

Repair Tools

The following table summaries the repair tools we have talked about in this chapter:

Repair Tools					
Tool	**Produced By**	**Cost**	**Download**	**Usable on the Internet**	**Comments**
AccRepair	HiSoftware	Yes	Yes	Yes	There is a version available as an plug-in for Microsoft FrontPage and an API for integration into web publishing and testing processes.
A-Prompt	Trace Center and the University of Toronto	No	Yes	Yes	
InFocus	SSB Technologies Inc.	Yes	Yes	Yes	
LIFT	UsableNet	Yes	Yes	Yes	This product comes in several flavors including at least two that work with Macromedia Dreamweaver.
PageScreamer	Crunchy Technologies Inc.	Yes, see Comments	Yes	Yes	There are plug-ins that will work with Microsoft FrontPage, Cold Fusion Studio, JRun Studio and HomeSite. The product comes in a regular as well as an enterprise version. There is also a management tool available.

Custom Presentation and Device Independence

Technologies and techniques are emerging that will let the user choose the way they want content displayed. In fact some of these are in use today.

Soon user-agents will be able to access web sites while specifying an appropriate mode of content presentation. This has obvious accessibility benefits. This can already be done with CSS stylesheets for specific presentation formats, but in most cases the formats must be manually chosen and there are a limited number of presentations available. Although stylesheets are not functional in every browser, they offer useful accessibility options to authors and users who understand them. They are also the basis for much of the work that is being done in other areas of accessibility. A good portion of the work we look at in this section involves stylesheets or technology based on the stylesheet concept.

The next step forward will be to have the web site figure out what kind of presentation the user prefers, and standards and techniques are emerging that will allow the web site to figure out what type of presentation a user needs or desires. Technology such as CC/PP (Composite Capability/Preference Profiles) will allow the user to set up their own profile that will provide the information necessary for a web server to present information appropriately. This will be a useful technique once it is developed. It will not only help people with disabilities to access the Web in the way they need to, but will also allow people with alternative access devices or people in low bandwidth areas to access web sites more easily.

Also, as the devices that are being used to access the Web change, it is becoming apparent that there must be some way for these new devices to be able to read what is on a web site, without having to provide alternative pages for each type of device. The goal is to find a way to set up a web site simply and elegantly, so it will be readable by any kind of device. The advantage to people with disabilities will be that any kind of device or assistive technology that they might use would be included.

The importance of this cannot be overstated. New types of devices are being developed all the time, and older devices, such as televisions, mobile phones, PDAs, and even refrigerators, are being integrated into the Web as well. Each device has unique needs and, unless special web content is going to be written for each type of device, a way must be developed to allow these devices to access the same web content as everyone else. The activities below are some examples of what is going on in this area.

Alternative Interface Access Protocol (AIAP)

This protocol is under development (*http://www.ncits.org/tc_home/v2.htm*). It will provide access to both individual and networked systems and devices. With suitable middleware, AIAP allows interaction with workstations, with embedded devices (environmental controls, intelligent appliances, and consumer electronics), or with applications via home networking or the Internet. The protocol can also convey information about user interface functionality, preferences, and capabilities to other systems with which the user wants to communicate. Other interfaces can then be worked with or built, on the fly if necessary, giving basic access to computer services and electronic information no matter what limitations the user has. This will be a great advantage to people with disabilities as they will be able to access many more devices and services when it is implemented.

Accessibility Features

At the present time, there are four methods proposed for a user to change the user interface:

- By using an alternative user interface component instead of the native user interface component.

- By allowing a person to use a complete alternative user interface (which includes its own alternative input, control and display mechanisms) instead of the native input, control and display mechanisms on the product (a Remote Console).

- By allowing the user to cause their characteristics or user interface preferences to be communicated to the target product (either directly or by providing a code which the device uses to look up the user preference or characteristics), so the target product changes its own user interface behavior based on the user's preferences or needs.

- By allowing the user to cause new user interface software to be determined and downloaded onto the target device directly or indirectly.

Quoted from http://www.ncits.org/tc_home/v2htm/V2docs/v201011.htm

Using the Technology

As the technology begins to mature it will be integrated into devices such as PDAs, Cell Phones, PCs and perhaps even remote controls. It will enable the largest audience possible to use these and other devices. It will bring true accessibility to the web and the devices that read web pages.

W3C Device Independence Activities

There is an Activity group working with the W3C that is dealing with the subject of Device Independence (*http://www.w3.org/2001/di/*). It represents the amalgamation of several groups, and was chartered throughout January 2002. It has produced a Device Independence Principles document (*http://www.w3.org/TR/di-princ/*) that describes the concepts. This document offers a good base from which to understand the concepts behind the work being done in the area of device independence.

The group was proposed to the W3C membership in the latter part of 2000. It was launched in January 2001. The Television and the Web Interest Group, The Mobile Access Interest Group, and the Composite Capabilities/Preferences Profile (CC/PP) Working Group are included in this activity.

TV and the Web Interest Group

This group is working on new issues that are arising from the integration of TV and the Web (*http://www.w3.org/TV/*). While this activity may not be directly linked to accessibility efforts, it will have to make its output accessible to people with disabilities, and it will probably use such things as SMIL to accomplish this goal. It did help produce the specifications for XHTML Basic which are found at: *http://www.w3.org/TR/2000/WD-xhtml-basic-20000210/*.

This group has merged with the Device Independence group, but they do still have their own independent activities in which they are engaging. More information on their current and past activities can be found by accessing the mailing list archive for this group at: *http://lists.w3.org/Archives/Public/www-tv/*.

Accessibility Advantages

This group and whatever protocols it develops do not appear to provide any inherent accessibility advantages. However it will have to use other protocols to achieve accessibility of its output. The experience gained by the members of this group may well help to advance accessibility features markup languages such as SMIL. At the time of writing they are working on some Cascading Style Sheets especially designed for the needs and constraints of TV devices (*http://www.w3.org/TR/css-tv*) and some of the Timed Text issues involved with captioning. The Timed Text Format Requirements can be found at: *http://www.w3.org/AudioVideo/timetext.html*.

Using the Technology – Tools

Tools developed using SMIL can assist in making the convergence of the Web and TV accessible.

Mobile Access Interest Group

Mobile devices have many restrictions that PCs do not have. They have a smaller memory, they have less storage space, and they have a limited speed and smaller screen compared to a fixed device such as a computer. In most cases input devices such as keyboards and mice are at best limited and at worst non-existent. Simple and intuitive operation is a must with these types of devices. At the time of writing this wireless companies do seem to be moving towards more use of voice-activated technology on their handsets.

> *You can read more about the activities of this group at*
> *http://www.w3.org/2001/di/Mobile/.*

While this group has merged with the Device Independence Group, they too are still active. The best way to find out about their current activities is to visit the current page at: *http://www.w3.org/2001/di/Mobile/.* They also have a mailing list but you must be a member of the W3C to access it and its archives.

Accessibility Advantages

In the HTML4.0 Guidelines for Mobile Access (March 1999), which is a W3C Note, it clearly states that the W3C Web Accessibility Initiative's WCAG are applicable to mobile devices (*http://www.w3.org/TR/NOTE-html40-mobile/*). This is an interesting linkage between mobile devices and the guidelines that have been produced for building accessible web sites; if you build an accessible web site, the chances are that it will be accessible to mobile devices too.

Using the Technology – Tools

The best tool to use in keeping your web pages accessible to mobile devices is to keep them accessible according to the WCAG. Of course you should test your pages on a mobile device or an emulator and make sure they are accessible. This is the best test and should always be used.

It should be noted that many people who are deaf or hearing-impaired use mobile devices such as PDAs quite regularly.

WAP Emulators

Wireless Access Protocol or WAP is the name of the communications protocol that is used when mobile devices access the Internet. Mobile devices can access pages coded in Wireless Markup Language (WML), which is derived from XML. There are some excellent WAP emulators and other tools that can be used to help design pages for these devices such as:

- **The Gelon WAP Emulator** (*http://www.gelon.net/*). To use this emulator simply type in the URL for the WAP page you want to view.

- **WAP Tool V1.1** (*http://www.argogroup.com/waptool/*). This tool converts HTML pages into WAP so that they are accessible to mobile devices.

- **Deckit Emulator** (*http://www.pyweb.com/tools/*). A WAP emulator.

CC/PP Working Group

CC/PP profiles are a method that allows a description of device capabilities and user preferences that allows content to be adapted to the device according those capabilities and preferences. CC/PP is based on the **Resource Description Framework (RDF)**, developed by the W3C, and is general-purpose meta data description language. By the use of standard values and attributes, a server can determine the most appropriate form in which to deliver a resource to a user according to their profile.

For more on this Group, see http://www.w3.org/Mobile/CCPP/.

Accessibility Advantages

With CC/PP profiles a disabled person who relies on assistive technologies would receive the web site's content in a format most usable by them or their assistive technology. This technology will allow web site content to be delivered to a variety of devices and in a variety of ways, without the need for any special coding techniques.

The CC/PP working group do have a mailing list and a good way to find out what the current activity of this group is, is to look in the mailing list archives at: *http://lists.w3.org/Archives/Public/www-mobile/*, as well as checking their main page at: *http://www.w3.org/Mobile/CCPP/.*

Using the Technology

The main purpose of this technology is to provide the web server with information on the capabilities of a user agent. This might be a PDA, a standard browser, or an assistive technology for someone with a disability. Generic profiles can be accessed over the Web, which will reduce the information that must be sent to the server. The end result will be that the user supplies a profile in one way or another and the CC/PP profile helps the server deliver the content to the user in the desired way.

The protocol is being developed with the help of the manufacturers of mobile phones and others. Here are some resources that you can use to keep up with further developments:

- Composite Capability/Preference Profiles (CC/PP): Structure and Vocabularies (*http://www.w3.org/TR/CCPP-struct-vocab/*). While this document is fairly technical it does help explain what CC/PP is doing and how it accomplishes its goal.

- For a good list of resources and background material (*http://www.w3.org/Mobile/CCPP/ccpp-reading*).

- Charter (*http://www.w3.org/2001/01/ccpp/charter-20010118.html*).

- CC/PP By Kynn Bartlett (*http://www.icdri.org/ccpp.htm*).

User Interface Markup Language (UIML)

Unlike a few years ago, when the only feasible way to access the Web was with a PC and modem, a large variety of alternative access devices now exist, for example cell phones, PDAs, or assistive technology devices. It is not realistic to expect web developers to have the time or resources to build separate web pages to fit every known device, as well as every type of assistive technology. Furthermore, new languages have been proposed for specific devices, implying that each device will have to have a page built to its specific needs and design specifications.

Its developers propose that the User Interface Markup Language (UIML) is the solution to this issue. UIML is a markup language that defines user interfaces (*http://www.uiml.org/*). This means that the device you are using is irrelevant to UIML, it could be a desktop PC, a mobile phone, voice input, a Graphical User Interface (GUI), or any other user interface, even interfaces that have not been thought of yet.

Unlike many markup languages UIML is not used to describe documents, it is used to describe elements on the page such as buttons, menu lists, and other page elements generally used in graphical user interfaces (GUIs). It defines their placement on the page, and the action to be taken when certain events such as mouse clicks or keystrokes occur. This allows the designers to design the user interface in generic terms and leave the device-specific issues to stylesheets. Thus UIML keeps the designer from being burdened with considerations of different device types and device specific issue are dealt with by the use of stylesheets. UIML can be used with Java, VoiceXML, HTML, WML, and other markup and programming languages.

Accessibility Advantages

UIML can help facilitate the separation of content from presentation, creating device independence. Instead of having to write web pages for specific types of interfaces, the elements on the page can be described once in UIML, and then stylesheets can handle the specification needed for each type of user interface. This means that not only will UIML be able to handle current user interfaces, but will be usable with future interfaces and assistive technology as well.

Using the Technology – Tools

There are several tools that can help with the integration of UIML into web-based resources. One of the best places to find out about the current availability of tools online is at *http://www.uiml.org/tool/index.htm*. Here you will find the latest information and software to help with the implementing of UIML.

Biometrics

Biometrics, which is automatically identifying people by one or more bodily characteristics, holds great promise as a way to help improve the accessibility of web-based technologies and many other facets of electronic and information technology.

One of the problems with biometrics for people with disabilities is that if the ID system is dependent on a body part that could be missing, damaged, or non-functional, a person with a disability will be at a distinct disadvantage, and may be excluded altogether.

Facial thermography is one possible solution to this problem. This technique involves identifying individuals by the heat signature of the face, which is unique to each of us and does not change, even with injury. This method was proposed in a paper on the web site of the International Center for Disability Resources on the Internet (*http://www.icdri.org/let_me_in.htm*). It should be possible, using this technology, to uniquely identify any living person solely by the face, and no other parts of the body. This could be used in conjunction with a heat sensor to verify the identity of someone signing into a web site.

You can learn more about Biometrics at http://www.biometrics.org/ and more specifically its potential for accessibility at http://www.icdri.org/let_me_in.htm

Accessibility Advantages

Biometric systems can uniquely identify a person, using information that cannot be easily falsified or stolen and that does not depend on body characteristics that might become damaged or altered. This offers an opportunity for people with disabilities to be identified and have their web environment altered to suit their needs and preferences. Biometrics offers unique and secure ways to identify users and their needs.

Using the Technology – Tools

Much of what can be done will be dependent upon the tools that are available to the average user. At this time, biometrics is an expensive solution for most users. However, the important thing is to be aware of the possibilities and to avoid the limitations. Once again if we are aware of accessibility issues, the technology can be turned to the advantage of people with disabilities instead of "locking them out".

Problems with Using Emerging Technologies

There are a number of ongoing problems in using emerging technologies to produce web pages and sites that are accessible. The first is that emerging technologies can be complicated to use and require a great deal of knowledge to use them. This, at least at first, will keep them from being widely accepted. Some of these technologies have been developed by those who have little or no awareness of disability issues and they do not always lend themselves to accessible usage across the board.

Another problem is that web designers can sometimes be seduced into using a new technology before a proper assessment is made of its usefulness and practicality. Many of these new technologies are not designed with the principles of Universal Design in mind, making them difficult to use in a way that will produce a web site that is accessible to the largest number of people possible.

Designing the technology without Universal Design principles can force the designers of both the technology and the sites where it has been used to have to go back at a later date and "retrofit" accessibility features into the site, which is usually very expensive at this stage. Nevertheless, the effort to use emerging technologies in accessible ways or to improve accessibility must continue, because this is what will move these technologies forward.

Complexity

One barriers of using new technologies can be the sheer complexity of implementation. Highly complex solutions will require software to make them easier for the user to operate. The technology itself must be usable, or it may never be widely implemented. So along with a new technology, there must be easy-to-use tools to implement the technology.

Accessibility Awareness

One of the biggest problems for developers of new web-based technologies is that the designers and developers are often unaware that there are any issues with accessibility for people with disabilities. They simply do not know that the problems exist.

The way to change this is to increase awareness of accessibility issues among software developers. Many developers will embrace accessibility enthusiastically once they are aware of it. The more developers can be educated about accessibility issues, the more the technology that emerges from their efforts will be accessible. Ideally all accessibility features should be integrated into product design, not presented as a separate feature.

Purpose

One typical problem with emerging and exciting technologies, is that we become so fascinated by the technology itself forget the both of the purpose the technology, and where it is best used. Using this new technology becomes an end in itself and can detract from both the purpose of the web page or web site and its usefulness.

One way to avoid this is to look at each piece of new technology and decide how it can further the goal of your web site, and how it can make your site more accessible.

One example of this is the animation presentations that have become popular on web sites. Many people decry their use as being inaccessible to people with disabilities. However, if they are properly implemented and properly designed, they can actually improve accessibility for some groups. As long as we understand that an alternative means of presentation may have to be provided, and that, carefully designed and implemented, this new technology can increase accessibility for some groups, we can also use it to increase the retention of information for others who may not have any disability at all.

Design for All

Wherever possible developers should design web technology for the largest audience possible. Following the principles of Universal Design, this is not the impossible task it might seem. It has many benefits: it will give a larger audience an opportunity to use the technology, and it will make the development of the technology more cost-effective. The continued use of these principles will also help develop new products and services that can serve a larger audience.

These principles were first developed and codified by the Center for Universal Design at North Carolina State University. They state:

> *Universal design is the design of products and environments to be usable by all people, to the greatest extent possible, without the need for adaptation or specialized design.*

> *The intent of universal design is to simplify life for everyone by making products, communications, and the built environment more usable by as many people as possible at little or no extra cost. Universal design benefits people of all ages and abilities. " (http://www.design.ncsu.edu:8120/cud/univ_design/ud.htm)*

They were further developed by the Trace Center at the University of Wisconsin at Madison. The Trace Center helped to focus these principles on Electronic and Information Technology (EIT). In fact people from the Trace Center where also involved with the W3C WCAG guidelines, which are used extensively today.

It is also true that Universal Design does not assume the user has the latest browser and the fastest connection possible. This is a problem with some emerging technology and it does leave out those who cannot afford the most recent software.

Let's take a look at some of the Universal Design Principles and see how they apply to web pages.

Perceptible Information

The design communicates necessary information effectively to the user, regardless of ambient conditions or the user's sensory abilities.

GUIDELINES

- Use different modes (pictorial, verbal, tactile) for redundant presentation of essential information.

- Provide adequate contrast between essential information and its surroundings.

- Maximize "legibility" of essential information.

- Differentiate elements in ways that can be described (that is, make it easy to give instructions or directions).

- Provide compatibility with a variety of techniques or devices used by people with sensory limitations.

This design principle was obviously quite helpful in developing several design guidelines for accessible web pages. It suggests first that information should be presented in several modes; it then states that adequate contrast should exist between information (web page content) and its surroundings and the information should be legible. While this may seem obvious, there are a surprisingly high number of web pages that present light colored text on light colored backgrounds, or have such a "busy" background that the text is quite difficult to read.

It also suggests that compatibility with different devices or techniques used by people with sensory limitations is a good idea. This could translate into web pages that are easy to read by means of a screen reader, mobile phone, or that can be used with voice input programs.

Tolerance for Error

The design minimizes hazards and the adverse consequences of accidental or unintended actions.

GUIDELINES

- Arrange elements to minimize hazards and errors: most used elements, most accessible; hazardous elements eliminated, isolated, or shielded.

- Provide warnings of hazards and errors.

- Provide fail-safe features.

- Discourage unconscious action in tasks that require vigilance.

Obviously this applies to web pages where people will be filling out forms or performing other critical operations. They could not only be warned if the form is not filled out correctly, the form should be designed so that it is easy to fill out.

These are two examples of how the principles of Universal Design can be applied to web page design.

If you are interested in reading the rest of the principles, they are located at: http://www.design.ncsu.edu:8120/cud/univ_design/princ_overview.htm. They have heavily influenced most of the accessibility guidelines that are in use today and their influence continues. They are most definitely part of the basis for web accessibility guidelines wherever they are found.

Retrofitting

In many cases pressure is placed on developers to retrofit new technologies that become popular to make them accessible. A far more cost-effective way is to design the new technology to be usable by the largest number of people possible, regardless of disability. This will save an enormous amount of time and effort over the life of the product or service.

If a product must be retrofitted, it is recommended that the retrofit be made an integral part of the design, and that the design be brought into adherence with the principles of Universal Design. This will insure that the product will be flexible enough to withstand the implementation of future changes and enhancements without having to be totally redesigned to make it accessible to the largest audience possible.

Summary

The solution is simple in concept but more difficult in implementation. Simply stated the developers and implementers of new technology must be made aware of the issues involved in web accessibility. This will require an ongoing training program directed at several levels: management, programmers, designers, and implementers of web-based technology.

There must also be a good set of resources that they can use to understand the issues and to develop their products to meet the needs of the largest possible audience. These resources should be collected on an ongoing basis and made available to your entire organization. There should also be a means of submitting new resources and techniques to this knowledge base so that others can use them.

As the Internet expands, accessibility issues, sometimes called "universal access", will become more critical not just for people with disabilities, but for those who do not speak your language, and for those who are going to access content with an alternative access device such as a phone or a voice-activated device or a computer in a car. People may want to control their air conditioning system, their sprinkler system, and turn their lights on and off with a single device. All of these things will require some kind of alternative access to the Internet and all alternative access is going to face similar problems to that which people with disabilities are facing today.

In solving the issues of accessibility of the Web for people with disabilities, many exciting solutions are going to be found. *Stay Tuned!*

13

- Americans with Disabilities Act

- Section 255 of the Telecommunications Act

- Electronic and informationtechnologyaccessibility

- Section 508

- WCAG guidelines

Author: Cynthia D. Waddell

US Web Accessibility Law in Depth

Through the American disability rights tradition, access to electronic and information technology has emerged as a civil right. As technology advanced, it was only a matter of time before a federal law would establish accessible design specifications for a broad class of electronic and information technology. Today, there are significant legal incentives for ensuring that Internet and intranet web sites designed for US entities meet accessible web requirements.

Ever since the passing of the 1964 Civil Rights Act prohibiting discrimination on the basis of race, legal protections for persons with disabilities have emerged and expanded through a patchwork of civil rights laws prohibiting discrimination on the basis of disability (for more, see *The Accessible Future*, National Council on Disability, June 21, 2001, at *http://www.icdri.org./accessible_future.htm*).

The Americans with Disabilities Act of 1990 (ADA), Section 255 of the Telecommunications Act of 1996 (Section 255), and Section 508 of the Rehabilitation Act Amendments of 1998 (Section 508) form the basis for discussion in this chapter. These federal laws and their accompanying regulations, interpretative guidance and case law, are only a few of many US disability rights laws impacting technology and access to information. As such, this body of law is complex and cannot be fully addressed in a chapter on accessible web design. In fact, I do not believe it would necessarily be helpful for web design technologists to delve into this complexity.

This chapter introduces the reader to the current state of US accessibility law as it pertains to the design of a web site. All decision makers, whether they are web developers, their clients, or policymakers need to understand the legal reasons for designing accessibly and the legal liability for ignoring the issue – this is especially important since ignorance of the law is not a defense. Therefore, we will examine the ADA accessible web cases and briefly discuss Section 255. The meat of this chapter, however, concerns the new US legislation addressing accessible web design in Section 508 – the Electronic and Information Technology Accessibility Standards.

Having established a foundation and core understanding, we will then take a look at how to decide when to apply the W3C **Web Content Accessibility Guidelines** (**WCAG**) as opposed to a Section 508 accessible web design rule. And lastly, an in-depth chapter would not be complete without discussing current legal hot topics for accessible web design and challenges ahead.

As Lawrence Lessig commented on page 6 of *Code and Other Laws of Cyberspace* (New York: Basic Books, ISBN: 046503912X):

> *We can build, or architect, or code cyberspace to protect values that we believe are fundamental, or we can build, or architect, or code cyberspace to allow those values to disappear. There is no middle ground.*

> This chapter is an introduction to US web accessibility law in depth and is not intended to be a complete discussion of the complex legal issues involved, nor does it intend to be the "final word" regarding the changing regulatory and technological environment. When reading this, be aware that comments in this chapter should not be construed as legal advice or opinion on specific facts, since particular legal questions can best be answered by seeking the advice of legal counsel.

Americans with Disabilities Act and the Internet

This year the US celebrates the twelfth anniversary of the passing of that landmark civil rights legislation, the Americans with Disabilities Act of 1990 (ADA). When former President Bush signed the ADA, it marked a watershed moment: now persons with disabilities would have access to facilities, programs, services, and employment just like any other person.

One major goal of the ADA is to remove barriers in society, both physical and programmatic, so that the quality of life would be improved. This effort has created side benefits for those beyond the community of persons with disabilities, but that topic is reserved for another time. Many Americans are aware that one of the most significant impacts has been the establishment of a building code specifying the accessible elements for designing buildings, public pathways, and car parks. Members of the construction industry, building code societies, and disability organizations came to the table to draft this important regulation after the ADA was enacted.

> *I recall that at that time it frequently did not occur to many as to why there were no people with mobility disabilities in inaccessible buildings. People would say, "Why should we remove barriers in construction? I don't see anyone needing access!"*

Similarly, many who do not understand the subject of this book have said the same about accessible web design. But hopefully the reader has reached this chapter fully informed and ready to implement an accessible web site that has been validated by end users with disabilities.

Another significant impact of the ADA has been the use of technology in the workplace. Technology has enabled people with disabilities to demonstrate their ability to perform the essential functions of the job – leading many to become independent and self-reliant. This is done through the "reasonable accommodation" process along with the requirement that "effective communication" and "auxiliary aids and services" be provided. These ADA concepts will be discussed later in this chapter when we look at ADA web cases.

The ADA is a complex law and so this chapter only touches the surface of important issues. For more information, please visit the US Department of Justice ADA home page at *http://www.usdoj.gov/crt/ada/adahom1.htm.*

Accessible Web ADA Myths

Perhaps this is a good time to point out three myths or erroneous views that have found their way into ADA legal literature about our topic:

- Accessible web requires the cost-prohibitive use of audio-streaming and high bandwidth

- Accessible web requires two versions of the same web site – one text and one graphical

- Web developers cannot be held liable if their client told them to ignore accessible web design

The first myth that accessible web requires audio-streaming and high bandwidth comes from not understanding how a screen reader or voice browser operates when viewing web pages. I have observed legal arguments against accessible web design built upon this myth – all the way from Congressional law and policy memoranda to law review articles!

As to the second myth, in certain cases there may be the need to show two versions of web site content, but technology has now brought us to the point that we have the knowledge and the means to design accessibly without segregation and without driving up the cost for implementation and maintenance. In my opinion, having two versions of a web site is not a best practice and we have coding solutions to enable someone using a text browser, such as Lynx, to reach the content of a graphical web page. In fact, the W3C WAI FAQ states that having two versions is counter-productive and not necessary (see *http://www.w3.org/1999/05/WCAG-REC-fact#text*).

The third myth – that web developers cannot be held liable for inaccessible web design due to client instructions and pocketbook – is subject to debate. Under the ADA, architects of buildings subject to new construction or remodeling have been held liable for failure to design and construct accessible facilities, although courts have not been consistent in their findings. However, the US Department of Justice has consistently maintained that architects can be held liable for violating the ADA. See *Legal Rights of Persons with Disabilities: An Analysis of Federal Law* (Tucker and Goldstein, LRP Publications, ISBN: 0934753466).

Similarly, it is now highly likely that web developers could also be held liable, both for the construction of a web site and any time they modify it. This is because the ADA imposes an ongoing duty to remove barriers and to maintain accessible features. Now that Section 508 Electronic and Information Technology Accessibility Standards is law, the ADA will be informed about what it means to design accessible web sites. Even though Section 508 only directly impacts federal agencies, there is also an indirect impact on other entities for a variety of reasons as discussed later in this chapter under *When Does a Web Developer Follow Section 508 Rules?*

Before the Section 508 Electronic and Information Technology Accessibility Standards became law, the ADA did not provide for specific accessible web design standards for web site conformance. Instead, the 1996 US Department of Justice policy ruling that the ADA applied to the Internet was the only guidance. This is why it was so significant that this author implemented the first accessible web design standard for local government in 1995, as discussed in *Chapter 2, Overview of Law and Guidelines*. ADA web site complaints were being filed, people with disabilities needed access, and there was no standard to follow.

Now that the Section 508 Electronic and Information Technology Accessibility Standards have become law, these standards will inform ADA entities on how to create accessible web sites and services, including the Help Desk and all product documents. As a result, web developers may be liable, as discussed later in this chapter under the *Section 508 Overview*.

I attribute these myths to lawyers not understanding technology and what it means to design accessibly. But we should not discount the possibility that these lawyers consulted the technical community, or that these erroneous views may have originated from the technical community. So watch out for variations of these myths!

US Department of Justice Policy Ruling: Applying the ADA to the Internet

Under the ADA, covered entities are required to furnish appropriate auxiliary aids and services where necessary to ensure effective communication with individuals with disabilities, unless doing so would result in a fundamental alteration to the program or service, or an undue burden. Auxiliary aids include taped texts, Brailled materials, large print materials, captioning, and other methods of making audio and visual media available to people with disabilities.

On September 9, 1996, the US Department of Justice (USDOJ) issued a policy ruling applying the ADA to the Internet. Under the rationale of "effective communication," the USDOJ Letter states that *State and Local Governments* (ADA Title II), as well as *Public Accommodations (nongovernmental) and Commercial Facilities* (ADA Title III), must provide effective communication whenever they communicate through the Internet.

"*Public Accommodations*" include private entities that offer goods and services to the public such as sales or rental establishments; service establishments; places of exhibition or entertainment, public gatherings, recreation, and education.

> The policy ruling stated that: "Covered entities under the ADA are required to provide effective communication, regardless of whether they generally communicate through print media, audio media, or computerized media such as the Internet. Covered entities that use the Internet for communications regarding their programs, goods, or services must be prepared to offer those communications through accessible means as well."

The USDOJ continued in the policy ruling by discussing a variety of ways to provide accessibility such as a text-only page, or the provision of accessible instructions on the web page so that a person with a disability could request the same web information in an accessible format such as Braille, large print, diskette, or audio-tape.

It should be noted that prior to the prevalent use of the Internet, entities met ADA requirements by providing accessible information in alternative formats such as those stated above. My office quickly experienced a cost saving of staff time and alternative format expenses when we began to provide accessible information through the Internet.

In addition, as we will see, the definition of "effective communication" was eventually further refined to be a three-pronged definition including "timeliness of delivery." It would be no longer an option to design an inaccessible web site and post instructions on how to request the same web content in an accessible format. Stay tuned for the California Community College case as discussed later in this chapter at *3. OCR Letter of Resolution, Docket No. 09-97-6001 (January 22, 1998).*

Lastly, it is interesting to note that the policy ruling came as a result of a letter initiated by a web designer who also was a lawyer. He was knowledgeable about the ADA, the prohibition against discrimination against persons with disabilities and wanted "to do the right thing." He wrote to his Senator who then made an inquiry to the USDOJ. The policy ruling was in response to the inquiry by Senator Harkin on behalf of this web designer. So web designers can make a difference!

Note that the policy ruling includes a list of resources on how to design accessible web pages. It was at the Center for Information Technology Accommodation of the US General Services Administration where visitors were pointed to resources, including this author's accessible web design standard at the City of San Jose, California. See *http://www.icdri.org/city_of_san_jose_world_wide_web_.htm*

> *See the United States Department of Justice Policy Ruling, 9/9/96: ADA Accessibility Requirements Apply to Internet Web Pages at 10 NDLR 240 or at http://www.usdoj.gov/crt/foia/tal712.txt, for more on the inquiry from a web designer.*

Introduction To the ADA Complaint Process

In the US, disability rights cases are complaint driven and are either administrative or filed in court. If an entity refuses to remediate the web site upon inquiry from a person with a disability, then a complaint must be filed in order to remedy the problem.

At times USDOJ will initiate a lawsuit, but only after it has first unsuccessfully attempted to settle the dispute through negotiations. However, the USDOJ may file lawsuits to enforce the ADA and may obtain court orders including compensatory damages and back pay to remedy discrimination. Under Title III (applicable to public accommodations and commercial facilities), the USDOJ may also obtain civil penalties of up to $55,000 for the first violation and $110,000 for any subsequent violation.

Another way an ADA federal enforcement agency might become involved would be, if they decided to initiate a compliance review that included the correction of a web site deficiency. We will see an example of this activity when we look at the California Community College case, later in this chapter.

Also, under the ADA, a person with a disability need not hold American citizenship to file the complaint. Since at least 1995, many ADA web cases have been filed, but as of the time of writing of this book, none has gone to trial. Instead, parties in these cases have entered into settlement agreements, some private and some public.

Because there have been no legal challenges under the ADA on the issue of inaccessible web pages, there have been no cases reported in commercial legal publications to inform attorneys about this issue. This is one of the reasons why members of the legal profession may not necessarily be knowledgeable about this issue. Because of my concern for educating the business and legal community about inaccessible technologies and their impact, I have authored a number of papers and articles currently posted at *http://www.icdri.org/cynthia_waddell.htm*. One such paper, *Applying the ADA to the Internet: A Web Accessibility Standard* (see *http://www.icdri.org/applying_the_ada_to_the_internet.htm*), was requested by the American Bar Association in 1998 because of the need for education. This paper has been frequently cited in legal literature as well as in reports to the US President and Congress, such as *The Accessible Future*, referenced in the beginning of this chapter.

Current ADA Case Law

Hooks v. OKBridge: Although there have been no court decisions on point, there is a USDOJ appellate brief outlining the ADA enforcement agency position. On 30 June 2000, the USDOJ filed a friend of the court appellate brief in *Hooks v. OKBridge* arguing that ADA Title III applied to the Internet. See *Hooks v. OKBridge, Inc.* 99-50891 (5th Cir.2000); also see *USDOJ amicus curiae brief* at *http://www.usdoj.gov/crt/briefs/hooks.htm.*

OKBridge is a commercial web site where customers can play bridge and participate in online discussion groups regarding the game for a fee. The USDOJ argues that a commercial business providing services over the Internet is subject to the ADA's prohibition against discrimination on the basis of disability because:

- The language of the ADA does not limit it to services provided at a company's physical facility

- The services "of" a place of public accommodation need not be provided "at" the place of public accommodation

- The definition of "public accommodation" is not limited to entities providing services at their physical premises

- The absence of specific mention in the ADA of services provided over the Internet does not restrict the ADA's coverage

- This court has already rejected the view that the ADA is limited to services performed at a physical place

The USDOJ points out that a growing number of services are being provided over the Internet creating modes of commerce that are replacing physical buildings. In addition, many businesses provide services at places other than their premises and they are not relieved from the prohibition from discriminating on the basis of disability; for example, services provided over the telephone or through the mail, such as travel agencies, banks, insurance companies, catalog merchants, and pharmacies. They also point out that many other businesses provide services in the homes or offices of their customers, such as plumbers, pizza delivery and moving companies, cleaning services, business consulting firms, and auditors from accounting firms.

In short, it is the USDOJ's position that the entertainment or recreation services provided by OKBridge make it a place of public accommodation. However, the Fifth Circuit Court ruling did not reach the question on whether or not the ADA applied to the Internet.

Other ADA Cases

Current case law finds courts disagreeing as to whether or not the ADA definition of "place of public accommodation" is limited to actual physical structures. In *Carparts Distribution Center v. Automotive Wholesalers Association of New England*, the First Circuit held that places of public accommodation are not limited to physical facilities – see 37 F.3d 12 (lst Cir. 1994). The court based its conclusion on legislative history and the purpose of the ADA and stated, "It would be irrational to conclude that persons who enter an office to purchase services are protected by the ADA, but persons who purchase the same services over the telephone or by mail are not. Congress could not have intended such an absurd result." (See page 19 of the decision, or see *http://www.harp.org/carparts.txt.*)

Similarly, the Seventh Circuit in *Doe v. Mutual of Omaha Insurance Company* stated in their discussion that web sites are a place of public accommodation. In *"Doe"*, the court said: "The core meaning of this provision, plainly enough, is that the owner or operator of a store, hotel, restaurant, dentist's office, travel agency, theater, *web site*, or other facility (*whether in physical space or in electronic space*) that is open to the public cannot exclude disabled persons from entering the facility and, once in, from using the facility in the same way that the non-disabled do."

> See *http://lw.bna.com/lw/19990615/984112.htm* cited as 179 F.3d 557 at (7th cir. 1999)(emphasis added and citations omitted).

On the other hand, both the Third and Sixth Circuits have held that the ADA does not cover services outside a physical location. See *Ford v. Schering-Plough Corporation*, 145 F.3d 601, 614 (3d Cir. 1998) and *Parker v. Metropolitan Life Insurance Company*, 121 F. 3d 1006 (6th Cir. 1997).

Selected ADA Accessible Web Complaints

As discussed, there has not been a legal challenge on accessible web design. However, there have been many ADA accessible web complaints that have been filed both administratively and in court and many have settled. Some of the settlements are private but some are public. We will take a look at the public settlements, mediations, and legal compliance reviews underway in chronological order.

Office for Civil Rights, US Department of Education

There are eight different federal agencies responsible for enforcing the ADA and this responsibility is assigned according to the function of each agency. For example, the US Office for Civil Rights (OCR), US Department of Education, is responsible for disability rights enforcement at public school districts, public colleges and universities, public vocational schools, and public libraries.

Each year the OCR receives approximately 5,000 complaints claiming discrimination on the basis of race, color, national origin, sex, disability, and age. These complaints involve some of the most important issues affecting equal access to quality education. For example, the disability discrimination issues range from accessibility of school facilities and programmes to auxiliary aids and accessible web design.

Access to the learning environment is a critical, front-line issue requiring immediate resolution. Library reference services are being transformed by the application of Internet access to information systems and search engines. Professors are teaching long-distance learning courses over the Internet, and even if a student is physically in class, homework assignments and resources are being posted on classroom web pages. Yet, even if a library terminal has assistive computer technology installed for students or visitors with disabilities, Internet research is not possible with inaccessible web page design.

The following is a summary of four California OCR, US Department of Education Letters of Resolution, which impact Internet accessibility:

1. OCR Letter of Resolution, Docket No. 09-95-2206 (January 25, 1996)

(see *http://www.icdri.org/sjsu.htm*)

This case concerned a student complaint that a university failed to provide equivalent access to the Internet. A student with a visual disability was required to make appointments with personal reader attendants as the exclusive mechanism for access to the Internet. The University also failed to complete the "Self-Evaluation Plan" as required by ADA Title II.

According to the finding, "the issue is not whether the student with the disability is merely provided with access, but rather the extent to which the communication is actually as effective as that provided to others. Title II of the ADA also strongly affirms the important role that computer technology is expected to play as an auxiliary aid by which communication is made effective for persons with disabilities. OCR notes that the "information superhighway" is fast becoming a fundamental tool in post-secondary research."

See Letter of Resolution, pp. 1-2; 38 C.F.R.§35.160(a).

2. OCR Letter of Resolution, Docket No. 09-97-2002 (April 7, 1997)

(see *http://www.icdri.org/csula.htm*)

This case concerned a student complaint that a university failed to provide access to library resources, campus publications, open computer laboratories, training on adaptive computer technology, and computer test-taking.

According to the finding, "Title II of the Americans with Disabilities Act (Title II) requires a public college to take appropriate steps to ensure that communications with persons with disabilities "are as effective as communications with others" [28 C.F.R. § 35.160(a)]. OCR has repeatedly held that the term "communication" in this context means the transfer of information, including (but not limited to) the verbal presentation of a lecturer, the printed text of a book, and the resources of the Internet. Title II further states that, in determining what type of auxiliary aid and service is necessary, a public college shall give primary consideration to the requests of the individual with a disability [28 C.F.R. § 35.160(b)(2)]."

In further clarifying what is meant by "effective communication," OCR held that the three basic components of effective communication are: "timeliness of delivery, accuracy of the translation, and provision in a manner and medium appropriate to the significance of the message and the abilities of the individual with the disability." (*Letter of Resolution, page 1*).

It is the first prong of the definition, "timeliness of delivery", that strengthened the legal requirement for accessible web design. Previous practices of posting information on the web site to tell people with disabilities that they could get the web content in an accessible format by phoning or e-mailing a request, no longer met the ADA definition of "effective communication." While one person could access the content of a web site within seconds, another, with a different disability, might have to make a phone call and have the content snail mailed to them in an accessible format. The "timeliness of delivery" prong of the definition was now going to play an important role in the civil right to information.

We also see the emergence of policy that later becomes law in Section 508: an accessible technology plan. In this Letter of Resolution, OCR points out that the courts have held that a public entity violates its obligations under the ADA when it only responds on an ad-hoc basis to individual requests for accommodation. There is an affirmative duty to develop a comprehensive policy in advance of any request for auxiliary aids or services – see *Tyler v. City of Manhattan*, 857 F. Supp. 800 (D.Kan. 1994). Moreover, according to OCR "[a] recognized good practice in establishing such a comprehensive policy is to consult with the disability community, especially those members most likely to request accommodations." (*Letter of Resolution, page 2*).

The bottom line, according to OCR, is that effective communication imposes a duty to solve barriers to information access that the entity's purchasing choices create. Whenever existing technology is "upgraded" by a new technology feature, it is important to ensure that the new technology either improves accessibility or is compatible with existing assistive computer technology. Web-authoring software programs that erect barriers in their coding of web pages fall under this scrutiny.

Lastly, OCR states that when an entity selects software programs and/or hardware equipment that is not adaptable for people with disabilities, "the subsequent substantial expense of providing access is not generally regarded as an undue burden when such cost could have been significantly reduced by considering the issue of accessibility at the time of the initial selection." (*Letter of Resolution, page 2*).

When applied to accessible web design, there is all the more reason to ensure that the initial design and any subsequent "updates" meet with accessibility requirements. If the problem of accessibility is not addressed at this stage, then the money to address the burden of expense afterwards may not be available. Therefore, all technology improvements must take into account the removal of existing barriers to access and ensure that new ones do not occur. Covered entities preparing to retrofit their web sites need to be aware of this requirement.

3. OCR Letter of Resolution, Docket No. 09-97-6001 (January 22, 1998)

(see *http://www.icdri.org/ocrsurltr.htm*)

Because OCR recognizes that not all illegal discrimination situations can be addressed by relying on complaints filed from the public, OCR conducts agency-initiated cases, or compliance reviews. According to OCR, these compliance reviews "permit OCR to target resources on compliance problems that appear particularly acute, or national in scope, or which are newly emerging." (See *http://www.ed.gov/offices/OCR/docs/ensure99.html*).

In March 1996, the OCR notified the California Community Colleges that it was about to begin a statewide compliance review under Title II of the ADA. The purpose of the review and subsequent OCR Report was to assess how 106 California Community Colleges meet their obligations to students with visual disabilities in providing access to print and electronic information. In OCR's letter dated January 22, 1998, the comprehensive review suggested nine strategies to address:

- Cost-effective approach to purchasing adaptive technology

- Adaptive technology training

- Access guidelines for distance learning and campus web pages as well as tools for training faculty and staff

- Inclusive language in the distribution of standard technology grants/funds addressing college responsibility to ensure technology access and compatible upgrades

- Print materials translated into alternative formats such as electronic text and Braille

- Central registry of textbooks in alternative formats

- Library technology initiatives for access to both students and patrons with disabilities

- Follow-up to OCR survey initiated in 9/18/96 to determine compliance progress

- Annual reviews of Disabled Student Programs and Services to include attention to the removal of barriers in electronic technology

The Community College Chancellor agreed to implement OCR's recommendations to help the colleges meet their obligations under the ADA and Section 504 of the Rehabilitation Act. See 9 March 1999 Letter from Ralph Black, General Counsel for the California Community Colleges, to Paul Grossman, Chief Regional Attorney, US Department of Education, OCR re: Case Docket No. 09-07-6001.

Whereas the assistive computer technology training, support, and services for students with disabilities was once limited to staff exclusively working with the Office of Disabled Student Programs, a systematic plan is now required for mainstreaming this knowledge campus-wide: "Technology access, like architectural access, must be addressed institutionally as an integral part of the planning process." (*Letter of Resolution, page 5*).

Just as the removal of architectural barriers requires a plan for implementation, the removal of technological or digital barriers in programs and services requires a comprehensive institutional plan impacting every campus office. We will again see this concept of a plan for accessible technology when we visit our discussion on Section 508.

Today, a standard for long-distance learning has been established by the CA Community Colleges as a direct result of this compliance activity. The 1999 "Distance Education: Access Guidelines for Students with Disabilities" are considered a model for the nation and can be found at *http://www.htctu.fhda.edu/dlguidelines/final%20dl%20guidelines.htm*.

4. OCR Letter of Resolution, Docket No. 09-99-2041 (April 20, 1999)

(see *http://www.icdri.org/lbeach.htm*)

This was a student complaint that the university failed to provide access to the College of Business curriculum and other educational programs, including computer laboratories and classes in the College of Business.

> *OCR noted that, although the academic community has heavily relied upon centralized units on campus to house and maintain assistive computer technology: "[S]uch sole reliance upon a single centralized location (when not limited to adaptive technology training, but instead used for instructing disabled students in course subject matter) may run counter to the strong philosophy embodied in [ADA]Title II and Section 504 regarding the importance of fully integrating students with disabilities into the mainstream educational program, unless such services cannot be otherwise effectively provided [see 34 C.F.R. § 104.4(b)(iv); 28 C.F.R. § 35.130(b)(iv).] Thus, OCR assumes that in most cases computer access will be effectively provided to the student with the disability in an educational setting with his or her non-disabled peers and classmates at the various computer laboratory sites scattered throughout the campus."*

OCR went on to point out that by April 1, 1999, the University provided OCR with a voluntary resolution plan, which resolved the issues raised in this case. The plan included the following commitments by the University to:

- Develop and implement a written procedure describing which campus units are responsible for installing and maintaining adaptive workstations situated in College and central computer laboratories.

- Develop and implement a systematic method for ensuring that the issue of accessibility to persons with disabilities, particularly persons who are blind, is taken into account when colleges purchase computer technology (software and hardware).

- Develop and implement a systematic method for informing campus employees who design/select web pages for use by students to make sure the web pages are in accordance with principles known to maximize accessibility to users with disabilities, including visual impairments.

As a result, the mainstreaming of students with disabilities created the need for appropriate technology tools for access to the learning environment. And as students with disabilities move into the workforce as employees, employers, or consumers, accessible web design, accessible web authoring tools, and an accessible Internet platform remain significant issues to be addressed. In other words, overcoming barriers in web design requires appropriate policies, technology tools and education for accessible design and implementation.

National Federation of the Blind v. America Online (November 1999)

In November 1999, the **National Federation of the Blind** (**NFB**) filed suit against **America Online, Inc.** (**AOL**), charging that AOL's proprietary browser and Internet web site was inaccessible to consumers who were blind.

According to the complaint, screen readers were encountering accessibility barriers to AOL services due to the use of unlabeled graphics, keyboard commands that had to be activated through a mouse, customized graphical controls, and channels hidden within unlabeled graphics.

Some of the web design barriers included:

- An inaccessible AOL service sign-up form that was not designed to inform the user as to the content requested for each blank field.

- A "Welcome" screen with features such as "*favorites*", "*parental control*", and "*chat rooms*", where the text was hidden within graphics.

- The required use of browser software designed to operate so that screen readers did not know when the browser was operating, thus making it very difficult for users who are blind to enter a keyword search, a web address, or even tab through the links.

- Barriers to the ADA requirement of "effective communication" where the user could not benefit from a significant number of AOL service features.

According to the complaint, service features that the user could not use included: electronic mail services; "buddy list" feature; public bulletin boards; public and private "chat rooms" and "auditorium" events; AOL's nineteen "channels" providing informational content; and commerce and community opportunities relating to news, sports, games, finance, shopping, health, travel, kids, and other subjects; and AOL's personalization and control features for users such as those for updating stock portfolios or blocking their children's access to inappropriate web sites

For additional discussion on this case, please see the following:

- *Suit Targets Cyberspace for ADA Compliance*, by *Cynthia D. Waddell, National Disability Law Reporter, Highlights, Volume 16, Issue 5, December 16, 1999.*

- *The National Federation of the Blind Sues AOL*, by *Cynthia D. Waddell, Human Rights, Volume 27, No. 1, Winter 2000, American Bar Association Magazine for the Section of Individual Rights and Responsibilities at http://www.abanet.org/irr/hr/winter00humanrights/waddell2.html.*

On the 26th of July 2000, NFB and AOL announced that the first ADA Internet complaint against an Internet service provider had been dismissed by mutual agreement. It was no accident that the joint press release was released on the 10th anniversary of the ADA. As I reviewed the Agreement, I found that although the complaint was dismissed without prejudice, NFB expressly reserved their rights to renew their ADA action against AOL. This means that the agreement should not be regarded as a settlement.

However, the Agreement set forth a number of remedies to assist AOL in addressing accessibility. For example, AOL committed to an **America Online Accessibility Policy**, now found on their web site at *http://corp.aol.com/access_policy.html*. The AOL Accessibility Policy has three components:

- Raising employee awareness of information technology accessibility issues

- Taking responsibility for developing accessible products and services

- Collaborating with the disability community for input and feedback on AOL products and services

For other discussion about AOL, see *Will the National Federation of the Blind Renew Their ADA Web Complaint Against AOL? by Cynthia D. Waddell, National Disability Law Reporter, Volume 18, Issue 5, August 24, 2000.*

Online Banking Settlements (Bank of America and Fleet)

If you have ever wondered why a Bank ATM has Braille labels on LCD displays, you are not alone. Although the ADA Accessibility Guidelines requires this "accessibility feature," few members of the blind and low-vision community can benefit from this feature, since it does not tell them what content the window displays.

In March 2000, a settlement was reached between the **California Council of the Blind** and **Bank of America** (see *http://www.icdri.org/bank_of_america_atm_settlement_a.htm*). Bank of America not only agreed to install more than 2500 talking ATMS in Florida and California, but few people realize that they also agreed to design their web sites to be in conformance with Priority Levels One and Two of the W3C WCAG 1.0.

This was the beginning of a series of talking ATM settlements that have continued today. A 28 February 2001 press release announced an agreement by **Fleet National Bank** to install talking ATMs and ensure accessible online banking services. According to their agreement, Fleet was to use its best efforts to design its web pages to comply with Priority 1 of the W3C Web Content Accessibility Guidelines 1.0 by 1 June 2001, and to eventually comply with Priority 2 of the Guidelines by 31, December 2001. For more, see *http://www.dlc-ma.org*.

Also, remember that accessibility effort in Australia? Currently, under the leadership of the **Australian Bankers' Association**, a draft Industry Standard for improving accessibility of electronic banking services has been developed. For more on this, see *http://www.bankers.asn.au?ABA/html/webdraft42.htm*.

Online Voting (March 2000)

In March 2000 the Arizona Democrat Presidential Primary was conducted online for the first time. Members of the blind community went to the polls expecting to vote for the first time independently and in private, but found that the web site ballot was not accessible to screen readers.

A now-defunct web site posted information about the incident, and so I interviewed a number of the complainants in order to understand the scope of the voting accessibility problem. In fact, I had predicted this very outcome the previous year in a paper commissioned by the US Department of Commerce and the National Science Foundation for the first national conference on the impact of the digital economy. I had noted that Fortune 500 companies were already using the Internet as an option for shareholder participation in annual or special business meetings and appeared to be unaware of the accessibility problems at their web site ballot. I had pointed out that this problem should be a reminder for governments that Internet voting for local, State, or national elections requires accessible web design to prevent the disfranchisement of people with disabilities. (See: *The Growing Digital Divide in Access for People with Disabilities: Overcoming Barriers to Participation* by Cynthia D. Waddell at *http://www.icdri.org/the_digital_divide.htm*.)

Election.com had provided the Internet voting web site for the Arizona Democrat Presidential Primary and in response to the complaints, top level *election.com* officials issued a press release in April 2000 stating that they would "take definite steps toward greater accessibility for blind voters." See *http://www.election.com/us/pressroom/pr2000/0419.htm*.

The following year, a US government federal agency, the US General Accounting Office, issued a report in October 2001 entitled *Voters with Disabilities: Access to Polling Places and Alternative Voting Methods*, GAO-02-107. This report pointed out that one advantage for Internet voting was that voters who are blind could vote independently when the Web ballot is designed according to Section 508 standards. See *http://www.gao.gov*.

Online IRS Tax Filing Services Settlement (April 2000)

April 2000 also brought an announcement by the Connecticut Attorney General's Office and the National Federation of the Blind that four online tax filing companies had agreed to make their Internet sites accessible to the blind. Four companies, HDVest, Intuit, H & R Block, and Gilman & Ciocia agreed to implement changes to conform to the W3C Web Content Accessibility Guidelines by the 2000 tax filing season. The popular online tax filing services had been listed on the Internal Revenue Service's official web site as online partners. See *http://www.cslib.org/attygenl/press/2000/health/blind.htm*.

Credit Card Company Monthly Statements (June 2001)

In the USDOJ April-June 2001 report, *Enforcing the ADA-Update*, it was reported that a successful ADA mediation was concluded between a credit card company and a person who was blind from Colorado. The credit card company agreed to change their practice when a customer who was blind complained that the large print credit card statement routinely provided by the company was too small to read. The credit card company agreed to maintain an accessible web site and worked with the complainant so he can now access the web site to enlarge and print his monthly statements in a format usable by him. The credit card company also paid the complainants' attorney's fees. See *http://www.usdoj.gov/crt/ada/aprjun01.htm*.

Suffice it to say that the Internet has made transactions so transparent that it is now very obvious to the community of people with disabilities when they cannot access the content of a web site due to inaccessible design. In my opinion, the emergence of Section 508 Electronic and Information Technology Accessibility Standards was a logical step in an evolution of disability rights. It seeks to level the playing field in access to the powerful tools that information and technology have become in our global economy.

Section 255 of the Telecommunications Act of 1996

The Telecommunications Act of 1996 was the first major revision of our nation's communications policy in 62 years. Section 255 requires that manufacturers of telecommunications and customer premises equipment as well as vendors of telecommunications services make their products and services accessible to, and usable by, persons with disabilities, unless it is not "readily achievable" to do so. See the February 1998 Telecommunications Act Accessibility Guidelines at *http://www.access-board.gov/telecomm/html/telfinal.htm.*

This is not a federal procurement law and it has a lower burden for compliance than Section 508, as we shall see, because "readily achievable" means without significant difficulty or expense. It also has one major limitation in that Section 255 does not cover every function or service in the scope of the telephone network.

This was the first product design law to attempt to drive the market to create accessible products. It is not a traditional civil rights law since it is an accessible design law that does not depend on the filing of a complaint for its requirements to be enforced. Although persons with disabilities can file a complaint with the Federal Communications Commission, this law does not provide for damages and lawsuits are not authorized.

On 22 September 2000, the FCC reminded manufacturers and providers of voice mail and interactive products that they were subject to Section 255. (for more on this, see *http://www.fcc.gov/eb/Public_Notices/da002162.html.*) As we watch the boundaries blur between the Internet and telecommunications, web developers should be reminded that interactive voice response (IVR) features on web sites need to meet the accessibility requirements of Section 508. Let's discuss section 508 next.

Electronic and Information Technology Accessibility Standards (Section 508) Overview

Understanding that technology was becoming integral to the quality of life for persons with disabilities, former President Clinton signed the **1998 Amendments to the Rehabilitation Act** into law. By strengthening Section 508 of the Rehabilitation Act, it provided an enforcement mechanism for the procurement of accessible electronic and information technology. I call this significant law the **ADA of Cyberspace**.

A week before Section 508's effective date, 25 June, 2001, President George W. Bush visited the Pentagon's Computer/Electronic Accommodations Program Technology Evaluation Center and spoke about these new rules:

"I'm pleased to announce that when Section 508 . . . becomes effective for all federal agencies next Monday, there will be more opportunities for people of all abilities to access government information. . . . Increasingly, Americans use information technology to interact with their government. They rely on thousands of government web pages to download forms, learn about federal programs, find out where to turn for government assistance, and communicate with elected officials, such as the President. And because of Section 508, government web sites will be more accessible for millions of Americans who have disabilities. Section 508 will also make the federal government a better employer, as roughly 120,000 federal employees with disabilities will have greater access to the tools they need to better perform their jobs. This is one example of the successful public-private partnerships that are removing barriers to full community participation by Americans with disabilities. I thank the leaders of the technology industry who are with us today for your innovation and your ongoing cooperation."

See *http://www.access-board.gov/news/508.htm.*

For the first time in US history, we have a procurement law that prohibits federal agencies (with limited exceptions) from developing, purchasing, using, or maintaining electronic and information technology that is inaccessible to persons with disabilities. Broad in scope, it requires functionality in the design of electronic and information technology including hardware, software, operating systems, web-based intranet and Internet information and applications, phone systems, video and multimedia products, and self-contained products such as fax machines, copiers, hand-helds, and kiosks. It covers both products and services.

On 21 December 2000, the US Access Board published the Electronic and Information Technology Accessibility Standards, which are now part of the Federal government's procurement regulations. Provisions in the standards identify what makes these products accessible to persons with disabilities, including those with vision, hearing, and mobility impairments. The Board includes technical criteria specific to various types of technologies as well as performance-based requirements, which focus on a product's functional capabilities. See *http://www.access-board.gov/sec508/508standards.htm* for more.

As the world's largest consumer of electronic and information technology, the federal government is required to use the power of the purse to push the electronic and information technology industries to design accessible products. All vendors, whether they be US or foreign, must design according to Section 508 if they want to participate in the federal government market.

Section 508 seeks to create a market-place incentive to design for accessibility. In fact, a vendor may protest the award of a contract to another vendor if they believe their product or service is more accessible. In addition, an agency can terminate a vendor's contract for non-compliance or require the vendor to provide a compliant version of the product or service. Lastly, a growing number of State governments are adopting Section 508 policies or legislation, since they also want their products and services to reach the widest possible audience.

With respect to legal liability, compliance with the accessibility standards is required except where it would pose an "undue burden" or where no complying product is commercially available. Undue burden is defined as "significant difficulty or expense". Certain technologies related to national security are exempt. The law allows federal employees and members of the public with disabilities to file a complaint with the appropriate Federal agency concerning access to products procured after the effective date. Alternatively, individuals may file suit against an agency seeking injunctive relief and attorneys' fees alleging non-compliance with the accessibility requirements.

343

In addition, web developers should not need to be reminded that if they knowingly misrepresent compliance with accessibility standards, they may find themselves subject to a False Claims Act (FCA) violation. Under the FCA, the government may impose penalties up to $10,000 for each false "claim" and recover treble damages. (A false claim could constitute each invoice for accessible web design services.) In addition, the FCA permits individuals to file whistleblower actions on behalf of the government. Such actions would enable the individual to receive up to 30 percent of the government's recovery. The operative word here is "knowingly" misrepresenting compliance with Section 508; a definition that includes deliberate ignorance or reckless disregard of the truth. So there is all the more reason to read this book!

State of Federal Accessibility Report To the President

Implementation of Section 508 requires periodic compliance reviews and reports. Under the leadership of the USDOJ, every federal agency will periodically evaluate the accessibility of its electronic and information technology. In addition, the USDOJ will also evaluate agency responses to Section 508 discrimination complaints.

The first report, *Information Technology and People with Disabilities: The State of Federal Accessibility*, was presented to the President and Congress in April 2000. All executive agencies and departments, including the United States Postal Service, were required to conduct self-evaluations to determine the extent to which their electronic and information technology is accessible to persons with disabilities. One theme that emerged, which was discussed earlier in this chapter under the OCR, US Department of Education cases, was that the USDOJ has determined that accessibility issues cannot continue to be addressed exclusively on an "ad hoc" or "as needed" basis. A systematic accessibility plan must be in place for electronic and information technology.

According to the April 2000 US Attorney General report on the state of federal accessibility:

> *"Data provided by the agencies suggest that the majority of agencies continue to handle IT accessibility issues exclusively on an "ad hoc" or "as needed" basis, instead of integrating accessibility into the development and procurement of their mainstream IT products. Many IT officials hold the mistaken belief that persons with disabilities can always be accommodated upon request by using widely available assistive technology devices (for example, screen readers, screen enlargers, volume control apparatuses, pointing devices that serve as alternatives to a computer mouse, voice recognition software, etc.) in conjunction with mainstream technology applications. Indeed, the goal of section 508 is to ensure that the agency will always be able to provide reasonable accommodations. Without adequate planning, however, the possibility of providing an accommodation to persons with a disability may be foreclosed. See, for example, the discussions of accessibility barriers created by certain uses of Adobe Acrobat's Portable Document Format, in section III, n. 19. Use of an "ad hoc" or 'as needed' approach to IT accessibility **will** result in barriers for persons with disabilities. A much better approach is to integrate accessibility reviews into the earliest stages of design, development, and procurement of IT. Once an accessible IT architecture is established, then and only then can persons with disabilities be successfully accommodated on an 'as needed' basis."*

(Excerpt from the April 2000 Report of the US Attorney General *Information Technology and People with Disabilities: The Current State of Federal Accessibility*, Section II, General Findings and Recommendations, p. 7, at *http://www.usdoj.gov/crt/508/report/intro.htm*.)

US Access Board Guide To the Standards

The Electronic and Information Technology Accessibility Standards, 36 CFR Part 1194, contain four Subparts:

- Subpart A – General

- Subpart B – Technical Standards

- Subpart C – Functional Performance Criteria and

- Subpart D – Information, Documentation, and Support.

Web developers should especially become familiar with B and D. Let's discuss these further.

Subpart B – Technical Standards

- 1194.21 Software applications and operating systems

- 1194.22 Web-based intranet and Internet information and applications

Subpart D – Information, Documentation, and Support

- 1194.41 Information, documentation, and support

The US Access Board provides technical assistance for the implementation of Section 508, and web developers should first review and apply this information before inserting their own independent interpretations on the application of each rule. It is expected that additional guidance will be made available as the implementation moves forward.

There are two approaches to compliance with Section 508. First, a web site would be in compliance if it met *§1194.22(a) through (p)*. Second, a web site would also be in compliance with Section 508 if it met the WCAG 1.0, Priority One checkpoints AND *1194.22(l), (m), (n), (o), and (p)* of these standards. See 36 Part 1194, page 80510.

Because WCAG 1.0 was not developed within the US regulatory enforcement framework, it was not possible for the US Access Board to adopt it as a standard for accessibility. However, the US Access Board acknowledged that at the publication of the Section 508 Electronic and Information Technology Accessibility Standards, the **Web Accessibility Initiative** (**WAI**) was developing the next version, WCAG 2.0. The US Access Board stated that they plan to work with the WAI in the future on the verifiability and achievability of WCAG 2.0.

Appendix C of this book provides the specific guidance provided by the US Access Board for the implementation of the Subpart B web-based rules. The accessibility rules for software applications are also included. This is because the Section 508 web-based rule at 1194.22(m) requires plug-ins, applets, or other applications to meet all of the software application accessibility standards at *1194.21(a) through (l)*.

At the time of this writing, the US Access Board has not provided Subpart D rule guidance. However, web developers should be aware that if their web site contains product support documentation or Help Desk services for a federal agency, then they must meet the requirements under Subpart D.

US Access Board Comments for Not Adopting Selected WAI Rules

According to the US Access Board, the first nine rules in *§1194.22, (a) through (i)*, incorporate the exact language recommended by the WAI in their comments to this rulemaking, or they contain language not substantially different from WCAG 1.0, supported by the WAI.

Rules *§1194.22(j) and (k)* were meant to be consistent with WCAG 1.0, but the US Access Board needed to use language consistent with enforceable regulatory language.

Rules *§1194.22(l), (m), (n), (o) and (p)* are different from WCAG 1.0 due to the need to require a higher level of access or prescribe a more specific requirement.

The US Access Board commented on certain WCAG checkpoints and the reason for not adopting them:

- **WCAG 1.0 Checkpoint 4.1 (natural language)**: Not adopted due to the fact that only two assistive technology programs could interpret such coding or markup and that the majority of screen readers utilized in the US do not have the capability of switching to the processing of foreign language phonemes.

- **WCAG 1.0 Checkpoint 14.1(clearest and simplest language):** Not adopted because it is difficult to enforce since a requirement to use the simplest language can be very subjective.

- **WCAG 1.0 Checkpoint 1.3 (auditory description of visual track):** Not adopted in the web rules because a similar provision was adopted in the video and multimedia product rules.

- **WCAG 1.0 Checkpoint 6.2 (dynamic content):** Not adopted because "the meaning of the provision is unclear."

See 36 CFR Part 1194, p. 80510.

When Does a Web Developer Follow Section 508 Rules?

So now we have two sets of technical specifications for accessible web design – the W3C Web Content Accessibility Guidelines 1.0 (WCAG) and the federal Electronic and Information Technology Accessibility Standards. Which should a web developer apply?

The answer depends on who owns the web site. If it is a US federal agency, or if the web site is a vendor web site that is accessed as a part of a Help Desk or vendor product documentation for federal agency services, then Section 508 applies.

If the web site is for a State or local government agency, then it will depend on whether or not that agency has adopted Section 508. It will also depend on whether or not the enforcement agency of another federal law, the Assistive Technology Act of 1998 (Tech Act), requires States to comply. At the time of this writing we are awaiting guidance from the US Department of Education since they have stated in the Section 508 rulemaking that they intend to require States to comply or lose Tech Act funding.

However, it is my opinion that State and local government agencies should implement Section 508 since they are subject to the ADA and Section 504 of the Rehabilitation Act of 1973. This is because the ADA requires accessible web sites for "effective communication" and Section 508 tells us how to design accessible web sites. This does not mean that an entity cannot also implement additional WCAG to maximize accessible design. Many States have already adopted WCAG for ADA-compliance reasons and so now Section 508 will provide the minimal legal requirements for accessibility.

If the web site is an educational institution, then it is highly likely that Section 508 applies indirectly through the Tech Act as discussed above. This is why a number of educational institutions have already adopted Section 508. For example, the California Community Colleges have taken steps to ensure that information technology or services procured, leased, or developed with State or federal funding meet the Section 508 requirements. This includes long-distance learning as well as campus web sites. See their 11 June 2001 Legal Opinion at *http://www.resna.org/taproject/policy/education/cccc508letter.doc*.

And what about everyone else? If they are subject to the ADA or receive federal funding, then it is the author's opinion that a "best practice" would be to follow Section 508 in addition to WCAG. Section 508 informs entities covered under the ADA and Section 504 of the Rehabilitation Act on what it means to design accessible web sites to meet the "effective communication" mandate. Section 508 enables commercial businesses to meet certain ADA responsibilities for their employees with disabilities by designing accessible Internet and intranet web sites. Section 508 also enables their web site services to reach the widest possible audience of consumers.

Legal Hot Topics for Web Developers and Policymakers

In this section we review some of the most common web site features that cause problems for Web users in their access to web content and services. After all, accessible Web design enables your web site to reach the widest possible audience, including older adults, people with disabilities, and people using alternative Internet access devices. Web developers need to be especially careful when designing these features and policymakers need to be knowledgeable of the features and functionality required for enabling access to content and services.

Electronic Forms

One positive impact of e-Government has been the streamlining of governmental transactions through the use of electronic forms. Because of the prevalence of forms utilized by governmental agencies, it should not be a surprise that electronic forms are specifically addressed in Section 508. Frequently, an electronic form is posted on the Web to be printed and completed off line. Even if online submittal is not an option, enabling the form to be completed online would be of great benefit to many people. Web developers should note that regardless as to whether or not the form is to be submitted online, it is important that the form be designed so that a person using assistive technology can fill it out and understand the directions for completing and submitting it. For this reason, Section 508 covers electronic forms under both the software and web technical standards at *§1194.21(l) and §1194.21(n)*.

As we shall see in our discussion of portable document formats (PDF), there are accessibility issues with PDF. Until PDF issues are fully resolved, it is highly recommended by both this author and the USDOJ that if a web developer posts a PDF electronic form, then they should also post an accessible electronic form complying with Section 508 rules.

Applets, Plug-ins and Applications

One of the most frustrating experiences for persons with disabilities has been the requirement at various web sites to utilize inaccessible applets, plug-ins, or other applications to access the content of the web page. Plug-ins can interfere with the functionality of assistive technology and can even cause the application to crash. Plug-ins may also have features and functionality that are inaccessible by design. Section 508 addresses the problem by requiring that web developers utilizing these applications meet the software standards at §1194.21. It is very important to note the guidance at §1194.22(m) from the US Access Board: "This provision places a responsibility on the web page author to know that a compliant application exists, before requiring a plug-in."

This means that web developers must not use plug-ins that do not meet the Section 508 software accessibility requirements. Likewise, applets and applications are subject to the Section 508 software technical requirements for accessibility, so be sure to become familiar with the US Access Board material in Appendix C.

PDF and Posted Documents

Since this is a chapter about legal requirements, this is not the place to discuss the various methods for creating PDF documents and how to minimize accessibility problems in their creation. Remember, it was the posting of City Council documents in PDF that brought an ADA complaint to the City of San Jose. Today, although Adobe has taken great strides to ensure that a PDF document has structure for assistive technology to access, there are still difficulties, especially in the conversion of complex documents to accessible HTML. Recognizing that there are benefits to having a print version of a document in PDF, the US Department of Justice recommends that if a document is posted in PDF, that an accessible version be posted as well:

> "Agencies should also test the accessibility of their pdf documents using screen readers before posting them to their web sites. Adobe's accessibility site includes includes [sic] the latest recommendations for making pdf files accessible (http://access.adobe.com). Finally, agencies should be careful that non-text content be accompanied by text descriptions in pdf files. Agencies that choose to publish web-based documents in pdf should simultaneously publish the same documents in another more accessible format, such as HTML."

See *http://www.usdoj.gov/crt/508/web.htm* for more.

Therefore, a good practice is to not solely rely on the user to utilize plug-ins and PDF conversion tools to convert a PDF document to an accessible format. Setting aside the issue of accessibility for people with disabilities, imagine the frustration experienced by people using alternative Internet access devices such as cell phones and personal digital assistants who encounter documents that they cannot access. The US Department of Justice recommendation for web developers to do the conversion to ensure accessibility should be followed until we solve this problem. Moreover, it is essential that organizations review their processes for document creation and formatting as part of their overall strategy for addressing accessibility.

Multimedia, Audio Broadcasts, and Captioning

Prior to Section 508, one web design technique to meet the ADA requirement for access to the President's State of the Union video clip was to post the text version of the speech. As a result, people who were deaf or hard of hearing could watch the video, not understanding what was said and when, and then read the static transcript.

Today Section 508 requires that text equivalents be provided for sound and that it be synchronized with multimedia presentations. See *§1194.22(a) and (b)*. Excellent free software tools such as Media Access Generator (MAGpie) are available to the web developer to make multimedia accessible to persons with disabilities. See *http://ncam.wgbh.org/webaccess/magpie/index.html* for more.

But another challenge for web developers is the requirement that audio broadcasts be captioned so that the deaf and hard of hearing community can have equal and timely access to the content. According to The US Access Board guidance found in Appendix C *for rule §1194.22(a)*, it might appear that the guidance is correct when it says, "If the presentation is audio only, a text transcript would meet this requirement." This is in error.

In response to my request to the US Access Board for clarification concerning this rule and live audio broadcasts that do not contain video, I received the following communication:

"If an audio file is on a web site, it is considered a nontext element and therefore needs a text alternative such as a transcript. If the audio instead of being a file, is an audio feed of a live event, even if it is only audio, the audio should be captioned as that is the only way to provide an equivalent alternative. A text transcript posted after the live session would mean that while the session was taking place, there would be no text equivalent and the web site would be in violation of 1194.22(a)." Email dated 22 January 2002 from Doug Wakefield, US Access Board.

Remember, audio is a non-text element that is required to be just as accessible as images. Many governmental agencies have been broadcasting public meetings on the Internet without realizing that they had failed to provide access to people who were deaf or hard of hearing. Government employees or members of the public who are required to listen to audio broadcasts for their work or for appearance before legislative hearings, may need real-time captioning. The web developer should be aware that real-time captioning services might need to be contracted to meet accessibility requirements. In some cases, governmental agencies may also need to arrange for the display of captioning on a screen in the public hearing room so that people present at the meeting as well as those on the Internet can have access to the content of the audio. At this time, real time captioning services are required for this functionality since the voice input to text output technology solution is not at a level where it can be applied to meet this type of need.

This should be a reminder that accessible web design is a cross-disability issue. Accessible web solutions based solely on one sensory mode (such as speech output for hearing) may be helpful for the blind and low vision community who may use a screen reader to hear the web page. But this solution will not meet the needs of those who are deaf and hard of hearing. So remember that technologies such as interactive voice response may not be the complete solution to accessible web design; especially if any of the interactive voice response content and service is not available on the web site.

And since we are on the topic, interactive multimedia has its own challenges for accessibility. For example, Macromedia has made a commitment to make Flash more accessible as well as to make Flash Player accessible to assistive technology.

Links To Inaccessible Content Off-Site

Now that there are legal requirements for accessible web design in the US, it is my opinion that the web developer should consider ways to indicate to the user when the content is not their own. This prevents being drawn into an ADA or Section 508 complaint process by the complainant. One method is to signal to the user at the link that they are leaving the web site. However, if the web site significantly relies on the content of an inaccessible web site, the web developer should consider seeking legal counsel.

Summary and Challenges Ahead

In summary, the ADA and Section 508 principles tell us that entities must adopt accessible web design policies and procedures for consistent implementation:

- A comprehensive policy must be implemented so that staff do not continue to respond to access issues on an ad hoc basis

- Web developers and managers must receive training, design tools, and resources

- There must also be a process within all organizations to handle and monitor web site access concerns and complaints

- The community of people with disabilities must be consulted as we address challenges ahead

One impact of Section 508 is that it seeks to prevent proprietary extensions of accessibility in technology. Although technology changes, civil rights do not. We have now defined the commons where everyone can work and play through effective communication. But as technology evolves, it will be important to continually assess the state of accessibility for our electronic and information technology. Without accessibility, we cannot have effective governance.

Section 508 places the US on the threshold of building accessibility into our Internet and intranet environments. Amidst all the technical and legal maze of requirements, standards, and guidelines, it is important to keep one fact clear: accessible web design offers opportunities to provide services to the widest possible audience, to the greatest extent possible, in ways that have been inconceivable until now.

The economic, political, and ethical benefits far outweigh the cost of this effort. The cost of being inaccessible – missing the boat on the coming age of thin clients, failing to serve our most needful citizens and employees, and legal liability – can be incalculable.

This millennium offers unprecedented opportunities for efficient, effective governance. The Internet should be accessible to all. It is the right thing to do.

Appendix A

Quick Reference Guide

This appendix is a quick reference to help you make your site usable and, more specifically, accessible. If you follow all the guidelines listed below, your site should be a long way towards compliance with the section 508 and WCAG guidelines.

General Site Design

- Know the purpose of your web site – make sure you know who the majority of your target audience is, and what they will want the site to do for them.

- Have a plan for building your web site – following on from the last point, when you know what your site is for, you should know what you need to do to make the site serve its purpose successfully, including what resources you will need, and how much time it will take.

- Design for all browsers, not just one or two – at least try to make it function in most browsers, if not perfectly.

- Use more than one way to represent important information, whenever possible.

- Avoid designing your pages for only the latest browsers.

Page Layout Design

- Make sure each page has a meaningful `<title>` element to describe the page

- Organize long documents so they can be easily navigated with or without assistive technology

- Make sure your documents are clear and simple

- Use default font types rather than specific fonts

- Use relative font sizes and try to avoid specifying exact font sizes

- Don't rely on color alone to convey the meaning of your message

- Don't use font colors that do not contrast well with the page background

- Use real text rather than images of text

- Use default heading and font sizes

- Use heading tags

Navigation

- Have a consistent navigation scheme with everything in the same place on each page.

- Use "skip navigation" techniques to help users with assistive technology skip over groups of navigation links. Please refer to Chapter 5 for more details about this.

- Make sure links are meaningful. Use hyperlinked text that is meaningful when read by a user or assistive technology—avoid non-descriptive text such as "click here".

- Use meaningful `title` attributes on frames, as well as giving each frame a meaningful name. This was covered in some detail in Chapter 5.

- Provide an accessible site map.

- Make your home page a directory to your site.

- Build your site so it can be navigated using a keyboard or other device besides a mouse.

Images

- Use `alt` attributes on images. Make sure the `alt` text gives an accurate description of the image, or its function on the page. On spacer images include blank `alt` text (`alt=""`).

- Use **D-links** or other ways to provide longer descriptions of images, when needed.

- Use client-side image maps where possible, and use appropriate `alt` text on all `<area>` tags of the `<map>` as detailed in Chapter 4.

- When using server-side image maps, also provide the user with equivalent text links.

- Avoid using images of text instead of actual text.

Tables

Lay out **tables** so that a screen reader will be able to read the cells in the proper order.

- Formatting tables should be designed so that, when linearized, the main content is read before the navigation bars, otherwise provide a skip navigation link that takes screen reader users straight to the main content.

- For simple data tables (defined in Chapter 4) identify row and column headers by placing them in column one and row one. In all cases use `<th>` or `scope` to identify which cells are row and or column headers.

- For complex data tables (defined in Chapter 4) use the `headers` attribute to explicitly associate header information with data cells.

- Use the Lynx browser or Lynx Viewer (*http://www.delorie.com/web/lynxview.html*) to test how your page linearizes.

Forms

Design **forms** so that they are accessible.

- For **edit fields and select menus** place prompt to the left or above the control.

- For **checkboxes and radio buttons,** place the prompt to the right of the control.

- For **buttons,** the prompt is part of the control, the `value` attribute.

- If this cannot be done then use the `<label>` tag to associate prompt text with the appropriate form element or the `title` attribute of the `<input>` element to clarify the purpose of each `<input>`. Please see Chapter 6 for more details.

Scripting Technologies and Applets

- Use the `<noscript>` option with scripting for those who do not have browsers that support scripting or who have it turned off.

- Provide alternative content where applets may not be accessible.

- Avoid using flashing animated objects on the page.

- Avoid making content available only through client-side scripting languages without providing accessible alternatives.

Testing

- Test your site with assistive technology, with as many different browsers as you can, and without images.

- Use the Lynx browser or Lynx Viewer (*http://www.delorie.com/web/lynxview.html*) to test how your page linearizes.

- Test your site with stylesheets and client-side scripting turned off.

Multimedia

- Caption and describe streaming video and audio where appropriate. The MAGPie tool can help with this task: *http://ncam.wgbh.org/webaccess/magpie*. See also Chapter 12.

- Offer a text equivalent to all non-text elements on the page.

Appendix B

Glossary of Terms

Many terms used by those who work with accessibility techniques to build web sites accessible to people with disabilties have other meanings, which may be confusing. This glossary should help eliminate this confusion, and act as a quick reference to anyone needing a quick definition for a technology, or a standards body, for example.

As much as possible, the context of these terms has been kept within the scope of accessible web-based technology. It is also available online, at *http://www.glasshaus.com*, so it can be kept current with changing technology.

We invite comments on this glossary – please send any feedback to *icdri@icdri.org*.

A

- Accessibility– the quality of a web site (or any entity) that makes it usable by the largest audience possible, regardless of disability.

- Americans with Disabilties Act (ADA) – a United States law passed in 1990 that prohibits discrimination against people with disabilties .

- Adaptive Technology – technology used to adapt an already existing computer device or piece of software. A good example would be a Head Pointer that allows a person with limited mobility to use the computer.

- Alternative Interface Access Protocol (AIAP) – a technology under development by the V2 committee of the National Committee on Information Technology; it will allow a user to get web pages in the form they choose for the device they choose.

- alt text – an alt attribute allows descriptive text to be attached to certain objects on a web page written in HTML (usually these objects are images), not only providing visual clues as to the purpose of said objects, but also providing a description that can be read out by a screen reader so that a person with visual impairment can know the nature of such objects too.

- Applet – a Java program or application designed to be embedded in, and invoked from, a web page, or other application. It cannot be run by itself.

- Assistive Technology – equipment or software that assists people with disabilities in performing every-day activities. Examples include screen readers and voice input software.

B

- Biometrics – the practice of automatically identifying people by one or more bodily characteristics.

- Bobby – a web site accessibility assessment tool developed by CAST, and located at *http://www.cast.org/bobby*.

- Browser – the software on a computer that allows web sites to be rendered so they can be displayed to users. There are two types of visual browsers (some, like Internet Explorer 6, render all content including the latest technologies while others, like Lynx, are text-only) but many other types exist, some of which produce voice output.

C

- Cascading Stylesheets (CSS) – a means of applying styling/formatting to markup (for example, XML or HTML). This has many advantages over using HTML formatting tags such as <b> and <font>. For a start, CSS formatting is more powerful, and allows more flexibility. Secondly, CSS styles are identified by a unique ID, which is used in the HTML to apply a style to content. If you want to change a style, you need only change its definition in the style sheet, rather than changing every instance of it in the HTML. Lastly, it has great uses for accessibility – for example, you can use an alternative stylesheet to make the text on a web site bigger, for the benefit of people with visual impairment.

- Center for Applied Special Technology (CAST) – This organization developed the web site accessibility checker Bobby. For more information, see *http://www.cast.org*.

- Composite Capabilities/Preference Profiles (CC/PP) – CC/PP profiles are a method that allows a description of device capabilities and user preferences to be delivered to the server, so that content can be adapted to the device according to the preferences of the user.

D

- Design forAll – see *Universal Design*

- Disability Discrimination Act (DDA) – a name shared by two laws passed in Australia (1992) and the United Kingdom (1995). They both prohibit discrimination against people with disabilities.

- Digital Divide – the gap that exists between those who have access to Electronic and Information Technology, and those who do not.

- Disability – a physical or mental impairment that renders tasks performed by an individual more difficult or impossible to achieve.

- D-LINK – a link that takes the form of a capital D near an image. It provides a longer description of the image or its purpose than is feasible using `alt` text.

- Document Type Definition (DTD) – a file that defines how applications interpreting a document should present the content. It is used in HTML, XML, and other markup languages.

- Dyslexia – a language-based learning disability that is often characterized by difficulties with understanding written language, and being more attuned to a graphical or object-based learning style.

E

- Electronic and Information Technology (EIT) – this term encompasses any of a number of devices and device types. It is basically any device or technology that uses electronic means to transmit and present information to the user. Examples include computers, PDAs, cell phones, information kiosks, televisions, and many other devices.

F

- Frames – a feature of HTML that allows a web author to divide a page into two or more separate windows. If the frame does not have a `<title>` element, or the `<title>` element is not meaningful, this can cause accessiblity issues. In addition, some browsers do not support frames.

H

- Head Pointer – a device attached to the user's head, that allows them to move the pointer on the screen, (usually moved by the mouse, a pointing device, the arrow keys, or with the movement of their head). It is useful for people who have limited mobility.

- HyperText Markup Language (HTML) – the markup language that is used on most of the World Wide Web to create web pages. The standards for HTML are controlled by the *W3C*.

I

- Image Maps – areas of an image on a web page that have links to other areas of the Web. Some types of images map can have `alt` tags on the areas, while others must have text links.

- Information and Communications Technology (ICT) – a generic name for all of the technologies involved in communicating with computers.

J

- Java – Java is an object-oriented programming language developed by Sun Microsystems. It was specifically designed for the distributed environment of the Web and can be used to create applications that can run on a single computer, or distributed among several computers in a network. It can also be used to write applets.

- JavaScript – a scripting language commonly used on web pages. It has many uses, including validating fields in a form, or writing information to the user's screen.

L

- Lynx – a text-only browser that is popular amongst Unix users, and commonly used by people with disabilities and those in low bandwidth areas. It can be downloaded from *http://lynx.isc.org/release/*.

M

- Multimedia – using a computer to present multiple types of media simultaneously, in an integrated manner. These can include sound, graphics, video, text, animation, or any other form of information representation.

O

- On Screen Keyboard – a keyboard that appears on screen so a user who cannot use their hands can use Assistive Technology (such as a *Head Pointer*) to enter keyboard input.

P

- Portable Document Format (PDF) – this was developed by Adobe Systems Inc, as a way to publish documents electronically, with good formatting for printing, and document security (documents are generally read-only). Originally it was in an image format, and this presented major accessiblity issues. Recently however, Adobe has made large strides in making the PDF format accessible to people with disabilities.

- Plugin – a module (either hardware or software) that adds a special feature to a larger system or program. For example, a program to play movies on a browser, or the plug-in that allows browsers to display Flash content.

S

- Screen Magnifier – a device (or software) that will make images and text on a screen larger for the benefit of visually impaired users.

- Screen Reader – a computer program that reads the screen to a user. It can be used to surf the Web, write a spreadsheet or document, or just to read pages. It is closely related to *Voice Output*.

- Section 508 – this is a common name for Section 508 of the Rehabilitation Act. This is an amendment to a US law that basically says all Electronic and Information Technology purchased or developed by the US Government must be accessible to people with disabilities. See *Chapter 13* of this book for more on this.

- Synchronized Multimedia Integration Language (SMIL) – a markup language under development by the W3C that will allow web developers to separate the content of multimedia into distinct files and transmission streams such as text, images, audio, and video. They can then be sent to the user's computer separately, reassembled and displayed as intended.

- Spacer Images – also called spacer GIFS. These are small transparent images placed on a page, usually in a table used layout. They help to position text and images on the page for a good visual effect.

- Style Guide – a Style Guide is a document that sets out the rules for your web site. All your developers must follow it and the Webmaster should enforce it. Accessibility rules and standards can be included in this Style Guide – this is a good idea, as when a style guide is implemented, accessibility becomes part of the basic parameters for your web site and becomes much less of an issue.

- Stylesheets – see *Cascading Stylesheets* and *Extensible Stylesheet Language (XSL)*.

- Scaleable Vector Graphics (SVG) – a languagefor vector graphics coded in XML. XML documents can have these graphics placed directly into the document, with many advantages – SVG produces graphics that are smaller, transmit more quickly, are scaleble without loss of resolution, can have searchable text labels, and allow links to part of an image. It is being developed by the W3C.

T

- Text Equivalent – this term is used to describe the technique of providing a text alternative that will be the same in both content and function as a non-text object on a web page, such as an image map.

- Text Only Browser – a browser that does not show images. It does not have images turned off; rather it just doesn't display them. A good example of this type of browser is Lynx.

U

- Universal Access – the idea that all things (on the Internet) should be accessible by the largest audience possible, regardless of disability, location, device, or speed of connection to the Internet.

- Universal Design – Designing for the largest audience possible regardless of disability or ability to speak the native language. This is a process rather than an end in itself.

- Usability – the idea that a web site or web page is easily used by a web user.

- User Centered Design (UCD) – the design process that places the user at the center of the design rather than the object to be designed. It is a philosophy and process rather than an end in itself.

- User Interface Markup Language (UIML) – unlike many markup languages UMIL is not used to describe documents, rather it is used to describe elements on the page such as buttons, menu lists, and other page elements generally used in graphical user interfaces. It is used to define their placement on the page, and the actions to be taken when certain events such as mouse clicks or keystrokes occur.

V

- Voice Input – software that recognizes voice commands, and responds accordingly.

- Voice Output – computer programs that read the screen to a user.

- Voice Recognition – programs that recognize a person's voice and its various characteristics. Closely related to Voice Input.

- VoiceXML – a type of XML that allows the user to interact with a web page using Voice Recognition software.

- Voice Recognition Software – software that can be trained to recognize a person's voice, and either execute commands, or turn the voice into text or other forms of media such as sign language for the deaf.

W

- World Wide Web Consortium (W3C) – an international consortium of companies and organizations involved with the Internet and the World Wide Web, responsible for maintaining web technology standards, such as HTML and CSS. See *http://www.w3.org/* for more.

- Web Accessibility Initiative (WAI) – started by W3C and its members, it addresses web accessibility issues. It can be found at: *http://www.w3.org/WAI.*

- Wireless Application Protocol (WAP) – A specification that allows users to access information via wireless handheld devices. These devices usually have small screens.

- Web Content Accessibility Guidelines (WCAG) – these are the guidelines built by the W3C/WAI to address issues in building accessible web pages.

- WAVE – the WAVE was developed by Temple University Institute on Disabilities. It has a number of excellent features that are not included with other assessment tools. It shows which images have the `alt` attribute missing and it also shows the order in which a screen reader will read a page. It can be found at *http://www.temple.edu/inst_disabilities/piat/wave/.*

X

- Extensible Markup Language (XML) – a language specification from the W3C that allows users to develop their own markup languages (often called vocabularies), and format their documents using stylesheets to be presented on a browser if desired. XML has a very strict set of rules that must be adhered to, allowing lots of control over document format. XML is most useful, however, as a completely language/platform-agnostic data format, but that is beyond the scope of this book.

- Extensible Hypertext Markup Language (XHTML) – this is a reformulation of HTML as an XML vocabulary – this is a good idea, as it eliminates a lot of the problems that arose from the existence of proprietary or badly coded HTML, because it must now follow the strict rules of XML.

- Extensible Stylesheet Language (XSL) – XSL is a W3C specification that contains 3 parts – Extensible Stylesheet Language Transformations (XSLT) for changing the formatting and structure of markup according to a set of rules, Extensible Stylesheet Language Formatting Objects (XSL-FO) for applying a strong set of rules to a document to ensure reliable formatting when printed, and XPath to select the elements required by XSLT.

Appendix C

Section 508 Guidelines

Guide To the Section 508 Standards for Electronic and Information Technology

Subpart B – Technical Standards
Excerpt from *http://www.access-board.gov/sec508/guide/index.htm*

Software Applications and Operating Systems (36 CFR 1194.21)

Updated: June 21, 2001

These provisions are applicable to both software applications and operating systems. They address program features that must be contained in software for the product to meet the standards. Because there are many programming languages from which a software producer may select, it is impossible to give specific coding techniques. In some cases it is possible that a particular programming language may not possess the features necessary to fulfill these requirements. In those instances, another language for creating the program would most likely have to be considered for the product to meet the standards.

All electronic and information technology contains software of some type. Do these provisions apply to all software with no exceptions?

To meet the standards, a product can either build all accessibility features in, or be compatible with assistive technology. Many of the provisions in this section are required to make software compatible with assistive technology. For example, how text is to be written to the display is required so assistive technology can read the text output of a program. Therefore, if the software is running on a product such as a desktop computer, where it is possible to add assistive technology, the software must comply with this section.

Are these provisions the only feasible approach for making software work with assistive technology?

No. By studying these provisions, a software producer can gain an understanding of what is to be achieved. However, as stated in 1194.5, equivalent facilitation, the provisions are not intended in any way to discourage producers from developing their own approach to achieving the end result. Alternative approaches through equivalent facilitation are allowed, as long as the alternative provides equivalent or greater access than the approach specified in these provisions.

(a) Executing Function from Keyboard	(b) Accessibility Features
(c) Input Focus	(d) User Interface Element
(e) Bitmap Images	(f) Textual Information
(g) User Selected Attributes	(h) Animation
(i) Color Coding	(j) Color and Contrast Settings
(k) Flashing or Blinking Text	(l) Electronic Forms

1194.21(a). When software is designed to run on a system that has a keyboard, product functions shall be executable from a keyboard where the function itself or the result of performing a function can be discerned textually.

Note: Illustration is a variation of the actual image published by the US Access Board and is provided for clarity purposes. To view the published illustration, visit http://www.access-board.gov/sec508/guide/1194.21.htm#(a).

Why is keyboard access to software required?

When keyboard access to programs' controls and features is provided, a person who cannot use a mouse or other pointing device will still be able to run the product. For example, a person with a disability that affects dexterity may find it impossible to move or hold a pointing device with enough accuracy to activate desired features. A person who cannot see the screen, therefore relying on assistive technology, may have no problems moving the pointer but will be unable to determine what is being pointed to.

Does this provision prohibit the use of "mouse-only" functions in any software?

All actions that can be identified or labeled with text are required to be executable from a keyboard. For example, most of the menu functions even in common drawing programs that allow a user to open, save, size, rotate, and perform other actions on a graphic image, can all be performed from the keyboard. However, providing keyboard alternatives for creating an image by selecting a "drawing tool", picking a color, and actually drawing a design would be extremely difficult. Such procedures require the precise level of control afforded by a pointing device (for example, a mouse) and cannot be given text labels because there is no way to predict what action the user plans to perform. Therefore, when a programmer is determining which functions need keyboard access, the best rule of thumb is to add keyboard shortcuts to any feature where the function can be identified with a text label.

Many applications utilize toolbars with buttons. Do these buttons all need keyboard access?

Not necessarily. Most toolbars give a visual shortcut to functions that also exist in the menu structure of a program. If the feature activated by a control on a toolbar is a duplicate of a menu function that already has a keyboard shortcut, then the toolbar control does not need its own keyboard access. However, if the control on the toolbar is unique and cannot be accessed in any other way, the control will be required to have a keyboard shortcut. Although not in the toolbar, a scroll feature that is not available in a menu bar must have keyboard alternatives. Typically, the use of the *page up*, and *page down* keys will provide keyboard access to scroll bars.

1194.21(b). Applications shall not disrupt or disable activated features of other products that are identified as accessibility features, where those features are developed and documented according to industry standards. Applications also shall not disrupt or disable activated features of any operating system that are identified as accessibility features, where the application programming interface for those accessibility features has been documented by the manufacturer of the operating system and is available to the product developer.

What is the application programming interface?

The **Application Programming Interface** (**API**) refers to a standard way for programs to communicate with each other, including the operating system, and with input and output devices. For instance, the application programming interface affects how programs display information on a monitor or receive keyboard input via the operating system.

What are accessibility features?

Many commercially available software applications and operating systems have features built into the program that are labeled as accessibility features. These features can typically be turned on or off by a user. Examples of these features include: reversing the color scheme (to assist people with low vision), showing a visual prompt when an error tone is sounded (to assist persons who are deaf or hard of hearing), or providing "sticky keys" that allow a user to press key combinations (such as *control-C*) sequentially rather than simultaneously (to assist persons with dexterity disabilities). This requirement prohibits software programs from disabling these features when they have been activated prior to running the application.

1194.21(c). A well-defined on-screen indication of the current focus shall be provided that moves among interactive interface elements as the input focus changes. The focus shall be programmatically exposed so that assistive technology can track focus and focus changes.

What is the importance of the focus for assistive technology?

The position on a screen where an action will take place is referred to as the "focus". For example, when a menu item in a program is highlighted – meaning that if the user clicks the mouse or presses the *enter* key – the feature will activate and that item has the focus. Providing a visual indication of the focus allows someone who is viewing the screen to accurately access the programs' features. When a computer is operated by a person who is also running a screen enlargement program or a speech or Braille output system, the assistive technology must discern the focus point. This provision requires that the position of the programs' focus be made available through its code to assistive technology. When, for example, a screen enlargement program magnifies a section of the screen, it must be able to follow the focus as the focus changes. If the magnified area does not move with the focus, the user may easily move down through a list of choices with the arrow keys but the magnified area remains stationary and very shortly the user has no idea what items will be activated if an action is taken.

1194.21(d) Sufficient information about a user interface element including the identity, operation, and state of the element shall be available to assistive technology. When an image represents a program element, the information conveyed by the image must also be available in text.

What is considered a "user interface element"?

Examples of user interface elements include button checkboxes, menus, toolbars, scroll bars, and any other feature of a program that is intended to allow the user to perform some action.

What does this provision require to be done with these elements?

This provision requires that text must be associated with each element. The text must identify the element and its current state or condition. For example, a button that shows a hand for getting more help must have the word "help" associated with the button. If a checkbox is present, a text label must indicate what is being checked, and whether the checkbox is checked or unchecked. There are many ways to accomplish this depending on the program language being used.

1194.21(e) When bitmap images are used to identify controls, status indicators, or other programmatic elements, the meaning assigned to those images shall be consistent throughout an application's performance.

What forms of bitmap images are affected by this provision?

This provision applies to those images which are used to indicate an action. An image used strictly for decoration is not covered by this provision.

Why is the provision important for accessibility?

Most screen reading programs allow users to assign text names to bitmap images. If the bitmap image changes meaning during a program's execution, the assigned identifier is no longer valid and is confusing to the user.

1194.21(f) Textual information shall be provided through operating system functions for displaying text. The minimum information that shall be made available is text content, text input caret location, and text attributes.

Can an application programmer develop unique display techniques for writing text on the screen or using graphics?

The operating system is the "core" computer software that controls basic functions, such as receiving information from the keyboard, displaying information on the computer screen, and storing data on the hard disk. Other software programs use the standard protocols dictated by the operating system for displaying their own information or processing the output of other computer programs. When programs are written using unique schemes for writing text on the screen or using graphics, other programs such as software for assistive technology may not be able to interpret the information. This provision does not prohibit or limit an application programmer from developing unique display techniques. It requires that when a unique method is used, the text should also be written to the screen through the operating system.

1194.21(g). Applications shall not override user-selected contrast and color selections and other individual display attributes.

How does this requirement improve accessibility for people with disabilities?

Often, persons with disabilities can increase their efficiency with a system by selecting colors, contrast, keyboard repeat rate, and keyboard sensitivity settings provided by an operating system. When an application disables these system-wide settings, accessibility is reduced. This provision is aimed at allowing users to select personalized settings, which cannot be disabled by software programs.

Does this provision mean that programs may not use any custom settings?

This provision allows programs to have unlimited options for customizing the display of the programs' content. However, there must be a section in the software that tells the program not to use its own setting, but to use whatever settings are already in place before the program starts. A simple menu selection, for example under a view or options menu, might be a checkbox that lets the user check "*use system display setting.*"

1194.21(h). When animation is displayed, the information shall be displayable in at least one non-animated presentation mode at the option of the user.

How can screen animation affect accessibility for people with disabilities?

The use of animation on a screen can pose serious access problems for users of screen readers or other assistive technology applications. When important elements such as push-buttons or relevant text are animated, the user of assistive technology cannot access the application reliably. This provision requires that in addition to the animation, an application shall provide an option to turn off animation.

1194.21(i). Color coding shall not be used as the only means of conveying information, indicating an action, prompting a response, or distinguishing a visual element.

Note: Illustration is a variation of the actual image published by the US Access Board and is provided for clarity purposes. To view the published illustration, visit *http://www.access-board.gov/sec508/guide/1194.21.htm#(i)*.

How can color coding create accessibility difficulties?
A software program that requires a user to distinguish between otherwise identical red and blue squares for different functions (for example, printing a document versus saving a file) would pose problems for anyone who was color-blind and would generally be very difficult to run with assistive technology. Screen reading software can announce color changes. However, this is an "on/off" feature. This means that if a user had to identify a specific color, they would have to have all colors announce which would greatly reduce the usability of the software for that person.

Does the provision prohibit the use of colors?
No. This provision does not prohibit the use of color to enhance identification of important features. It does, however, require that some other method of identification, such as text labels, be combined with the use of color.

1194.21(j). When a product permits a user to adjust color and contrast settings, a variety of color selections capable of producing a range of contrast levels shall be provided.

Do all products have to provide color selections?
No. This provision is applied to those products that already allow a user to adjust screen colors.

What is the desired outcome of this requirement?
This provision requires more than just providing color choices. The available choices must also allow for different levels of contrast. Many people experience a high degree of sensitivity to bright displays. People with this condition cannot focus on a bright screen for long because they will soon be unable to distinguish individual letters. An overly bright background causes a visual "white-out". To alleviate this problem, the user must be able to select a softer background and appropriate foreground colors. On the other hand, many people with low vision can work most efficiently when the screen is set with very sharp contrast settings. Because there is such a variance in individual needs, it is necessary for a program to have a variety of color and contrast settings.

1194.21(k). Software shall not use flashing or blinking text, objects, or other elements having a flash or blink frequency greater than 2 Hz and lower than 55 Hz.

Why are flashing or blinking displays limited by this provision?
This requirement is necessary because some individuals with photosensitive epilepsy can have a seizure triggered by displays that flicker or flash, particularly if the flash has a high intensity and is within certain frequency ranges. The 2 Hz limit was chosen to be consistent with proposed revisions to the ADA Accessibility Guidelines which, in turn, are being harmonized with the International Code Council (ICC)/ANSI A117 standard, "Accessible and Usable Buildings and Facilities", ICC/ANSI A117.1-1998 which references a 2 Hz limit. An upper limit was identified at 55 Hz.

1194.21(l). When electronic forms are used, the form shall allow people using assistive technology to access the information, field elements, and functionality required for completion and submission of the form, including all directions and cues.

Why are electronic forms so difficult for some people with disabilities to access?
At present, the interaction between form controls and screen readers can be unpredictable, depending upon the design of the page containing these controls.

How can forms in a software application meet this provision?
If keyboard alternatives are provided for navigating through a form, and all elements of the form are labeled with text located in close proximity to the field that is to be completed, the form will most likely meet this provision. Attention must be paid to the placement of field labels. On a web page, a label can have a direct association with a particular field that is indicated in the HTML code.

Assistive technology can interpret the HTML and correctly announce the appropriate label. There is no similar method for forms in software programs. Therefore, the label must be in a logical position relative to the input areas. For example, placing labels to the immediate left of where the user is to enter information is by far the most logical position for the label.

Web-Based Intranet and Internet Information and Applications (36 CFR 1194.22)

Updated: June 21, 2001

These provisions of the standards provide the requirements that must be followed by Federal agencies when producing web pages. These provisions apply unless doing so would impose an undue burden.

The key to compliance with these provisions is adherence to the provisions. Many agencies have purchased assistive software to test their pages. This will produce a better understanding of how these devices interact with different coding techniques. However, it always should be kept in mind that assistive technologies, such as screen readers, are complex programs and take extensive experience to master. For this reason, a novice user may obtain inaccurate results that can easily lead to frustration and a belief that the page does not comply with the standards.

For example, all screen reading programs use special key combinations to read properly coded tables. If the novice user of assistive technology is not aware of these commands, the tables will never read appropriately no matter how well the tables have been formatted.

A web site will be in compliance with the 508 standards if it meets paragraphs (a) through (p) of Section 1194.22. Please note that the tips and techniques discussed in the document for complying with particular sections are not necessarily the only ways of providing compliance with 508. In many cases, they are techniques developed by the Board, the Department of Education, and the Department of Justice that have been tested by users with a wide variety of screen reader software. With the evolution of technology, other techniques may become available or even preferable.

(a) Text Tags	(b) Multimedia Presentations
(c) Color	(d) Readability (style sheets)
(e) Serve-Side Image Maps	(f) Client-Side Image Maps
(g) & (h) Data Table	(i) Frames
(j) Flicker Rate	(k) Text-Only Alternative
(l) Scripts	(m) Applets and Plug-Ins
(n) Electronic Forms	(o) Navigation Links
(p) Time Delays	

1194.22(a). A text equivalent for every non-text element shall be provided (for example via alt or longdesc attributes, or in element content).

What is meant by a text equivalent?

A text equivalent means adding words to represent the purpose of a non-text element. This provision requires that when an image indicates a navigational action such as "move to the next screen" or "go back to the top of the page," the image must be accompanied by actual text that states the purpose of the image. This provision also requires that when an image is used to represent page content, the image must have a text description accompanying it that explains the meaning of the image. For example:

HTML Source Code: `<img src="art/logo-green.gif" alt="Access Board Logo">`

How much information actually needs to be in the text equivalent?

The text information associated with a non-text element should, when possible, communicate the same information as its associated element. For example, when an image indicates an action, the action must be described in the text. The types of non-text elements requiring actual text descriptions are limited to those elements that provide information required for comprehension of content or those used to facilitate navigation. Web page authors often utilize transparent graphics for spacing. Adding a text description to these elements will produce unnecessary clutter for users of screen readers. For such graphics, an empty `alt` attribute is useful.

Example of source code: `<img src="transparent.gif" alt="">`

What is meant by the term, non-text element?

A non-text element is an image, graphic, audio clip, or other feature that conveys meaning through a picture or sound. Examples include buttons, checkboxes, pictures and embedded or streaming audio or video.

HTML Source Code: `<img src="art/logo-green.gif" alt="Access Board Logo">`

How should audio presentations be treated?

This provision requires that when audio presentations are available on a multimedia web page, the audio portion must be captioned. Audio is a non-textual element, so a text equivalent of the audio must be provided if the audio is part of a multimedia presentation, Multimedia includes both audio and video. If the presentation were audio only, a text transcript would meet this requirement.

What are ways of assigning text to elements?

There are several ways of providing textual information so that it can be recognized by assistive technology devices. For instance, the `<img>` tag can accept an `alt` attribute that will enable a web designer to include text that describes the picture directly in the `<img>` tag.

HTML source code:

```
<img src="image/ab_logo1.gif" alt="The Architectural and Transportation Barriers
Compliance Board emblem-Go to Access Board website">
```

Similarly, the `<applet>` tag for Java applets also accepts an `alt` attribute, but it only works for browsers that provide support for Java. Often, users with slower Internet connections will turn support for Java applets off. A better alternative for providing textual descriptions is to simply include the alternative text between opening and closing `<applet>` or `<object>` tags. For instance, if a web designer wanted to include an applet called `MyCoolApplet` in a web page, and also include a description that the applet shows a stock ticker displaying the current price of various stocks, the designer would use the following HTML coding for example:

```
<applet code="MyCoolApplet.class" width="200", height="100">
</applet>
This applet displays current stock prices for many popular stocks.
```

Finally, yet another way of providing a textual description is to include it in the page in the surrounding context:

```
<p> Below is a picture of me during my great vacation!</p>
<img src="pictureofme.jpg">
```

1194.22(b). Equivalent alternatives for any multimedia presentation shall be synchronized with the presentation.

What are considered equivalent alternatives?
Captioning for the audio portion and audio description of visual information of multimedia presentations are considered equivalent alternatives. This provision requires that when an audio portion of a multimedia production is captioned, as required in provision (a), the captioning must be synchronized with the audio. Synchronized captioning would be required so someone reading the captions could also watch the speaker and associate relevant body language with the speech.

If a web site offers audio files with no video, do they have to be captioned?
No, because it is not multimedia. However, since audio is a non-text element, a text equivalent, such as a transcript, must be available. Similarly, a (silent) web slide show presentation does not need to have an audio description accompanying it, but does require text alternatives to be associated with the graphics.

If a Federal agency official delivers a live audio and video webcast speech, does it need to be captioned?
Yes, this would qualify as a multimedia presentation and would require the speech to be captioned. For example, go to:

National Endowment for the Humanities
www.neh.gov/media/scottcaptions.ram

National Center for Accessible Media (NCAM)
http://main.wgbh.org/wgbh/access/dvs/lion.ram

1194.22(c). Web pages shall be designed so that all information conveyed with color is also available without color, for example from context or markup.

Note: Illustration is a variation of the actual image published by the US Access Board and is provided for clarity purposes. To view the published illustration, visit http://www.access-board.gov/sec508/guide/1194.22.htm#(c).

Why is this provision necessary?
When colors are used as the sole method for identifying screen elements or controls, persons who are color-blind as well as those people who are blind or have low vision may find the web page unusable.

Does this mean that all pages have to be displayed in black and white?
No, this provision does not prohibit the use of color to enhance identification of important features. It does, however, require that some other method of identification, such as text labels, must be combined with the use of color. This provision addresses not only the problem of using color to indicate emphasized text, but also the use of color to indicate an action. For example, a web page that directs a user to "press the green button to start" should also identify the green button in some other fashion than simply by color.

Is there any way a page can be quickly checked to ensure compliance with this provision?
There are two simple ways of testing a web page to determine if this requirement is being met: by either viewing the page on a black and white monitor, or by printing it out on a black and white printer. Both methods will quickly show if the removal of color affects the usability of the page.

1194.22(d). Documents shall be organized so they are readable without requiring an associated stylesheet.

What are the potential problems posed by stylesheets?
Stylesheets can enable users to define specific viewing preferences to accommodate their disability. For instance, users with low vision may create their own stylesheet so that, regardless of what web pages they visit, all text is displayed in an extra large font with white characters on a black background. If designers set up their pages to override user-defined stylesheets, people with disabilities may not be able to use those pages. For good access, therefore, it is critical that designers ensure that their web pages do not interfere with user-defined stylesheets.

In general, the "safest" and most useful form of stylesheets are "external" stylesheets, in which the style rules are set up in a separate file. An example of an external stylesheet is:

Example of source code:

```
<link rel="stylesheet" type="text/css" href="section508.css">
```

1194.22(e). Redundant text links shall be provided for each active region of a server-side image map.

How do "image maps" work?

An "image map" is a picture (often an actual map) on a web page that provides different "links" to other web pages, depending on where a user clicks on the image. There are two basic types of image maps: "client-side image maps" and "server-side image maps." With client-side image maps, each "active region" in a picture can be assigned its own "link" (called a URL or "Uniform Resource Locator") that specifies what web page to retrieve when a portion of the picture is selected. HTML allows each active region to have its own alternative text, just like a picture can have alternative text (see §1194.22(a)). By contrast, clicking on a location of a server-side image map only specifies the coordinates within the image when the mouse was depressed. The ultimate selection of the link or URL must be deciphered by the computer serving the web page.

Why is this provision necessary?

When a web page uses a server-side image map to present the user with a selection of options, browsers cannot indicate to the user the URL that will be followed when a region of the map is activated. Therefore, the redundant text link is necessary to provide access to the page for anyone not able to see or accurately click on the map.

1194.22(f). Client-side image maps shall be provided instead of server-side image maps except where the regions cannot be defined with an available geometric shape.

Why do client-side image maps provide better accessibility?

Unlike server-side image maps, the client-side image map allows an author to assign text to each image map "hot spots." This feature means that someone using a screen reader can easily identify and activate regions of the map. An explanation of how these image maps are constructed will help clarify this issue.

Creating a basic client-side image map requires several steps:

- Identify an image for the map. First, an image must be used in a client-side image map. This image is identified using the `<img>` tag. To identify it as a map, use the "`usemap`" attribute.

- Use the `<map>` tag to "areas" within the map. The `<map>` tag is a container tag that includes various `<area>` tags that are used to identify specific portions of the image.

- Use `<area>` tags to identify map regions. To identify regions within a map, simply use `<area>` tags within the `<map>` container tags. Making this client-side image map accessible is considerably easier to describe: simply include the `alt` attribute and area description inside each `<area>` tag. The following HTML demonstrates how to make a client-side image map:

```
<img src="navbar.gif" border="0" usemap="#Map">
<map name="Map">
  <area shape="rect" coords="0,2,64,19" href="general.html"
       alt="information about us">
  <area shape="rect" coords="65,2,166,20" href="jobs.html"
       alt="job opportunities" >
  <area shape="rect" coords="167,2,212,19" href="faq.html"
       alt="Frequently Asked Questions">
```

377

```
    <area shape="rect" coords="214,2,318,21" href="location.html"
         alt="How to find us">
    <area shape="rect" coords="319,2,399,23" href="contact.html"
         alt="How to contact us">
  </map>
```

1194.22(g). Row and column headers shall be identified for data tables.

1194.22(h). Markup shall be used to associate data cells and header cells for data tables that have two or more logical levels of row or column headers.

Why are these two provisions necessary?

Paragraphs (g) and (h) permit the use of tables, but require that the tables be coded according to the rules of the markup language being used for creating tables. Large tables of data can be difficult to interpret if a person is using a non-visual means of accessing the web. Users of screen readers can easily get "lost" inside a table because it may be impossible to associate a particular cell that a screen reader is reading with the corresponding column headings and row names. For instance, assume that a salary table includes the salaries for federal employees by grade and step. Each row in the table may represent a grade scale and each column may represent a step. Thus, finding the salary corresponding to a grade 9, step 5 may involve finding the cell in the ninth row and the fifth column. For a salary chart of 15 grade scales and 10 steps, the table will have at least 150 cells. Without a method to associate the headings with each cell, it is easy to imagine the difficulty a user of assistive technology may encounter with the table.

Section 1194.22 (g) and (h) state that when information is displayed in a table format, the information shall be laid out using appropriate table tags as opposed to using a preformatted table in association with the `<pre>` tag. Web authors are also required to use one of several methods to provide an association between a header and its related information.

How can HTML tables be made readable with assistive technology?

Using the "Scope" Attribute in Tables – Using the "scope" attribute is one of the most effective ways of making HTML compliant with these requirements. It is also the simplest method to implement. The scope attribute also works with some (but not all) assistive technology in tables that use `"colspan"` or `"rowspan"` attributes in table header or data cells.

Using the Scope Attribute – The first row of each table should include column headings. Typically, these column headings are inserted in `<th>` tags, although `<td>` tags can also be used. These tags at the top of each column should include the following attribute:

```
scope="col"
```

By doing this simple step, the text in that cell becomes associated with every cell in that column. Unlike using other approaches (notably `id` and `headers` attributes) there is no need to include special attributes in each cell of the table. Similarly, the first column of every table should include information identifying information about each row in the table. Each of the cells in that first column are created by either `<th>` or `<td>` tags. Include the following attribute in these cells:

```
scope="row"
```

By simply adding this attribute, the text in that cell becomes associated with every cell in that row. While this technique dramatically improves the usability of a web page, using the scope attribute does not appear to interfere in any way with browsers that do not support the attribute.

For example, the following simple table summarizes the work schedule of three employees and demonstrates these principles.

```
<table>
  <tr>
    <th> </th>
    <th scope="col">Spring</th>
    <th scope="col">Summer</th>
    <th scope="col">Autumn</th>
    <th scope="col">Winter</th>
  </tr>
  <tr>
    <td scope="row" >Betty</td>
    <td>9-5</td>
    <td>10-6</td>
    <td>8-4</td>
    <td>7-3</td>
  </tr>
  <tr>
    <td scope="row">Wilma</td>
    <td>10-6</td>
    <td>10-6</td>
    <td>9-5</td>
    <td>9-5</td>
  </tr>
  <tr>
    <td scope="row">Fred</td>
    <td>10-6</td>
    <td>10-6</td>
    <td>10-6</td>
    <td>10-6</td>
  </tr>
</table>
```

This table would be displayed as follows:

	Spring	Summer	Autumn	Winter
Betty	9-5	10-6	8-4	7-3
Wilma	10-6	10-6	9-5	9-5
Fred	10-6	10-6	10-6	10-6

The efficiency of using the scope attribute becomes more apparent in much larger tables. For instance, if an agency used a table with 20 rows and 20 columns, there would be 400 data cells in the table. To make this table comply with this provision without using the scope attribute would require special coding in all 400 data cells, plus the 40 header and row cells. By contrast, using the scope attribute would only require special attributes in the 40 header and row cells.

Using the ID and Headers Attributes in Tables

Unlike using the scope attribute, using the id and headers attributes requires that every data cell in a table include special attributes for association. Although its usefulness for accessibility may have been diminished as browsers provide support for the scope attribute, the id and headers attributes are still very useful and provide a practical means of providing access in smaller tables.

The following table is much more complicated than the previous example and demonstrates the use of the id and headers attributes and then the scope attribute. Both methods provide a means of complying with the requirements for data tables in web pages. The table in this example includes the work schedules for two employees. Each employee has a morning and afternoon work schedule that varies depending on whether the employee is working in the winter or summer months. The "*summer*" and "*winter*" columns each span two columns labeled "morning" and "afternoon". Therefore, in each cell identifying the work schedule, the user needs to be told the employee's name (Fred or Wilma), the season (*Summer* or *Winter*), and the shift (morning or afternoon).

```
<table>
  <tr>
    <th> </th>
    <th colspan="2" id="winter">Winter</th>
    <th colspan="2" id="summer">Summer</th>
  </tr>
  <tr>
    <th> </th>
    <th id="am1">Morning</th>
    <th id="pm1">Afternoon</th>
    <th id="am2">Morning</th>
    <th id="pm2">Afternoon</th>
  </tr>
  <tr>
    <td id="wilma" >Wilma</td>
    <td headers="wilma am1 winter">9-11</td>
    <td headers="wilma pm1 winter">12-6</td>
    <td headers="wilma am2 summer">7-11</td>
    <td headers="wilma pm2 summer">12-3</td>
  </tr>
  <tr>
    <td id="fred">Fred</td>
    <td headers="fred am1 winter">10-11</td>
    <td headers="fred pm1 winter">12-6</td>
    <td headers="fred am2 summer">9-11</td>
    <td headers="fred pm2 summer">12-5</td>
  </tr>
</table>
```

This table would be displayed as follows:

	Winter		Summer	
	Morning	Afternoon	Morning	Afternoon
Wilma	9-11	12-6	7-11	12-3
Fred	10-11	12-6	9-11	12-5

Coding each cell of this table with `id` and `headers` attributes is much more complicated than using the `scope` attribute shown below:

```
<table>
  <tr>
    <th> </th>
    <th colspan="2" scope="col">Winter</th>
    <th colspan="2" scope="col">Summer</th>
  </tr>
  <tr>
    <th> </th>
    <th scope="col">Morning</th>
    <th scope="col">Afternoon</th>
    <th scope="col">Morning</th>
    <th scope="col">Afternoon</th>
  </tr>
  <tr>
    <td scope="row">Wilma</td>
    <td>9-11</td>
    <td>12-6</td>
    <td>7-11</td>
    <td>12-3</td>
  </tr>
  <tr>
    <td scope="row">Fred</td>
    <td>10-11</td>
    <td>12-6</td>
    <td>9-11</td>
    <td>12-5</td>
  </tr>
</table>
```

This table would be displayed as follows:

	Winter		Summer	
	Morning	Afternoon	Morning	Afternoon
Wilma	9-11	12-6	7-11	12-3
Fred	10-11	12-6	9-11	12-5

Is the summary attribute an option?
Although highly recommended by some web page designers as a way of summarizing the contents of a table, the `summary` attribute of the `<table>` tag is not sufficiently supported by major assistive technology manufacturers to warrant recommendation. Therefore, web developers who are interested in summarizing their tables should consider placing their descriptions either adjacent to their tables or in the body of the table, using such tags as the `<caption>` tag. In no event should web developers use summarizing tables as an alternative to making the contents of their tables compliant as described above.

1194.22(i). Frames shall be titled with text that facilitates frame identification and navigation.

Why is this provision necessary?

Frames provide a means of visually dividing the computer screen into distinct areas that can be separately rewritten. Unfortunately, frames can also present difficulties for users with disabilities when those frames are not easily identifiable to assistive technology. For instance, a popular use of frames is to create "navigational bars" in a fixed position on the screen and have the content of the web site retrievable by activating one of those navigational buttons. The new content is displayed in another area of the screen. Because the navigational bar doesn't change, it provides a stable "frame-of-reference" for users and makes navigation much easier. However, users with disabilities may become lost if the differences between the two frames are not clearly established.

What is the best method for identifying frames?

The most obvious way to accomplish this requirement is to include text within the body of each frame that clearly identifies the frame. For instance, in the case of the navigation bar, a web developer should consider putting words such as "*Navigational Links*" at the beginning of the contents of the frame to let all users know that the frame depicts navigational links. Providing titles like this at the top of the contents of each frame will satisfy these requirements. An additional measure that should be considered by agencies is to include meaningful text in the `<frame>` tag's `title` attribute. Although not currently supported by major manufacturers of assistive technology, the `title` attribute is part of the HTML 4.0 specification and was intended to let web developers include a description of the frame as a quote-enclosed string. Demonstrating the use of the "`title`" attribute requires a basic understanding of how frames are constructed. When frames are used in a web page, the first page that is loaded must include a `<frameset>` tag that encloses the basic layout of the frames on the page. Within the `<frameset>` tag, `<frame>` tags specify the name, initial contents, and appearance of each separate frame. Thus, the following example uses the `title` attribute to label one frame "*Navigational Links Frame*" and the second frame "*Contents Frame*".

```
<frameset cols="30%, 60%">
   <frame src="navlinks.html" name="navlinks" title="Navigational Links Frame">
   <frame src="geninfo.html" name="contents_page" title="Contents Frame">
</frame>
```

While assistive technology does not yet widely support the `title` attribute, we recommend including this attribute in web pages using frames.

For example: see right – the ADA Technical Assistance Program (*http://www.adata.org*) – this demonstrates the use of frames with "No Frames Link".

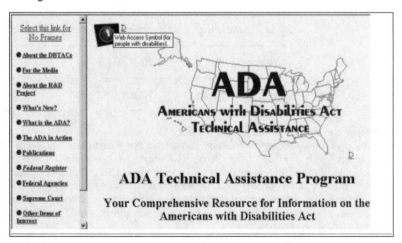

1194.22(j) Pages shall be designed to avoid causing the screen to flicker with a frequency greater than 2 Hz and lower than 55 Hz.

Why is this provision necessary?

This provision is necessary because some individuals with photosensitive epilepsy can have a seizure triggered by displays that flicker, flash, or blink, particularly if the flash has a high intensity and is within certain frequency ranges. The 2 Hz limit was chosen to be consistent with proposed revisions to the ADA Accessibility Guidelines which, in turn, are being harmonized with the International Code Council (ICC)/ANSI A117 standard, "*Accessible and Usable Buildings and Facilities*", ICC/ANSI A117.1-1998 which references a 2 Hz limit. An upper limit was identified at 55 Hz.

How can flashing or flickering elements be identified?

Flashing or flickering elements are usually added through technologies such as animated `GIF`'s, Java applets, or third-party plug-ins or applications. Java applets and third party plug-ins can be identified by the presence of `<applet>` or `<object>` tags. Animated GIF's are images that download in a single file (like ordinary image files), but have content that changes over short periods of time. Like other images, however, they are usually incorporated through the use of the `<img>` tag.

1194.22(k). A text-only page, with equivalent information or functionality, shall be provided to make a web site comply with the provisions of these standards, when compliance cannot be accomplished in any other way. The content of the text-only page shall be updated whenever the primary page changes.

What must a text-only page contain to comply with this provision?

Text-only pages must contain equivalent information or functionality as the primary pages. Also, the text-only page shall be updated whenever the primary page changes.

For example: *http://www.disability.gov/* displays a text-only page on the home page (see below).

HTML source code:

```
<div ID="textonly">
  <p>
    <a HREF="../textonly/default.asp">Text Only</a>
  </p>
</div>
```

1194.22(l). When pages utilize scripting languages to display content, or to create interface elements, the information provided by the script shall be identified with functional text that can be read by assistive technology.

What accessibility problems can scripts cause?

Web page authors have a responsibility to provide script information in a fashion that can be read by assistive technology. When authors do not put functional text with a script, a screen reader will often read the content of the script itself in a meaningless jumble of numbers and letters. Although this jumble is text, it cannot be interpreted or used.

How can web developers comply with this provision?

Web developers working with JavaScript frequently use so-called JavaScript URLs as an easy way to invoke JavaScript functions. Typically, this technique is used as part of <a> anchor links. For instance, the following link invokes a JavaScript function called myFunction:

```
<a href="javascript:myFunction();">Start myFunction</a>
```

This technique does not cause accessibility problems for assistive technology. A more difficult problem occurs when developers use images inside JavaScript URLs without providing meaningful information about the image or the effect of the anchor link. For instance, the following link also invokes the JavaScript function myFunction, but requires the user to click on an image instead of the text "*Start myFunction*":

```
<a href="javascript:myFunction();"><img src="myFunction.gif"></a>
```

This type of link, as written, presents tremendous accessibility problems, but those problems can easily be remedied. The <img> tag, of course, supports the "alt" attribute that can also be used to describe the image and the effect of clicking on the link. Thus, the following revision remedies the accessibility problems created in the previous example:

```
<a href="javascript:myFunction();"><img src="myFunction.gif" alt="picture link for
starting myFunction"></a>
```

Another technique advocated by some developers is to use the "title" attribute of the <a> tag. For instance, the following example includes a meaningful description in a "title" attribute:

```
<a title="this link starts myFunction" href="javascript:myFunction();"><img
src="myFunction.gif"></a>
```

This tag is supported by some but not all assistive technologies. Therefore, while it is part of the HTML 4.0 specifications, authors should use the "alt" tag in the enclosed image.

Finally, the browser's status line (at the bottom of the screen) typically displays the URL of any links that the mouse is currently pointing towards. For instance, if clicking on an anchor link will send the user to *http://www.usdoj.gov*, that URL will be displayed in the status line if the user's mouse lingers on top of the anchor link. In the case of JavaScript URLs, the status line can become filled with meaningless snips of script. To prevent this effect, some web developers use special "event handlers" such as onmouseover and onmouseout to overwrite the contents of the status line with a custom message. For instance, the following link will replace the content in the status line with a custom message "*Nice Choice*".

```
<a href="javascript:myFcn();" onmouseover="status='Nice Choice'; return true;"
onmouseout="status='';"><img src="pix.gif"></a>
```

This text rewritten into the status line is difficult or impossible to detect with a screen reader. Although rewriting the status line did not interfere with the accessibility or inaccessibility of the JavaScript URL, web developers should ensure that all important information conveyed in the status line also be provided through the alt attribute, as described above.

JavaScript uses so-called "event handlers" as a trigger for certain actions or functions to occur. For instance, a web developer may embed a JavaScript function in a web page that automatically checks the content of a form for completeness or accuracy. An event handler associated with a "*submit*" button can be used to trigger the function before the form is actually submitted to the server for processing. The advantage for the government agency is that it saves government resources by not requiring the government's server to do the initial checking. The advantage for the computer user is that feedback about errors is almost instantaneous because the user is told about the error before the information is even submitted over the Internet.

Web developers must exercise some caution when deciding which event handlers to use in their web pages, because different screen readers provide different degrees of support for different event handlers. The following table includes recommendations for using many of the more popular event handlers:

- onClick – The onClick event handler is triggered when the user clicks once on a particular item. It is commonly used on links and button elements and, used in connection with these elements, it works well with screen readers. If clicking on the element associated with the onClick event handler triggers a function or performs some other action, developers should ensure that the context makes that fact clear to all users. Do not use the onClick event handlers for form elements that include several options (for example, select lists, radio buttons, checkboxes) unless absolutely necessary.

- onDblClick – The onDblClick event handler is set off when the user clicks twice rapidly on the same element. In addition to the accessibility problems it creates, it is very confusing to users and should be avoided.

- onMouseDown and onMouseUp – The onMouseDown and onMouseUp event handlers each handle the two halves of clicking a mouse while over an element – the process of (a) clicking down on the mouse button and (b) then releasing the mouse button. Like onDblClick, this tag should be used sparingly, if at all, by web developers because it is quite confusing. In most cases, developers should opt for the onClick event handler instead of onMouseDown.

- onMouseOver and onMouseOut – These two event handlers are very popular on many web sites. For instance, so-called rollover GIFs, which swap images on a web page when the mouse passes over an image, typically use both of these event handlers. These event handlers can neither be accessed by the mouse nor interfere with accessibility – a screen reader simply bypasses them entirely. Accordingly, web designers who use these event handlers should be careful to duplicate the information (if any) provided by these event handlers through other means.

- onLoad and onUnload – Both of these event handlers are used frequently to perform certain functions when a web page has either completed loading or when it unloads. Because neither event handler is triggered by any user interaction with an element on the page, they do not present accessibility problems.

- onChange – This event handler is very commonly used for triggering JavaScript functions based on a selection from within a <select> tag. Surprisingly, it presents tremendous accessibility problems for many commonly used screen readers and should be avoided. Instead, web developers should use the onClick event handler (associated with a link or button that is adjacent to a <select> tag) to accomplish the same functions.

- onBlur and onFocus – These event handlers are not commonly used in web pages. While they don't necessarily present accessibility problems, their behavior is confusing enough to a web page visitor that they should be avoided.

1194.22(m). When a web page requires that an applet, plug-in, or other application be present on the client system to interpret page content, the page must provide a link to a plug-in or applet that complies with §1194.21(a) through (l).

Why is this provision necessary?
While most web browsers can easily read HTML and display it to the user, several private companies have developed proprietary file formats for transmitting and displaying special content, such as multimedia or very precisely defined documents. Because these file formats are proprietary, web browsers cannot ordinarily display them. To make it possible for these files to be viewed by web browsers, add-on programs or "plug-ins" can be downloaded and installed on the user's computer that will make it possible for their web browsers to display or play the content of the files. This provision requires that web pages that provide content such as Real Audio or PDF (Adobe Acrobat's Portable Document Format) files also provide a link to a plug-in that will meet the software provisions. It is very common for a web page to provide links to needed plug-ins. For example, web pages containing Real Audio almost always have a link to a source for the necessary player. This provision places a responsibility on the web page author to know that a compliant application exists, before requiring a plug-in.

How can plug-ins and applets be detected?
Plug-ins can usually be detected by examining a page's HTML for the presence of an <object> tag. Some plug-in manufacturers, however, may require the use of proprietary tags. Like plug-ins, applets can also be identified by the presence of an <object> tag in the HTML source for a web page. Also, an <applet> tag may signal the inclusion of an applet in a web page.

1194.22(n). When electronic forms are designed to be completed online, the form shall allow people using assistive technology to access the information, field elements, and functionality required for completion and submission of the form, including all directions and cues.

Why do electronic forms present difficulties to screen readers?

Currently, the interaction between form controls and screen readers can be unpredictable, depending upon the design of the page containing these controls. HTML forms pose accessibility problems when web developers separate a form element from its associated label or title. For instance, if an input box is intended for receiving a user's last name, the web developer must be careful that the words "*last name*" (or some similar text) appear near that input box or are somehow associated with it. Although this may seem like an obvious requirement, it is extremely easy to violate because the visual proximity of a form element and its title offers no guarantee that a screen reader will associate the two or that this association will be obvious to a user of assistive technology.

The following form demonstrates these problems. Visually, this form is part of a table and each field is carefully placed in table cells adjacent to their corresponding labels (note: formatting forms with tables are by no means the only situation presenting the accessibility problems inherent in forms; tables merely illustrate the problem most clearly).

While the relationship between the titles "*First Name*" or "*Last Name*" and their respective input boxes may be obvious from visual inspection, the relationship is not obvious to a screen reader. Instead, a screen reader may simply announce "input box" when encountering each input box. The reason for these difficulties is revealed from inspecting the HTML source for this table. The following code is a simplified version of this table.

```
<form>
  <table>
    <tr>
      <td><b>FIRST NAME: </b></td>
      <td><input type="text" name="firstname"> </td>
    </tr>
    <tr>
      <td><b>LAST NAME: </b></td>
      <td><input type="text" name="lastname"> </td>
    </tr>
  </table>
<p></p>
<input type="submit" value="submit">
</form>
```

The problem created by laying out form elements inside of this table is now clear – the form elements are separated from their labels by the formatting instructions for the table.

How can developers provide accessible HTML forms?

The first rule of thumb is to place labels adjacent to input fields, not in separate cells of a table. For the web developer who does not wish to place form elements immediately adjacent to their corresponding titles, the HTML 4.0 specification includes the `<label>` tag that lets web developers mark specific elements as "labels" and then associate a form element with that label. There are generally two ways to use the label tag: explicit labels and implicit labels.

"Explicit Labels" Work Well

Experience has shown that explicit labeling works extremely well with all popular assistive technology and is recommended in all but the very simplest of tables. We recommend that all agencies ensure that their web developers are familiar with these important concepts. Using "explicit" labels involves two distinct steps:

Use the `<label>` tag and associated `for` attribute to tag labels. In other words, identify the exact words that you want to use as the label for the form element and enclose those words in a `<label>` tag. Use the `form` attribute to uniquely identify that element.

Use the `id` Attribute in the associated form element. Every form element supports the `id` attribute. By setting this attribute to the identifier used in the `form` attribute of the associated `<label>` tag, you "tie" that form element to its associated label. For instance, we have rewritten the HTML code for our simple form-inside-a-table to include explicit labels below:

```
<form>
  <table>
    <tr>
      <td><b><label for="first"> first name:</label> </b></td>
      <td><input type="text" name="firstname" id="first"></td>
    </tr>
    <tr>
      <td><b><label for="last"> last name:</label> </b></td>
      <td><input type="text" name="lastname" id="last"></td>
    </tr>
  </table>
<p></p>
<input type="submit" value="submit">
</form>
```

In a nutshell, that's all there is to making HTML form elements accessible to assistive technology. Experience has shown that this technique works extremely well in much more complicated and convoluted forms and it should work well in all agency HTML forms.

Avoid Using "Implicit Labels"

In "implicit" labels, the form element and its associated label are contained within an opening `<label>` tag and a closing `</label>` tag. For instance, in the table above, an implicit label to associate the words "*First Name*" with its associated input cell, we could use an implicit label as follows:

```
<label>
  <tr>
    <td><b>first name:</b></td>
    <td><input type="text" name="firstname"></td>
  </tr>
</label>
```

Experience has shown that implicit labeling should be avoided for two reasons. First, implicit labeling is not reliably supported by many screen readers and, in particular, does not work well if explicit labels are simultaneously used anywhere on the same web page. Often, the output can be wildly inaccurate and confusing. Second, if any text separates a label from its associated form element, an implicit label becomes impractical and confusing because the label itself is no longer easily identified with the form element.

1194.22(o). A method shall be provided that permits users to skip repetitive navigation links.

Why do navigational links present impediments to screen readers and other types of assistive technologies?

This provision provides a method to facilitate the easy tracking of page content that provides users of assistive technology the option to skip repetitive navigation links. Web developers routinely place a host of routine navigational links at a standard location – often across the top, bottom, or side of a page. If a non-disabled user returns to a web page and knows that he or she wants to view the contents of that particular page instead of selecting a navigation link to go to another page, he or she may simply look past the links and begin reading wherever the desired text is located. For those who use screen readers or other types of assistive technologies, however, it can be a tedious and time-consuming chore to wait for the assistive technology to work through and announce each of the standard navigational links before getting to the intended location. In order to alleviate this problem, the section 508 rule requires that when repetitive navigational links are used, there must be a mechanism for users to skip repetitive navigational links.

For example: As seen below, the USDA Target Center (*http://www.usda.gov/oo/target.htm*) and DOL (*http://www.dol.gov/dol/odep/*) web sites use the *Skip Repetitive Navigational Links*.

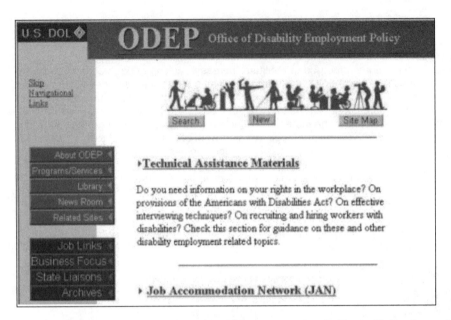

1194.22(p). When a timed response is required, the user shall be alerted and given sufficient time to indicate more time is required.

Why do timed responses present problems to web users with disabilities?

Web pages can be designed with scripts so that the web page disappears or "expires" if a response is not received within a specified amount of time. Sometimes, this technique is used for security reasons or to reduce the demands on the computer serving the web pages. Someone's disability can have a direct impact on the speed with which he or she can read, move around, or fill in a web form. For instance, someone with extremely low vision may be a slower-than-average reader. A page may "time out" before he is able to finish reading it. Many forms, when they "time out" automatically, also delete whatever data has been entered. The result is that someone with a disability who is slow to enter data cannot complete the form. For this reason, when a timed response is required, the user shall be alerted via a prompt and given sufficient time to indicate whether additional time is needed.

For an example of this, see the Thrift Savings Plan at *http://www.tsp.gov*.

Index

A Guide to the Index

The index is arranged alphabetically in word-by-word order (so that New York would sort before Newark). An unmodified heading represents the principal treatment of a topic. Acronyms have been preferred to their expansions as main headings on the grounds that they are easier to recall.

D

E

e-commerce
   benefits to people with transportation difficulties, 4
   e-banking, e-education and e-government, 34
e-Europe 2002 Action Plan, 42
EASI accessibility training, 290
edit fields
   correct prompt positioning for, 149
educational institutions
   complaints about accessibility to disabled
      students, 335
   Section 508 applies through the Tech Act, 346
effective design and efficiency
   aspects of web site usability, 7
EIT (Electronic and Information Technology)
   see also Section 508.
   glossary entry, 361
   standards, 15
elderly people
   see also seniors.
   Japanese accessibilty concerns, 48
Election.com, 341
Electronic Signatures in Global and National
   Commerce Act
   accessibilty problems associated with, 35
Elisa Communications
   supporters of WAI, 41
<em> element
   preferred to <i>, 19
em measurements
   problems with older browsers, 239
   relative font sizes, 238
Emacspeak browser, 246
   availability for UNIX, 56
embedding stylesheets, 234
emerging technologies, 305
   problems with, summarized, 323
empowerment
   Accessibility Organization within an enterprise, 286
empty alt attributes, 374
empty text input controls, 141
enforcement and rewards
   accessible enterprise web development, 297
enlightened self-interest, 26
enterprises
   implementing accessibility in, 283
epileptic seizures
   flicker as possible cause of, 107
   photosensitive epilepsy, 372, 383
equivalent facilitation principle
   Section 508 provisions, 368
error tolerance
   universal design principles, 325
error tones
   visual prompts shown with
      Section 508 provision relating to, 369
errors and warnings
   W3C CSS Validation Service, 259
ESC (European Economic and Social
Committee), 43
European Commission
   Information Society Technologies Programme, 41
European Union
   implementation status of WCAG 1.0, 42
European Year of Disabled People, 2003, 43

evaluation tools see assessment and repair tools.
event handlers
   browser status line and, 385
   DHTML accessibility and, 198
Ewers, Neal
   screen reader video demonstration, 55
explicit labels, 387

F

facial thermography, 322
FCA (False Claims Act) violations
   misrepresentation of Section 508 compliance, 344
FCC (Federal Communications Commission)
   role with respect to Section 255, 342
feedback mechanisms, AO, 291
<fieldset> element
   GoLive Web authoring tool, 218
   grouping form controls, 155
   Microsoft FrontPage tag support, 212
fieldset.html, 156
file types
   algorithmic testing for text equivalents, 166
Finland
   implementation status of WCAG 1.0, 44
firewalls
   W3C Validation Service and, 257
FirstGov web site
   code for invisible navigation links, 120
   web site with invisible navigation links, 119
fixed-size text, 23
Flash, 267
   accessibility challenges, 349
   built-in Dreamweaver support, 209
   objects need accessible alternatives, 199
Flash movies
   accessible elements, 271
   avoiding rapid screen changes, 280
   interactive movies should be keyboard-
      navigable, 280
   looping movies, 280
   providing text equivalents, 273
Flash MX, 268
   accessibility hints, 280
   Accessibility panel for text equivalents, 268
      keyboard shortcuts, 275
   auto-labeling, 274
   support for form components
      creating accessible forms, 276
Flash Player 6, 267
   buttons and forms in, 274
   exposes text elements to screen readers, 269
flashing see flicker.
Fleet National Bank
   accessible banking services, 340
flicker, 107
   algorithmic and judgmental testing of Section 508
      compliance, 171
   caused by DHTML use, 199
   Section 508 provision related to, 372, 383
focus changes
   Section 508 provision relating to, 370
focus groups, 291
focus rectangles
   navigation using, 134

Information Society Technologies Programme
supporters of WAI, 41
initial assesment
enterprise web accessibility, 299
web technology review components, 300
inline stylesheets, 235
to be avoided, 237
inline text
long image descriptions, 88
<input> element
src attribute, 72
title attribute
carrying form control information, 153
type attributes, 79
value attribute
use by JFW, 80
input forms *see* forms.
InSight assessment tool, 316
enhancing the GoLive Web authoring tool
with InSight LE, 217, 219
instance names
Flash tab order, 276
integrating accessibility, ATAG 1.0 guideline, 194
ATAG 1.0 guideline
Dreamweaver 4.0 and Dreamweaver MX, 207
BBEdit, 228
GoLive Web authoring tool, 220
Microsoft FrontPage, 214
integration strategy, AO, 298
interactive movies
Flash, should be keyboard-navigable, 280
internal standards, 296
Internet
ADA applicability to, 332
changes in characteristics of users, 16
proportion of users with disabilities, 16
Section 508 provisions relating to, 373
voting by, 341
Internet Industry Association
Maguire v SOCOG, 38
Internet Society
comments on the Electronic Signatures in Global and
National Commerce Act, 35
Intranet information
Section 508 provisions relating to, 373
invisible images
form controls with no text prompts, 152
invisible buttons, 275
invisible navigation links, 119
Jim Thatcher's own site, 133
LexisNexis web site, 122
use for indentation, 242
use in skip over navigation links, 117
use in stylesheets for screen readers, 238
viewing an invisible GIF, 118
"Invisilink" class, 121
IPO (International Program Office)
W3C, WAI and, 40
Ireland
implementation status of WCAG 1.0, 45
IRS (Internal Revenue Service)
form 1040, PDF form example, 158
online IRS tax filing services, 341
ismap attribute
server-side image maps, 129, 168

Italy
implementation status of WCAG 1.0, 45
ITTATC (Information Technology Technical Assistance
and Training Center)
accessibility training course, 290
assessment and repair tool review, 187
web site with invisible skip navigation links, 121
<acronym> tag, 121
IVR (Interactive Voice Response), 342, 349

J

J-WAS web accessiblity evaluation tool, 47, 49
Japan
HPR developed first for Japanese characters, 58
implementation status of WCAG 1.0, 47
Java, 309
glossary entry, 362
JavaScript
checking as distinction between Section 508 and
WCAG, 186
DHTML accessibility and, 198, 199
disabling on IE and Netscape, 63
form-based menus
web authoring tool problems from, 199
glossary entry, 362
invoking JavaScript URLs from <a> links, 384
not supported by Lynx browser, 61
Section 508 provisions relating to, 384
self-refreshing pages, 199
JAWS (Jobs Access With Speech) *see* JFW.
JFW (JAWS for Windows)
cost and availablilty, 55
demonstration version available on web site, 68
Dreamweaver accessibility through, 208
forms reading mode example, 146
frame support, 127
help text, 146
listening to tagged PDF forms, 159
performance in finding prompts, 143
performance reading image buttons, 79
without alt text, 80, 81
performance reading image maps, 77
Yahoo! home page, 79
performance reading title markup forms, 155
performance with non-tabular forms, 149
performance with skip over navigation links, 123
reading a badly-captioned table, 102
setting up to read tables cells, 100
support for headers attribute, 106
techniques for using, 56
use of src attributes, 73
won't select alt text for radio button arrays, 153
JFW 4.01
Dreamweaver accessibility problems, 208
Microsoft FrontPage accessibility, 215
Jobs Access With Speech *see* JFW.
judgment
needed with assessment and repair tools, 314
role in accessibility testing, 165
jump menus
web authoring tool problems from, 199
jumps *see* next text jumps; table jump mode.

K

L

logos
  Bobby assessment tool, 175
  Flash MX, adding a text equivalent, 270
  promoting accessible sites, 25
longdesc attribute
  algorithmic testing for section 508 compliance, 166
  Flash MX Description field corresponds to, 270
  LIFT Online tool evaluation results, 184
  text equivalents for charts and graphs, 71, 86
look and feel
  integrating accessibility into, 194
  web site appearance and customer feedback, 291
looping movies, 280
Luxemburg
  implementation status of WCAG 1.0, 45
Lynx browser
  disabling stylesheets, 251
  frame support, 126
  glossary entry, 362
  investigating page linearization using, 59
  investigating table linearization using, 97
  JavaScript not supported, 61
  Montanaboat.com rendered by, 251
Lynx Viewer, 97
  inconsitent web site views with Lynx browser, 61
  investigating page linearization using, 59
  Montanaboat.com, 254

M

Mac OS *see* Apple Macintosh.
Macromedia
  see also Dreamweaver; Flash; HomeSite web editor.
  commitment to accessibility, 200
Macromedia Accessibility Resource Center, 280
magnified displays *see* screen magnification.
MAGpie (Media Access Generator), 312, 349
Maguire v SOCOG
  complaint over inaccessible web design, 37
mainstreaming disability concerns, 33
Make Child Objects Accessible option
  Accessibility panel, Flash MX, 271, 272
Make Object Accessible option
  Accessibility panel, Flash MX, 275
management
  need for overview of accessibility obligations, 3
<map> elements
  adding alt text, 78
  client-side image maps, 377
  position isn't significant, 75
markup editors
  text-based markup editors, 221
  WYSIWYG markup editors, 194
markup preservation, ATAG 1.0 guideline, 193
  BBEdit, 225
  Dreamweaver 4.0 and Dreamweaver MX, 200
  GoLive, 217
  HomeSite Web editor, 221
  Microsoft FrontPage, 210
markup validity, ATAG 1.0 guideline, 193
  BBEdit, 225
  Dreamweaver 4.0 and Dreamweaver MX, 201
  GoLive, 217
  HomeSite Web editor, 222
  Microsoft FrontPage, 210

<marquee> element
  possible cause of flicker, 108
media attribute
  <link> element, 249
  <style> element, 248
@media rule
  specifying media dependencies, 247
media-specific stylesheets
  CSS2 specification supports, 236
media types, 247
  recognized media attributes tabulated, 250
  specifying within a document, 249
Medium option
  W3C CSS Validation Service, 260
memorability
  aspect of web site usability, 7
meta languages
  CC/PP as, 321
  User Interface Markup Language, 321, 364
meta text
  inserted by HPR and JFW, 76, 123
Microsoft Corporation
  see also IE; MSAA; SAMI.
  supporters of WAI, 41
Microsoft FrontPage, 210
  AccVerify SE validator, 213
  assessment and repair tools, 315
  documentation and help text, 214
  keyboard accessibility, 215
  pitfalls to avoid, 215
  support for VML instead of SVG, 211
Microsoft Local District Information
  web site, client-side map example, 131
Mobile Access Internet Group, W3C, 320
mobile devices *see* handheld devices.
mobility impairment
  see also timed responses.
  Dreamweaver Timelines, 209
monochrome displays
  color contrast and, 92
Montanaboat.com
  case study, 251
    HTML source, 252
  default heading examples, 240
  effects of turning off CSS, 241
  font style examples, 239
  media types example, 248
  results from W3C CSS Validation Service, 260
  results from WDG CSSCheckUp validation, 264
Moore, Donald L
  concerns for deaf people, 160
motivation
  for providing accessible web sites, 14
mouse-only functions
  Adobe GoLive Web authoring tool, 220
  DHTML accessibility and, 198
  Dreamweaver Design View, 208
  Section 508 provision relating to, 369
movies *see* Flash movies.
MSAA (Microsoft Active Accessibility)
  blank input screens detectable using, 141
  IE effectiveness with screen readers and, 56
  MSAA Application Mode, Window-Eyes, 56
  used with Flash Player 6, 267
MTIC (Mission pour les Technologies de l'Information
    et de la Communication), 44

online forms *see* forms.
online guide to Section 508, 68
online HTML validators, 193
online resources, 29
    Access Board's Section 508 standards and online
        guide, 68
    ADA, 330
    AIAP, 319
    Assistive Technology products, 68
    ATAP comparison of Section 508 and WCAG, 68
    Authoring Tool Accessibility Guidelines, 192
    California OCR Letters of Resolution, 335
    CC/PP, 321
    color contrast checking, 93
    device independence principles, 319
    discussion of color contrast, 93
    Electronic Signatures in Global and National
        Commerce Act, 35
    Flash Player 6 download, 267
    HPR free trial, 98
    HTML tag listing, 19
    HTML Validator, 20
    human judgment, 314
    IBM Web Accessibility Guidelines, 68
    Java Accessibility API, 309
    legal aspects of accessibility, 15
    listing accessible products, 25
    logos for accessible sites, 25
    Lynx browser and Lynx Viewer, 97
    MAGpie, 312
    Maguire v SOCOG, 38
    neiljohan.com on tags causing flicker, 108
    Section 508, 295
    statistics on prevalence of disabilities, 16, 18
    survey on internet use by the disabled, 16
    SVG and related tools, 310, 311, 312
    Tablin tool for linearization, 98
    technology trends comment from Judy Brewer, 28
    universal design, 324
        principles, 325
    US Department of Education report on the San José
        complaint, 36
    US disability rights legislation, 329
    WAI techniques document, 105
    WAVE analysis, 82
    WCAG checkpoints, 42, 67
    XHTML, 308
    XML, 307, 308
    XSLT, 308
Opera browser
    treatment of alt text, 9
    turning off animation, 107
operating systems
    providing textual information through
        Section 508 provision relating to, 371
    Section 508 provisions relating to, 367
Optavia
    accessible web site, usable on handheld devices, 18
organizational benefits, 29
organizational reputations
    improved by accessible products, 25
organizations
    implementing accessibilty in, 283.
OSM (Off-Screen Model)
    used by screen readers, 54
OutSpoken screen reader, 55

P

<p> element
    class attribute, 235
    text-indent property, 242
page layout *see* layout.
page refreshes, 162
    web authoring tool problems from automatic
        refreshes, 199
PageScreamer assessment and repair tool,
    315, 316, 317
    included in ITTATC review, 188
partially-sighted *see* visually impaired.
PC Magazine Top 100 sites
    informal survey on missing alt text, 89
PDA (Personal Digital Assistant) *see* handheld devices.
PDF (Portable Document Format) files
    glossary entry, 362
    inaccessible using markup editors, 200
    need for plug-ins with, 386
    require accessible alternatives, 348
PDF forms, 158
    complaint over inaccessible web design, 36
    don't allow reviewing of entries, 159
    forms require accessible alternatives, 347
    identified as a barrier to accessiblity, 37
percentages
    relative font sizes, 238
perceptible information
    universal design principle, 325
performance
    advantages of stylesheets, 21
periodic objective reviews
    enterprise web accessibility, 292
    tools and techniques for, 297
Photo Gallery
    Microsoft FrontPage, 216
photosensitive epilepsy, 372, 383
    flicker as possible cause of seizures, 107
pixels
    relative font sizes, 238
"place of public accommodation"
    disputed ADA definition, 334
plug-ins
    algorithmic and judgmental testing of Section 508
        compliance, 172
    detectable by presence of <object> tags, 386
    glossary entry, 362
    Section 508 requirements for, 160, 345, 348, 386
policymakers
    legal hot topics for, 347
Portugal
    implementation status of WCAG 1.0, 46
positioning
    see also prompts.
    field labels
        Section 508 provision relating to, 373
    identifying table headers using, 107
    problem with stylesheets disabled, 242
    stylesheets allow precise positioning, 232, 240
<PRE> element
    inappropriate use for tabular data, 243, 378
precedence
    embedded, linked and imported stylesheets, 235
preferences section
    Bobby assessment tool customization, 179
    LIFT Online, 185

413

Notes

Notes

Notes

Notes

Notes

Notes

Notes

Also from glasshaus:

glasshaus

web professional to web professional

Usable Web Menus

Andy Beaumont, Dave Gibbons, Jody Kerr, Jon Stephens

1-904151-02-7

March 2002

US: $19.99
C: $ 29.95
UK: £15.99

When developing a web site, one of the most important things to consider is the navigation menu, to allow your users to find their way around it. It needs to be usable, informative, and well implemented, but this can take time.

This book will take all the hassle out of implementing web menus, in whatever style and technology you wish, by providing full code samples, along with walkthrough tutorials on how they work to allow easy customization for your own needs.

Includes

- Guidelines on designing usable web menus, with 12 common-sense rules to follow
- Information Architecture for menus (including identifying your target user), and user testing
- Easy to Follow tutorials on building menus with HTML, JavaScript, CSS, and Flash
- Advanced tutorials on dynamically populating menus from XML and databases with server-side scripting, including PHP and ASP
- Extensive web support including fully adaptable downloadable code for your own use and a gallery of working menu examples

Practical JavaScript for the Usable Web

Paul Wilton, Stephen Williams, Sing Li

1-904151-05-1

March 2002

US $ 39.99
C $ 52.95
£ 28.99

This is a new kind of JavaScript book. It's not cut'n'paste, it's not a reference, and it's not an exhaustive investigation of the JavaScript language. It is about client-side, web focused, and task-oriented JavaScript.

JavaScript is a core skill for web professionals, and as every web professional knows, client-side JavaScript can produce all sorts of glitches and bugs. 'Practical JavaScript for the Usable Web' takes a two pronged approach to learning the JavaScript that you need to get your work done: teaching the core client-side JavaScript that you need to incorporate usable interactivity into your web applications, including many short functional scripts, and building up a complete application with shopping cart functionality.

When you have finished working with this book, you'll have a thorough grounding in client-side JavaScript, and be able to construct your own client-side functionality quickly, easily, and without falling into any of the usability traps that this technology leaves wide open.

glasshaus

web professional to web professional

glasshaus writes books for you. Any suggestions, or ideas about how you want
information given in your ideal book will be studied by our team.
Your comments are always valued at glasshaus.

Free phone in USA 800-873 9769
Fax (312) 893 8001

UK Tel.: (0121) 687 4100   Fax: (0121) 687 4101

Constructing Accessible Web Sites – Registration Card

Name _____

Address _____

_____

_____

_____

City _____ State/Region_____

Country _____ Postcode/Zip_____

E-Mail _____

Occupation _____

How did you hear about this book?

❏ Book review (name) _____

❏ Advertisement (name) _____

❏ Recommendation _____

❏ Catalog _____

❏ Other _____

Where did you buy this book?

❏ Bookstore (name) _____ City_____

❏ Computer store (name) _____

❏ Mail order_____

❏ Other _____

What influenced you in the purchase of this book?

❏ Cover Design ❏ Contents ❏ Other (please specify):

_____

How did you rate the overall content of this book?

❏ Excellent ❏ Good ❏ Average ❏ Poor

What did you find most useful about this book? _____

_____

_____

What did you find least useful about this book? _____

_____

Please add any additional comments. _____

_____

What other subjects will you buy a computer book on soon?

_____

What is the best computer book you have used this year?

_____

> **Note:** This information will only be used to keep you updated
> about new glasshaus titles and will not be used for
> any other purpose or passed to any other third party.

glasshaus

web professional to web professional

Note: If you post the bounce back card below in the UK, please send it to:

glasshaus, Arden House, 1102 Warwick Road,
Acocks Green, Birmingham B27 6HB. UK.

Computer Book Publishers

NO POSTAGE
NECESSARY
IF MAILED
IN THE
UNITED STATES

BUSINESS REPLY MAIL

FIRST CLASS MAIL   PERMIT#64   CHICAGO, IL

POSTAGE WILL BE PAID BY ADDRESSEE

glasshaus
29 S. LA SALLE ST.,
SUITE 520
CHICAGO IL 60603-USA